The Politics of Public Budgeting

Getting and Spending, Borrowing and Balancing

THIRD EDITION

IRENE S. RUBIN
Northern Illinois University

CHATHAM HOUSE PUBLISHERS, INC.
Chatham, New Jersey

THE POLITICS OF PUBLIC BUDGETING:
Getting and Spending, Borrowing and Balancing
THIRD EDITION

CHATHAM HOUSE PUBLISHERS, INC.
Post Office Box One
Chatham, New Jersey 07928

PUBLISHER: Edward Artinian
COVER DESIGN: Antler & Baldwin Design Group
PRODUCTION SUPERVISOR: Katharine Miller
COMPOSITION: Bang, Motley, Olufsen
PRINTING AND BINDING: R.R. Donnelley and Sons Company

LIBRARY OF CONGRESS CATALOGING-IN-PUBLICATION DATA
Rubin, Irene.
    The politics of public budgeting : getting and spending, borrowing and balancing / Irene S. Rubin. — 3rd ed.
        p.   cm.
    Includes bibliographical references and indexes.
    ISBN 1-56643-033-x
    1. Local budgets—Political aspects—United States. 2. Budget—Political aspects—United States.   I. Title.
HJ9147.R83 1997
336.73—dc20   96-32924
                                                        CIP

Manufactured in the United States of America
10 9 8 7 6 5 4 3 2 1

Contents

Acknowledgments

I would like to thank particularly the people who read and critiqued the manuscript for me in its various stages: Aaron Wildavsky, Allen Schick, Naomi Caiden, Tom Lauth, and Herb Rubin. They have been good and helpful colleagues. Aaron is gone now, but may those of us who remain continue to challenge and encourage one another. I would like to acknowledge particularly the assistance of Professor Schick, whose scholarship and intellectual integrity have been a model for the profession and an inspiration to me.

Preface to the Third Edition

The scene: The guest house opposite the White House in Washington, D.C. Negotiators from Congress and from the White House meet. Each side makes demands the other side is publicly committed to reject. The talks fall apart; recriminations fly. Negotiators will try again tomorrow, but the president, the majority leader in the Senate, and the Speaker of the House will not be present. They will probably return to the talks only when there is some hope of progress. Until they work out an agreement, many government offices will remain closed, their employees furloughed. Employees in many other offices will work, but without pay.

This scenario actually took place in December 1995. Controversy about how to balance the federal budget derailed budgetary decision making, resulting in tense, highly publicized negotiations. Republicans in Congress were determined to pressure the White House into complying with their plan to balance the budget by 2002, and so they refused to pass temporary legislation to keep the government going until formal appropriations could be passed. Without permission to spend, many agencies of the federal government closed for the second time since the beginning of the fiscal year on 1 October. Veterans and welfare recipients feared for their benefit checks. People who needed a passport were stymied. And people on vacation were locked out of federal museums and national parks and monuments.

More important than the short-term consequences of disagreement on priorities, this most recent effort to balance the federal budget will result in major cutbacks in programs, reorganization of agencies, and restructuring of entitlements.

An entitlement is an especially strong claim on the budget. Under an entitlement program, whoever meets certain conditions specified in the law, such as being above a certain age or below a certain income level, is eligible for benefits. Now these programs are being cut back and the strength of their claim on the budget weakened. What the American people have come to expect from their government may not be there the next time they need it. And what they get, especially in health care, may be vastly different from what they used to get, and it may cost more. Many of these changes will fall more heavily on the poor, but the middle classes also will feel the burden, especially of changes in health-care spending.

Something had to be done. Entitlements, especially those for health care, were pushing up spending, driving out other priorities, and contributing to the swelling deficit. The willingness of Congress and the president to grapple with the difficult choices of what to cut back has been encouraging. Whether the correct choices are being made, or the best choices, and whether important government programs will survive is less clear. People of different political beliefs may have different opinions of the outcomes.

This has been an exciting time to study public budgeting. The president and Congress are openly fighting out a series of dramatic issues. Questions of the government's role in the redistribution of income upward or downward; of its role in education, commerce, and housing; and of its ability to assure the safety of food and drugs and the cleanliness of water and air are all on the table. Seldom is budgeting confronted simultaneously with so many crucial decisions. This book helps explain the dramatic efforts to balance the budget and the resulting conflicts that closed down federal agencies twice in 1995 for the longest times on record.

The book does not focus exclusively on the national level. As in previous editions, the goal is to explain the politics of budgeting at all levels of government in the United States. The third edition adds current examples, deletes some older ones, updates tables, and reorganizes the material slightly, so the chapters do not get longer and longer as research accumulates and the real world of budgeting continues to change.

Describing public budgeting in recent years has been like painting a moving train. To the extent that this book captures the underlying budgetary politics, it should help the reader understand what is happening in public budgeting, no matter how fast the train goes by.

1. The Politics of Public Budgets

Public budgets describe what governments do by listing how governments spend money. A budget links tasks to be performed with the amount of resources necessary to accomplish those tasks, ensuring that money will be available to wage war, provide housing, or maintain streets. Budgets limit expenditures to the revenues available, to ensure balance and prevent overspending. Most of the work in drawing up a budget is technical, estimating how much it will cost to feed a thousand shut-ins with a Meals-on-Wheels program or how much revenue will be produced from a 1 percent tax on retail sales. But public budgets are not merely technical managerial documents; they are also intrinsically and irreducibly political.

□ Budgets reflect choices about what government will and will not do. They reflect general public consensus about what kinds of services governments should provide and what citizens are entitled to as members of society. Should government provide services that the private sector could provide, such as water, electricity, transportation, and housing? Do all citizens have a guarantee of health care, regardless of ability to pay? Are all insured against hunger? Are they entitled to some kind of housing?

□ Budgets reflect priorities—between police and flood control, day care and defense, the Northeast and the Southwest. The budget process mediates between groups and individuals who want different things from government and determines who gets what. These decisions may influence whether the poor get job training or the police get riot training, both as a response to an increased number of unemployed.

□ Budgets reflect the relative proportion of decisions made for local and constituency purposes, and for efficiency, effectiveness, and broader public goals. Budgets reflect the degree of importance legislators put on satisfying their constituents and the legislators' willingness to listen to interest-group demands. For example, the Defense Department may decide to spend more money to keep a military base open because the local economy depends on it and to spend less money to improve combat readiness.

□ Budgets provide a powerful tool of accountability to citizens who want to know how the government is spending their money and if government has generally followed their preferences. Budgeting links citizen preferences and governmental outcomes.

□ Budgets reflect citizens' preferences for different forms of taxation and different levels of taxation, as well as the ability of specific groups of taxpayers to shift tax burdens to others. The budget reflects the degree to which the government redistributes wealth upward or downward through the tax system.

□ At the national level, the budget influences the economy, so fiscal policy affects the level of employment—how many people are out of work at any time.

□ Budgets reflect the relative power of different individuals and organizations to influence budget outcomes. Budgetary decision making provides a picture of the relative power of budget actors within and between branches of government, as well as the importance of citizens in general and specific interest groups.

In all these ways, public budgeting is political. But budgeting is not typical of other political processes and hence one example among many. It is both an important and a unique arena of politics. It is important because of the specific policy issues reflected in the budget: the scope of government, the distribution of wealth, the openness of government to interest groups, and the accountability of government to the public at large. It is unique because these decisions have to take place in the context of budgeting, with its need for balance, its openness to the environment, and its requirements for timely decisions so that government can carry on without interruption.

Public budgets clearly have political implications, but what does it mean to say that key political decisions are made in the context of budgeting? The answer has several parts. First, what is budgeting? Second, what is public budgeting, as opposed to individual or family budgeting or the budgeting of private organizations? Third, what does *political* mean in the context of public budgeting?

What Is Budgeting?

The essence of budgeting is that it allocates scarce resources and hence implies choice between potential objects of expenditure. Budgeting implies balance, and it requires some kind of decision-making process.

MAKING BUDGETARY CHOICES

All budgeting, whether public or private, individual or organizational, involves choices between possible expenditures. Since no one has unlimited resources, people budget all the time. A child makes a budget (a plan for spending, balancing revenues and expenditures) when she decides to spend money on a marshmallow rabbit rather than a chocolate one, assuming she has money enough for only one rabbit. The air force may choose between two different airplanes to replace current bombers. These examples illustrate the simplest form of budgeting because they involve only one actor, one resource, one time, and two straightforward and comparable choices.

Normally, budgeting does not take place by comparing only two reasonably similar items. There may be a nearly unlimited number of choices. Budgeting usually limits the options to consider by grouping together similar things that can be reasonably compared. When I go to the supermarket, I do not compare all the possible things I could buy, not only because I cannot absorb that number of comparisons, but because the comparisons would be meaningless and a waste of time. I do not go to the supermarket and decide to get either a turkey or a bottle of soda pop. I compare main dishes with main dishes, beverages with beverages, desserts with desserts. Then I have a common denominator for comparison. For example, I may look at the main course and ask about the amount of protein for the dollar. I may compare the desserts in terms of the amount of cholesterol or the calories.

There is a tendency, then, to make comparisons within categories where the comparison is meaningful. This is as true for governmental budgeting as it is for shoppers. For example, weapons might be compared with weapons or automobiles with automobiles. They could be compared in terms of speed, reliability, availability of spare parts, and so on, and the one that did the most of what you wanted it to do at the least cost would be the best choice. As long as there is agreement on the goals to be achieved, the choice should be straightforward.

Sometimes, budgeting requires comparison of different, and seemingly incomparable things. If I do not have enough money to buy a whole balanced meal, I may have to make choices between main dishes and desserts. How do I compare the satisfaction of a sweet tooth to the nourishment of turkey? Or, in the public sector, how do I compare the benefits of providing shelters for the homeless with buying more helicopters for the navy? I may then move to more general comparisons, such as how clearly were the requests made and the benefits spelled out; who got the benefits last time and whose turn is it this time; are there any specific contingencies that make one choice more likely than the other? For example, will we be embarrassed to show our treatment of the homeless in front of a visiting dignitary? Or, are

THE POLITICS OF PUBLIC BUDGETING

disarmament negotiations coming up in which we need to display strength or make a symbolic gesture of restraint? Comparing dissimilar items may require a list of priorities. It may be possible to do two or more important things if they are sequenced properly.

Budgeting often allocates money, but it can allocate any scarce resource, for example, time. A student may choose between studying for an exam or playing softball and drinking beer afterward. In this example, it is time that is at a premium, not money. Or it could be medical skills that are in short supply, or expensive equipment, or apartment space, or water.

Government programs often involve a choice of resources and sometimes involve combinations of resources, each of which has different characteristics. For example, some federal farm programs involve direct cash payments plus loans at below-market interest rates, and welfare programs often involve dollar payments plus food stamps, which allow recipients to pay less for food. Federal budgets often assign agencies money, personnel, and sometimes borrowing authority, three different kinds of resources.

BALANCING AND BORROWING

Budgets have to balance. A plan for expenditures that pays no attention to ensuring that revenues cover expenditures is not a budget. That may sound odd in view of huge federal deficits, but a budget may technically be balanced by borrowing. Balance means only that outgo is matched or exceeded by income. The borrowing, of course, has to be paid off. Borrowing means spending more now and paying more in the future in order to maintain balance. It is a balance over time.

To illustrate the nature of budget balance, consider me as shopper again. Suppose I spend all my weekly shopping money before I buy my dessert. I have the option of treating my dollar limit as if it were more flexible, by adding the dimension of time. I can buy the dessert and everything else in the basket, going over my budget, and then eat less at the end of the month. Or I can pay the bill with a credit card, assuming I will have more money in the future with which to pay off the bill when it comes due. The possibility of borrowing against the future is part of most budget choices.

PROCESS

Budgeting cannot proceed without some kind of decision process. Even in the simplest cases of budgeting, there has to be some limit set to spending, some order of decision making, some way to structure comparisons among alternatives, and some way to compare choices. Budget processes also regulate the flow of decisions so they are made in a timely manner.

4

Back to my shopping example: If I shop for the main course first, and spend more money than I intended on it because I found some fresh fish, there will be less money left for purchasing the dessert. Hence, unless I set a firm limit on the amount of money to spend for each segment of the meal, the order in which I do the purchasing counts. Of course, if I get to the end of my shopping and do not have enough money left for dessert, I can put back some of the items already in the cart and squeeze out enough money for dessert.

Governmental budgeting is also concerned with procedures for managing tradeoffs between large categories of spending. Budgeters may determine the relative importance of each category first, attaching a dollar level in proportion to the assigned importance, or they may allow purchasing in each area to go on independently, later reworking the choices until the balance between the parts is acceptable.

The order of decisions is important in another sense. I can determine how much money I am likely to have first and then set that as an absolute limit on expenditures, or I can determine what I must have, what I wish to have, and what I need to set aside for emergencies and then go out and try to find enough money to cover some or all of those expenditures. Especially in emergencies, such as accidents or other health emergencies, people are likely to obligate the money first and worry about where it will come from later. Governmental budgeting, too, may concentrate first on revenues and later on expenditures, or first on expenditures and later on income. Like individuals or families, during emergencies such as floods or hurricanes or wars, governments will commit the expenditures first and worry about where the money will come from later.

Governmental Budgeting

Public budgeting shares the characteristics of budgeting in general but differs from household and business budgeting in some key ways. First, in public budgeting, there are always people and organizations with different perspectives and different goals trying to get what they want out of the budget. In individual budgets, there may be only one person involved; and in family and business budgets, there may be only a limited number of actors and they may have similar views of what they want to achieve through the budget.

Second, public budgets are more open to the environment than budgets of families or businesses are. Public budgets are open not only to the economy but also to other levels of government, to citizens, to interest groups, to the press, and to politicians.

Third, budgets form a crucial link between citizen taxpayers and government officials. The document itself may be a key form of accountability. This function does not apply to businesses, families, or individuals.

Fourth, public budgeting is characterized by a variety of constraints, legal limits, perceived limits imposed by public opinion, rules and regulations about how to carry out the budget, and many more. Public budgeting is far more constrained in this sense than budgets of individuals or businesses.

An example should give the reader a feeling for governmental budgeting. The example is from a local government that was trying to work out its response to the elimination of a federal grant program on which it had become dependent. While the illustration is not necessarily typical of other public budget making, the minicase illustrates the need for balance, the choice between competing objects of expenditure, and the process for making budgetary decisions. It also illustrates some of the specific characteristics of public budgeting.

MINICASE: MAKING CHOICES IN THE BUDGET PROCESS

DeKalb, Illinois, is a council-manager city, which means that the elected city council members hire a professional manager to run the city and report to them for policy guidance. The manager's formal responsibilities include drawing up a budget proposal, and submitting it to the council for examination and approval. Council members typically have little budgetary expertise and little time to pore over the budget. In recent years, they have responded to these problems by creating a finance advisory board, with citizen and council representation, and staffed by the city manager, the finance director, and the city clerk. The members of this board are selected for financial expertise and political representativeness. Their responsibilities are to examine the budget, request supplemental information, consider options, and make policy recommendations to the council. The board tests both political and technical feasibility of proposals. The compromises worked out by the board are normally accepted by the council as a whole.

The annual budget cycle begins with a meeting between the city manager, the members of the council, and the whole finance advisory board. The council members and the manager discuss their priorities for the year and constraints on revenues. When the finance advisory board meets to examine the manager's proposed budget, it already has a good idea what revenue problems are likely to arise and how the council views certain issues, such as increased taxation or particular spending cuts. The proposed budget is several hundred pages long, and the finance advisory board discusses it section by section, department by department, and program by program. Most of the discussion focuses on special problems that occur and the financial implications of possible policy responses.

The central problem in 1986 was that federal revenue sharing was about to end as a program, reducing the city's revenue by more than $600,000. The money had been used for two kinds of expenditures: $400,000 for debt service, to pay back loans for large construction projects; and $200,000 for social services including day care, transportation for the elderly, and emergency care and counseling for battered spouses. The city was strapped for funds. Other revenue sources were not growing rapidly enough to cover the lost money, so some difficult choices had to be made.

One option was simply to cut the expenditures out of the budget—no more debt service, no more social services. But, legally, the debt service could not be dropped. So at least $400,000 had to come from somewhere, either from new revenues (a politically unpopular option repeatedly rejected by the city council) or from cutting other programs. City officials could not cut legal obligations such as pensions or city-run businesses such as the water fund. But cuts could be taken from fire, police, public works (street repairs, snow plowing, sweeping, etc.), building and code inspection, or general management.

The choices about the social services program were difficult because there is no legal requirement that they be maintained. If the city wished, it could cut the social services and reduce its anticipated shortfall by $200,000. These social services tend not to benefit everyone in the community; they benefit small groups such as the elderly, handicapped, single working mothers, and abused spouses. How badly did these groups need the city's subsidy, and how much support did these groups have in the community as a whole?

Representatives from the social service agencies made presentations to the finance advisory board, describing their work, how many clients they served in the city, the history of past funding from the city, other sources of funding they had sought, and the potential impact of reduced aid from the city. (The city manager had sent them a list of questions so the information on each service agency was relatively uniform.) Their presentations sparked heated debate.

One council member on the board argued that revenue sharing had been spent on social services with the understanding that if the money dried up, the subsidy would be terminated. He opposed spending the city's regular tax revenues for social services, presumably because they lacked widespread political support. He argued that the social services were frivolous anyway, nice to have but not necessary, not livelihood related. He implied that the women running the spouse-abuse center were lesbians and men haters, and did not deserve public funds. A citizen member shot back that transportation for the elderly to and from doctors and shopping was as basic to living as economic development.

7

The advisory board was split on the issue of retaining the social services, but it was clear that there was some support for the social services, and the mayor threw his weight behind retaining them in the city budget. The council gave the advisory board the task of coming up with $600,000 in cuts from the budget or a new funding scheme, or some combination of cuts and new funding.

The city manager framed the alternatives to emphasize the capital budget, money set aside for construction and repair projects, as the only source of potential cuts that would not involve layoffs or major reductions in services. He argued against such cuts because the capital budget was already seriously underfunded, leading to broken and rough pavement and high costs for rebuilding roads. The city had budgeted only half what was needed as it was, without additional cuts.

The manager was interested in maintaining capital projects because of their implications for operating costs—delayed maintenance meant higher operating costs and, ultimately, heavier repair and replacement bills. The council was interested in maintaining the capital budget because large visible improvements in their districts make them look effective to their voters. Because there was support for maintaining the capital budget, if the social services were to be preserved, it looked as if there would have to be a tax increase. But there was very little support for a tax increase that would go only for social services; everyone would feel that they were being taxed to benefit the few. But when social services and debt service costs were combined, and a tax increase proposed to cover both, the coalition of potential supporters was larger. To make the package more acceptable to taxpayers, the finance advisory board proposed to raise the sales tax enough to cover the social services and capital projects, with a little left over to reduce the property tax.

The city sales tax in DeKalb falls proportionately more on the poor than the wealthy, there are no exemptions for food or medicine, and there is a ceiling on expensive items, so there is proportionately less sales tax on expensive cars and boats than on food. The property tax is very roughly proportional to wealth so that people who are richer—if they have more expensive homes—pay more tax. Reducing property taxes and increasing sales taxes shifted the burden of taxation slightly more toward the poor. The cost of saving the social services, which serve the elderly, the poor, and the handicapped, was to shift the burden of taxation more on to the poor. This was a compromise everyone was willing to live with, and it passed the council intact.

The story of one city's response to the end of a federal grant program illustrates a number of themes about public budgeting. First, budgeting is constrained. It is constrained by the availability of revenues and the requirement of budgetary balance; it is constrained by legal obligations that frame the choices of what to cut out of the budget. And the budget is constrained by the stated policy goals of the city council and the acceptability of various forms of taxation to the public. Major policy decisions have to be made within these technical and political constraints.

Budgeting does not occur in a vacuum, divorced from other political considerations or from other levels of government. Cities are legally created by and dominated by their state governments, which can add burdens to the cities, reduce or add to the scope of the services they perform, or provide financial aid. Both cities and states may receive aid from the federal government or may have that aid withdrawn. Governments have to worry not only about the performance of the economy and how the economy will affect their revenues but also about political and budgetary decisions made at other levels of government. Money coming from other levels of government may require a local match—a dollar given by the donor has to be matched by money contributed by the recipient; or it may come with strings attached and thus can be spent only for certain things. Grants from other levels of government may be highly uncertain from year to year. Each revenue dollar is not equal from a budgetary perspective; it depends where it comes from, what it may be spent on, and how certain it is.

The minicase also illustrates that within the constrained and somewhat unpredictable and uncontrollable budget environment, policy choices are made, tradeoffs are framed, and public support levels expressed. The external environment changed, reducing revenue levels, but since the budget had to be balanced, some choices had to be made about the scope of government and about comparisons of the worth of different kinds of expenditures. Salaries and staff positions were put off limits; only capital expenditures were considered, and they were vigorously defended by the manager and the council. Economic development and so-called basic services were compared to social services in terms of intrinsic worth and importance. And then expenditure cuts were compared with revenue increases, and the issue of who should pay more was raised in the choice of which tax to increase. It is hard to imagine a sequence of more important policy issues at the local level. These issues are not considered every year but only occasionally when the environment forces a choice.

It was impossible to talk about budgetary decision making without describing a budget process, a collection of actors, a number of decisions, an assignment of tasks to actors, an emphasis on revenue constraints or on spending requirements. The role of the city manager, the role and composition of the finance advisory board, and the role of the city council were all important in describing the decision making. If revenues had been determined before expenditures, the outcome might have been different. The board tried to figure out how and where to cut, met with frustration at the difficulty of the task, and ended up arguing that despite the difficulty, revenue increases were the better option. The process regulated the access of interest groups and the public. The public, for example, was formally represented on the finance advisory board, but taxpayers' associations were not formally represented. The process influenced the information available for decision making, and it influenced the amount and kind of scrutiny various proposals received. The process also regulated the points at which the council could intervene with policy guidelines.

The minicase described only one city, and only one instance of policy making as part of the budget process. But it is suggestive of a number of characteristics of public budgeting at all levels of government.

More formally, public budgeting has five characteristics that differentiate it from other kinds of budgeting. First, public budgeting is characterized by a variety of budgetary actors who often have different priorities and different levels of power over budget outcomes. These actors have to be regulated and orchestrated by the budget process. Second, in government there is a distinction between those who pay taxes and those who decide how money will be spent—the citizens and the elected politicians. Public officials can force citizens to pay taxes for expenditures they do not want, but citizens can vote politicians out of office. Third, the budget document is important as a means of public accountability. Fourth, public budgets are very vulnerable to the environment—to the economy, to changes in public opinion, to elections, to such local contingencies as natural disasters like floods, or political disasters such as the police bombing of MOVE headquarters in Philadelphia, which burned down part of a neighborhood. Fifth, public budgets are incredibly constrained. Although there is a built-in necessity to make budgets adaptable to contingencies, there are many elements of public budgets that are beyond the immediate control of those who draw up budgets.

A VARIETY OF ACTORS

The first characteristic of public budgeting was the variety of actors involved in the budget and their frequently clashing motivations and goals. On a regular basis, bureau chiefs, executive budget officers, and chief executives are involved in the budget process, as are legislators, both on committees and as a whole group. Interest groups may be involved at intervals, sometimes for relatively long stretches of time, sometimes briefly. Sometimes citizens play a direct or indirect role in the budget process. Courts may play a role in budgets at any level of government at unpredictable intervals. When they do play a role in budgetary decisions, what are these actors trying to achieve?

Bureau Chiefs. Many students of budgeting assume that agency heads always want to expand their agencies, that their demands are almost limitless, and that it is up to other budget actors to curtail and limit their demands. The reasons given for that desire for expansion include prestige, more subordinates, more space, larger desks, more secretaries, and not incidentally, more salary. The argument presumes that agency heads judge their bureaucratic skills in terms of the satisfaction of their budget requests. Successful bureaucrats bring back the budget. Agency expansion is the measure of success.

Recent research has suggested that while some bureaucrats may be motivated by salaries, many feel that one of their major rewards is the opportunity to do good for people—to house the homeless, feed the hungry, find jobs for the unemployed, and send out checks to the disabled.[1] For these bureaucrats, efforts to expand agency budgets are the result of their belief in the programs they work for.

Recent research has also suggested that the bureaucracy has become more professional, which introduces the possibility of another motivation, the desire to do a good job, to do it right, to put in the best machinery that exists or build the biggest, toughest engineering project or the most complicated weapons.

The generalization that bureaucrats always press for budget increases appears to be too strong. Some agencies are much more aggressive in pushing for growth than others. Some are downright moribund. Sometimes agency heads refuse to expand when given the opportunity,[2] suggesting there are some countervailing values to growth. One of these countervailing values is agency autonomy. Administrators may prefer to maintain autonomy rather than increase the budget if it comes down to a choice between the two. A second countervailing value to growth is professionalism, the desire to get the job done, and do it quickly and right. Administrators generally prefer to hire employees who have the ability to get the job done, plus a little, a spare amount of intelligence, motivation, and energy just in case they need to get some extra work done or do it fast in response to a political request.[3] Administrators may refuse to add employees if the proposed employees do not add to the agency's capacity to get things done.

A third countervailing value is program loyalty. Expansion may be seen as undesirable if the new mission swamps the existing mission, if it appears contradictory to the existing mission, or if the program requires more money to carry out than is provided, forcing the agency to spend money designated for existing programs on new ones or do a poor job.

A fourth countervailing value is belief in the chain of command. Many, if not all, bureaucrats believe that their role is to carry out the policies of the chief executive and the legislature. If those policies mean cutting back budgets, agency heads cut back the agencies. Agency heads may be appointed precisely because they are willing to make cuts in their agencies.[4]

Bureaucrats, then, do not always try to expand their agencies' budgets. They have other, competing goals, which sometimes dominate. Also, their achievements can be measured by other than expanded budgets. They may go for some specific items in the budget without raising totals, or may try for changes in the wording of legislation. They may strive to get a statutory basis for the agency and security of funding. They may take as a goal providing more efficient and effective service, rather than expanded or more expensive service.

The Executive Budget Office. The traditional role of the budget office has been to scrutinize requests coming up from the agencies, to find waste and eliminate it, and to discourage most requests for new money. The executive budget office has been perceived as the naysayer, the protector of the public purse. Most staff members in the budget office are very conscious of the need to balance the budget, to avoid deficits, and to manage cash flow so that there is money on hand to pay bills. Hence they tend to be skeptical of requests for new money.

In recent years, however, there has been a change in the role of budget office. At the national level under President Ronald Reagan, budgeting became much more top-down, with the director of the Office of Management and Budget (OMB) proposing specific cuts and negotiating them directly with Congress, without much scrutiny of requests coming up from departments or bureaus. OMB became more involved in trying to accomplish the policy goals of the president through the budget.[5] At state levels too, there has been an evolution of budget staff from more technical to more political and more policy-related goals. When the governor is looking for new spending proposals, these may come from the budget office.

Chief Executive Officers. The role of chief executive officers (the mayor or city manager, the governor, the president) is highly variable, and hence these executives' goals in the budget process cannot be predicted without knowledge of the individuals. Some chief executives have been expansive, proposing new programs; others have been economy minded, cutting back proposals generated by the legislatures. Some have been efficiency oriented, reorganizing staffs and trying to maintain service levels without increases in taxes or expenditures.

Legislators. Legislators have sometimes been described as always trying to increase expenditures.[6] Their motivation is viewed as getting reelected, which depends on their ability to provide constituents services and deliver "pork"—jobs and capital projects—to their districts. Norms of reciprocity magnify the effects of these spending demands because legislators are reluctant to cut others' pork lest their own be cut in return. At the city level, a council member described this norm of reciprocity, "There is an unwritten rule that if something is in a councilman's district, we'll go along and scratch each other's back."[7]

For some legislators, however, getting reelected is not a high priority. They view elected office as a service they perform for the community rather than a career, and while they may be responsive to constituents' needs, they are simply not motivated to start new projects or give public employees a raise in order to get reelected. Also, some legislators feel secure about the possibility of reelection, and hence have no urgent need to deliver pork in order to increase their chances of reelection.[8]

Even assuming the motivation to get reelected, holding down taxes may be as important to reelection as spending on programs and projects. The consequence of tax reduction is usually curtailed expenditures. Legislators are bound to try to balance the budget, which puts some constraints on the desire to spend.

The tendency to provide pork is real, but there are counterbalancing factors. Some legislators are more immune to pressures from constituents because they are secure electorally, and legislators can organize themselves in such a way as to insulate themselves somewhat from these pressures. They can, for example, select more electorally secure representatives for key positions on appropriations committees; they can separate committees that deal extensively with interest groups from those that deal with expenditures; they can set up buffer groups to deal with interest groups; they can structure the budget process so that revenue limits precede and guide spending proposals.

Moreover, legislators have interests other than providing pork. Some legislators are deeply concerned about solving social problems, designing and funding defense and foreign aid systems, and monitoring the executive branch. The proportion of federal budget spent on pork-type projects has declined in recent years, despite reforms in Congress that decentralized control and allowed pressure for pork to increase.[9] "Congressmen are not single-minded seekers of local benefits, struggling feverishly to win every last dollar for their districts. However important the quest for local benefits may be, it is always tempered by other competing concerns."[10] The pull for local benefits depends on the program. Some, like water projects, are oriented to local payoffs; others, like entitlement programs for large numbers of people, are not. Programs with local pull account for smaller and smaller proportions of the budget[11] and the trend has accelerated since 1978.[12]

Interest Groups. Interest groups, too, have often been singled out as the driving force behind budget increases. They are said to want more benefits for their members and to be undeterred by concerns for overall budget balance or the negative effects of tax increases. Moreover, their power has been depicted as great. Well-funded interest groups reportedly wine and dine legislators and provide campaign funding for candidates who agree with their positions.

There is some truth to this picture, but it is oversimplified. Interest groups have other policy goals besides budget levels. In fact, most probably deal with the budget only when a crisis occurs, such as a threat to funding levels. Because they can be counted on to come to the defense of a threatened program, they reduce the flexibility of budget decision makers, who find it difficult to cut programs with strong interest-group backing. But many areas of the budget do not have strong interest-group backing. For example, foreign aid programs have few domestic constituencies. Agencies may even have negative constituencies, that is, interest groups that want to reduce their funding and terminate their programs. The American Medical Association sought for years to eliminate the Health Planning Program.

Often when there are interest groups, there are many rather than one, and these interest groups may have conflicting styles or conflicting goals, canceling one another out or absorbing energy in battles among themselves. A coalition of interest groups representing broad geographic areas and a variety of constituencies is likely to be more effective at lobbying.

Hence coalitions may form, but individual members of the coalition may not go along with measures supported by others, so the range of items lobbied for as a unified group may be narrow. Extensive negotiations and continual efforts are required to get two or more independent groups together for a lobbying effort, and the arrangement can then fall apart. In short, interest groups are often interested in maintaining their autonomy.

Individuals. Individuals seldom have a direct role in the budget process, as they did in the DeKalb case, but they often have an indirect role. They may vote on referenda to limit revenues, forbid some forms of taxation, or require budgetary balance. They voice their opinions also in public opinion polls, and more informally by calling or writing their elected representatives and giving their opinions. Their knowledge of the budget is not usually detailed, but their feelings about the acceptability of taxation are an important part of the constraints of public budgeting. Their preferences for less visible taxes and for taxes earmarked for specific approved expenditures have been an important factor in public budgeting.

The Courts. Another budget actor that plays an intermittent role in determining expenditures is the courts.[13] The courts get involved when other actors, often interest groups, bring a case against the government. Suits that affect the budget may involve service levels or the legality of particular forms of taxation. If a particular tax is judged unconstitutional, the result is usually lost revenues. If there are suits concerning levels of service, governments may be forced to spend more money on that service. There can also be damage suits against governments that affect expenditures. These suits are usually settled without regard to the government agencies' ability to pay. The result may be forced cuts in other areas of the budget, tax increases, or even bankruptcy. When the courts get involved, they may determine budget priorities. They introduce a kind of rigidity into the budget that says do this, or pay this, first.

Typical areas in which courts have gotten involved and mandated expenditures for state and local governments are prison overcrowding (declared cruel and unusual punishment) and deinstitutionalization of mentally ill and mentally handicapped patients. In each case, the rights of the institutionalized population required more services or more space, often involving expenditures of additional funds. From the perspective of the courts, the priority of rights outweighs immediate concerns for budget balances, autonomy of governmental units, and local priorities.

These various actors not only have different and potentially clashing budgetary goals, but they typically have different levels of power. Thus, at times, the budget office may completely dominate the agencies; at times, Congress may differ from the president on budgetary policy and pass its own preferences. The courts may preempt the decision making of the executive and the legislature. Some particular interest groups may always be able to get tax breaks for themselves.

The combination of different preferences and different levels of power has to be orchestrated by the budget process in such a way that agreement is reached, and the players stay in the game, continuing to abide by the rules. If some actors feel too powerless over the budget, they may cease to participate or become obstructionist, blocking any agreements or imposing rigid, nonnegotiable solutions. Why participate in negotiations and discussions if the decision will go against you regardless of what you do? If some actors lose on important issues, they may try to influence budget implementation to favor themselves. Or the actors with less budget power may try to change the budget process so that they have a better chance of influencing the outcomes.

OPENNESS TO THE ENVIRONMENT

Public budgets are open to the environment. The environment for budgeting includes a number of different factors including the overall level of resources available (the amount of taxable wealth, the existing tax structure, current economic conditions); the degree of certainty of revenues; and a variety of emergencies such as very heavy snowfall, tornadoes, wars, bridge collapses, droughts, chemical explosions, and water pollution. The environment also includes rigidities resulting from earlier decisions, which may now be embodied in law. For example, rapid inflation in housing prices in California resulted in a citizen referendum to protect against rapidly rising property taxes. The result of the referendum was incorporated in the state constitution, limiting the taxing options of local governments. Constitutional restrictions to maintain a balanced budget or limit expenditures or put a ceiling on borrowing operate in a similar manner. Prior borrowing creates a legal obligation for future budgets, an obligation that may press other possible expenditures out of consideration or require higher levels of taxation. The environment in this sense may frame policy issues and limit alternatives. Public opinion is also part of the budgetary environment, and the perception of change in public opinion will be reflected in changing budgets.

The intergovernmental system is also a key part of the environment for budget actors. The legal sources of revenues, limits on borrowing, strings attached to grants, and mandated costs are but a few of the budgetary implications of the intergovernmental system. The requirement that some grants be spent on particular items or that a recipient match expenditures on grants may result in a pattern of spending different from what the state or local government would have preferred.

THE BUDGET DOCUMENT AND ACCOUNTABILITY

The third feature of public budgeting is that decisions about how money will be spent are made not by those providing the money but by their representatives. The payers and the deciders are two distinct groups. The payers are not given a choice about whether they want to pay or how much they want to pay. The power of the state may force them to pay. They may protest if they do not like how their money is being spent, and elect new representatives. They cannot, generally, take their money and do something else with it.

The distinction between the payers and the deciders leads to two crucial characteristics of public budgeting: public *accountability* and political *acceptability*. Accountability means to make sure that every penny of public money is spent as agreed and to report accurately to the public on how money was spent. Acceptability means that public officials who make budget decisions are constrained by what the public wants. Sometimes they will do precisely what they think the public wants, even if the results are inefficient or inequitable, and sometimes they will present the budget so that it will be accepted by the public, even if they have not precisely followed public will. This effort may involve persuasion or deception.

Because public demands may not be clearly expressed, and because different segments of the public may make different and competing demands, and because public officials themselves may have other priorities, officials may not be able or willing to be bound tightly to public opinion. Nevertheless, if politicians knowingly make decisions that differ from what the public seems to want, there is pressure to present the budget in a way that makes it appear acceptable. That pressure creates a tension between accountability, which requires nearly complete openness, and acceptability, which sometimes involves hiding or distorting information or presenting it in an unclear fashion.

Because of the separation of payer and decider, the budget document itself becomes an important means of public accountability. How did the public's representatives actually decide to spend taxpayer money? Did they waste it? Did they spend it on defense or police or on social services? The streets are in terrible shape—how much money did they spend on street repair? Citizens do not typically watch the decision making, but they and the press have access to the budget document and can look for the answers. They can hold the government accountable through the budget, to see that what officials promised them was actually delivered.

But budgets do not always present a complete and accurate picture. One example of how budgets can lose information happened recently in a state university. A university president decided to expand the big-time sports program, in an environment of overall financial scarcity. While some faculty members undoubtedly favored the action, many would have opposed it if they had been asked. The president did not ask their opinions, however; instead, the full costs of the program were disguised to make the budget appear acceptable. Because of progressive underestimates of costs in the sports program, some pundits labeled the sports program the case of the disappearing budget.

To obscure the real costs, the president broke up the costs for the program and scattered them among different portions of the budget. To complicate the picture further, he drew on different pockets of revenue, including student athletic fees, bond revenues, and voluntary donations. When asked, he said money going to the athletic programs was earmarked and could not be spent on other programs, so that professors trying to get more money to teach history or biology would look elsewhere than to sports. The amount of money showing as costs in the athletic program remained constant every year, although the program costs were expanding. Fearing conflict and disapproval, the president hid the costs in the budget.

The more complicated the budget, the more different activities and accounts, the greater the discretion of the administrators. As one university president offered, "Not a day goes by when we do not wish we had a more complex budget." The complexity allows for choice of where to report expenditures, and which revenues to use, to highlight some expenditures and gloss over others.

It would be misleading to suggest that the tension between accountability and acceptability always leads to more distortion or more secrecy. Sometimes the balance tends toward more accountability and budgets become clearer and more representative of true costs. The federal budget, for example, has moved toward clearer and more comprehensive portraits of public expenditures in recent years. But the tension is always present, and each budget represents some degree of selectivity about what it will present and how. The art of selective revelation is part of public budgeting.

BUDGET CONSTRAINTS

Openness to the environment creates the need for budgets to be flexible. Public officials have to be able to adapt quickly, reallocating funds to meet emergencies, spending more now and making up the difference later, cutting back expenditures during the year to meet sudden declines in revenues or increases in expenditures. But the same openness to the environment that creates the need for flexibility may simultaneously subject budgeting to numerous constraints.

For example, in California, a statewide referendum limited the rate of growth of local assessments, restraining the growth of property tax revenues. Federal grants provide budgetary constraints when they can be spent only on particular programs. The courts may create budgetary constraints by declaring programs inadequate or taxes illegal. Legal obligations to repay debt and maintain public businesses separate from the rest of the budget also create constraints.

The need for flexibility and the number of budgetary constraints contest with one another, creating patterns typical of public budgeting. For example, local officials may press for home rule, which gives more independence and autonomy to local governments to manage their own affairs and adapt to changing conditions. But state officials may erode home rule through continually mandating local costs. State universities may try to squirrel away contingency funds outside those appropriated by the legislature so that they can respond to emergencies; the legislature may then try to appropriate and hence control this new local source of revenues.

The Meaning of Politics *in Public Budgeting*

Public budgets have a number of special characteristics. These characteristics suggest some of the ways that the budget is political. Political is a word that covers a number of meanings, even when narrowed to the context of budgetary decision making. The purpose of this book is to clarify the meaning of politics in the context of budgeting by sorting out some key meanings and showing how these meanings apply to different parts of budgetary decision making.

The literature suggests at least five major ways of viewing politics in the budget: reformism, incrementalist bargaining, interest-group determinism, process, and policymaking.

□ The first is a reform orientation, which argues that politics and budgeting are or should be antithetical, that budgeting should be primarily or exclusively technical, and that comparison between items should be technical and efficiency based. Politics in the sense of the opinions and priorities of elected officials and interest groups is an unwanted intrusion that reduces efficiency and makes decision making less rational. The politics of reform involves a clash of views between professional staff and elected officials over the boundary between technical budget decisions and properly political ones.

□ The second perspective is the incrementalist view, which sees budgeting as negotiations among a group of routine actors, bureaucrats, budget officers, chief executives, and legislators, who meet each year and bargain to resolution. To the extent that interest groups are included at all in this view, they are conceived of in the pluralist model. The process is open, anyone can play and win, and the overall outcome is good; conflict is held down because everyone wins something and no one wins too much.

□ The third view is that interest groups are dominant actors in the budget process. In its extreme form this argument posits that richer and more powerful interest groups determine the budget. Some interests are represented by interest groups, and others either are not, or are represented by weaker interest groups; the outcome does not approximate democracy. There may be big winners and big losers in this model. Conflict is more extensive than in the incrementalist model. This view of politics in budgeting raises the question whether these interest groups represent narrow or broad coalitions, or possibly even class interest. To what extent do these interest groups represent oil or banking or the homeless, and to what extent do they represent business and labor more broadly?

□ The fourth view of politics in the budget is that the budget process itself is the center and focus of budget politics. Those with particular budget goals try to change the budget process to favor their goals. Branches of government struggle with one another over budgetary power through the budget process; the budget process becomes the means of achieving or denying separation and balance between the branches of government. The degree of examination of budget requests, and the degree to which review is technical or political, cursory or detailed, is regulated by the budget process. The ability of interest groups to influence the budget, the role of the public in budget decisions, the openness of budget decision making—all these are part of the politics of process. In this view of politics, the individual actors and their strategies and goals may or may not be important, depending on the role assigned to individual actors in the budget process, and depending on whether the external environment allows any flexibility.

□ The fifth view is that the politics of budgeting centers in policy debates, including debates about the role of the budget. Spending levels, taxing policies, and willingness to borrow to sustain spending during recessions are all major policy issues that have to be resolved one way or another during budget deliberations. Budgets may reflect a policy of moderating economic cycles or they may express a policy of allowing the economy to run its course. Each is a policy. Similarly, budgets must allocate funding to particular programs, and in the course of doing so, decide priorities for federal, state, and local governments. This view of politics in the budget emphasizes tradeoffs, especially those that occur between major areas of the budget, such as social services and defense or police. This view also emphasizes the role of the budget office in making policy and the format of the budget in encouraging comparisons between programs.

These five views of politics have been developed over time, and like an ancient document, the messages have been written over one another. Surely they are not all equally true, and certainly they often contradict each other. Parts of each may still be true, and they may be true of different parts of budgetary decision making, or true of budgetary decision making at different times or at different levels of government.

Budgetary Decision Making

The focus of the book is to explore the kind of politics that occurs in budgetary decision making. What is budgetary decision making like? We have already discovered that public budgeting is open to environmental changes and deals with policy conflicts. Policy conflicts can delay particular decisions or prevent them from being made at all; other budget decisions must be independent enough to be made without the missing pieces. They can be corrected later when missing pieces fall into place. Environmental emergencies can reorder priorities and alter targets that have already been determined. As a result, public budgeting must be segmentable and interruptible. The need for segmentation and interruptibility is satisfied by dividing budgeting into separate but linked decision clusters: revenues, process, expenditures, balance, and implementation.

Decision making in each cluster proceeds somewhat independently while referring to decisions made in the other clusters, or in anticipation of decisions likely to be made in other clusters. These decision clusters are ultimately interdependent, but do not occur in a fixed sequence. The decision one needs to have in one decision cluster may not be made by another decision cluster in time to use. Then one may guess, or use an old figure, and then change when the new figure is determined. Sometimes decision making alternates between estimates of revenues, estimates of expenditures, new estimates of revenues, and new estimates of expenditures, in an iterative process.

Each cluster attracts a different characteristic set of actors and generates its own typical pattern of politics. Some clusters have heavy interest-group activity, while others have virtually none; some clusters are marked by intense competition and negotiations and efforts to bind future decisions to restrict open competition; some are marked by deep ideological splits, while others seem not to be ideological at all. Some are marked by dominance of a technical perspective, while others are clearly determined by the priorities of elected officials and the public, and still others represent a blend of the two.

THE REVENUE CLUSTER

Revenue decisions include technical estimates of how much income will be available for the following year, assuming no change in the tax structures, and policy decisions about changes in the level or type of taxation. Will taxes be raised or lowered? Will tax breaks be granted, and if so, to whom, for what purpose? Which tax sources will be emphasized, and which deemphasized, with what effect on regions, and economic classes, or on age groups? How visible will the tax burden be? Interest groups are intensely involved in the revenue cluster. The revenue cluster emphasizes the scarcity of resources that is an essential element in budgeting and illustrates the tension between accountability and acceptability that is a characteristic of public budgets. Revenues are also extremely sensitive to the environment because changes in the economy influence revenue levels and because the perception of public opinion influences the public officials' willingness to increase taxes.

THE BUDGET PROCESS

The process cluster concerns how to make budget decisions. Who should participate in the budget deliberations? Should the agency heads have power independent of the central budget office? How influential should interest groups be? How much power should the legislature have? How should the work be divided, and when should particular decisions be made? Normally the legislature takes a key role in establishing budget process, although the chief executive may propose desired changes. Interest groups play a minor role, if any role at all. The politics of process may revolve around individuals or groups trying to maximize their power through rearranging the budget process. This jockeying for power rises to importance when the competing parties represent the executive and legislative branches and involve the definition of the separation and balance between the branches of government. The politics of process may revolve around the policy issues of the level of spending and the ability of government to balance its budget.

THE EXPENDITURE CLUSTER

The expenditure cluster involves some technical estimates of likely expenditures, such as for grants that are dependent on formulas and benefit programs whose costs depend on the level of unemployment. But many expenditure decisions are policy relevant—which programs will be funded at what level, who will benefit from public programs and who will not, where and how cuts will be made, and whose interests will be protected. Agency heads are more involved in these decisions than in taxation or process decisions, and interest groups are also often active. This portion of the budget emphasizes the element of choice between items of expenditures in the definition of budgeting and illustrates the nature of the constraints on choices that are characteristic of public budgeting in particular.

THE BALANCE CLUSTER

The balance cluster concerns the basic budgetary question whether the budget has to be balanced each year with each year's revenues, or whether borrowing is allowed to balance the budget, and if so, how much, for how long, and for what purposes. The politics of balance deals with questions whether balance should be achieved by increasing revenues, decreasing expenditures, or both, and hence reflects policies about the desirable scope of government. Sometimes the politics of balance emphasizes definitions, as the group in power seeks to make its deficits look smaller by defining them away. The balance cluster also deals with questions of how deficits should be eliminated once they occur and their amounts are pinned down. At the national level, because deficits may be incurred during recessions in an effort to help the economy recover, the ability to run a deficit is linked to policies favoring or opposing the role of the budget in controlling the economy and, in particular, the use of the budget to moderate unemployment. These issues—whether budgets should balance, the proper scope of government and level of taxation, and the role of government in moderating unemployment—are issues that the general public cares about. Citizens may participate in this decision cluster through referenda and opinion polls; broad groups of taxpayers and interest-group coalitions representing broad segments of society may be involved in lobbying on this issue. Political parties may even include their policies toward deficits in their election platforms.

BUDGET IMPLEMENTATION

Finally, there is a cluster of decisions around budget implementation. How close should actual expenditures be to the ones planned in the budget? How can one justify variation from the budget plan? Can the budget be remade after it is approved, during the budget year? The key issues here revolve around the need to implement decisions exactly as made and the need to make changes during the year because of changes in the environment. The potential conflict is usually resolved by treating implementation as technical rather than policy related. Executive branch staff play the major role in implementation, with much smaller and more occasional roles for the legislature. Interest groups play virtually no role in implementation. The allowance for technical changes does open the door to policy changes during the year, but these are normally carefully monitored and may cause open conflict when they occur.

Microbudgeting and Macrobudgeting

The five clusters of decision making outline the nature of the decisions actually being made, but tell little about how and why the decisions are made. On the one hand there are a number of budget actors, who all have individual motivations, who strategize to get what they want from the budget. The focus on the actors and their strategies is called microbudgeting. But the actors do not simply bargain with one another or with whomever they meet in the corridor. The actors are assigned budget roles by the budget process, the issues they examine are often framed by the budget process, and the timing and coordination of their decisions are often regulated by the budget process. The budget actors are not totally free to come to budget agreements in any way they choose. Individual actors are bound by environmental constraints. There are choices they are not free to make because they are against the law, or because the courts decree it, or because previous decision makers have bound their hands. The total amount of revenue available is a kind of constraint, as is popular demand for some programs and popular dislike of others. Budgetary decision making has to account not just for budgetary actors but also for budget processes and the environment. This more top-down and systemic perspective on budgeting is called *macrobudgeting*. Contemporary budgeting gives more emphasis to macrobudgeting than exclusively to microbudgeting.

One way of viewing the determinants of budgetary outcomes is as a causal model, depicted in figure 1.1. In this schema, the environment, budget processes, and individuals' strategies all affect outcomes.

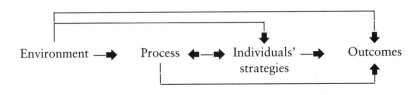

FIGURE 1.1

DECISION MAKING: ENVIRONMENT, PROCESS, AND STRATEGIES

The environment influences budgetary outcomes directly and indirectly, through process and through individual strategies. The environment influences outcomes directly, without going through either budget process or individual strategies, when it imposes emergencies that reorder priorities. Thus a war or a natural disaster preempts normal budgetary decision making.

The environment influences the budget process in several ways. The level of resources available—both the actual level of wealth and the willingness of the citizens to pay their taxes—influences the degree of centralization of budgeting. When resources are especially scarce and there is apparent need to either cut back according to a given set of policies or make each dollar count toward specific economic goals, there is no room for bottom-up demands that result in compromises and a little bit of gain for everyone regardless of need. When resources are abundant, a more decentralized model of process may hold, with less emphasis on comparing policies and less competition between supporters of different policies.

The environment may influence the format of the budget as well as the degree of centralization of decision making. When revenues are growing, there may be more emphasis on planning and on linking the budget to future community goals, to stimulate public demands for new spending. When there is little new money, the idea of planning may seem superfluous. Changing direction, or setting new goals, may seem impossible in the face of declining revenues that make current goals difficult to sustain.

Environment in the sense of the results of prior decisions may also influence process. If there is a huge accumulation of debt and little apparent way to control it, or if the budget has been growing very rapidly for reasons other than war, there may be attempts to change the budget process in an effort to control spending and debt. In contrast, if the environment suggests the need for additional spending, and the current budget process is delivering very slow growth, the process may be changed to make spending decisions quicker and easier.

The environment influences not only the budget process but also the strategies of the budget actors. Clearly, the level of resources available determines whether actors press for new programs and expansion of existing ones or if they strive to prevent cuts and protect their revenue sources from encroachment by other programs.

The level of certainty of funding influences strategies as well. If whatever an agency was promised may never arrive, agency heads are likely to engage in continuous lobbying for their money, and continual rebudgeting internally every time circumstances change. Long-term or future agreements will be perceived as worthless; the possibility of toning down conflict by stretching out budget allocation times will disappear. Attention will focus on what is available now, and going after whatever it is, whether it is what you want or not, because what you really want may never show up and hence is not worth waiting for.

The intergovernmental grant structure is part of the environment that may influence strategies. Because some grant money may seem free, state and local governments may focus their energies on getting grants instead of raising local revenues. Or they may seek to decrease the amount of match required for a grant or increase their authority over how the money can be spent. Intergovernmental grants may make some expenditures relatively cheap, and some cutbacks relatively expensive, and hence frame constraints and choices for state and local budget officials.

The legal environment also influences strategies. For example, if public school teachers want tax raises to fund education and there is a provision in the state constitution forbidding income taxes, the teachers must either campaign for a constitutional revision (a time-consuming and difficult task) or support a tax they know to be more burdensome to the poor. Thus the environment frames choices and influences strategies.

In figure 1.1, the budget process influences strategies directly and, to a lesser extent, outcomes directly. But there is a double-headed arrow on the linkage between budget processes and strategies, suggesting that individuals' strategies also influence budget processes.

Budget processes influence strategies in some fairly obvious ways. If the budget structure allows for lengthy detailed budget hearings, open to the public and interest groups, at which decisions are often made, then various actors are likely to concentrate their efforts on making a good impression at these hearings. If the chief executive prepares the budget, which is subject to only superficial scrutiny and pro forma hearings before being approved by the legislature, anyone who wants to influence the budget—including the legislators themselves—must make their opinions heard earlier in the process, before the final executive proposal is put together. Informal discussion with department heads, or even telephone calls to the budget office, may be the route to influence. If the budget is made two or three times, with only the last one effective, then strategies may be to play out the first time or two with grandstanding—extreme positions to attract media attention—and more detailed and moderate positions later when the final decisions are made. The budget process orders the decisions in such a way that some of them are critical and determine or influence those that come afterward. Budget strategies naturally gravitate to those key decisions no matter where they are located.

When budget outcomes contradict some group's preference, the group may try to change the budget process to help it get the outcomes it prefers. When coalitions of the dissatisfied can agree on particular changes, fairly substantial changes in process may result. A change in process will bring about a change in outcome if the change in process shifts power from one group of individuals who want to accomplish one goal to another group with different goals.

The final link in the figure is between the strategies of budget actors and outcomes. The effect of different strategies on the outcomes is hard to gauge. It seems obvious, however, that strategies that ignore the process or the environment are doomed to failure. Budget actors have to figure out where the flexibility is before they can influence how that flexibility will be used. Strategies that try to bypass superiors or fool legislators generally do not work; strategies that involve careful documentation of need and appear to save money are generally more successful.

Summary and Conclusions

Public budgeting shares the characteristics of all budgeting. It makes choices between possible expenditures, it has to balance, and it has a decision-making process. But public budgeting has a number of additional features peculiar to itself, such as its openness to the environment; the variety of actors involved in budgeting, all of whom come to it with different goals; the separation of taxpayers from budget decision makers; the use of the budget document as a means of public accountability; and the numerous constraints typical of public budgeting.

Public budgeting is both technical and political. Politics takes on some special meanings in the context of budgetary decision making. Budgetary decision making must be flexible, adaptive, and interruptible, which leads to a structure of five semi-independent strands of decision making: revenues, process, expenditures, balance, and implementation. Each such strand generates its own political characteristics.

Budget outcomes are not solely the result of budget actors negotiating with one another in a free-for-all; outcomes depend on the environment, and on the budget process as well as individual strategies. Individual strategies have to be framed in a broader context than simply perceived self-interest.

Budgeting is not well described as an annual process with little change from year to year. Budgetary decision making changes over time: interest group power waxes and wanes, competition in the budget increases and decreases, and the budget process itself varies over time. Changes in process take place in response to individuals, committees, and branches of government jockeying for power; in response to changes in the environment from rich to lean, or vice versa; in response to changes in the power of interest groups; and in response to scandals or excesses of various kinds.

Chapters 2 to 8 describe the patterns of politics associated with each of the decision streams, and the sources and patterns of change over time. The final chapter integrates the decision streams into one model of budgetary decision making and points out the commonalities and differences among the decision streams.

Notes

1. Patricia Ingraham and Charles Barrilleaux, "Motivating Government Managers for Retrenchment: Some Possible Lessons from the Senior Executive Service," *Public Administration Review* 43, no. 3 (1983): 393–402. They cite the Office of Personnel Management Federal Employee Attitude Surveys of 1979 and 1980, extracting responses from those in the Senior Executive Service, the upper ranks of the civil service and appointed administrators. In 1979, 99 percent of the senior executives said that they considered accomplishing something worthwhile was very important; 97 percent said the same in 1980. By contrast, in response to the question "How much would you be motivated by a cash award," only 45 percent said either to a great extent or a very great extent.

2. Twelve percent of LeLoup and Moreland's Department of Agriculture requests between 1946 and 1971 were for decreases. See Lance LeLoup, *Budgetary Politics,* 3d ed. (Brunswick, Ohio: King's Court, 1986), 83. For a more recent case study of an agency requesting decreases, see the case study of the Office of

Personnel Management, in Irene Rubin, *Shrinking the Federal Government* (New York: Longman, 1985). See Irene Rubin, *Running in the Red: The Political Dynamics of Urban Fiscal Stress* (Albany: State University of New York Press, 1982), for an example of a department refusing additional employees.

3. For a good discussion of this phenomenon, see Frank Thompson, *The Politics of Personnel in the City* (Berkeley: University of California Press, 1975).

4. See Rubin, *Shrinking the Federal Government,* for examples during the Reagan administration.

5. U.S. Senate, Committee on Governmental Affairs, *Office of Management and Budget: Evolving Roles and Future Issues,* Committee Print 99–134, 99th Cong., 2d sess., prepared by the Congressional Research Service of the Library of Congress, February 1986.

6. See, for example, Kenneth Shepsle and Barry Weingast, "Legislative Politics and Budget Outcomes," in *Federal Budget Policy in the 1980s,* ed. Gregory Mills and John Palmer (Washington, D.C.: Urban Institute Press, 1984), 343–67.

7. Rubin, *Running in the Red,* 56.

8. For a vivid account of the relationship between pork-barrel spending and building political coalitions, see Martin Shefter, "New York City's Fiscal Crisis: The Politics of Inflation and Retrenchment," *Public Interest* 48 (Summer 1977): 99–127.

9. See John Ellwood, "Comments," in Mills and Palmer, *Federal Budget Policy in the 1980s,* 368–78.

10. Douglas Arnold, "The Local Roots of Domestic Policy," in *The New Congress,* ed. Thomas Mann and Norman Ornstein (Washington, D.C.: American Enterprise Institute, 1981), 252, quoted by Ellwood, in Mills and Palmer, *Federal Budget Policy in the 1980s.*

11. Arnold, "Local Roots," 282.

12. Ellwood, in Mills and Palmer, *Federal Budget Policy in the 1980s,* 370.

13. Linda Harriman and Jeffrey Straussman, "Do Judges Determine Budget Decisions? Federal Court Decisions in Prison Reform and State Spending for Corrections," *Public Administration Review* 43, no. 4 (1983): 343–51.

2. Revenue Politics

We ... seem to be able to defy what is supposed to happen. The nay-sayers all said Social Security was in such trouble, and the Ways and Means Committee pulled it together. It was a doctrine of politics that tax increases could not happen in an election year. We have done it quite often in the last years. ... There is no doubt we can make tough decisions.

— Representative Barbara Kennelly

Public budgeting involves a separation of the tax payers and the decision makers who determine tax and spending levels. This separation sets up the possibility of some radical disagreements. Citizens would undoubtedly be happier about paying taxes if they could choose which services they wanted and pay no more for them than they felt the programs were worth. They might be even happier if they could get others to pay the taxes while they received the services. Individual taxpayers usually do not control the mix of services, however, and thus may have to pay for some programs they do not want. Moreover, many citizens are convinced that they are paying for waste and mismanagement. In addition, taxpayers often feel that others are getting away with paying less taxes than they are. They resent being forced to pay more than their share.

Elected officials have the legal power to raise taxes, but they can easily be turned out of office if they raise taxes beyond the limits that citizens formally or informally set. Angry citizens and activated interest groups can, and sometimes do, revolt against taxes. Some politicians respond to this kind of threat by promising not to raise taxes, no matter what.

Never raising taxes is a difficult position to maintain, since expenditures are likely to increase. Even when government does not expand functions, inflation increases the costs of equipment, such as fire trucks and airplanes, and the costs of salaries. Revenue sources that do not grow with inflation, such as water and sewer fees, have to be raised periodically to keep up with the gradually rising costs. When government does add functions, it has to find new sources of taxation or increase existing revenues to cover the increased costs. And when general taxes are eroded by special exceptions or other changes in the laws, some provision has to be made to replace the lost revenues, or decrease the size or scope of government. Changes in the environment, such as termination of grant income or a decline in the economy or a natural disaster or war, can create the need for more revenues.

The necessity of increasing revenues and the public's reluctance to be taxed, especially for services they do not want, leads to three major characteristics of revenue politics. The first is that when public officials determine that additional revenues are necessary, they go about getting support very carefully. They may work out a set of strategies, adapt budget processes specifically for taxation purposes, and choose their timing so that overwhelming environmental pressures seem to require tax increases. The second characteristic of revenue politics is that it develops an underside, a mirror image, a politics of protection from taxation and of tax reductions and exceptions. Third, the efforts to raise taxes carefully and to protect individuals, interest groups, and regions from taxation leads to a piecemeal, complicated, inconsistent, and inequitable tax structure that periodically needs overhauling. Revenue politics is characterized by periodic efforts at reform.

Increasing Taxes

Garnering support for increasing revenues is much more difficult than gaining support for spending proposals. Taxation creates a set of opponents and has few supporters. To get taxes passed requires major efforts to create support and defuse opposition.

What follow are two examples of efforts to increase taxes. One was only partly and temporarily successful (in Illinois), while the other (in Dayton, Ohio) worked quite well. Both efforts show the tremendous effort that goes into trying to gain support for a tax increase.

The problem in the Illinois case was partly procedural. By initially setting up a blue-ribbon committee to come up with technical solutions, the process stirred up interest-group opposition rather than toning it down. But the more important problem was that there was no irrefutable evidence of need; the governor's past manipulations of the budget created distrust that he just could not overcome. Part of the reason for the success of the Dayton tax increase was the care with which the opposition was defused, by making the increases revokable in the future, by widely airing the need, by guaranteeing the lack of waste to those most suspicious of it, and by linking revenues to specific desired service levels.

MINICASE 1: INCOME TAX INCREASES IN ILLINOIS

In 1983, the State of Illinois needed more revenues.[1] The state had granted several tax-relief measures, including an expansion of the eligibility for the circuit breaker, a tax-relief measure for the elderly. The state inheritance tax had been repealed in 1982. Both measures lowered revenues. Inflation and recession squeezed state finances, and a long-term decline in heavy industry was eroding the state's economic base.

Cash-flow problems and deficits were revealed immediately after the 1982 election, creating the impression that the governor had hidden the true fiscal condition of the state until after the election was over. This feeling of having been deceived increased the unpopularity of the tax proposal in the state legislature.

The governor set up a blue-ribbon task force to examine the revenue situation. The commission made twenty far-ranging recommendations, including increased revenues, decreased tax breaks, increased fairness, and some economic stimulation. The bipartisan recommendations drew "protests from nearly every special interest group in the state."[2] That was the last that was heard of the seriously thought through bipartisan package.

Governor James Thompson then presented his own proposal for a $1.9 billion tax increase, raising the personal income tax from 2.5 percent to 4 percent and the corporate income tax from 4 percent to 5.6 percent. He also proposed increases in the gasoline tax, license plate fees, and liquor taxes.

The governor's second step was to present his budget proposal for the following year without the tax increases. His so-called doomsday budget included massive cuts in education, local government, public aid, and mental health. It was intended to rouse the beneficiaries of the services facing cuts, to get them to lobby the legislature for the tax increase. The doomsday budget succeeded in rousing these interest groups. The education lobby, the American Federation of Federal, State, and Local Employees, and social service providers all supported various provisions of the tax increase. The Chamber of Commerce, representing an alliance of small business people, predictably opposed the increases, as did the Illinois Association of Manufacturers.

The third step in the governor's strategy was to delay his announcement of how he would allocate the new tax revenues. He wanted to give the impression that many legislators' programs would be funded, without specifically saying yes to one and no to another.

The outcome of the negotiations was partially successful. The legislature granted only a temporary surcharge on the income tax, but the governor was reelected. The financial problems of the state remained and the governor had to go back to the legislature to request increases again in 1987.

MINICASE 2:

A SUCCESSFUL MUNICIPAL TAX INCREASE IN DAYTON, OHIO

In March 1984, voters of Dayton, Ohio, voted overwhelmingly for an increase in the city's income tax.[3] The tax was presented as part of a package, including property tax relief of $50 per person, a tax benefit amounting to more than $1.5 million. Other elements of the approved package included a pledge to reduce municipal employment by more than 100 positions over the next five years, a pledge to maintain services at present levels, a limit on the city's cash reserves, and the establishment of a Chamber of Commerce review committee to study city expenditure patterns. The increase in the income tax was passed with a sunset provision, that is, it was set to terminate in 1990.

City officials engaged in a three-year campaign for acceptance of the increase. The campaign included quarterly reports to council members to build awareness of the problem, reduction of 300 city positions by attrition, and meetings with a group of chief executive officers of businesses in the city, to explain the need and ask for support. For the nine months immediately prior to the increase, the mayor and the city manager publicized financial problems, talked to neighborhood groups, and explained the plan to the city unions. The final package was put together by the city council, based on talks with these groups, and then the package was publicized, using "lots of personal contact, targeted selling techniques, and endorsements to explain and sell the package to the voters."[4]

Tax increases need to be planned carefully; consideration must be given to the timing, the choice of budget process, and the selection of the particular elements that will be proposed in a tax increase package.

MONITORING THE ENVIRONMENT

The environment affects the timing of tax increases. For example, executives have been more likely to propose increases when the risks were relatively low—when there was no major opposition party to take advantage of taxpayer discontent or when the overall need for more revenues was very clear, as during a depression or war.[5] When the federal income tax became legal after a constitutional amendment in 1913, most people had to pay no income tax. The law had graduated rates as income rose. The top rate, on incomes over $500,000, was 7 percent.[6] To pay for World War I, the exemption was lowered, so more people with moderate incomes had to pay some tax. Rates were also increased, and the degree of progressivity was increased so that wealthier people paid much higher tax rates. The high rates of progressivity were dropped after the war. But during the Great Depression of the 1930s, revenues fell off because of the shrinking economy and mass unemployment; the need for more revenues resulted in proposals to restore some of the taxes that had been cut. The new proposals shared the burden rather widely.[7] And again during World War II, when the need for additional revenues was acute and unquestionable, the income tax expanded, changing from an elite to a mass tax, vastly increasing its revenue yield.

CHOOSING A PROCESS

The process of increasing taxes has to be somewhat buffered from interest groups in order to be effective. Individuals and interest groups tend to be both well informed and highly interested in tax proposals; they lobby intensively against increases and for changes that will help them. When information about proposals is open to the public, the public in its various forms tends to turn considered technical proposals into mash. This is what happened with the governor's blue-ribbon panel proposal in Illinois.

But tax-writing legislative committees can buffer themselves against interest groups in a variety of ways. Key elements in the process have to do with openness of the decision making to the public and interest groups, the kind of discipline leaders can exert or rewards they can provide, and the rules under which bills are considered. Open rules allow large numbers of often unrelated amendments, and closed rules prevent amendments after a bill has been passed by committee.

At the national level, the central role in tax decisions of the Ways and Means Committee in the House of Representatives has stimulated much thought on the effect of process on outcomes. For years, the Ways and Means Committee was dominated by its chairman, Wilbur Mills. He carefully worked out compromise legislation that had the full support of his committee; his recommendations were reported to the floor under a closed rule forbidding amendments, and had full committee backing; they were seldom turned down by the House of Representatives.[8] The closed rule prevented House members from sticking a number of tax breaks for special interests onto the tax measure when it came to the floor for a vote, while it enhanced the power of the committee chairman. The closed rule, considerable secrecy in committee deliberations, and the selection of members to the Ways and Means Committee who were from safe districts made the committee less accessible to interest groups. Members of the committee were hand picked, not only because they were from safe districts, but also because they were known to be party loyalists with discipline.[9] The committee operated as a committee of the whole, so the committee chair did not share authority with subcommittee heads. The chair offered support on special-interest tax legislation to get backing on major issues. Once he had forged a coalition of support, it held through the legislative process.

33

The relative inaccessibility of the deliberations gave the impression of secrecy and of the dominance of an old-boy power structure in tax legislation. The congressional reforms of the 1970s opened up the committee procedures. The chair no longer had the freedom to select members, the committee was expanded in size, and specialized subcommittees were formed. The decision-making process was more open to the public and the press. The ability of committee members to go directly to the press, and their greater independence in getting legislation through, made them less dependent on the chair's support for their special-interest legislation, and hence they were less responsive to his rewards for their loyalty. Members were no longer selected to sit on the Ways and Means Committee because of party loyalty or because they had safe seats. Committee members became more vulnerable to interest groups.

Tax legislation did not markedly improve under this structure; the tendency to give away tax breaks (sometimes called tax expenditures) seems to have increased. "Between 1975 and 1980 the revenue losses for tax expenditures rose faster—14 percent a year—than direct outlays, which increased 11 percent annually during that period. From fiscal 1974 to fiscal 1980, tax expenditures grew by 162 percent while outlays rose by 111 percent. In fiscal 1982 total tax expenditures exceeded $260 billion."[10]

Under the reforms of the 1970s, Ways and Means bills came to the floor under an open rule, meaning that House members could add amendments to a bill when it reached the floor of the House. The Ways and Means bills were more likely to be amended. The Senate sometimes added amendments to House-passed bills, bypassing the Ways and Means Committee completely; these amendments went directly to conference, without any committee consideration. "The process has become so manipulable that in some ways it resembles an open caucus that can be taken over by virtually any group."[11] This environment strengthened interest groups.

After 1980, the structure changed back in the direction of more committee control over the tax process. Representative Dan Rostenkowski took firmer control over Ways and Means Committee members, negotiating support for committee positions and threatening punishment for those not supporting the final agreement. The open rule of the 1970s was replaced by a modified open rule, which allows a few specific and germane amendments, but not an unlimited number for a range of purposes. In addition, more of the committee markups are now done in closed sessions, often without a formal vote. Appointments to the committee increasingly include more senior representatives from safer districts. These changes helped to insulate the committee from interest-group pressure and have been credited with helping Ways and Means to design and pass the 1986 tax reform, which reduced the number of tax breaks.[12] After the 1986 tax reform, the rate of increase in tax losses slowed from 14 percent to approximately 6 percent a year (calculated from *The Budget of the United States, 1991*).

The similarities between tax policy and trade policy are instructive. In trade policy, generous giveaways in the form of tariff increases prevailed for a number of years before the Great Depression of the 1930s. The higher a trade barrier, the more protected domestic businesses and industries felt because foreign goods were too expensive, once their producers paid the tariffs, to compete with domestic goods. But the Smoot-Hawley tariff bill, which put tariffs on many items, brought on a world trade war and economic disaster, creating a new consensus for free trade. The consequences of excessive protection were so striking and so negative that the need to change policy was widely accepted. Congress then restructured its trade policy process to bring about the desired outcomes, responsiveness without capitulation to special interests. Congress successfully insulated itself from direct interest-group pressure on bills.[13]

Process by itself cannot control politicians' desires to do favors. If the consensus to provide sound tax policy is there, the structure can be created to allow it to occur. The consensus tends to form when the environment leaves no doubt about the urgency of the need and when the environment suggests that tax increases are low risk, as when there is no effective opposition party. Interest groups do not always determine the outcomes if legislators choose to insulate themselves in the interest of avoiding a clear public policy disaster. But when legislators choose not to create such a structure, they can be overrun by interest groups.

Tax-Raising Strategies

Public officials use a wide variety of strategies to try to get tax increases passed by the legislature and accepted by the voters. Some of these strategies have been suggested in the cases of Illinois and Dayton—for example, the strategy of convincing the public that there is a need for a tax increase and the strategy of proving to citizens that their money will not be wasted.

The chief executive who supports a tax increase can try to trade support on unrelated bills for support on the tax increase. If legislators feel the threat of being thrown out of office, such promises are often inadequate; the tax package has to be structured in such a way as to maximize support. There are basically two ways to do that: (1) tie the tax increase to some highly desired service(s) or capital project(s), which is called earmarking; (2) raise more revenue than is immediately needed to cover costs and distribute the extra income in such a way as to garner the needed votes.

35

Earmarking. Earmarking revenues means raising them for a specific purpose so that the money must be spent on that purpose and not on anything else. If the purpose is popular, such as repaving miles of broken residential streets, citizens may be more willing to pay the extra tax for that desired purpose than for general purposes over which they have little control. Earmarking revenues for popular causes can be one way of overcoming popular resistance to tax increases. Those who support a particular program are often eager to have earmarked resources because it means that they do not have to compete with other expenditures in the budget; they can protect their program's funding into the future if they manage to earmark revenues for it. Sometimes powerful lobby groups actually get earmarking into the state constitution to lock in a revenue source for the future.

Earmarking is a major part of revenue politics with program supporters trying to get revenues earmarked. At the national level, one of the major examples of earmarking is social security taxes, which are levied on individuals' paychecks and put into a trust fund that can be spent on nothing else. This arrangement is meant to protect social security funding from the demands of other government programs or demands to reduce taxation. There are also special earmarked revenues at the federal level for airport construction, highways, and public transportation. In 1994, $690 billion of federal revenues, or 47 percent of total receipts from the public, were earmarked.[14] Earmarking is also prevalent at the state level. Looking only at taxes and not at all revenues, the National Conference of State Legislatures found a decrease over time from 51 percent earmarked in 1954, to 41 percent in 1963, 23 percent in 1979, 21 percent in 1984, 23 percent in 1988, and 24.4 percent in 1993. While average earmarking at the state level remains much lower than at the national level, recent years have seen a slight rise in earmarking at the state level, primarily for primary and secondary education.[15]

The decrease in the proportion of earmarked state funds from 1954 to 1984 was less a matter of policy choice to reduce earmarking than a side effect of the adoption of broad-based sales and income taxes that occurred in many states between 1950 and 1971. These sales and income taxes were adopted with relatively low levels of earmarking[16] and grew more quickly than earmarked revenue sources.[17] The slight increase in earmarking since 1984 has been a matter of policy choice: "... it is clear that legislators now turn somewhat more readily to earmarking taxes than they did in the recent past."[18]

Sometimes taxes are earmarked for the purposes of easing adoption, but then the earmarking is gradually eroded and eventually dropped. One reason this may occur is that earmarking works for popular programs but not for less popular ones. The costs of carrying out routine housekeeping tasks, such as hiring an attorney, become incredibly difficult to pay for if a major portion of revenue is earmarked for the most popular and visible programs. Revenues may not be shifted from earmarked purposes, limiting the flexibility of managers to deal with housekeeping matters, severe needs of small groups, or changing political or technical priorities. Hence there is internal pressure to eliminate and reduce earmarking.

If the earmarking cannot be reduced or eliminated, there may be enormous pressure to take away from the recipient of earmarked revenues any general revenues (nonearmarked revenues) that it may have received, to spend on needy but less popular programs. A recent study indicated that in all seven states studied—New York, New Hampshire, Ohio, Michigan, California, Montana, and Florida—lottery revenues substituted for general revenue that had been going to education.[19] In Florida, after the introduction of the lottery, the proportion of state dollars going to education dropped from 62 to 53 percent.[20] Taxpayers are likely to become angry at such maneuvers. They voted to tax themselves more heavily in order to increase the funding for schools, only to find that the additional earmarked taxes are substituted for the original state funding. When they find themselves in this kind of situation, voters may well refuse to approve future tax increases. A less harmful way of using earmarked funding to pay for less popular programs is to group more and less popular programs together and ask for one earmarked tax increase to pay for both of them. This bundling of more and less popular programs is what happened in the DeKalb, Illinois, case described in chapter 1 when capital expenditures and social services were linked and an increase in the sales tax was earmarked to pay for them.

Although earmarking can help get a tax passed, it has a number of disadvantages. It prevents comprehensive budgeting. It links specific revenue sources with specific spending programs, but often without any connections between the amount of revenues produced and the amount of revenues needed for the program. Often there is little programmatic connection either. A portion of the income tax may be spent on local government, as in Illinois, or a portion of income from pari-mutuel betting may be earmarked for mental retardation or indigent patients, as in Arkansas, or taxes on tobacco may be earmarked for education and welfare, as in Alabama.[21] These shortcomings may have helped keep down the level of designating taxes for specific expenditures, despite the temptations of easing public approval of new taxes by earmarking.

Distributing Benefits from a Tax Increase. A second alternative for making revenue increases more palatable is to raise more revenues than needed for the immediate problem and then design a package of expenditures that will gain support for the tax increase. Sometimes, as in recent efforts in Illinois to increase taxes, this may be done by keeping the new expenditures secret, allowing many legislators to think that their projects will be included; or the new revenue may be tentatively allocated, pending approval of the tax, to get the new recipients to lobby for the tax increase.

Some revenue-raising proposals have sought to reduce some taxes while increasing others, to gain supporters among those who would benefit from the tax reduction. Thus, in the Dayton case, property taxes were to be reduced for a large number of people; a similar arrangement allowed for increases in sales taxes in DeKalb, Illinois, by reducing the property tax. The net amount of revenues is increased, but a large number of people feel they are getting something positive out of the tax increase.

Some other strategies that public officials use when raising taxes include making the increase temporary, spelling out carefully what the increase will be used for, ensuring that any tax increases are gradual and predictable, and taxing those who lack the power or the means to protest.

Temporary Taxes. Specific tactics used to disarm the opposition include making the tax increase temporary and including a variety of safeguards to show that the spending is not wasteful. Temporary taxes are distinctly easier to pass than permanent ones, but if the need is not temporary (e.g., a short-term recession continues longer than expected) the problem recurs and the scene plays itself out again.

Accountability. The secrecy with which the Illinois governor handled the finances of the state before his request for tax increases eroded the trust necessary to pass the increases. In this case, accountability was a prerequisite for acceptability. Accountability also frequently plays a role in local school financing elections when citizens' distrust is caused by accumulated deficits and ambiguous statements about how the money will be used. Citizens often want to know what their money is going to be used for, and that it will be well spent, before they willingly part with more of their earnings. Thus openness about government's finances may be part of a successful campaign for tax increases.

Predictability. Successful campaigns to increase taxes are also sensitive to the need for increasing taxes in a gradual, predictable, and unobtrusive manner. Taxes that increase in unpredictable jumps are apt to arouse the most vociferous opposition because people are likely to be unable to pay for them without making major sacrifices. Sudden high increases in property taxes have often preceded tax revolts. Rather than raise one tax by a large and visible amount, politicians may raise a number of smaller taxes by a small amount so that no one group is seriously hurt and citizens feel that the burdens are being widely and equitably shared. In Illinois, the governor proposed moderate increases in an array of taxes rather than larger increases in just one source of funds.

Taxing the Politically Weak. Another way of gaining acceptability for increases in taxation is to place the burden for paying for them on those who have relatively little political power. When business is relatively dominant, it shifts the burden of taxation away from business and on to consumers; when labor is dominant, it shifts the tax burden more on to business and the wealthy. Another version of taxing those too weak to fight back is taxing outsiders. "Outsiders" are those who do not vote and hence cannot throw politicians out of office. Severance taxes on natural resources is one way to pass taxes on to others. For example, states rich in natural resources tax those resources, and the tax is passed on as part of the price to residents in other states who consume the final product. At the local level, sales taxes in shopping centers are popular in part because they tax shoppers from other cities and towns. Hotel and motel taxes are also popular because they tax the out-of-town traveler rather than the resident.

To summarize, public officials plan very carefully for tax increases. They plan the timing, taking advantage of a lack of organized opposition and an environment that seems to require tax increases. They devise and use processes that insulate them somewhat from interest groups. And they strategize to minimize the pain to voters and build coalitions of support. When tax increases are necessary, public officials must be accountable for the way they have been spending money, in terms both of the quality of management (lack of waste) and of following the spending preferences of the public. Their strategies often include conveying to the public the appearance of good management, and tying new revenues to particular popular programs. They may back off from these efforts after the tax increase is passed. Hence the need for periodic tax increases is an important linkage between the taxpayers and the spenders, to keep the spenders in line with the desires of the payers.

The Politics of Protection

The politics of raising revenues has a mirror image, that of protecting the population in general or specific groups from taxation, or lowering tax levels for individuals or groups. Just as raising taxes necessarily brings a certain amount of blame, the lowering of taxes brings, if not praise, at least a measure of gratitude. Interest groups may hire lobbyists to help deflect needs for more taxation on to others, or even contribute to election campaigns to find candidates who will protect them from tax increases.

The acceptability of taxation is at least in part a function of where the burden falls. Choices revolve around three issues: (1) which taxes to consider; (2) what definition of taxable wealth is used; (3) what pattern of exceptions to grant to broad-based taxes.

THE CHOICE OF REVENUES TO CONSIDER

Part of revenue politics involves pressure to adopt or increase reliance on tax sources that burden others more than oneself. The major forms of revenue currently in use are income and wage taxes, sales taxes of various sorts, tariffs, property taxes, and user fees. Although there are many kinds of each, with somewhat different characteristics, each of these revenue sources works differently and affects the population differently.

Income taxes are taxes paid on different forms of income, including wages and interest on investments, and they are paid by virtually everyone except the very poor. They can be progressive; that is, they may tax the rich more heavily than the poor. Or they can be proportional, taxing everyone the same percentage regardless of income. Income taxes are tied to ability to pay. Wage taxes are also tied to ability to pay, but they are a little different, since they are taxes only on wages (earned income), and they tax those who earn their income in the jurisdiction whether they live there or not. Wage taxes are one way of taxing outsiders, commuters to a city who work there but live and vote elsewhere.

Sales taxes are consumer taxes, taxes paid when people or businesses buy something, usually (but not always) a finished product. Sales taxes do not affect wholesale and manufacturing businesses directly, but retailers, who are the ones who collect the tax, may be inconvenienced, and they have to deal with price increases and a possible reduction in demand. Consumers are the most directly affected, but they pay sales taxes in small, almost invisible amounts during the year, so they tend not to mind them too much. Sales taxes are not very tightly linked to ability to pay; they often fall more heavily on the poor than the wealthy because the poor pay a larger proportion of their incomes on taxable items.

Tariffs are fees required for foreign producers to be allowed to market their goods in this country. Tariffs are another revenue form that taxes outsiders. Tariffs protect domestic industries from foreign competition by raising the price of imported products, but they also raise prices for consumers.

Tariffs are ultimately paid by the consumer, without much regard to the ability to pay. Tariffs are levied only by the national government.

Property taxes are those that tax a proportion of the worth or sales value of property owned. This may be personal property (e.g., cars or horses) or real estate (land and houses and buildings). Property taxes on real estate are loosely related to ability to pay because wealthier persons are likely to own more expensive homes, but the relationship is not tight. Older persons on fixed incomes may find property taxes rising because the value of their homes is increasing over time, for example. Or a business may own expensive property and equipment, but not be making much income on it proportional to the value of the property. Owners of commercial property may pass the tax on to their tenants, who may have less income than the owners.

User fees are a revenue source that depends on how much citizens use the service. The fee is supposed to be in some way proportional to use. If you use the local swimming pool, you help pay for it; if you do not use it, you do not pay. Water bills are a form of user fee. User fees have the advantage of allowing those who pay to select only the services they want, and not to use them, and not pay, if the cost is too high. But they have several disadvantages as well. First, they often have little to do with ability to pay. And second, others may benefit although they are not currently using the service, and without their support, the costs of providing some services may be too high for the users to pay. For example, only those currently attending public schools are using the service directly, but every employer of a graduate benefits from the service, and every voter benefits from the education level of other voters. If the whole cost of public schools were placed on those currently taking classes, the costs might easily exceed the students' ability to pay, increasing the number of drop-outs and illiterate unemployables.

Business groups often prefer sales taxes on consumers and oppose income taxes, especially those levied on corporate incomes. Labor groups usually favor income taxes, but as labor's wages have risen, the rank and file have become more reluctant to support high individual income taxes and more supportive of higher corporate income taxes. Many groups support user fees because they seem to be so fair, on the one hand, and so voluntaristic, on the other; if you do not want a service, you do not have to pay for it, and if you use less, you pay less. Those who favor smaller government tend to favor user fees.

The effort to lobby for or against certain forms of taxation becomes particularly visible when a new tax is proposed. For example, when a new tax on imported oil was proposed at the federal level, representatives from the New England states opposed it vigorously because it would raise the cost

THE POLITICS OF PUBLIC BUDGETING

of gasoline and fuel oil, but the oil-producing states of the South and West supported the tax, because it would help raise the price of domestically produced oil.[22]

DEFINING TAXABLE WEALTH

The choice of which revenue source to use often revolves around the definition of taxable wealth. In theory, one can levy taxes against any form of wealth. Historically, tax collectors counted windows in houses and taxed people with more windows more heavily. The number of windows was a rough indicator of wealth and one that was less subject to hiding than cash or animals. Choosing the basis for taxation is not merely a technical decision, however; it is also a political decision, and it necessarily hurts some and helps others.

Politicians can protect particular groups of people from taxation by defining their sources of wealth as not taxable. To protect one group, public officials may shift the burden of taxation to some other group or reduce the level of taxation for everyone.

Since particular forms of taxation affect different kinds of wealth, and different regions of the country have been based on different kinds of wealth, the politics of taxation has historically revolved around the choice of taxes that would affect particular regions of the country. Until the late 1930s, ". . . the Northeast favored first tariffs (which protected their industrial goods) and excise, license and land taxes if needed; the South and West resisted all these taxes, whose impact fell disproportionately on them, and favored taxes on income and wealth, of which they had little."[23]

The urban-rural split has also been important in the history of taxation, especially property taxes. Rural areas wanted to make sure the basis of taxation, the measure of wealth, was something they had little of and cities had much of. They worked to define property taxes in terms of both realty (houses, buildings, machinery) and personalty (other forms of wealth, including bonds, mortgages, and other money instruments.) The farmers wanted to define the base of taxation to include the new wealth of the cities, of which the farmers had little; they also sought exemptions of various kinds for their own equipment and herds.[24]

Defining the base of taxation in order to control the burden, especially on the business classes, has a long history within cities. San Francisco during the latter part of the nineteenth century, a city experiencing rapid economic and population growth, illustrates how the tax base may be defined or limited through political choices. Politicians defined the new wealth of the city as not taxable. "In effect, local leaders built a wall between socioeconomic structural development and fiscal policy, refusing to act on the demands created by such development or to accept additional resources provided by such development."[25]

More generally, in the 1800s U.S. cities were growing rapidly, experiencing huge migrations of the poor. The need for revenues to provide infrastructure, especially for streets, water and sewer, and housing, was urgent. The middle and upper classes felt that they were unduly taxed to support the poor and that the burden might be limitless. In response, they tried to buffer the public sector from demands and put their own wealth off limits. By the early 1900s, however, the Progressive movement was strong; part of its thrust was to devise technical solutions to the problems of the cities and to find the resources required to implement them. The Progressives were much more willing to tax the rich to get the capital they needed for public infrastructure.

The effort to define some sources of wealth as nontaxable has continued over the years. In Oakland, California, in the 1960s and early 1970s, an artificially low definition of how much citizens could be taxed kept the scope of services limited, and kept City Hall in a perpetual scramble to balance the budget.[26] At the state level, protests by taxpayers in the 1970s reinforced the notion that property taxes are unacceptable to voters. In these instances, the definition of the taxable base was politically negotiated; those who had more political power at the time managed to protect their own wealth. Part of this process involved the systematic discouragement of government response to existing problems. To keep the level of taxation down, the scope of government services had to be kept narrow.

Those who manage to define taxable wealth or acceptable levels of taxation to their own advantage are likely to want to lock in that definition for a long time. One way of doing this is to write tax limits or unacceptable forms of taxation into constitutions and charters. For example, Proposition 13 in California, which limited the property tax, was an amendment to the California constitution. For many years, the U.S. Constitution had a prohibition against an income tax, as did a number of state constitutions.

Writing such constraints into constitutions slows down the rate of change, but constitutions can be amended or rewritten.[27] Introducing a new tax in the face of constitutional restrictions may require larger legislative majorities, public referenda, or even constitutional conventions. The courts are often involved to determine if a new tax is constitutional. Thus the number of actors is often greater, the size of potential veto groups often smaller, and the time lag longer for new tax sources than for increases in traditional sources. Consequently, there is a tendency for historical tax choices to have long-term impact; governmental units tend to stay with whatever taxes they have and marginally increase them as needed; only major economic problems or massive changes in opinion or political strength are likely to provide the background for major changes in the definition of taxable wealth.[28]

Tax Breaks

A tax, once passed, may place the burden of taxation on one group or another, but the location of that burden may change throughout the life of the tax as politicians grant exemptions from the tax. The exemptions are then viewed as political protections for certain groups or economic classes. The nature and politics of tax breaks, sometimes called tax expenditures, vary considerably from one level of government to another, but regardless of the level of government at which they occur, tax breaks share some common features.

First, they represent dollars that the government is theoretically owed that it has decided not to collect. Absent dollars are much more difficult to count and account for than dollars one receives in one's hands. Tax breaks do not always meaningfully add to one another and hence are not always comparable to dollar outlays for expenditures. The amount of revenue lost is based on an estimate of the amount of money the taxpayer would owe if the tax break did not exist, but if a particular tax preference were eliminated, the government might not receive all the money it lost because of the tax break; the money could be spent on something else that was tax deductible instead.

A second characteristic of tax breaks is that there is a general tendency for all broad taxes gradually to be eroded by exceptions for particular groups. Sometimes when a tax is passed or the structure of the tax is changed in a way that hurts some particular group, that group tries to get tax breaks so that the new burden on them is lessened. Politicians may respond to what they perceive as hardship among a particular group affected by a tax. Those who wish to lower their tax burdens may lobby effectively for exceptions for themselves, regardless of hardship. How responsive lawmakers are to these pressures depends somewhat on the political strength of the group making the demands. At the state level, state officials are often responsive to pressure from the dominant industries in their states. California taxes the movie industry lightly, and Wisconsin favors the beer industry. North Carolina favors the tobacco industry, and Michigan protects its auto industry.[29]

The third characteristic of tax breaks is that during a period of economic stress, there is often a tendency to give specific tax breaks to businesses. When the economy began to falter in the middle 1970s, pressure increased for government to stimulate investment and capital formation. The national government responded with a number of tax breaks, aimed prima-

44

rily at businesses and upper-income taxpayers. The number of tax expenditures greatly increased between 1975 and 1981, compared to the preceding twenty-nine years.[30] Many states have responded to economic problems in similar ways. In the middle 1970s, when unemployment hit 8 percent, governors were "under tremendous pressure to do something—anything. Most states responded with conventional medicine: they cut taxes and offered large firms in other states a host of tax and financial incentives to open new plants across state lines."[31] Cities have responded to weakening economies in similar ways.[32]

A fourth characteristic of tax expenditures is that the money is granted, often with the idea that public policy objectives will be achieved through them, without any supervision or evaluation to see if the policy objective is being achieved. Thus the federal government provides a tax break for investors who loan money to cities so that cities can borrow at lower expense than private-sector companies. The public purpose is to encourage the building of infrastructure, such as streets, buildings, and drainage, that are needed for the economy to function. But there is no supervision to see if the borrowing has indeed gone for such purposes or whether cities are spending money to subsidize private-sector businesses, preparing sites for them, paying for moving costs, or even constructing buildings for private-sector businesses.

Within these overall similarities, there is considerable variation in the nature, use, and politics of tax expenditures at the federal, state, and local levels.

Federal Level. At the national level, the federal income tax has gone through a number of changes since its inception. These changes have been of two basic kinds: (1) the structure of the tax; and (2) the number of exceptions granted.[33] The structure of the tax includes the definition of taxable wealth, policy decisions such as how to treat marriage or children, and the percentage rates applied to families with high, middle, or low incomes. The exceptions are reductions in taxes for those to whom the tax would normally apply. A single individual or a class of people with certain characteristics or certain forms of wealth might get such a reduction, or a company or a particular industry might get a particular tax break.

When the structure of a tax changes, it creates new burdens for different groups of people. As the burden on a group increases, the demand for exceptions for that group is likely to increase. The federal income tax illustrates the relationship between the structure of a tax, the relative burdens it imposes, and the nature of the exceptions granted.

In the early years of the income tax, which was passed in a period of working-class dominance, tax rates burdened the rich particularly. When business dominance was reasserted in the 1920s, the tax structure was modified somewhat and extensive tax breaks were granted to the wealthy. One example of a tax break for the well-to-do was the lower rate of taxation applied to capital gains compared to wages.

Capital gains taxes offer a separate rate of taxation for income resulting from increases in the value of investments held for a specified period of time, sometimes as short as six months. When the rate of taxation applied to this source of revenue is markedly lower than the rate applied to wages, those who own capital pay lower tax rates than those who earn salaries. This tax break was supposed to provide an incentive for the public to invest money rather than spend it, but it has been available equally during times of capital shortage and abundance.

The capital gains tax was created in 1921. Between 1913 and 1921, there was no differentiation between other income and capital gains. The maximum rate rose from 7 percent to 77 percent between 1913 and 1919, and it was 73 percent between 1919 and 1921. In 1921, the top rate was reduced to 58 percent, in response to the end of World War I and the reduction in revenue needs, and as part of the early period of business dominance. Simultaneously, a separate rate was fixed for long-term capital gains.[34] Initially the special rate for capital gains was set at 12.5 percent, considerably lowering the tax liability of well-to-do investors. This benefit was not eliminated until the tax reform of 1986.

The Oil and Gas Depletion Allowance, first granted in 1913, allows special deductions for taxpayers who derive their income from natural gas or oil.[35] These taxpayers may deduct a substantial proportion of their wells' income each year. This special tax privilege is supposed to compensate for the fact that oil and gas are limited resources and can be used up. Later, such depletion allowances expanded to include sand and gravel, brick clay and monumental stone, and clam and oyster shells. The benefits were not as high as those for gas and oil, but they were still substantial.

The benefits to the oil companies were lessened as a reaction to the gasoline shortages of the 1970s, when the public reacted with furor to price gouging and opportunistic profits for the oil companies at the expense of the public. But only the biggest companies lost their benefits; smaller companies, which were scattered around the country and had better political support, maintained their benefits. The estimated dollar loss to the Treasury Department in 1983 from oil and gas depletion allowances was $375 million for corporations and $1.4 billion for individuals. When combined with another special benefit for oil and gas companies that allows them to subtract costs of exploration and development, the losses are $1.035 billion for corporations, and $2.3 billion for individuals. The U.S. budget listed the estimated losses from both tax breaks as $2.495 billion for 1985, and about $2.140 billion in 1986. Estimates for 1991 were less than $1 billion.[36]

There were a number of special benefits to the rich and to businesses in the 1920s besides the capital gains tax and the oil and gas depletion allowances, but special tax benefits have not been exclusively for the rich. Major changes occurred in the structure of the income tax during World War II as rates and numbers of taxpayers increased in 1940, 1941, and 1942. The income tax became a mass tax, including many more people of moderate and lower incomes, and rates for higher incomes became steeper. These changes were not repealed or reversed after the war. As a result, after the war, exemptions were addressed to a wider group of citizens. More concern was shown for whether people could afford to pay the tax, and so exemptions were created for the elderly, for people with medical problems, and the blind. (Deductions for medical expenses were passed in 1942, special allowances for the blind in 1944, and additional exemptions for the elderly in 1948. These benefits were expanded during the 1950s.) In 1983, the cost to the Treasury of these tax breaks was about $2.5 billion.[37] According to the 1991 budget, the deductibility of medical expenditures was estimated to cost about $3 billion in outlay equivalent dollars, the benefit to the blind was estimated to cost about $15 million, and the benefit to the elderly and disabled about $15 million.

The broad scattering of tax benefits passed in 1954 may have been a direct response to the changes in the tax structure during World War II. "Prior to the war there was little need for child care provisions or a retirement credit because most people affected by such rules did not pay any income taxes. Moreover, the stakes of the game had increased for those with higher incomes. When the top marginal rate is 25 percent, whether 20 or 30 percent of adjusted gross income can be deducted as charitable giving does not make that much difference. When rates are 91 percent, however, it does."[38]

While much of the pattern of tax breaks can be explained as reactions to a changing tax structure, in which those suddenly feeling the impact of higher tax burdens successfully pressure for reductions for themselves, some of the tax breaks have been policy responses to currently perceived problems, such as the gasoline shortages of the 1970s. In 1978, as part of its response to the energy crisis, the Carter administration passed a tax-incentive package for individuals and businesses to insulate their homes and save energy. The estimated cost to the Treasury in 1979 was $935 million.[39]

There have been tax breaks virtually throughout the history of the income tax, but the rate of granting exceptions and the impact on the revenue base have accelerated since the 1950s. The 1954 tax reform, which gave many benefits to many people, was an acceleration of the tendency that always exists in taxation to generate consensus by giving away the store. "In the earlier periods the benefits were limited by the range of constituents affected and by the relatively simpler structure of the code. As the number of those affected increased and the code became more complex, the Christmas tree grew."[40]

By the 1980s, the rate of growth of tax breaks was described as out of control. "There had been a tenfold increase in the amounts since 1960."[41] The 1981 tax cuts under the Reagan administration contained major tax breaks for businesses, including accelerated depreciation allowances for equipment purchases and reductions in the tax rate on capital gains. Twenty-nine tax preferences were added to the tax code between 1975 and 1981.[42] Most preferences passed at this time were aimed at businesses and upper-income citizens, and had the effect of reducing taxes much more for the wealthy than for the poor.

By 1983, tax expenditure estimates were in the range of $295 billion. After 1983, the rate of increase slowed down, and the 1986 Tax Reform Act eliminated a number of tax breaks completely and reduced the value of a number of others. A crude estimate of the impact of the tax reform on tax expenditures is that it reduced tax expenditures by $190 billion, or about 40 percent. About 60 percent of this reduction was the result of lowering the tax rates for citizens with higher incomes, rather than from eliminating or reducing tax breaks. Still some $76 billion of the estimated reduction reflected the elimination or reduction of tax breaks.[43] The Congressional Budget Office estimated the value of eliminated tax expenditures somewhat higher, at $100 billion.[44]

The rate of growth in tax expenditures after 1986 has generally been moderate, motivated in part by the decrease in 1986 in the top bracket of the income tax. When the top bracket is lower, taxpayers have less motivation to look for tax breaks; moreover, the dollar value, in outlay equivalents, of existing tax breaks drops. The 1990 Budget Enforcement Act, which required that any increase in tax expenditures be offset by increased taxes or reduced spending, may also have helped keep the level of increases down.

Despite the relatively moderate rates of growth, concern was building by 1993 about the overall size of the tax expenditures, which had reached over $400 billion. Congress had passed more than twenty new tax expenditures between 1986 and 1993.[45]

The average rate of increase in dollar losses to the treasury from tax expenditures was moderate from 1988 to 1994, but the losses were accelerating. Accounting problems and changes in reporting over time make it difficult to come to conclusions about how rapidly tax expenditures are growing, so the following numbers are approximate. Using the reports from the Joint Committee on Taxation, tax expenditures increased only 15.5 percent over the six years from 1988 to 1994, but a little over 9 percent over the two years from 1992 to 1994. Moreover, one expert predicted that tax expenditures would increase from about $400 billion in 1993 to about $525 billion in 1998, or about 30 percent over five years.[46]

Another reason for increased uneasiness about tax expenditures was that while Congress examined existing tax expenditures as part of revenue packages in 1982, 1983, 1984, 1986, and a little in 1987, the major tax actions in 1990 did not include a review of or reduction in tax expenditures.[47] At the same time that the deficit seemed to be growing out of control, tax expenditures were getting less, rather than more, scrutiny. A number of congresspersons knew from experience that not all tax expenditure proposals were for worthy public purposes. Congressman Thomas Barrett of Wisconsin supported a line-item veto for tax expenditures—giving the president the right to cut them out after Congress put them in—because he saw firsthand the special-interest tax provisions that had been written into the previous year's tax bill.[48]

The increase in revenue losses from tax expenditures resulted from some new benefits granted and the expansion of some old ones. One major change had to do with the reintroduction of a separate and lower tax for income derived from capital gains on investments. A major outcome of the 1986 tax reform had been to lower the top bracket of the income tax and make the tax on earned income and income from sale of capital assets the same. But in 1990, and again in 1993, the top bracket of the income tax for earned income was increased, from 28 percent in 1986 to 31 percent in 1990, and 36 percent in 1993. Also, in 1993, a surcharge of 10 percent was put on very high incomes, creating a top-top bracket of 39.6 percent. Capital gains taxes were capped in 1990 at 28 percent. Money from sales of investments held for more than a year was again taxed at a lower tax rate than money earned from wages. As the top bracket of the income tax increased, the value of the cap on the rate of taxation for capital gains increased proportionately.

While some of the increase in tax expenditures resulted from intentional policy choices, most of the recent increases in tax expenditures have resulted from increased costs of existing legislation. Tax expenditures are a lot like entitlements. They represent open-ended obligations for all those who are eligible and who take advantage of the break. If more people take advantage of the break, or more people in top brackets take advantage of the break, the costs to the government increase. These increases can be the result of changes in the economy, or changes in people's behavior so that they can take advantage of the breaks, or even changes in the rate of inflation.

Comparing the reports of the Joint Committee on Taxation for 1994 and 1995, the major increases in tax breaks occurred in the following areas: deductibility of mortgage interest, lower tax rates for capital gains than for earned income, depreciation of equipment, the exclusion for medical insurance and medical payments by employers, the net exclusion for pension contributions and earnings for employer plans, and an increase in the earned income tax credit. The deductibility on mortgage interest increased $8 billion, or about 17 percent; the increase due to the capital gains break was about $5.3 billion, or almost 140 percent; excess depreciation of equipment increased about $4.7 billion, or about 30 percent; and the increase in the dollar value of the employer health benefits provision was about $9.1 billion, or about 25 percent. The exclusion for employer-granted pension benefits increased $14.1 billion, or about 25 percent. The earned income tax credit increased from $1.3 billion to $3.5 billion, almost 170 percent.

Of these, only two can be clearly traced to explicit legislative changes in 1993: the increase in the value of the capital gains tax cap and the increase in the earned income tax credit. The size of the deduction for mortgage interest necessarily reflects the health of the housing market, the cost of mortgages, and the number of home buyers each year. The recent increase in the cost of this tax expenditure may also reflect the extension of home equity to consumer purchases, such as car loans based on home equity, and credit cards with home equity backing. Interest on these consumer loans becomes tax deductible if it is backed by home equity because it is treated as mortgage interest. The value of this tax break thus depends on the economy and changes in behavior as taxpayers scramble to get the benefit of this tax break. The value to employees of not treating health insurance provided by employers as taxable income has gone up as medical and insurance costs have risen at a much faster rate than the economy at large. Thus increases in this tax break depend on the rate of inflation in medical costs and the expense of health insurance benefits that employers decide to provide. If employers decide to grant less expensive health insurance, the cost of this tax break would go down or increase more slowly.

While the rate of change is attention getting, the total amount of tax expenditures is stunning. Estimates for tax expenditures for 1994 calculated from the Joint Committee on Taxation's report were in the range of $410 billion; estimates in terms of outlay equivalents calculated from the 1996 budget were in the range of $568 billion for 1994.[49] Regardless of whether one focuses on estimating the revenue losses to the Treasury or how much it would cost in dollars to provide the same benefits that individuals receive from tax expenditures, the amounts involved are over $400 billion, considerably larger than the size of the deficit.

Some in Congress have noted the size of the tax expenditures compared to the size of the deficit. They have begun to encourage reforms. Some legislators of a more liberal bent note that most of the benefits from tax expenditures go disproportionately to the well-to-do, who need the benefits the least, and that protecting tax benefits while cutting direct outlays that are more likely to benefit the poor will have major redistributional consequences. Those who take this view of tax expenditures and the deficit urge more regular congressional review of existing tax expenditures and the paring back of existing totals. For example, Representative Lee Hamilton of Indiana argued that all tax expenditures should be examined (not just new tax breaks). He linked the deficit, the rate of growth of tax expenditures, and the need for reforms to help control spending on tax breaks.[50] Others, who are more protective of existing tax expenditures, agree that they are often granted as favors to particular businesses or constituencies with little redeeming public policy purpose. This group is more concerned with strengthening prohibitions against adding future tax breaks or expanding existing ones. This approach is likely to have a far smaller impact on the deficit given the amount of growth that is due to existing tax breaks rather than new ones or policy-based expansions.

A number of congresspersons have recently called for and supported reforms that would make tax expenditures more visible and make them vetoable by the president by breaking them out as separate legislation. When the Republicans took a majority of seats in the House and the Senate in the fall of 1994, it became less likely that major reductions in existing tax expenditures would be forthcoming in order to balance the budget. Republicans argued that reductions in tax expenditures are increases in taxes and that the budget should be balanced by reducing direct outlays instead. With respect to specific changes in tax expenditures, they have proposed major reductions in tax expenditures for the working poor and major increases in tax expenditures for the well-to-do. They have also argued for increased tax deductions for each child. While the budget balancing proposals are unlikely to eliminate many major tax breaks, flat-tax proposals, which are circulating independently of the budget balancing negotiations, would eliminate all tax breaks and have everyone pay the same rate.

Tax breaks at the federal level are often justified in terms of achieving programmatic goals. They are, in this sense, the equivalent of direct outlays. Thus tax reductions to homeowners for the interest on their mortgage payments are explained in terms of encouraging a stable homeowning class and widespread hope of future homeownership. The good to be achieved also includes stimulation of the economy, since homebuilding requires not only lumber and other raw materials but also products such as washing machines, refrigerators, air conditioners, and heaters, each of which requires raw materials and processing. Such tax breaks benefit the homebuilding industry and realtors, but they are rationalized in terms of a national good.

This attempt to use tax breaks as a policy tool and/or rationalize them in terms of national goals opens tax breaks to a series of tests. Will this tax break help resolve some existing social or economic problem? Would some other form of subsidy achieve more of the goal less expensively than this tax break? When evaluated in these terms, tax breaks often do not look very good.

Lower taxes on capital gains have been justified in terms of encouraging investment and capital formation, but they have been used in periods when capital was generally available as well as when capital was in short supply. This anomaly makes one question whether this tax break was really intended to solve an economic problem or whether it was a redistribution upward, to those earning substantial income from investments.

Even when tax breaks are clearly intended to solve a problem, they may be much more expensive than other forms of subsidy to achieve similar ends. For example, the federal government allows local governments to borrow using tax-free municipal bonds. This lowers the cost of borrowing for cities because investors do not have to pay income tax on the earnings from these municipal bonds. The federal government loses revenues that it would otherwise have earned; wealthy individuals and corporations that invest in municipal bonds get a substantial portion of the benefit; only a limited portion of the money the federal government loses goes to cities to help lower borrowing costs. It would be cheaper for the federal government to give dollars to local governments to build infrastructure than to subsidize construction through tax breaks.

When tax breaks do not meet tests of efficiency and effectiveness, one wonders why they are used instead of more efficient and effective alternatives. One possibility is that the policy goals stated for creating the tax break were just a loose cover for granting favors. The purpose of allowing meals with clients to be deducted as a business expense is, in part, to make business more profitable for restaurateurs by making nice meals in restaurants cheaper for business people. Whether the tax break does or does not achieve the stated policy goals may be irrelevant because it is achieving the desired political (distributional) goals.

Another reason for using inefficient tax breaks is that they sometimes increase the number of people and institutions that benefit from a program and hence enhance the political support for that program. For example, the tax break on interest from municipal bonds creates a large pool of beneficiaries of a program ostensibly designed to reduce the borrowing costs of local governments. Local governments alone in recent years have not had enough political power to maintain their direct program benefits from the federal government, but the subsidy on bonds has proven difficult to remove because all those who invest in tax-free municipal bonds become a potential lobby to maintain this subsidy to local government. Local governments are aware of this political advantage and have tried to prevent a shift of their subsidy to the direct spending side of the budget, which they see as more vulnerable to cutbacks.

Another possible reason for preferring tax breaks over direct outlays is that they are somewhat less visible to the public. Since 1974, the Congressional Budget Reform Act has required that tax expenditures be listed and at least roughly summarized in the budget, and tax expenditures have to be passed by Congress and the president just like other legislation. The federal government is much more open about tax expenditures than other levels of government are. Nevertheless, it is in the nature of tax breaks to be less visible than program outlays. With welfare payments, it is reasonably easy to estimate the benefit to a mother with five children in a particular state, but it is very difficult, if not impossible, for a journalist or citizen to figure out what the dollar benefit to a business is from combined tax breaks. The public is generally not aware that benefits to the middle class from tax breaks equal or exceed direct spending for the poor in some program areas. Partly because of the lower visibility of tax expenditures to the public, tax expenditure programs can be passed that would not be passed if they were open to the same kind of scrutiny and examination as direct outlays. Paul McDaniel spelled out the policy implications of the tax break for employer-provided health insurance, and then asked if a direct spending program with these features would pass Congress. For example, the tax expenditure covers only those who are employed; the unemployed are not covered. The decision whether employees will participate in the program is left to the discretion of the employer—neither the government nor the employee has any say. There is no limit on the size of the tax expenditure. The federal contribution is proportional to the marginal tax rate of the taxpayer; thus wealthier folks get a bigger subsidy on their health insurance. If a couple earn $80,000 a year, the federal government will pay $31 per $100 of premium; if the couple's taxable income is below $10,000 a year, the federal government will pay none of the couple's premium. It seemed to McDaniel that Congress was unlikely to design a health-care spending program that would have these features.[51]

One characteristic of federal tax expenditures, then, is their programmatic focus and the resulting comparison between direct program outlays and tax breaks to achieve similar goals. A second characteristic of tax expenditures at the federal level is that they are granted on an entitlement basis. That means that everyone who meets the stated criteria is eligible for the benefit. Consequently, it is very difficult to estimate how much revenue will be lost in any given year as a result of tax expenditures. How many builders will take advantage of subsidies for rental housing for the poor in any year and how much this subsidy will cost are extremely difficult to estimate with any accuracy. The amounts are open ended, which makes budgeting for balance extremely difficult. On the other hand, the availability of tax breaks is generally known in advance, and anyone who meets the requirements can take advantage of them, which makes planning possible for the taxpayers.

A third characteristic of federal tax expenditures is that the rationale used to justify them can be used to expand the benefit to others. If the depletion of oil supplies is a reason to give a break to oil companies on their taxes, then why not give a break for the depletion of other natural resources? This logic has proved difficult to resist, although the consequences can be absurd, such as granting tax breaks for the depletion of sand or shells (used for paving in parts of the country). A particularly powerful lobby can negotiate benefits for an industry that are then expanded to much weaker interests by the logic of the rationale used to cover the initial grant.

To summarize, because the federal government's budget is so large, tax breaks, even relatively small ones, can have impacts on the economy and on people's behavior, in buying a house or drilling an oil well. Tax breaks can have legitimate policy goals, including improving the equity of the tax burden and stimulating the economy. But this legitimate federal function can easily become confused with more mundane political matters, such as responding to pressure from an interest group that wants to reduce its tax liability. These latter tax expenditures are often rationalized in terms of national goals to be achieved. When programs funded through tax breaks are compared with programs funded with direct outlays, they may be less efficient and less effective, but they may be more politically potent. The rationalizations used to legitimize political giveaways to powerful lobbies can be used by others to leverage further tax breaks.

Nevertheless, federal level tax breaks are not uncontrollable. The amounts involved are clearly listed in the budget. Congressional committees now buffer themselves from interest groups, and requirements to offset every reduction in revenues put pressure on legislators to watch the number and size of tax breaks awarded.

State Level. On the state level, tax expenditures expanded during the 1970s and 1980s. They were primarily used to protect key industries and powerful lobbies, to stimulate the economy, and to alleviate protests against taxes. The protection of key industries has been a function of state tax systems for many years, but the other two sources of tax breaks became more prominent in the 1970s when the economy began to falter. Many governors were desperate to do something when unemployment increased; at the same time, because taxation was increasing more rapidly than people's incomes, tax protest accelerated and many state officials felt that if they did not respond with tax breaks, they would be confronted with rigid, publicly mandated tax limitations.

For example, in Illinois, twenty-eight tax breaks were enacted between 1979 and 1989. Of them, twenty were enacted between 1979 and 1984, just after Proposition 13 in California and the deep recession of the early 1980s. Roughly categorized by purpose, nine of the tax breaks were to encourage economic development; six were efforts to make taxes more equitable or otherwise reduce pressure for tax limits; nine were responses to powerful local industries; and five were responses to other requests or worthy causes.[52]

To encourage economic development and to help head off pressure for tax limits, states have passed a number of tax breaks, in sales, income, and property taxes. Maryland, for example, has constantly eroded the base of its sales and use tax; almost every session of the legislature has added exemptions.[53] As a result, "only approximately 18 percent of consumer income is subject to the sales and use tax."[54]

Maryland also granted breaks from its income tax. To give some idea of the cost of these tax breaks, five discretionary modifications of the tax base for which detailed information was available reduced the state revenues by nearly $1.9 billion in 1987.[55] The largest of the breaks was for exclusion from taxation of income derived from capital gains; that tax break alone cost the state of Maryland $898 million in 1987.[56]

Tax breaks on the property tax have also been widespread. Efforts to head off tax revolts resulted in both homestead exemptions and circuit breakers. By 1992, thirty-six states had adopted circuit breakers, which are provisions to reduce the property taxes of the poor, elderly, or disabled. Most of these provisions were adopted between 1971 and 1977, a time of rapid inflation in housing prices and massive discontent with property taxation. An even higher proportion of states (forty-five out of fifty plus the District of Columbia) adopted homestead exemptions. Of these, nineteen provide benefits to all homeowners who live in their own homes, and most provide additional benefits to the poor, the elderly or disabled, or veterans. The amount of revenue lost by these exemptions was significant, especially in states where eligibility for benefits was broad. Michigan lost $773 million in revenue to circuit breakers in 1990, and five states (including Michigan) lost over $100 million. For homestead exemptions, California lost $3.2 billion in revenues in 1992, Florida lost $1.7 billion in 1991, while Texas school districts lost $1.1 billion in 1990. These are the high-end figures; most states lost considerably less than these amounts. See tables 2.1 and 2.2 for details.

States are less able than the federal government to stimulate the economy. Their orientation has been less one of stimulating demand for purchases or increasing the amount of capital available through tax breaks and more one of responding to direct competition with other states. The federal government may feel that it is in competition with other countries, but it has not yet yielded to the easy policy of saying "other countries subsidize this industry, so we have to too." States, however, use this logic extensively and expensively.[57]

This competition increasingly led states to offer the same set of tax breaks as incentives to lure potential industries. For example, in 1974, six

TABLE 2.1

STATE CIRCUIT BREAKER PROGRAMS, ESTIMATED COSTS

State (fiscal year)	Amount ($000)	State (fiscal year)	Amount ($000)
Arizona (1991)	12,743	Nevada (1991)	2,636
Arkansas (1992)	3,950	New Jersey (1990)	n.a.
California (1992)	16,699	New Mexico (1991)	3,903
Colorado (1992)	14,462	New York (1989)	50,800
Connecticut (1991)	27,916	North Dakota (1992)	2,381
District of Columbia (1992)	8,854	Ohio (1991)	56,094
Hawaii (1991)	5,819	Oklahoma (1991)	398
Idaho (1992)	6,031	Oregon (1990)	6,365
Illinois (1990)	104,354	Pennsylvania (1991)	108,681
Indiana (1991)	n.a.	Rhode Island (1991)	653
Iowa (1990)	10,737	South Dakota (1991)	1,000
Kansas (1992)	8,700	Tennessee (1992)	7,026
Maine (1992)	7,494	Utah (1991)	n.a.
Maryland (1991)	48,397	Vermont (1992)	22,010
Michigan (1990)	773,555	Washington State	n.a.
Minnesota (1991)	133,500	West Virginia (1991)	n.a.
Missouri (1992)	17,973	Wisconsin (1992)	105,505
Montana (1990)	4,090	Wyoming (1992)	n.a.

SOURCE: Advisory Commission on Intergovernmental Relations, *Significant Features of Fiscal Federalism, 1994*, vol. 1 (Washington, D.C.: Government Printing Office, 1994), table 39.

states offered tax exemptions to encourage research and development, but
by 1992, thirty-one states offered this tax break. In 1974, eighteen states offered an exemption to industries on the corporate income tax, but by 1992,
thirty-five states offered this break. The trend is uniform across a variety of
tax breaks, with most of the competition and resulting imitation taking
place before 1989.[58] As the tax incentives became more similar, in order to
compete successfully, states had to outbid each other in the size of the tax
breaks. The costs of tax breaks per job created in the automobile industry
increased from $11,000 in 1980 (the Nissan plant in Tennessee) to $65,000
per job in 1992 (the BMW plant in South Carolina) to $200,000 per job in
1993 (Alabama, Mercedes).[59]

Tax incentives for economic development may or may not be phrased as
entitlements. Some benefits, such as reduced taxes to companies that expand
and hire twenty or more additional employees, are generally available to all

TABLE 2.2
STATES' LOSSES FROM HOMESTEAD EXEMPTIONS

State (fiscal year)	Amount ($000)	State (fiscal year)	Amount ($000)
Alaska (1991)	9,585	Montana (1990)	1,400
Arizona (1990)	162,744	Nebraska (1991)	29,300
California (1991–92)	3,290,000	New Jersey (1991)	59,583
Connecticut (1991)	18,522	New Mexico (1986)	8,400
District of Columbia (1989)	21,758	North Carolina (1990–91)	19,072
		Oklahoma (1991)	56,639
Florida (1991)	1,700,000	South Carolina (1991)	37,650
Illinois (1989)	451,498	Texas (school districts 1990)	1,169,665
Indiana (1991)	274,501		
Iowa (1991)	99,613	Utah (1990)	1,847
Kentucky (1989)	9,711	Vermont (1991)	1,000
Louisiana (1991)	438,494	Washington State (1991)	39,200
Maine (1991)	3,024	West Virginia (1991)	25,829
Minnesota (1989)	660,000	Wisconsin (1992)	177,600
Mississippi (1990)	110,387	Wyoming (1992)	0

SOURCE: Compiled from Advisory Commission on Intergovernmental Relations, *Significant Features of Fiscal Federalism, 1991*, vol. 1 (Washington, D.C.: Government Printing Office, 1991), table 42.

NOTE: Other states have homestead exemptions, but their estimates of revenue losses were un-available.

and are phrased as entitlements. Other tax breaks are enabled by the state government but are negotiated by state and local governments on a case-by-case basis. Each case is treated as unique, with a specific package of reductions and incentives. Granting benefits to one company does not spill over by logic into granting benefits to other companies. States and local governments can grant more benefits to the first company to get things moving and fewer to companies that come later, after the momentum is established.

Sometimes the design of an individual deal does open up the path for other companies to use the same tax break. For example, in the Alabama-Mercedes case, to benefit Mercedes the state passed a law that would allow any company that was investing over $5 million and creating at least fifty jobs to use the money it would have paid in state income taxes to pay off its debt. Similarly, the law allowed such companies to use the income taxes deducted from employee wages to pay for land, equipment, and plant.[60]

The model of competing with other states in awarding tax breaks may be both expensive and ineffective because if the surrounding states all offer the same incentives, the incentives lose their drawing power. After 1986, states shifted their economic development strategies more toward entrepreneurial efforts, such as loans and loan guarantees and equity or near-equity investments in businesses. This shift occurred at least in part because by then the more traditional incentive approaches, including tax expenditures, had been adopted by most states and failed to distinguish between possible locations for businesses.[61] In the 1990s, there has been some resurgence of interest in tax breaks as a tool because the recession created a sense of greater urgency than long-term high risk investments could address. Even when tax expenditures did not work well, they allowed political credit taking that longer-term strategies did not, and recessions have increased the perceived urgency of creating jobs or bringing jobs into the state.[62]

Visible competition and negotiated settlements often create pressure to bring a deal to a successful completion, defined by the company locating or expanding in the state or constructing a building, almost regardless of the cost. The justification is, we have to do this because of the competition (i.e., we will lose the deal if we do not give them what they want), and it is for economic development. While tax breaks for economic development are given one deal at a time, states and local governments avoid a project-by-project cost-benefit analysis by arguing that each project will generate future growth that will not be subsidized or will be subsidized at a lesser rate. The amount and timing of this additional growth is no more than a wild guess, so it is impossible to figure out how much in concessions to give. Any amount conceivably can be justified. Researcher Sam Nunn estimated that it would require anywhere between 750 and 7300 jobs created by an economic development project to justify a tax abatement of $1 million, if a city had a sales tax. The variation in number of jobs required to break even depended on the assumptions about the income level of the jobs to be created and how much of that income would be spent in the community.[63] The only test of the outcome is whether the company carries out the project; any failure only reinforces the notion that not enough was given away.

The bargaining perspective tends to foster secrecy. Dealings with business, and economic development more generally, are likely to be more secret than other government transactions. The reason given is that business demands secrecy. Presumably, if you want what business has, you do things its way. Nevertheless, by 1992, twenty-one states had reported their tax expenditures. In most cases, the reporting requirement was recently adopted.[64] Many states increased tax breaks in response to tax protests in the 1970s and then confronted the declining revenues of the recession of 1981–82. The recession forced some states to raise revenues and cut spending. In that context, some state officials began to rethink their tax expenditures and report on them.[65]

When states began issuing their reports on tax expenditures, the results were startling. Of nine states reporting from 1982 to 1984, the ratio of tax expenditures to total revenues varied from a low of 35 percent in California in 1984 to a high of 116 percent in Nebraska in 1982.[66] The average ratio was 69 percent of total revenues. These states may not be typical of other states because those with higher tax expenditures would be more likely to see them as a problem that needed public documentation and scrutiny.

Even granting that the states with tax expenditure reports are more extreme than other states, the amounts reported are dramatic. California reported tax expenditures of about $16.9 billion in fiscal year 1988, equal to about 45 percent of the governor's proposed 1987–88 budget for direct expenditures.[67] The state had 230 individual state-level tax expenditure programs. California's report concluded that the tax expenditure budget was growing more quickly than direct expenditures. Tax expenditure programs grew 8 percent in 1988, while direct outlays grew only 3 percent in the governor's proposed budget. The reason for the expansion was not only the number of tax breaks but also the expansion of the economic base on which tax expenditures were computed.[68] Maryland reported tax expenditures of $4.5 billion in 1987. Tax expenditures in the income tax amounted to 47 percent of income taxes in 1987, and 42 percent in 1988. Foregone sales and use taxes amounted to 34 percent of these revenue sources in both 1987 and 1988.[69]

Texas reported $12 billion in sales and franchise tax exemptions in fiscal year 1991. This figure compares with total general revenue expenditures of $15.1 billion.[70] Louisiana estimated about $3.9 billion in tax expenditures for the fiscal year ending in 1992; this figure was more than 100 percent of the net tax revenues collected.[71] Ohio provides data for its tax expenditures across revenue sources for the general fund. The estimates for 1995 were $5.8 billion in tax expenditures compared to $12.5 billion in general fund tax revenues, or about 46 percent.[72] (Note: These figures are not comparable across states. The dollar totals of tax expenditures are only estimates; some figures are given for general revenues and others for total revenues across funds; and what is counted as a tax expenditure in one state might not be counted in another state.)

In Ohio, sales taxes constituted about 37 percent of total general fund taxes, but over 70 percent of the tax expenditures. Ohio's tax expenditure report lists forty-seven different sales tax breaks. In recent years, however, the direction of change seems to be not toward narrowing the base but broadening it, including more services in the taxable category. The grand total for tax expenditures across funds was $6.7 billion in 1992 and $7 billion in 1993, but it had dropped to about $5 billion in 1994 and $5.8 billion in 1995.

The experiences of Ohio suggest that some states, perhaps especially those with tax expenditure reports, have seen how expensive tax breaks can be and have begun to curtail them. Detailed data from Washington State support this idea. As shown in table 2.3, the number of tax breaks granted per year has steadily increased from one period to the next, but the average cost per tax break has varied considerably. The tax breaks granted during the Great Depression of the 1930s are far and away the most costly. The number and cost dropped after World War II, during a general period of

TABLE 2.3

STATE OF WASHINGTON, HISTORY OF THE COST
OF TAX BREAKS

Period	Average number of breaks granted per year	Current cost of breaks	Average cost
1871–1929	.37	$1,605,472,000	$72,976,000
1931–1945	4.46	18,056,605,000	269,501,000
1947–1970	3.39	1,616,713,000	20,727,000
1971–1985	7.64	2,510,970,000	23,467,000
1986–1991	10.20	185,488,000	3,636,000

SOURCE: Calculated from State of Washington, Department of Revenue, *Tax Exemptions 1992*, Revenue Research Report.

prosperity, but increased somewhat during the fiscal stress of the 1970s and 1980s. While the number of tax breaks granted has continued to go up in the most recent period, the average cost of each new break granted has dropped precipitously.

While many states are reporting their tax expenditures, the majority are still not doing so. The overall costs of tax expenditures over time may not be clearly set down anywhere. The result is that it may be impossible to see trends toward more or less tax expenditures or correlate changes in levels of tax expenditures with increased investment, tax yield, or employment. It is also impossible in many states to calculate the distributional impact of tax expenditures.

Local Level. At the local level, tax breaks are normally used to encourage economic development projects. They are seldom used to head off tax protests because cities have other means to do that, including the assessment procedures, reduced dependence on property taxes, and increased reliance on sales taxes, utility taxes, user fees, and, in some cases, wage or income taxes.

Partly because of the focus on economic development, tax expenditures at the local level are even less visible than at the state level. They seldom appear in budgets or financial reports,[73] and they are generally granted on a one-at-a-time basis. The costs of each deal tend to be clear to the government making the deal, but the tradeoff between costs and benefits may be obscure. The dealmaking aspect of tax breaks means that benefits are not known or knowable in advance; builders, contractors, and businesses are encouraged to ask for the moon and see how much they can get. The element of competition that was apparent at the state level is exaggerated at the local level because the government has so little possibility of influencing the economy and the bargaining tends to take place when the local community is desperate for jobs. Companies can promise jobs or threaten to take them away unless they get most of what they ask for. The bargaining power tends to be one-sided.

There are no aggregate estimates of the amounts of tax expenditures at the local level, but particular examples that have been studied suggest that individual large projects can be very expensive to both the state and local governments. The Diamond Star automobile plant in Bloomington and Normal, Illinois, illustrates the size of total incentive packages and the proportion of the packages that involve tax breaks.[74] The short-term cost of the total incentive package was $5.384 million for the municipalities concerned; of that amount, $1.2 million was for sales tax breaks, $206,000 was in local utility reductions, $234,000 was in reduction in local fees, $78,000 was in reduction in sewer collection fees, and $486,000 was in reduction in local property tax collections. Over the life of the project, the two cities would be committing $9.2 million. Of the total package, reductions in utility charges will cost the two cities $2.4 million and property tax reduction will cost the two municipalities $5.8 million. Bloomington and Normal are two small midwestern communities, so these costs are substantial. One tax abatement granted in 1989 in Fort Worth, Texas, was estimated to result in an annual loss of revenue of about $6.8 million for fifteen years. The relocation of Sears' corporate headquarters from downtown Chicago to suburban Hoffman Estates cost about $6 million in tax abatements.[75]

Additional evidence of the amounts of local tax expenditures is spotty. In the early 1980s, New York City was reported to have abated $44 million in property taxes in a single year; St. Louis, a major user of property tax exemptions, was reported to have exempted nearly $1 billion worth of real estate, about half the city's tax base.[76] A recent study of a single tax break for industrial property in Cook County, Illinois, estimated that for the ninety-five firms receiving tax benefits between 1981 and 1985 for the duration of those tax breaks, $68 million in property taxes will be lost.[77] Losses from this one benefit amounted to $5.7 million in 1985, and the amount of loss was estimated to increase over the next few years as additional firms were granted reductions and old reductions had not yet begun to expire.

Local government tax abatement is characterized primarily by one-on-one bargaining, from a position of weakness with respect to business, and a squishiness about estimates of future benefits to be received that encourages local governments to give the maximum benefits allowed by law. An additional feature of local tax breaks occurs because of the multiplicity of federal, state, and local governments. Sometimes the tax breaks the cities give away are not from their own revenues. For example, cities have extended their tax-free borrowing status to businesses in order to save them money. These breaks are called Industrial Development Revenue Bonds, and they cost the federal government money.[78] Cities also give away property taxes belonging to school districts. In the Diamond Star case, the school districts negotiated for themselves and chose a shorter maturity for the tax breaks offered than the cities did. But in many cases, the school districts are not negotiating for themselves; cities may make economic development deals that are good for the cities but reduce the property taxes that school districts would otherwise receive.

There are no reliable estimates of the extent to which cities reduce the tax revenues of school districts, but some individual cases are suggestive. In Corpus Christi, Texas, in 1990 there were $900,000 in tax losses to school districts reflecting tax breaks for corporations. Wichita, Kansas, school districts lost $1.6 million to tax concessions during fiscal year 1991. In Ohio, school systems are routinely excluded from participating in city or county decisions on tax exemptions for economic development. In one recent project in Cleveland, the city abated $8 million in property taxes, 60 percent of which would have gone to the school system, which is facing a $34 million deficit for the next fiscal year. An attorney for the school district argued, "Our city council hasn't seen a tax abatement it didn't like."[79] Of the $68 million in lost property taxes from one tax break in Cook County, Illinois, 40 percent will come from the Board of Education.[80]

Thus a peculiarity of local-level tax abatements is that cities and counties can often take the lead in economic development and negotiate with other governments' or districts' revenues, sometimes exacerbating their fiscal stress. The cities are encouraged to offer larger incentives because the money they offer is not their own. As a result, the school districts may look badly managed and may have to come to the public more often for tax increases.

The Politics of Reform

The gradual erosion of the integrity of general taxes is part of a larger process that also includes reform and at least the temporary curtailing of interest groups. Tax expenditures reduce revenues, which means cutting back spending, finding alternative revenue sources, or tolerating chronic deficits. Each of these alternatives has negative political consequences. The more extreme each potential response to the reduction in revenues, the greater the pressure to stop awarding tax breaks or curtail the number of existing tax breaks. Tax expenditures also give the impression of unequal treatment of equals, which upsets taxpayers and encourages them to try to reduce their own tax payments. In the extreme, it may lead to tax protests. When voluntary compliance with tax laws diminishes, the cost of tax collection increases. Thus, despite the political coalitions that support existing tax benefits, there are often counterpressures to reform the tax structure.

The main goal of such reforms is to simplify taxes and reduce special exceptions. The resulting revenue increases may be used to reduce tax rates for everyone, or to reduce the size of the deficit or sustain services and programs. For some, the goal of tax reform has been to see to it that the poor do not pay a disproportionate burden of taxation and that taxes overall are apportioned according to the ability to pay. Since tax breaks are often relatively inefficient ways of accomplishing program goals, curbing tax expenditures may also be seen as an effort to improve efficiency.[81]

Such reforms are difficult but not impossible to achieve. Politically, they have the general weakness that those whose benefits are taken away are likely to be hopping mad, while those whose tax burden is lessened are likely to feel that they deserved it all along. Opponents are likely to be outspoken, and supporters likely to be passive.[82] In addition, the amount of money gained from a large loophole to a relatively small number of people is not enough when spread around to the entire taxpaying audience to win much applause. One way to make tax reform politically attractive is to take away enough tax benefits to moderate substantially the tax burden of large numbers of people.

There was nothing inevitable about the timing of the federal 1986 tax reform, but the conditions were certainly favorable for a tax reform by the middle 1980s. Several decades of accelerated granting of tax expenditures had eroded the revenue base, and the president's 1981 tax reduction had gotten completely out of hand, with Democrats and Republicans competing to add more tax breaks. The result was an increase in the size of the national deficit, despite President Reagan's campaign promises to eliminate the deficit within several years. Reagan made tax reform an early priority of his second term, and his support helped push the reform through, especially when the legislation stalled in the House when Republicans (the president's own party) would not support it.

The White House and the Treasury, where such proposals normally originate, wanted a proposal that would give tax reductions to 80 percent of taxpayers, and set that figure as a guideline. The Senate Finance Committee struggled to reduce the top bracket of the income tax, that is, the maximum rate applied to the wealthiest people, from 50 percent to close to 27 percent. (The final figure was 28 percent.) They wanted to drop the top rate significantly in order to gain enough support in Congress and among the interest groups to pass. The reduction of the top rate was very attractive to business groups, so while many of the individual groups opposed specific reductions in their tax breaks, others supported the whole package because of the attractiveness of the overall rate reductions. "The movement to overhaul the U.S. Tax Code, now sputtering its way through the Senate Finance Committee, has survived so far in part because of Congress's perception that large sectors of American business favor going ahead with it."[83]

Rather than a mobilized opposition and quiet supporters, the 1986 tax reform had active interest groups on both sides. Business groups were split over the issue. Those in danger of losing benefits lobbied heavily against the reform.

Chief executive officers of major corporations, such as IBM, Pepsico, and Reynolds, were active in support of tax reform. Taxpayer groups also created a politically powerful presence. Citizens for Tax Justice, a tiny union-financed group, turned out reports on the amount of taxes paid by major

U.S. corporations, many of whom paid nothing at all. The reports received major publicity in the two years preceding the tax reform and helped persuade Congress to remove some of the beneficial tax treatment of these corporations. Citizens for Tax Justice "gave us the fuel for tax reform and for tax increases on the business community," said Representative Robert T. Matsui (D-Calif.), an influential member of the Ways and Means Committee. "I'll bet every member" who favored overhauling the tax code "used CTJ statistics in speeches back home."[84] As an aide to the House Ways and Means Committee chairman remarked, sometimes legislation is based on a few good horror stories, and Citizens for Tax Justice provided those stories.[85]

Despite pressure from proreform interest groups, lobbying to retain tax breaks was fierce;[86] the first time the Senate Finance Committee tried to hammer out its version of reform, it was overwhelmed by resistance to eliminating a variety of preferences. The committee chairman, Robert Packwood (R-Oreg.), may have set the wrong tone initially by supporting Oregon's lumber industry. By the time other senators had protected their constituents, the proposal was no longer revenue neutral—more money was given away in tax decreases than was gained by eliminating or reducing tax breaks.

Senator Packwood went back to the drawing board and started again with a stricter revenue-neutral rule: No benefit could be added without closing a loophole or eliminating a special benefit to pay for it. The committee's recommended package arrived on the Senate floor with an understanding that any amendments would not change the total amount of revenues and would not increase the size of the deficit. This informal rule blocked many interest groups that would have tried to reinstate their benefits on the floor.

One of the particularly interesting aspects of the passage of the reform act was the major role of the conference committee set up to resolve the differences between the House and Senate versions. The many differences between the House and Senate bills created a relatively open conference. The chairs of both the House Ways and Means and the Senate Finance Committee were on the conference committee and conducted most of the negotiations themselves behind closed doors. Other members of Congress reported that such a procedure insulated them from interest groups because they could legitimately say they did not know what was going on.[87]

The final conference committee product did not eliminate all special tax benefits, but it reduced many of them and eliminated others outright. The top individual tax rate was dropped from 50 percent to 28 percent, and 80 percent of individuals and families would be taxed at no more than 15 percent. The top corporate rate was reduced from 46 percent to 34 percent.

In at least one case, the dynamics of income tax reform were similar at the state level. In Wisconsin in 1982, the cost of tax breaks was just about equal to the total taxes collected.[88] A major reform of the income tax occurred by 1985. The reform had the governor's support and was tied to tax reduction. The reduction was partly the result of eliminating deductions and exceptions and partly the result of a favorable revenue projection. The top income bracket was lowered, apparently as an essential part of gaining political support for reform. A high degree of centralization and closed decision rules helped block interest-group demands.[89]

To summarize, broad-based taxes are likely to be gradually eroded by the demands of the interest groups and individuals who feel the burden of the tax. The integrity of the revenue base and the perception that the tax applies equally to all gradually deteriorates. The growing complexity of the tax laws, revenue losses, and inequitable treatment of businesses and individuals in similar financial circumstances generate pressure for reform. When conditions are favorable, there may be a tax reform to eliminate or curtail the special exceptions and restore the tax base.

Tax reform by itself is not a politically attractive alternative, since it is likely to offend those who have received tax breaks, but not likely to attract many supporters. But if the reform can produce enough revenues to reduce the tax burden of large numbers of people, then interest groups in favor of the reform may spring up and help counter the interests of those whose tax break is being eliminated. Tax reform can be turned into distributive politics, allocating general tax reductions. One way to build a positive constituency for reform is boldly to eliminate a large number of expensive tax breaks, generating enough resources to lower the majority of other taxpayers' tax bills. The Wisconsin case suggests that tax reform is easier if it can be combined with a general tax reduction resulting from expanding revenues. In both the national tax reform of 1986 and the Wisconsin tax reform of 1985, tax reform and widespread tax reduction were intentionally linked to gain broader support for reform. The resulting pattern is a long, slow accumulation of tax breaks and gradually building pressure for far-reaching reforms that expand the tax base, reduce the top bracket (reducing at least temporarily pressure for tax breaks), reduce loopholes, and strengthen the procedure for resisting interest-group pressure for tax breaks.

Summary and Conclusions

The politics of taxation is not a politics of coercion, it is a politics of persuasion. When public officials plan to raise a tax or levy a new tax, they spend time gathering opinion, publicizing need, crafting deals that will gain political support. They often collect more new revenues than immediately needed in order to provide some resources with which to buy support, or they link tax reductions in other tax sources to the increase in the tax they are raising. When raising taxes by eliminating tax breaks, politicians may try to reduce the overall level of taxation to gain majority support. Failure to win broad support for a tax increase may result in loss of office for politicians and tax revolts among the public. The voting public plays a major, direct role in the politics of taxation.

Public officials need to raise taxes from time to time, but they confront a political minefield when they try to do it. The result is that they raise taxes with great care and try to place the burden of taxation in such a way as to minimize opposition and gain the maximum of support.

Raising taxes is public business that generally goes on with a lot of publicity because of the need for public support. The more open the government has been about its finances, and the greater the belief that the resources are really needed and will be spent on items approved by the taxpayers, the greater the acceptability of the tax increase. Tax increases may be precisely the time when the government is held to account. The greater ease of passing earmarked taxes suggests that the public wants the money spent for specific approved purposes and not others.

The relationship between accountability and acceptability in the politics of taxation is complex. On the one hand, the unpopularity of taxation tempts public officials either to keep it quiet or to distort it. Their strategies include choosing taxes that are not dramatically visible and raising taxes a little bit in a number of areas so that the total amount of taxes paid by individuals may be obscured. On the other hand, openness about financial matters in general makes taxes more acceptable by clarifying the need for additional revenue. Openness in decision making seems to exaggerate vulnerability to interest groups. Such openness comes and goes, depending on the need to insulate decision makers from interest-group pressures.

The actors involved in revenue decisions include the chief executive, the revenue committees of Congress and finance committees of legislatures and councils, interest groups, and the courts. Departments and agency heads are almost completely absent, except when the Treasury Department recommends tax reforms. Citizen commissions, blue-ribbon committees, and task forces of the Chamber of Commerce are also frequent actors, examining the overall need, the current revenue situation, and possible revenue alternatives. An array of interest groups is directly involved at different times. Public employees and service recipients get involved when service cuts are threatened; chambers of commerce and other groups of business representatives get involved when new taxation is being considered. Taxpayers' organizations, unions, and business associations represent broad groups, but there are clearly splits within each broad group. For example, business associations are deeply split about tax reform.

Interest groups are distinctly important actors in revenue politics, but their participation indicates that what kind of interest groups will be involved depends on the issue—threatened service cuts bring out service providers and recipients; tax breaks bring out specific industries and even specific companies or individuals; new taxes or shifts in the structure of taxes bring out coalitions of interest groups representing business or labor, the rich or the middle class or the poor.

The power that interest groups are able to wield does not depend solely on their finances; small, poor interest groups are sometimes more effective than larger, better financed ones. Small groups, with little financial backing, are sometimes able to manage major impacts through research and symbolic stories that catch the media's and legislators' attention. The ability of interest groups to form and maintain coalitions affects their success, as does the budget process itself. When legislators organize themselves and the budget process in such a way as to insulate themselves from interest groups, interest-group power may be curtailed. This does not happen all the time, but it certainly indicates that interest groups do not always call the shots.

The politics of taxation is characterized by a struggle to shift the burden of taxation away from one's own group, however defined. The pressure may be away from the relatively poor to the relatively rich, or vice versa. Alternatively, the pressure may be to shift taxation from individuals to corporations, or from homeowners to renters or owners of commercial property. Those in one region of the country may try to shift the burden of taxation to other regions. When representatives of any group are in power, they may shift the burden to other groups.

Overall, revenue politics is characterized by a relatively long time span, in which both narrow and broader societal interests compete for position, and by efforts to lock in benefits such as tax breaks and to lock out taxes on particular forms of wealth while backers are powerful enough to do so. Earmarking of revenues is another way of trying to lock in particular favorable patterns. These powerful locks tend to slow down the rate of major changes so that taxation changes by small amounts in many sources, or in small ways over time. At intervals, however, there are major changes. New taxes are passed; the burden of taxation shifts; and the definition of taxable wealth varies. These shifts may be precipitated by major changes in the dominant coalition or by major changes in the economy or huge deficits. To understand the politics of taxation, one needs to understand not only the motivations and strategies of the actors in the short run but also the history of changes in the environment and in the budget process.

Notes

1. This case study draws extensively on Joan Parker, *The Illinois Tax Increase of 1983, Summit and Resolution* (Springfield: Sangamon State University, Illinois Issues, 1984).

2. Ibid., 20.

3. This case study is taken from Timothy Riordan, "The Dayton Income Tax Increase: A Summary of Success," *Urban Fiscal Ledger* 1, no. 3 (August–September 1984): 1–3.

4. Ibid., 3.

5. Susan Hansen, "Extraction: The Politics of State Taxation," in *Politics in the American States: A Comparative Analysis,* 4th ed., ed. Virginia Gray, Herbert Jacobs, and Kenneth Vines (Boston: Little Brown, 1983), 434–36.

6. John F. Witte, *The Politics and Development of the Federal Income Tax* (Madison: University of Wisconsin Press, 1985), 77.

7. Ibid., 97.

8. Catherine Rudder, "Tax Policy: Structure and Choice," in *Making Economic Policy in Congress,* ed. Allen Schick (Washington, D.C.: American Enterprise Institute, 1983), 196–220.

9. Rudder argues that committee members tended to be party regulars, "with relatively high scores on party unity." Ibid., 197.

10. Ibid., 212. The reader should note that any attempt to add up the value of tax breaks is approximate. Nevertheless, this description of trends is probably fairly accurate.

11. Ibid., 211.

12. Randall Strahan, "Committee Politics and Tax Reform" (paper prepared for the 1987 meetings of the American Political Science Association, 3–6 September 1987). See also Randall Strahan and R. Kent Weaver, "Subcommittee Government and the House Ways and Means Committee" (paper presented at the Southern Political Science Association meetings, Memphis, Tennessee, 2–4 November 1989). Randall Strahan's book, *The New Ways and Means: Reform and Change in a Congressional Committee* (Chapel Hill: University of North Carolina Press, 1990), deals with these themes at length.

13. Robert Pastor, "The Cry and Sigh Syndrome: Congress and Trade Policy," in Schick, *Making Economic Policy in Congress,* 158–95.

14. General Accounting Office, *Budget Issues: Earmarking in the Federal Government* (Washington, D.C.: Government Printing Office, 1995).

15. Martha A. Fabricius and Ronald K. Snell, *Earmarking State Taxes,* 2d ed. (Denver: National Council of State Legislatures, September 1990), 26; Arturo Pérez and Ronald Snell, *Earmarking State Taxes,* 3d ed. (Denver: National Council of State Legislatures, 1995), 3, 5, 22.

16. Advisory Commission on Intergovernmental Relations, *Significant Features of Fiscal Federalism, 1988* (Washington, D.C.: Government Printing Office, 1989), 1:96–97.

17. Ibid., 1 and tables 7 and 8.

18. Pérez and Snell, *Earmarking State Taxes,* 3.

19. Charles Spindler, "The Lottery and Education: A Case of Having Your Cake and Eating Mine Too?" Forthcoming.

20. Susan MacManus, "Florida: Reinvention Derailed," in *The Fiscal Crisis of the States: Lessons for the Future,* ed. Steven Gold (Washington, D.C.: Georgetown University Press, 1995), 250.

21. Fabricius and Snell, *Earmarking State Taxes,* tables 4, 5, and 7.

22. Timothy Clark, "Taking a Regional Stand," *National Journal,* 22 March 1986, 700.

23. Witte, *Politics and Development of the Federal Income Tax,* 68.

24. C.K. Yearley, *The Money Machines: The Breakdown and Reform of Governmental and Party Finance in the North, 1860–1920* (Albany: State University of New York Press, 1970), 39.

25. Terrence J. McDonald, "San Francisco: Socioeconomic Change, Political Culture and Fiscal Politics," in *The Politics of Urban Fiscal Policy,* ed. Terrence J. McDonald and Sally K. Ward (Beverly Hills, Calif.: Sage, 1984), 51.

26. Arnold Meltsner, *Politics of City Revenue* (Berkeley: University of California Press, 1971). See also Charles Levine, Irene Rubin, and George Wolohojian, *The Politics of Retrenchment: How Local Governments Manage Fiscal Stress* (Beverly Hills, Calif.: Sage, 1981). The authors state that although Oakland's property tax base was rising very slowly during the 1960s and 1970s, the city reduced property tax rates whenever possible. The property tax rates declined in 1968, 1969, 1970, and 1971, and then again in 1976, 1977, and 1978. (After 1978, the city was affected by Proposition 13, which eliminated the city's discretion and forced further cuts in property tax rates.) These declines occurred despite increasing costs.

27. Hansen, "Extraction," 429.

28. Ibid., 434, and Susan Hansen, *The Politics of Taxation: Revenue without Representation* (New York: Praeger, 1983).

29. Hansen, "Extraction," 428.

30. Allen Schick, *Capacity to Budget* (Washington, D.C.: Urban Institute, 1990), 144.

31. David Osborne, *Laboratories of Democracy* (Boston: Harvard Business School Press, 1988), 27.

32. See Bryan Jones and Lynn Bachelor, with Carter Wilson, *The Sustaining Hand: Community Leadership and Corporate Power* (Lawrence: University Press of Kansas, 1986), for the relationship between economic decline and tax breaks for General Motors in Detroit; see Daniel Mandelker, Gary Feder, and Margaret R. Collins, *Reviving Cities with Tax Abatements* (New Brunswick, N.J.: Rutgers University, Center for Urban Policy Research, 1980), for the connection between economic decline and property tax abatements in St. Louis. For the relationship between declining economy and tax breaks in Cook County, where Chicago is located, see Arthur Lyons, Spenser Staton, Greg Wass, and Mari Zurek, "Reducing Property Taxes to Promote Economic Development: Does It Work?" Report prepared for the Comptroller of the City of Chicago, January 1988.

33. Stanley Surrey and Paul McDaniel, *Tax Expenditures* (Cambridge: Har-

vard University Press, 1985), 3, make this distinction. Tax exceptions are sometimes called tax expenditures because they reduce the revenues that would normally have been raised by the tax, and because the stated goal of such tax reductions is to achieve some programmatic goal using tax incentives instead of spending programs.

34. Louis Eisenstein, *The Ideologies of Taxation* (New York: Ronald Press, 1961).

35. Congressional Research Service, *Tax Expenditures: Compendium of Background Material on Individual Provisions* (Washington, D.C.: Committee Print of the Committee on the Budget, December 1994), 63.

36. The 1983 figures are from Surrey and McDaniel, *Tax Expenditures,* 9. Their source was the Congressional Joint Committee on Taxation, *Estimates of Federal Tax Expenditures for Fiscal Years 1983–88,* 7 March 1983, 10–18. The later figures are from the 1987, 1988, and 1991 budgets. Estimates of dollar losses due to tax expenditures are not very exact. It is hard to know exactly how much revenue the Treasury would get if a particular tax break were eliminated, since reliance on other forms of tax breaks might increase to compensate. When estimates for losses due to several tax expenditures are added up, the sponginess of the totals is even greater. These figures are therefore ballpark figures.

37. Surrey and McDaniel, *Tax Expenditures,* 22.

38. Witte, *Politics and Development of the Federal Income Tax,* 149.

39. Ibid., 214.

40. Ibid., 150.

41. Howard E. Shuman, *Politics and the Budget: The Struggle Between the President and the Congress* (Englewood Cliffs, N.J.: Prentice Hall, 1984), 105.

42. Schick, *Capacity to Budget,* 144.

43. Thomas Neubig and David Joulfaian, "The Tax Expenditure Budget Before and After the Tax Reform Act of 1986," OTA Paper 60, Office of Tax Analysis, Department of the Treasury, October 1988, 1–2.

44. Congressional Budget Office, *The Effects of Tax Reform on Tax Expenditures* (Washington, D.C.: Congressional Budget Office, 1988), cited in Schick, *Capacity to Budget,* 148.

45. Based on Statement by Paul R. McDaniel, "Overview of Tax Expenditures in the Budget," *Hearing Before the Committee on the Budget, Concurrent Resolution on the Budget for Fiscal Year 1994,* U.S. Senate, 1st sess., 3 February 1993, 360. McDaniel compared the tax expenditure report in the 1986 budget with the report in the 1993 budget.

46. Jane Gravelle, in Congressional Research Service, *Overview of Tax Expenditures, 1993* (Washington, D.C.: Government Printing Office, 1993), 376.

47. Eugene Steuerle, in Congressional Research Service, *Overview of Tax Expenditures, 1993,* 378.

48. *Congressional Record,* 25 January 1995, H.687.

49. Office of Management and Budget, *The 1996 U.S. Budget, Tax Expenditure Report: The Joint Committee on Taxation, Estimates of Federal Tax Expenditures for Fiscal Years 1995–1999* (Washington, D.C.: Government Printing

Office, 9 November 1994).

50. *Congressional Record,* 13 July 1994, E.1449.

51. McDaniel, "Overview of Tax Expenditures," 362.

52. Based on an analysis of information presented in "A Layman's Guide to Illinois Taxes," Illinois Department of Revenue, September 1989, 23–25.

53. Frederick W. Derrick and Charles E. Scott, *Maryland's Sales and Use Tax: Past, Present and Future* (prepared for the Maryland Commission on State Taxes and Tax Structure, 31 October 1989), 1.

54. Ibid., 9.

55. Jay Ladin, *The Maryland Personal Income Tax* (prepared for the Maryland Commission on State Taxes and Tax Structure, January 1990), 21.

56. Ibid., 19.

57. Lee Walker, *The Changing Arena: State Strategic Economic Development* (Lexington, Ky.: Council of State Governments, 1989); and Paul Peretz, "The Market for Industry: Where Angels Fear to Tread?" *Policy Studies Review* 5, no. 3 (February 1996): 624–33.

58. Charles Spindler, "Winners and Losers in Industrial Recruitment: Mercedes Benz and Alabama," *State and Local Government Review* 26, no. 3 (Fall 1994): 192–204.

59. Ibid., 202.

60. Ibid., 198.

61. Peter Eisenger, *The Rise of the Entrepreneurial State: State and Local Development in the United States* (Madison: University of Wisconsin Press, 1988).

62. Don Sherman Grant II, Michael Wallace, and William Pitney, "Measuring State-Level Economic Development Programs, 1970–92," *Economic Development Quarterly* 9, no. 2 (May 1995): 134–45; and Peter Eisenger, "State Economic Development Policies in the 1990s: Politics and Policy Learning," *Economic Development Quarterly* 9, no. 2 (May 1995): 146–58.

63. Samuel Nunn, "Regulating Local Tax Abatement Policies: Arguments and Alternative Policies for Urban Planners and Administrators," *Policy Studies Journal* 22, no. 4 (Winter 1994): 574–88.

64. J.E. Harris and S.A. Hicks, "Tax Expenditure Reporting: The Utilization of an Innovation," *Public Budgeting and Finance* 12, no. 3 (Fall 1992): 32–49; the figure of twenty-one states is cited on p. 33.

65. Karen Benker, "Tax Expenditure Reporting: Closing the Loophole in State Budget Oversight," *National Tax Journal* 39, no. 4 (December 1986): 403–17.

66. Ibid., 412.

67. Jon David Vasche, "Tax Expenditure Reporting: A Comment," *National Tax Journal* 40, no. 2 (June 1987): 255–57.

68. Ibid., 256.

69. Jesse Hughes and Janne Moteket, "Tax Expenditures for Local Government," *Public Budgeting and Finance* 8, no. 4 (Winter 1988): 68–73.

70. John Sharp, Texas comptroller of accounts, sales and franchise tax ex-

emptions, *A Report to the Governor and Texas Legislature,* January 1991; and letter from John Sharp, 16 December 1992.

71. Louisiana Department of Revenue and Taxation, table entitled "Comparison of Tax Revenues to Expenditures, FY 1992," n.d. Sent on request.

72. State of Ohio Executive Budget for the Biennium, 1 July 1993 to 30 June 1995, bk. 2, *Report on Tax Expenditures Prepared in 1993.*

73. Hughes and Moteket, "Tax Expenditures."

74. Ann H. Elder and Nancy S. Lind, "The Implications of Uncertainty in Economic Development: The Case of Diamond Star Motors," *Economic Development Quarterly* 1, no. 1 (February 1987): 30–40.

75. Nunn, "Regulating Local Tax Abatement Policies," 582.

76. Michael Barker, ed., *State Taxation Policy* (Durham, N.C.: Duke University Press, 1983), 94.

77. Lyons et al., "Reducing Property Taxes," 50.

78. For an account of the federal government's efforts to control this tax break, see Dennis Zimmerman, *The Private Use of Tax Exempt Bonds: Controlling Public Subsidy of Private Activity* (Washington, D.C.: Urban Institute Press, 1991).

79. William Celis III, "Schools Lose Money in Business Tax Breaks," *New York Times,* 22 May 1991, 1.

80. Lyons et al., "Reducing Property Taxes," 57.

81. One example of the relative inefficiency of tax expenditures as a means of achieving program goals occurred in housing. In 1975, Congress passed a tax credit for the purchase of new homes, reportedly to encourage building and sales of new homes, at a cost of $600 million. Housing was increased by fewer than 105,000 units, which amounted to a subsidy of $5700 per unit. More efficient subsidies could have been used, according to Thomas Reese, *The Politics of Taxation* (Westport, Conn.: Quorum Books, 1980), xvi.

82. Ibid., xix.

83. Timothy Clark, "Divided They Stand," *National Journal,* 19 April 1986, 928.

84. Timothy Clark, "How to Succeed Against Business," *National Journal,* 3 May 1986, 1059.

85. Ibid.

86. For an account of the lobbying to protect tax breaks, see Jeffrey Birnbaum and Alan Murray, *Showdown at Gucci Gulch: Lawmakers, Lobbyists, and the Unlikely Triumph of Tax Reform* (New York: Random House, 1987).

87. Eileen Shanahan, "Congress Expected to OK Tax Overhaul Bill," *National Journal,* 23 April 1986, 1951.

88. Benker, "Tax Expenditure Reporting," 412.

89. John F. Witte, "Wisconsin Income Tax Reform," in *State Policy Choices: The Wisconsin Experience,* ed. Sheldon Danzinger and John F. Witte (Madison: University of Wisconsin Press, 1988), 108–29.

3. The Politics of Budget Processes

If the budget process is to produce anything, it must produce honesty. Only then will the American people learn of and support the difficult choices the Congress and the President must make to restore fiscal discipline.

— Senator John Exon

The budget process divides budgetary decision making into parts and assigns the parts to different institutional actors. Once the work is divided up, the budget process has to coordinate the different streams of decision making by arranging sequences and feeding decisions from one stream into another. The budget process frames which decisions and which comparisons will be made, and determines the amount of information and the amount of time allowed for making the designated decisions.

Sometimes descriptions of budget processes seem like a list of reporting dates that are made on time or missed, but the budget process is more than a technical arrangement for the timely flow of decisions. The budget process is also political: (1) because it gives some participants more control over whether money is spent on one project or another, in one place or another; (2) because it structures the competition between agencies and programs; and (3) because it influences or is believed to influence policy outcomes, such as the overall size of the budget, the distribution of costs and benefits, and the relative size of expenditures on social services and defense or social control.

Control over budget decisions is widely sought after because it allows public officials to satisfy constituency demands and build a power base. Power over the budget gives budget actors resources to trade. The desirability of playing a role in budget decisions creates a pressure to divide decision making into numerous small pieces so that many actors can each get at least a little budget power. It also leads to jockeying to get into key decision-making positions and maintain the power of those positions against others who are trying to enhance their budget power. This competition occurs between individuals, between committees in the legislature, and between legislative and executive branches of government.

The budget process is responsible for grouping together items to be considered and determining which items will be compared with one another. It thus controls the degree and nature of competition in the budget. By framing which questions will be asked of each decision maker, the budget process also determines the level and kind of scrutiny that various requests get and the documentation required to support a request. The budget process controls the level of policy analysis in the creation of a budget.

The budget process is widely believed to influence policy outcomes. A particular process does not automatically produce a particular outcome, but by shifting budget power to actors who have particular interests or sets of demands, the process influences outcomes. Moreover, some processes emphasize the articulation and satisfaction of local interests, while others emphasize spending control or the articulation of overall policy concerns. Some budgetary actors believe that by shifting the degree of openness to various interests, or by shifting the degree of centralization of budget processes they can increase or decrease total spending levels and enhance or reduce the ability of the budget to perform as a tool to shape public policy.

Characteristics of Public Budgeting Processes

Public budgeting processes share a number of characteristics. Actors with different goals compete to design the budget process. In addition, the process is vulnerable to the environment. It adapts, more or less well, to environmental richness or leanness, to public attitudes toward government spending and taxation, and to accumulated deficits or high rates of growth in spending. Budget processes regulate the level and mechanisms of accountability to the public and openness to interest groups. Finally, budget processes embody the constraints typical of public budgeting, such as overall spending limits or mandated across-the-board cuts or formulas for the distribution of funds. Within this overall similarity, budget processes vary in terms of the amount of power granted to the executive, the degree of centralization, the degree of openness to the public and interest groups, the format of the budget, the amount of policy content, and the extensiveness of review.

MULTIPLE ACTORS WITH DIFFERENT GOALS
Elected officials and staff are the key actors in budget reform. Citizens and interest groups play almost no role, although not-for-profit research insti-

tutes such as the American Enterprise Institute at the national level or Bureaus of Governmental Research at the local level often generate reform proposals.

The chief executive may argue for strengthened executive powers, such as enhanced veto or rescission power; the legislature may argue for more legislative control over the policy in the budget. Legislative committees may jockey for more control over the process among themselves, or the leadership of the legislature may try to enhance its own power at the expense of the committees. Those who favor more or less spending may agitate for particular reforms they think will enhance those outcomes.

House Speaker Newt Gingrich centralized budget power in his own hands in 1995 by using the budget reconciliation process to bypass committees if they were deadlocked or could not come up with proposals that suited him. Many committee members were startled and some protested.

The reconciliation process was part of the 1974 Congressional Budget Reform Act. This step in the budget process gives targets to committees working on different parts of the budget. The committees are supposed to figure out ways to meet the targets. The committees' separate proposals are supposed to be rolled up into one inclusive or "omnibus" piece of legislation. Over the years, other legislation has crept into the omnibus bill, often without adequate or any committee consideration. In addition, in 1995, Gingrich took legislation out of the committees' hands. Congressman Lee Hamilton, among others, decried the threat to committee power. Hamilton, quoted in the *Congressional Record* on 31 October 1995, said:

> I am here today because I am troubled by the pattern of abuse of the legislative process that has been developing during this Congress. This bill exemplifies that abuse. . . . This reconciliation bill enters a new universe in its breadth, the sheer number and complexity of proposals, and the extent to which committees of jurisdiction—and thus, all members of the minority—were shut out of developing this package.
>
> The reconciliation package contains three large items and several smaller provisions that fall within the jurisdiction of the International Relations Committee. First, HR 2517 contains a major legislative proposal dramatically changing the configuration of the Commerce Department. The committee has jurisdiction over international trade issues, so the dismantlement of the Commerce Department causes great concern. The committee never considered the measure. Second, the bill "deems" enacted the entire

foreign affairs agencies' reorganization bill. Action has not yet been completed in the Senate. Third, the bill contains the text of HR 927, the Cuban Liberty and Democratic Solidarity Act, approved by the House [in late 1995]. This bill was altered substantially by the Senate and should be scheduled for conference.

The purpose of a reconciliation bill is to bring direct spending in line with the targets set by the budget resolution. Among the many problems with this bill, these items in the jurisdiction of the International Relations Committee have nothing to do with budget reconciliation. . . .

1. This process places enormous power in the leadership, who will consult only with those persons and groups they want to include. The committee is bypassed, an entire House of the Congress is bypassed. All decision making about the issues occurs behind closed doors in a group formed by the leaders of the majority. Final decisions are made by the Speaker. You have created a largely secret system. This is a system which reduces accountability. It is an entirely closed process. The average American has no way of learning which members are involved, which special interest groups are consulted or locked out, and what positions members have taken on a proposal until it is too late and the House has voted. Many members of both parties with significant expertise were simply not welcome to contribute to the process.

2. This process bypasses and undermines the entire committee system. When the chairman decides to waive consideration of bills that are central to the committee's jurisdiction, most members—including all members of the minority—are shut out. The Commerce proposal is a case in point. Our committee had no role in developing that proposal. We held no hearings on this proposal, there was no debate, we had no markup, no amendments were permitted, we did not vote. We defaulted on our responsibilities. The committee is also stripped of its responsibilities when items that it has considered and moved through the House are included in the reconciliation package. Moving the committee's foreign affairs reorganization bill or the Cuba bill through the reconciliation bill removes the committee from meaningful participation in a conference. It puts these major foreign policy bills into a conference with a mix of 1,000 other domestic items. The substance of these bills will not likely be discussed in a reconciliation conference. . . .

3. This process produces a monster bill. This bill is simply overwhelming. What we have before us—all 1,754 pages—is not really the entire bill. It does not yet include the Medicare package. There are several other bills that are hundreds of pages themselves—such as HR 1561 and the welfare reform package—that this bill incorporates by reference. This reconciliation package will include bills that majority votes in committees rejected. The

"Freedom to Farm" bill, for example. It includes bills the bulk of which the House has rejected, such as the mining patents and national park concessions proposals. It includes bills such as the Cuba bill, that have passed the House and Senate in very different forms. There is every reason to send this bill to conference under regular process. It includes bills—for instance, the Commerce proposal—created by a task force made up only of members of the majority party, after committees have reported out different measures and some committees—such as the International Relations Committee—were apparently instructed by the leadership not to act at all.

4. This process will include a tightly constrained rule. Reconciliation bills traditionally impose severe constraints on time for debate and the opportunity to amend. You will undoubtedly prescribe a restrictive rule, a rule designed to keep the package intact. The Senate accords only 20 hours of debate (12 minutes per member) on the bill. In this bill, that means just over one minute per page. We have had only a few days to digest this enormous bill. And the contents of the bill we take up on the floor are anyone's guess—I expect your rule will include significant "self-executing" changes. We will probably know even less about the contents of the reconciliation conference report before we must vote on it.

5. This process is not defensible because the ends do not justify the means. I understand that the current leadership has a very different view of the committee system. If the leadership is driven only by outcome, then process is irrelevant. Having the votes at the end of the day is all that matters. I believe that the essence of democracy is process, and that the end does not justify the means, that the means is as important as the end. That means a process that guarantees that all members will have an opportunity to be heard, if they do not have the chance to prevail. It means a process that allows every member to offer amendments and to vote, and every constituent to track how their representative has voted as a bill winds its way from committee, to the floor, to conference, and to the president. It means a process that allows those who have spent time developing expertise in a particular area to have a seat at the negotiating table. Eliminating consideration by committees, by one House, silencing voices, reducing the number of people at the negotiating table may get bills through the House faster. You may get bills out of conference more quickly. But in the end we will not get better laws. And we will erode the foundations of this institution.... I ask that you think very seriously about the entire way you're planning to move this reconciliation package. Subverting the legislative process does a grave disservice to this body, and to the American people.

Though the congressman complained in terms of harm to the legislative process and to public accountability, an underlying issue was that the committees, which had been used to exercising power, were suddenly denied that power.

VULNERABILITY TO THE ENVIRONMENT

Which goals will be emphasized in the budget process depends not only on the power of the budget actors trying to achieve particular budget goals but also on the environment. Huge deficits create pressure to adopt a budget process that emphasizes balance; rapid growth in expenditures creates pressure to adopt a process that makes spending decisions difficult, that buffers the process from interest groups, or that shifts decision making to particular actors who are able to resist spending demands. Sometimes major social changes, such as mass migrations, economic growth or decline, or widespread civil unrest, may set the stage for increased expenditures, and the budget process may be altered to facilitate such spending. A decline in revenues or general scarcity of government income may create an environment where spending must be carefully weighed against alternative uses for money, putting pressure on the budget process to provide adequate decision-making information and adequate time to consider alternatives. The degree of consensus among decision makers and within the society more broadly may influence the tolerance for conflict and competition in the budget process.

SEPARATION OF PAYER AND DECIDER

The budget process determines both the level of accountability to taxpayers and the mechanisms for providing accountability. For example, the budget process may actively solicit or ignore the opinions of citizens about what they want the budget to do. Citizen and interest-group input can be regulated by the location, timing, and openness of budget hearings, by the openness of deliberations to the public and the media, by the use of advisory boards with citizen and interest-group representation, and by the decentralization of decision making, which creates numerous locations for possible public input and influence. The budget process also determines the format and level of explanation in the budget document. A budget with a high level of accountability reports how public money was allocated and how efficiently and effectively public money was spent, and describes the budget in terms that ordinary citizens can understand.

CONSTRAINTS

The budget process introduces some of the many constraints that characterize public budgeting. One recent example at the federal level is legislation called (after its legislative sponsors) Gramm-Rudman-Hollings, which reorganized the budget process in 1985. It included new deadlines for decisions, targets for reductions in the deficit over a period of years, and an automatic series of cuts if deficit-reduction targets were not met. This process of deficit reduction framed decisions by requiring across-the-board cuts in particular categories of the budget, but exempted many programs from the across-the-board cuts. The Gramm-Rudman-Hollings process thus introduced a number of extremely constraining conditions under which budgeting was to take place. Gramm-Rudman-Hollings was modified in the fall of 1990, but the amended process is still highly constrained.

More generally, budget processes often set limits to expenditures or to revenues at the start of the budget process so that the decision making has to take place within those constraints. Or the process may begin with other kinds of constraints, such as goals for reallocation or productivity savings or constraints on cutting back capital or staff. The specific constraints depend on the conditions and policies then in effect, but they are embodied in the budget process and frame the decision making.

Constraints on decision making may exclude many key decisions from the budget process. The decisions that remain may be very narrow, despite the size of the budget. In one city with a multimillion-dollar budget, the most important decision the budget decision makers were asked to make was between increasing a contingency fund by $20,000 or increasing two part-time secretaries to full-time. The amount of money involved was small and the decision had no major policy implications.

The budget process also reflects constraints imposed by other levels of government. For example, the amount of budgeting autonomy granted to cities by the states varies enormously. Some states mandate uniform budget formats for local governments, while others allow each jurisdiction to work out its own format. States can mandate that the budget be put together by a finance director or budget officer, or allow the city clerk or city attorney to put together an appropriation ordinance (a simple list of anticipated expenditures to help estimate needed property taxes) in lieu of a budget. States can reduce the level of tradeoffs in the budget by allowing the creation of special-purpose governments, by earmarking revenues to local governments, and by mandating expenditures.

Variable Elements of Budget Processes

Budget processes are not fixed. If the actors do not like the outcomes, they can change the process. It is during efforts to change the budget process that the actors' goals are most apparent and the influence of the environment is most clear. Participants' efforts to change the process help make it clear how particular parts of the budget process are intended or expected to work to achieve particular budget outcomes.

One pressure for change in budget processes is the goal of individuals to enhance their power over the budget. Jockeying for power results in a variety of pressures, some of which cancel each other out. For example, because so many budget actors want some control over budget outcomes, there is pressure to disperse decision-making power widely. But counter to that pressure, those already in decision-making roles may work to concentrate the making of decisions more into their own hands. Members of particular legislative committees seek to increase their power, but members of other committees may try to thwart them and enhance their own power instead. If the only purpose of a proposed change is to enhance the power of one actor or small group, it may be difficult to get a majority to go along with the proposed change, especially if the change threatens the power of other groups. But a proposal to change the budget process to achieve different budget outcomes—such as a reduction in the size of the deficit—is likely to mobilize more actors. When such changes in the budget process are being considered, those whose power will be enhanced are likely to support the changes, and those whose power will be diminished are likely to oppose them. Jockeying for budget power between different budget actors thus becomes a kind of undertheme in the politics of budgeting, while efforts to change the budget outcomes is the overtheme, the central dominating explanation.

When budget outcomes are unacceptable, and more important causes cannot be easily attacked, there is pressure to change the budget process to favor particular outcomes. Budget processes can be designed to emphasize and facilitate any (or several) of the following goals:

1. Growth or reduction in expenditures
2. Balance or deficit spending
3. Tradeoffs between programs and goals
4. Competition or minimization of competition
5. Financial and managerial control (preventing overspending of targets and other forms of waste)

Because different budget actors have different goals, it may be difficult to come to a consensus about what goals should be emphasized. One group may want to emphasize economy and efficiency, while another wants to emphasize reduction in spending and shrinking the scope of government services. Another group may be interested in building a process that allows the chief executive to take an active stance in shaping policy through the budget.

Proposals for changing the budget process often emphasize several goals, to bring together a variety of backers. The environment may make coalition building easier if it presents overwhelming problems that force a variety of actors to submerge their differences and get on with a solution.

When designing budget processes, some basic elements of budgetary decision making are almost always present. Some actor makes a claim for resources, someone examines that claim or request, and someone approves or disapproves the requests. Within that framework, there is considerable variation. Who makes the initial proposal, with what kind of guidance? Who reviews the request? What kind of comparisons are made between requests, on the basis of what information? How are the decisions framed? Who gives the final approval? Who may exercise a veto, and how often is the veto invoked? Different answers to these questions create, or are believed to create, biases toward particular budgetary outcomes.

The politically significant variability between budget processes can be described in terms of six characteristics. These characteristics represent particular answers to the questions of who proposes, who frames choices, who examines what kind of information, and who makes final decisions. Each characteristic is generally believed to have some impact on outcomes.

1. Executive vs. legislative dominance
2. The degree of centralization; top-down or bottom-up initiatives
3. The level of access for citizens and interest groups
4. The format of the budget requests, and layout and kind of information used to justify the request
5. The extensiveness of the policy formulation and statements at the beginning of the budget process
6. The timing and nature of reviews of budget requests

EXECUTIVE VERSUS LEGISLATIVE DOMINANCE

Perhaps the most dramatic difference between budget processes is the degree to which they are dominated by the executive or the legislative branch. In the model of executive dominance, the chief executive is responsible for formulating the budget proposal, which reflects his or her priorities and policy agenda, if any. The chief executive may keep the executive branch agencies completely away from the legislature, other than to present the chief executive's approved version of the proposal. The legislature may rubber-stamp the executive budget, that is, approve it without detailed examination or emendation. Should the legislature make any changes that the chief executive opposes, the chief executive can veto the changes and sometimes even rewrite legislation. In the legislatively dominated budget process, the bureau chiefs write up their requests for spending with the assistance of legislators who want some particular expenditures. The requests are not scrutinized by the chief executive, but are handed directly to the legislature for review and approval. The role of the chief executive in the legislative dominance model is slight.

Budget processes normally fall between the extremes of total dominance either by the executive or by the legislature. Formally and legally, the legislatures often have the power to initiate spending and approve taxation and proposals for spending, but they may delegate much of that power to the executive. One reason for delegating that authority is the belief that expenditures are out of control and that the legislature cannot discipline itself, especially on capital projects and jobs for constituents. The chief executive is expected to be able to cut out proposals that legislators make to please constituents and impose discipline on the legislature. The belief that legislatures are more vulnerable to interest-group and constituent demands than the chief executive leads to pressure to shift budget power from the legislature to the chief executive.

One way that the executive is supposed to exercise control is to veto any increases the legislature adds to the executive's proposed budget. Strong executive veto powers usually indicate a strong executive and a weak legislature. The political power of the legislature over appropriations is conditioned by the executive's power to veto.

Governors generally have broader veto powers than the president. The president of the United States has to veto all of a bill or none of it, which permits Congress to package bills to discourage vetoes. Thirty-eight state governors have line-item vetoes that allow them to strike out any expenditure that appears as a separate line in the budget.[1] State legislatures have less ability to package bills to avoid a veto by the governor.

Some governors have other, more powerful veto powers, such as amendatory vetoes, which allow them to rewrite passages in the law, or reduction vetoes, which allow them to reduce the amount in any line by any amount. Reduction vetoes thus make it more difficult for legislators to pass bills that require new funding over the opposition of the governor. If they try, the governor can simply reduce the amount, thereby requiring a supermajority of the legislators (say, a two-thirds vote) to overturn the governor's veto.

CENTRALIZATION

A second politically significant characteristic of budget processes is their degree of centralization. Centralization refers to two related concepts: (1) the degree to which the budget process is bottom-up or top-down; and (2) the degree to which power is scattered among independent committees, commissions, and elected officials without an effective coordinating device.

Bottom-up procedures begin with the budget requests of bureau chiefs. These requests are scrutinized by either the chief executive and his budget staff or by the legislature, or by both, but the requests form the framework of decision making and set the agenda. There is little or no prioritizing between programs in this model in its extreme form. Each request is judged on its merits, independently of other requests. A loose coordination is achieved by setting revenue or spending limits at the beginning of the process; cost increases are kept within rough limits by giving no agency an increase much higher than the total percentage increase in revenues.

Top-down budgeting at its extreme virtually ignores bureau chiefs. The chief executive may not ask bureau chiefs for their budget requests or may give them detailed instructions on how to formulate their requests. The proposal can be made from whole cloth at the top of the executive branch by taking last year's actual budget and making changes in it in accordance with policy preference, giving more to one and less to another, regardless of what the bureau chiefs would have asked for themselves. A more moderate top-down procedure takes the bureaus' requests and gives more to one and less to another based on policy choices.

In the legislature too, budget processes can be more top-down or more bottom-up, depending on whether budget and revenue targets are given to spending and revenue committees to work with, or whether the revenue and spending committees do their own work and give the totals to the body as a whole.

Budgeting processes normally combine some top-down elements and some bottom-up elements. Budgeting tends to become more top down when there is a revenue problem or a defined budget crisis that requires reduction in expenditures. Top-down budgeting is associated with spending control and a policy orientation to the budget. That is, if the chief executive has a marked preference for achieving some goal, he or she is more likely to use a top-down process to select some programs and reject others as a means to achieve that goal.

The second dimension of centralization is the extent to which power is scattered among relatively independent actors. For example, the chief executive may have to share power with other elected executive branch officers or with independent commissions. When power is widely shared, the effect may be to immobilize decision making. No one has responsibility or can tell anyone else what to do; approval for any action has to go through a number of different actors. The purpose of a highly fragmented and decentralized budget process may be precisely to limit the amount of spending, and the amount of activist government. More centralization of budget processes is usually more activist and more policy oriented, but may be either economy oriented or spending oriented.

OPEN OR CLOSED PROCESS

Budget processes vary on the dimension of openness. The most open processes are those that make all decisions in plain public view, before the press, the public, and interest groups. Meetings are held at convenient times for visitors and are announced well in advance. Representatives of various interests are invited to share their views during budget hearings and on advisory boards. The process is closed if the public, the press, and interest groups are not permitted to watch the decision making or allowed to express their views during the budget process. Or their views may be solicited but routinely disregarded. Budget processes are seldom completely open or completely closed.

Open budget processes are more accountable to the public, but they are also more open to interest-group pressure. Closing the budget process is often considered one way to help control increases in expenditures; opening it is usually a way of increasing expenditures. Closing the process is also a way of helping to pass revenue bills, as noted in chapter 2, which means that a more closed process should favor budget balance as a goal.

FORMAT

The key goals of the budget are reflected in the budget format and its relative emphasis on expenditure control, management improvement and cost effectiveness, and policy and planning.[2] The major budget formats are the line-item budget, performance budgets, and program budgets.

A line-item budget lists each department and assigns a sum of money to the department. The money is not granted in a lump sum, to be spent as needed, but is divided into money for specific expenditures—travel, payroll, commodities, and the like. Each kind of expenditure is listed on a separate line; the department then has to spend the money in accordance with the requirements of each line. If the budget is broken into many detailed lines, such as paper supplies, pencils, desks and chairs, typewriters and stamps, the department head has very little discretion about how the money can be spent. This kind of budget emphasizes financial control. A line-item budget plays down competition because it never compares programs.

A performance budget lists what each administrative unit is trying to accomplish, how much it is planning to do, with what resources. It reports on how well it did with the resources it had last year. The emphasis is on getting the most service for the dollar.

A program budget divides expenditures by activities so that the costs for juvenile counseling are broken out from traffic patrol, and both of those are separated from crime detection. Sometimes program budgets are formally linked to a planning process where community (or national) goals are stated and expenditures allocated in an effort to reach those goals. The emphasis in this format is on the appropriateness of current spending priorities and the possible need for tradeoffs between programs. Program budgets have the most potential for allowing legislators to review the policy implications of spending decisions.

Zero-based budgeting is a particular kind of program budget. It associates service levels in each program with costs, and then it prioritizes all the options, treating high and low service levels as different program options. All those at the top of the priority list are funded. If there are more items than money, the ones on the bottom of the list are not funded. Zero-based budgeting formally allows for and creates a mechanism for reallocation, since one department may suggest a higher level of service or a new program that is ranked high on the priority list, while another department's programs are ranked low. The new proposal may be funded at the expense of the older. The potential for generating competition and conflict is enormous in this budget format, so that it is seldom used; but a modified version of it, target budgeting, which puts 5 or 10 percent of the departments' budgets at risk for reallocation, is used more often.

The information presented in each budget format allows different kinds of decisions to be made. The line-item budget forces comparisons along the lines of changes in accounting categories—why are office supplies more expensive this year than last? These are technical questions of limited focus. When a budget is line item only, it can be very difficult to examine proposed expenditures for sound management practice or the appropriateness of the expenditures.[3] The program budget, especially with its zero-based budget component, forces comparisons between programs on the basis of stated priorities. These priorities are usually statements of policy; for example, when comparing two programs, the one that benefits the poor should have a higher priority than the one that benefits the rich, or programs that emphasize prevention should receive funding before programs that emphasize suppression. Performance budgets lay out not only what programs cost and roughly what they achieve; they lay out the (implied) criteria of productivity for the choices between programs. Legislators, of course, may use other criteria as well.

Because the different budget formats have different strengths and weaknesses, many actual budgets combine formats.[4] Everyone has to be concerned about financial control, so there is often a line-item budget conforming to administrative units; but sometimes program budgets are added to line-item budgets, and, more rarely, performance budgets are added to the program budget.

In short, there is enormous variation in budget formats. Formats differentially emphasize control, management, or policy preferences. Different formats also influence the kind of review that spending proposals get and structure the level of competition between programs.

EXTENSIVENESS OF UP-FRONT POLICY FORMULATION

Some budget processes begin with a consideration of the overall policies that are to guide the budget that year, such as targets for spending or limitations on the raising of new revenues, or items that are absolutely off limits for cut-back or tradeoffs. Once these decisions are made, the rest of the decision making should be more mechanical and flow more smoothly.

The willingness to deal with major controversial policy issues first and in the open implies either a high level of consensus or a willingness to deal with conflict and controversy. The environment may impose circumstances that forge a degree of consensus if deficits are large or expenditures are growing at an alarming rate with respect to revenues. The need for policy decisions up front to curtail borrowing or limit spending may be widely accepted, and the potential controversy lessened. In the absence of consensus on goals, the budget process may tone down the level of controversy by bypassing the step of formulating common policy guidelines.

BUDGET REVIEW

While all public budget processes involve review, the location and intensity of review are variable. Sometimes the executive budget office (staff to the chief executive officer) carefully reviews each budget request coming up from the bureaus, looking for consistency with stated guidelines, the logic of the justification of expenditures, and the correctness of the calculations. Sometimes the budget office does not have the staff time or expertise for a detailed review of the requests, or lacks sensible standards against which to measure the reasonableness of requests. Depending on the format of the budget, legislators may give a superficial examination to the budget or a more detailed look.

Some budget processes involve hearings. These hearings may be in the executive branch as the budget requests are being examined; typically this kind of hearing involves only agency heads and representatives of the budget office. Or there may be hearings only in the legislature after the executive branch has delivered its requests to the legislature. These hearings may involve only agency heads as witnesses, or may also include citizens and interest groups; they may be far reaching in content and exploratory in nature, or they may stick closely to the numbers on the budget request; they may be used in making budget decisions, or they may have little to do with decision making. There can be hearings in both the executive branch and the legislative branch, one for the formation of the budget request and one for examination and review.

At the state level and sometimes at the local level, there may be joint hearings between the executive and the legislative branch before the budget is submitted to the legislature. In 1975, seventeen states had such joint hearings where the legislators or their staff participated in the hearings. Four more had joint hearings at which the legislators attended but did not participate. These hearings did not include interest groups or the public; they were typically for agency witnesses only.[5] Reportedly some legislators felt that it was difficult for them to add requests to the governor's proposal after it was prepared because the governor could so easily veto unwanted items. Consequently, these legislators chose to add items while the governor's budget was still in the formative stage.

The nature of the review determines whether there can be a policy focus in the budget and whether tradeoffs can be made based on analysis delivered during the budget process. If inadequate time is given to review, if the review is superficial or technical, the potential for tradeoffs and conflict is dampened.

Of the six characteristics of budget process discussed here, each is expected to have some impact on the outcomes, but they are often grouped for maximum impact. Several characteristics that have similar effects will be put together. For example, a budget process that was open to interest groups and the public, that was in the program format, that allowed sufficient time for review and included hearings at which a variety of actors could present their cases, that budget process would be full of conflict, lively, and probably policy oriented. A budget process that was decentralized and line item in format would tone down conflict and have little policy orientation. Such a process would facilitate gradual expenditure increases and fiscal control to prevent overspending. A top-down process with limited interest-group access and defined policy objectives at the beginning of budget deliberations would facilitate accomplishment of activist goals, regardless of the content of the goals. One could come up with numerous combinations that would facilitate one or more budgetary goals.

Variation between and among Federal, State, and Local Governments

For years, the federal budget process was used by scholars as a model against which other processes could be compared and understood. But during the 1980s, the federal budget was put together in a different way every year. The advent of ad hoc budgeting at the federal level shifted attention to the states and to local governments in the search for a pattern that would convey the idea of a budget process. But a survey of state and local budget processes reveals enormous variation. To come up with an idea of budget process based on this variation requires a description of that variation and the mechanisms that generated it. This section illustrates some of the key ways that budget processes differ from one another, while the final section of the chapter describes how and to some extent why federal, state, and local budget processes have changed and discusses some common themes in their evolution.

VARIATION BETWEEN LEVELS OF GOVERNMENT

There is so much variation in budget processes between levels of government, and so much variation within levels, that it is difficult to give a concise listing of differences that is at the same time meaningful. What follows is a sketch of some of the major differences in recent years.

One way of describing budget processes is to examine the balance between the executive and the legislature in drawing up and reviewing the budget. Over the past decade, at the federal level there has been more of an equal balance between the branches than at the state or local level. At the state level, the executive tends to be stronger than the legislature, with strong veto powers. At the local level, for all but the smallest cities, the model of executive dominance generally holds. Mayors often hold powerful vetoes and the councils are often prohibited from increasing the mayor's estimates. Councils have little or no budget staff. They do have to approve the budget in most cities, and in some cities they play a substantial role in reviewing the budget. Councils often are more subordinate to the executive than state legislatures or Congress are.

One aspect of the balance between the executive and legislature is the strength of the executive's veto power over the legislature. The president can veto only whole bills. Most governors can veto parts of bills, and some can even change amounts or wording in legislation. Because the president can veto only whole bills, Congress can seek to avoid vetoes by packaging legislation in such a way that the president cannot veto the whole bill without losing something he wants badly.

As differences between the president and Congress became acute during the 1980s, Congress resorted to omnibus legislation, huge packages of legislation combined in a single bill. This omnibus legislation included increased reliance on continuing resolutions. Such resolutions are intended to assure funding to agencies if one of the thirteen money bills is late, but they have increasingly been used instead of normal appropriations bills because they are more "veto proof." Congress also merged a variety of unrelated measures into omnibus reconciliation acts, which are the result of committee compliance with budget constraints assigned during the budget process. While the president technically could veto such omnibus measures, such a veto would leave the government without a budget and create a funding crisis.

At the state level, budgets may be passed in a single measure or in a series of separate bills—practice varies from state to state. But the use of omnibus legislation to avoid vetoes is virtually nonexistent. Only nine states have a mechanism for continuing last year's budget in case this year's budget is late.[6] Omnibus reconciliations are a peculiarity of the federal budget process. State legislatures lack the motivation to package legislation in large clumps; since the governor can generally veto parts of legislation, omnibus legislation provides no protection against a veto.

At the local level, most budgets are passed as a single ordinance, without any unrelated legislation. Agreement on the budget is often worked out in advance,[7] so the council approves the mayor's or manager's budget, and the need for a veto is slight. This is especially true where councils are forbidden to increase the executive's budget recommendations.

Executive staff members carefully monitor council statements throughout the previous year, weigh the spending and tax proposals embodied in such discussions, and incorporate the ones that make sense to them into the budget. By the time the council gets the budget, the ideas they wish to see are usually already incorporated. The executive branch generally lays aside a small amount of money for symbolic additions if council members insist on adding some project the mayor, manager, or budget office intentionally deleted. To the extent that the budget is negotiated with the council, it is generally done in advance, with little open confrontation.

Relations between the mayor and council over the budget can become confrontational if a council member is a potential rival for mayor; even then, the lack of budget staff for the council makes it difficult for council members to pull the budget apart and make their own proposals. The council can become a noisy opposition and, in some cases, can prevent the passage of the budget or force compromises as the price for their support.

In short, there are major differences in the formal powers and patterns of negotiations between the executive and legislative branches at the federal, state, and local levels. At the federal level where the balance is relatively even, executive and legislative members must engage in extensive formal or informal bargaining. The results of these negotiations tend to frame the budget and set limits for departments. While bottom-up budget requests

continue to be generated and examined, they may play a small role in determining outcomes because the agreements reached by the executive and legislative branches take priority over the expressed needs of the departments
and agencies.[8] The federal government has put a great deal of time and energy into trying to devise budget agreements across branches. The result has
been a considerable shift to top-down budgeting.

Top-down budgeting is not just a function of relations between the executive and legislative branches. It also reflects policy preferences of the
chief executive and to some extent the legislature. A mayor who wishes to
reduce property taxes may make that a policy priority and reduce available
revenues, and ignore a number of departmental requests. The more policy
oriented the executive or the legislature is, the more likely the budget process will take on some top-down elements.

The federal government is most sensitive to policy issues in the budget,
though some states and cities also focus on policy formation and expression
through the budget. The policy emphasis at the federal level is partly a function of its large size and the impact of the budget on the economy, so even
relatively small changes in taxation or spending have major policy impacts.
It is also to some extent a reflection of the more ideological budgeting that
characterized the Reagan-Bush era. The federal budget process also requires
an allocation of ceilings to functional areas of the budget, requiring explicit
tradeoffs between defense and domestic spending.

The states occupy an in-between position on policy making. State-level
spending has a much smaller impact on the economy, ideological budgeting
is less apparent (although it does occur), and the budget process typically
does not force the same level of explicit tradeoff between kinds of expenditures.

Cities do not influence the economy much with their expenditures, and
they seldom budget ideologically. The portion of the budget that would be
affected by ideological budgeting is relatively small in any event. Cities can
choose most of the time to obscure tradeoffs in spending completely. When
the environment forces a choice between social services and "basic" services
(police, fire protection, water, streets, and sanitation), the level of controversy may be suddenly jerked upward. The federal government has to make
such controversial decisions almost every year.

Despite the relatively top-down and policy orientation of the federal
budget, budgetary power is the most dispersed and fragmented at the national level, partly because the decisions are so important that everyone
wants a piece of the action. The dispersal of power is not only the result of
the division of budget authority between the executive and legislative
branches but also the result of highly fragmented power within Congress.

Before 1974, Congress divided up budget responsibility between legislative committees that designed and authorized programs, revenue committees, and appropriation committees; in 1974, it added budget committees to set spending and revenue targets and coordinate the other committees. The summit agreements between the executive branch and Congress that occurred from time to time during the 1980s added an additional level of fragmentation, since they performed some of the key roles of the budget committees, they occurred at unpredictable intervals, and they were negotiated by a shifting set of actors.

By contrast, state and local governments have simpler and less fragmented decision making, in part because the executive branch tends to dominate budgeting. Responsibility for budgeting in the legislature tends to be more concentrated in appropriations and revenue committees. The distinction between legislative authorization and appropriation is less clear at the state level, and new legislation for programs may appear in appropriations legislation.

The level of coordination between committees is relatively high in state legislatures. Fourteen states report a joint tax and expenditure committee in the house, and eighteen report such a joint committee in the senate. The formation of a single committee is probably the most powerful means of coordination. Another six states refer revenue bills to the appropriations committees, another powerful form of coordination. Seven states report a somewhat looser form of coordination through joint membership on committees and other means.[9]

At the local level, legislative consideration of the budget may be confined to a single finance committee that is also responsible for revenue and bill approval.

Federal budgeting is fragmented in another sense as well. Some expenditures are approved annually by the Appropriations committee, but a substantial portion of the federal budget is entitlements, which do not go through the appropriations process. Entitlements are special programs, the spending for which is determined by how many people or governments meet eligibility requirements. They are very difficult to budget for because they are generally open ended. If the economy worsens, the number of unemployed increases, pushing up the costs of some entitlements; if inflation increases, the costs of some entitlements increase; a long and deep recession increases the number of people entitled to some form of welfare. In essence, there are at least two different budget processes, one that applies to entitlements and one that applies to other spending.

States also have entitlements, some in cooperation with the federal government, and they cause problems at the state level as well, because they are unpredictable and mandatory. The state must find the money to pay for them, and spending for entitlements generally increases at precisely the time when the state's own revenues are falling. State governments are also the recipients of federal grants. Such grants are now generally appropriated by the legislature, but they used to form a kind of second budget that was handled differently from normal appropriations.

Much of the fragmentation in state budget making occurs in the executive branch, since many key executive branch officers may be elected independently. While the governor can tell his own subordinates what to do, he or she may have little ability to control other executive branch agencies.

Local governments generally do not have entitlements and appropriate all or nearly all their budgets every year. In many cities, grant revenues from state and local governments are merged into the budget, and appropriated like other funds. (Grant funds are treated separately in some cities, especially larger ones.) The relative uniformity and comprehensiveness of city budgets make it possible to use budget systems that classify programs and evaluate them comparatively. Many elaborate analytical budget systems that were tried and floundered in the federal government survived in simplified and modified form in some cities.

Cities experience some fragmentation in the handling of the budget, mostly because of enterprises and semi-independent functions for which the city may have responsibility, but little authority. It is common, for example, for cities to have some responsibility for education but little or no influence over the expenditures for education. Mass transit can also create imbalances between responsibility and control.

Partly as a result of format innovations, a less disparate budget process frequently dominated by a strong executive, and relatively inclusive appropriations, cities often have more explanatory budgets than the states or federal government. The budget is a more important tool for accountability at the local level. This is even more the case as the president uses the budget proposal to establish bargaining positions with Congress, rather than guide deliberations. The proposed federal budget may no longer be close to the final approved budget.[10] Governors also sometimes use the budget proposal to bargain with the legislature, which can reduce its relationship to a "real" budget.

Variation in Budget Processes among States and among Cities

Not only do federal, state, and local governments differ from one another in their budget processes, but states differ from states, and cities differ from cities. Two examples at the state level illustrate the range of possibilities. The budget process in Texas is legislatively dominated. The executive branch is

THE POLITICS OF PUBLIC BUDGETING

decentralized, with a number of committees and commissions sharing power. Broad coalitions of interest groups dominate key policy issues such as the scope of government and size of the budget. There is little explicit policy focus on programs because the intent of keeping costs down requires deemphasis on comparative needs and a structure that discourages specific interest groups from making program demands. The Wisconsin model is quite different. The budget proposal is prepared by the governor and his budget office, although the legislature also has a major role in the budget. There is considerable centralization in both the executive branch and the legislature, and an explicit program and policy focus. The executive budget office serves also as a policy shop, evaluating and recommending policies; the budget is in program format, allowing for policy tradeoffs in the consideration of the budget.

In Texas, the governor has little budget control, and the legislators have strong linkages directly to the departments.[11] The Budget and Planning Office in the Office of the Governor produces a revenue plan for financing state programs, which provides an expenditure ceiling.[12] The governor has the power to veto items to enforce revenue ceilings, but the plan for expenditures comes from the Legislative Budget Board, which consists of a ten-member, joint legislative committee composed of the legislative presiding officers, chairpersons of the appropriations and finance committees, and other members appointed by the legislative leadership. Though the governor is by statute the chief budget officer, the role has not been realized. The Legislative Budget Board creates a working outline. Budget preparation continues in the fiscal committees. The budget is not finished until it is out of conference committee. Then it is voted up or down as a whole by the legislature.

The process is marked by individualistic and personalistic politics in which interest groups "become unchallenged aggregators of political influences."[13] The system produces large amounts of unplanned spending and concentrates power in a small group of people who support one another. The integrity of the original plan is not defended as it goes through legislative committees, so "long range positive policy goals are difficult, if not impossible to make."[14] Administrators of spending agencies work with their boards (note the existence of independent boards, not cabinet-level gubernatorial appointees) and with the legislative leadership "to frame a budget which reflects the low-taxing, low-spending values of the dominant coalition of interest groups."[15] There is little debate over spending "because of the short time, and the lid on government spending and taxing."[16]

The Texas model is extreme in state budgeting. Only a few other states are still as legislatively dominated. Most states have more of an executive budget and more centralization in the executive branch. Wisconsin may come close to the other extreme, where the governor has good policy control over the budget and the office of the budget actually helps formulate and sometimes even helps sell the governor's policies in the legislature.[17] The budget office helps prepare a list of upcoming policy issues well before the receipt of the budget requests from the agencies and sorts the agency requests into level of impact on fiscal and policy issues. The state budget office directly negotiates with agency heads on minor and intermediate-level implications of budget proposals, while the governor negotiates directly on the major ones.[18] Select cabinet agency heads may participate in the development of the key policy issues, but noncabinet agency heads have little role. The policy process in the budget is not completely top-down, but is more top-down than bottom-up.

When the budget proposal reaches the legislature, it is reviewed by a fourteen-member standing committee called the Joint Committee on Finance. This committee holds public hearings on the recommendation. The hearings are held on the budgets of each state agency, regardless of size. "In addition to testimony from the Governor's budget staff and administrators of the respective agencies, representatives of particular interest groups and individual private citizens also may testify."[19] A Legislative Fiscal Bureau provides briefings to committee members before the hearings and provides issue papers for committee members to review. The Joint Committee on Finance prepares its proposals as a substitute for the executive proposal, incorporating whatever parts of the governor's recommendations they choose to keep. Then each house votes on the Joint Committee's recommendations.

Although the legislature's consideration is centralized, well staffed, and based on open hearings, the governor still has potent veto power. In Wisconsin, the governor has an item veto, which allows the governor to reject any item in the budget. Governors in Wisconsin have used the item veto extensively, vetoing dollar amounts, appropriations language, and programmatic language. It requires a two-thirds vote of both houses to overturn the governor's veto.

Most states have some form of executive budgeting, but it is common for agencies to submit budget proposals to the legislature either before or at the same time as the governor submits his or her proposal to the legislature.[20] The legislature can choose between the governor's proposals and the agencies' where these proposals differ. This arrangement dilutes executive power over the agencies, providing a ready-made procedure for agency end runs to the legislature.

The major systematic source of variation in municipal budget processes is the form of government. In the town meeting, citizens vote directly on the budget, providing the maximum imaginable level of accountability. This form is necessarily limited to small towns and relatively simple issues. In the commissioner form, which was widely adopted in the early 1900s, the department heads sit as the council and jointly make budget decisions. This form makes no distinction between the executive and legislative branches. It has become rare in recent years, in part because it created problems of accountability.

Most cities today have either a mayor-council form or a council-manager form. In mayor-council forms, the mayor may be chosen by the council and may have little more authority than other council members, or may be chosen by the citizens directly and may have considerably more power than other council members. While small cities may still budget legislatively, with spending recommendations coming from the departments to the council finance committee for review, in medium and large cities, generally the mayor and members of his staff prepare the budget proposal, and the council has limited ability to make changes or even to review the budget. In council-manager cities, the executive-legislative distinction is again blurred, because the city manager, who prepares the budget, is hired and fired by the council. If the manager insists on a budget that departs from council priorities, he or she is fired. Councils tend to play a more active role in budgeting in city-manager cities, at least to the point of making their policy preferences known and ensuring that their interests are represented in the budget. The council-manager form is more common in middle-size cities, while strong (independently elected) mayors are typical of larger cities.

Summary and Conclusions

Budget processes are partly technical, coordinating decision making and keeping the flow of resources to the agencies timely. But they have a political side as well. Because budget power is perceived as such an important component of overall political power, there is considerable jockeying for positions within the budget process and considerable effort to expand the power of some positions at the expense of others. More broadly, many budget actors try to change the budget process to help achieve the goals they value, whether those be growth or decline in the scope and size of government, expansion or contraction of the policy role of the budget, or excitement of or damping down of visible competition. But budget actors do not always act to promote their personal or ideological goals; they also try to solve public problems. When the need for solutions is acute and other solutions seem elusive, budget actors may try to change the budget process to facilitate certain outcomes, such as a reduction in the size of deficits or an increase in the amount of infrastructure.

96

One way of changing budget outcomes is to find budget actors who favor those outcomes and give them more budget power. Less directly, budget actors tamper with budget processes to change the level of access of interest groups, to change the level of centralization, to shift power between the executive and the legislature, to change the budget format, or to alter the structure and level of competition in the budget. A decentralized, legislative budgeting process is very open to interest groups and not open to policy concerns. A more top-down, executive-dominated process is more responsive to policy concerns. Budget formats that make comparisons between programs also encourage a policy orientation. The process can to some extent rein in interest groups; and it can exaggerate or tone down competition, and encourage and frame budget tradeoffs.

The budget process directly and sometimes indirectly influences outcomes. The budget process, in turn, is open to the environment. Budget processes are sensitive to broad reform movements, to wars, to past debts, to scandals. Cities are sensitive to actions taken by state governments, curtailing or increasing their autonomy. The level of activism of government, which mirrors the level of social and economic problems, is reflected in the increasing capacity to make budget policy.

Notes

1. Advisory Commission on Intergovernmental Relations (ACIR), *Significant Features of Fiscal Federalism* (Washington, D.C.: Government Printing Office, 1994), 12.

2. Allen Schick, "The Road to PPB: The Stages of Budget Reform," *Public Administration Review* 26 (December 1966): 245–56.

3. Thomas Anton, *The Politics of State Expenditure in Illinois* (Urbana: University of Illinois Press, 1966), 73.

4. See Gloria Grizzle, "Does Budget Format Really Govern the Actions of Budget Makers?" *Public Budgeting and Finance* 6, no. 1 (Spring 1986): 64.

5. ACIR, *The Question of State Government Capability* (Washington, D.C.: Government Printing Office, 1985), 256–58.

6. Tony Hutchison and Kathy James, *Legislative Budget Procedures in the 50 States: A Guide to Appropriations and Budget Processes* (Denver: National Conference of State Legislatures, 1988), 28.

7. Glenn Abney and Thomas B. Lauth, *The Politics of State and City Administration* (Albany: State University of New York Press, 1986), esp. chap. 9.

8. Allen Schick, *The Capacity to Budget* (Washington, D.C.: Urban Institute Press, 1990), chap. 6.

9. Hutchison and James, *Legislative Budget Procedures,* 73.

10. Schick, *Capacity to Budget,* 164.

11. Beryl Pettus and Randall Bland, *Texas Government Today: Structures, Functions, Political Process* (Homewood, Ill.: Dorsey Press, 1979).

12. Ibid., 341.

13. Ibid., 343.

14. Ibid., 344.

15. Ibid.

16. Ibid.

17. James Gosling, "The State Budget Office and Policy Making," *Public Budgeting and Finance* 7, no. 1 (Spring 1987): 51–65.

18. Ibid., 57.

19. Barbara Yondorf and B.J. Summers, *Legislative Budget Procedures in the 50 States,* Legislative Finance Paper 21 (Denver, Colo.: National Conference of State Legislatures, 1983), 198.

20. Hutchison and James, *Legislative Budget Procedures,* 43–44.

4. The Dynamics of Changing Budget Processes

Budget processes are highly variable because budget actors keep trying to change them. They are trying to enhance their own power, the power of their committees, and the power of the executive or legislative branch. They are also trying to solve problems immediately confronting them. The belief in the power of the budget process is so strong that actors recommend changes in the budget process to solve a variety of problems.

The belief in the efficacy of changing budget processes may be stronger than the reality. Even when there is a clear linkage between process and outcomes, the same process does not always lead to the same outcome. For example, if budget processes are relatively open to interest groups, that does not mean that expenditures will necessarily be high because the interest groups may be most interested in keeping expenditures and taxation levels down. This was the case in the Texas example; it is also true in a number of cities. Shifting power from the legislative branch to the executive branch need not reduce spending; at times, the chief executive is likely to be more aggressive in spending, and at other times, the legislature is likely to spend more. Centralizing legislative control over the budget—giving more power to budget committees to set revenue and spending limits—is no guarantee of smaller spending targets. It enhances the possibility of such action, but in no way guarantees it.

Simply shifting power from one location to another has no determinate outcome. Nevertheless, if a particular president is antispending, or is promilitary, shifting power to him is likely to influence outcomes over the period of his administration. If particular committees have been more prospending than others, shifting power to them is likely to increase the levels of spending. For example, in 1885 the House of Representatives reorganized its internal budget process by taking considerable budget power away from the Appropriations committee and giving it to the legislative committees.

The legislative committees were thought to be more program loyal and more interested in program expansion than the Appropriations committee, so the shift was seen as an attempt to increase expenditures. Expenditures did actually increase more quickly as a result of the change.[1] Later, in 1920, Congress recentralized control in the appropriations committees, in an effort to curtail the growth of expenditures.

Variation in budget processes reflects different adaptations to similar kinds of problems and similar responses adopted at different times. The strengthening of the chief executive officer's power over the budget was a widespread response to the need for increased fiscal and policy control, but it was adopted at different times in different governmental units. Some states adopted very little of the proposed reform, such as Texas, while others adopted most of the executive budget schema.

Overall, budget processes have become more top-down and more centralized, to facilitate financial control and a more explicitly policy-oriented review process. The practice of departments submitting budget requests directly to legislative committees with limited central review gradually yielded to a more executive-dominated budget, where the chief executive was responsible for reviewing the agency and departmental requests. As part of this change, executive budget offices were created, grew in professional staff, and became more politically sensitive and policy oriented. Cabinet government became more prevalent, so that there were fewer elected executive officers and more appointed by the chief executive and responsible to the chief executive.[2]

Over time, legislatures granted more power to chief executives to formulate and execute the budget. The effect was often to enhance the policy-making power of the executive. Depending on the personality of the executive and the degree of difference between the executive and the legislature, the policy-making power was sometimes used for purposes explicitly forbidden by the legislature or was used to bypass legislative approval. Legislators were reluctant to give up their influence over policy and their control over constituency-oriented spending. They responded by strengthening their own ability to perform the functions they assigned to the executive. They increased budget staff, improved their capacity to review budget proposals, and enhanced their capacity to evaluate executive branch performance.

Historically, two features of contemporary budget processes evolved together, the executive budget and increased centralization. On the legislative side, centralization was reflected in consolidating budget power more in a single committee. On the executive side, the increased central control reflected the formation of cabinet government, and especially the development of a budget office under the chief executive. This development aided the capacity of the chief executive to formulate and impose policy choices on the budget.

More recent changes include a rebalancing of the budgetary power between legislative and executive branches and a reshuffling of centralized executive control so that departments have greater control over managerial decisions. At the national level, recent changes in budget process have revolved around how to rebalance the budget; this issue has been of less concern to state and local governments.

Major Changes in the Federal Budget Process

The federal budget process has changed in important ways several times. In 1921, the executive budget process was adopted; in 1974, the Congressional Budget Reform Act was passed, limiting some of the president's budgetary discretion and enhancing Congress's ability to check executive branch revenue projections and economic assumptions; in 1985 Gramm-Rudman-Hollings was passed in an effort to curtail and shrink the deficit. After several iterations, GRH was replaced by the Budget Enforcement Act in a further effort to help strengthen the norms of balance. Throughout the 1980s and 1990s, the more equal budgetary power of Congress and the president combined with government frequently divided along party lines to result in budget negotiations at the summit between Congress and the president, eventually leading to more centralization of control in OMB and congressional leadership in order to reach and carry out agreements.

THE CREATION OF THE EXECUTIVE BUDGET AT THE NATIONAL LEVEL

At the national level, the 1921 Budget and Accounting Act created the executive budget and the Budget Bureau in the executive branch. This major change in budget processes illustrates both the competition for power over budgeting between branches of government and the role of the environment in fostering increases in expenditures and debt that presented problems that had to be addressed. The existence of a dominant reform movement created a specific agenda for change.

Two major pressures for change were the increase in spending that occurred from 1899 to 1912 and the growth of the reform movement. The level of spending during the last third of the nineteenth century was $200 to $400 million. From 1899 to 1912, the level jumped to $500 to $700 million a year.[3] The full proposal for reform in budgeting at the national level included not just presidential review of agency requests but also a line-item veto for the president and restricted powers of the Congress to change amounts proposed by the president. Clearly, one aim of the reform was to control expenditures.

President William Howard Taft and his secretary of the treasury were very supportive of the executive budget, but Congress did not initially approve of the idea. Part of the reason why Congress did not go along with Taft's plans was that there were budgetary surpluses in 1911 and 1912.[4] The pressure on Congress to give up some of its traditional power in the interest of economy was thus reduced.

President Woodrow Wilson, a Democrat, followed Taft, and Wilson's support of the presidential budget was less intense than Taft's. The Democratic Congress continued to oppose the idea; the Democrats preferred to strengthen Congress and let it do the job of controlling expenditures. World War I intervened, reducing the salience of the issue in the short run but raising the level of expenditures and deficits to such a point that congressional opposition to the presidential budget was reduced. Something needed to be done, and this reform promised lower taxes, lower spending, and elimination of deficits.

In the event, congressional budget reform was carried out in 1920, before the shift to the presidential budget. The House of Representatives consolidated appropriations into a single committee in 1920. Complete integration of revenues and expenditures and comparisons of spending between programs were not fully accomplished, "but the reconsolidation of appropriations power of several committees over the objection of the members of those committees and of the agencies and interest groups involved was still a considerable achievement."[5]

As a result of the congressional reorganization and centralization, some of the pressure for the executive budget was reduced, and the eventual shift of power to the president was not as extreme as originally envisioned by the reformers. The president got the Bureau of the Budget, which was transferred to the Executive Office of the President in 1939, and responsibility for preparing and presenting the budget, but Congress did not give the president a line-item veto and retained for itself its powers of accepting or rejecting or altering the president's proposed budget.

Between 1921 and 1974, Congress had tried unsuccessfully several times to centralize its budget process and make it more effective. During the Great Depression, in response to massive unemployment and resulting poverty, a new kind of program was initiated, which gave money to individuals who satisfied criteria established by the programs. Called entitlements, these programs bypassed the appropriations committees and were scrutinized only by the authorizing committees. Hence fragmentation of the budget process accompanied the creation of these new programs. Considerable spending power was shifted to authorizing committees, who often favor additional spending, and control over spending was divided up among a greater number of committees, making coordination more problematic. In addition, during the 1940s, there were massive expenditure increases caused by World War II. Congress responded to these problems by trying to integrate the revenue and expenditure process into a legislative budget. The Legislative Reorganization Act was passed in 1946. Had it been implemented, it might have enhanced congressional control over the budget, but Congress never succeeded in using the process and it was later formally abandoned.

In 1950, Congress tried a more moderate reform, to link all the regular appropriations bills into one omnibus package (except the appropriations for the District of Columbia); this effort failed also, under fire from the appropriations committees. Arguments against the procedure included claims that the size of the budget bill would make it difficult to amend and that the single bill would delay the budget and force Congress to pass continuing resolutions instead. Committee members' complaints about the difficulty of amending the omnibus measure meant that they were unwilling to lose power over particular programs in the budget.

The failure of these two efforts at centralization made it seem that any attempts to centralize budget control would be thwarted by members who would refuse to give up power to protect particular programs. These failures discouraged further efforts at reform until the 1970s.

From 1966 to 1973 several environmental changes took place that strained the budget process and gave additional impetus to congressional reform.[6] First were the increased costs of the Vietnam war. Rather than curtail domestic expenditures to help pay for the war and risk exacerbating domestic conflicts, the government ran deficits of increasing size. There was pressure to reduce both the overall level of spending and the size of the deficits. At the same time, there were major policy splits between Congress and the president over the conduct of the war and over domestic spending. President Nixon increasingly withheld billions of dollars of domestic spending that Congress had approved. Mistrusting the president and fearing the of loss of policy control over spending, Congress increased its budgetary role and enhanced its capacity to examine and determine budget policies.

These two pressures—to reduce spending and control deficits, and to enhance the congressional role over spending policy—combined into the 1974 Congressional Budget and Impoundment Control Act. Impoundment control prevented the president from unilaterally withholding congressionally approved spending. The budget reform moderately increased the level of centralization and coordination, but equally important, it provided a professional staff of budgeters to help Congress make budget policies.

To the existing authorizing, taxing, and appropriations committees, the 1974 budget reform act added budget committees, whose responsibility was to come up with overall estimates of revenues and spending and targets for spending in broad areas. The other committees were generally supposed to stay within the guidelines established by the budget committees. The new arrangement provided for some coordination between revenue and expenditure committees and some fiscal policy formation, and at the same time did not overly threaten the existing division of power.

Congress's reorganization of the budget process was also intended as a way of taking back some budget initiative from the president. The budget committees could accept presidential policies or, relying on the new Congressional Budget Office, could differ with the president on projections of the economy, the anticipated size of the deficits, and rates of inflation. Congress could make its own fiscal policy.

Though Congress tried to enhance its own power to devise and implement fiscal policy, most of the distribution of power within Congress was left as it was to ensure that threatened appropriations, tax, and authorizing committee members did not squash the whole proposal for change. The compromises reflected in the legislation resulted in budget committees that had little real power or influence. Their ability to act as a brake on spending was thus limited.

The influence of the budget committees gradually increased, however, as the size of the deficits continued to grow and began to seem out of control. The provision of *reconciliation,* which had been written into the 1974 law, was first used in 1980, then extensively used in 1981. Reconciliation is a process by which the budget committees can give targets to the other committees that they have to meet, in any way they choose. Reconciliation thus provides a mechanism other than voluntary compliance for enforcing a budget total lower than the desire of a spending committee or forcing a tax proposal higher than a revenue committee might choose.

Despite the new budget process, deficits continued to rise, taking an upturn at the end of the Carter administration and then growing even more rapidly throughout the Reagan administration, reaching historic highs. Some of the problem of deficits had to do with the slow growth of the economy and the effects of rapidly growing social entitlements programs, but deficits also had to do with tax reductions, military buildups, and overestimates of economic growth.

Since so many of the causes of deficits were seen as difficult to control or politically off limits, there was renewed activity to change the budget process. Proponents of discipline applied from the executive branch proposed stronger presidential vetoes; proponents of smaller government proposed taking discretion away from all public officials, of both branches, by passing a constitutional amendment requiring a balanced budget and revenue limitations. Proponents of congressional power suggested further reforms of the legislative budget process. What finally passed was a peculiar compromise that did not change the balance of power much between the Congress and the executive branch, but markedly limited the discretion of both branches if they could not meet guidelines on the reduction of the deficit.

The compromise legislation, called Gramm-Rudman-Hollings after its sponsors, was intended to reduce the annual deficit to zero in five years by setting targets that the budget had to reach each year. A failure to achieve the annual targets for deficit reduction triggered an automatic, across-the-board cut (with some exemptions for entitlements). Presumably the across-the-board cuts would be so obnoxious to all parties that they would choose to achieve the deficit-reduction targets on time, so the automatic feature of the cuts would not be invoked. Passed in 1985, the deficit-reduction law was declared unconstitutional in July 1986, because it gave power to determine cuts to the controller general (the head of the General Accounting Office, or GAO) and thus presumably violated the separation-of-powers doctrine because the controller general reports to Congress as well as to the president. In October 1987, Gramm-Rudman-Hollings was reinstituted, substituting the OMB for the GAO.

MINICASE:
COMMITTEE RESPONSE TO GRAMM-RUDMAN-HOLLINGS

Representative William Dickinson of Alabama reported in a hearing of the House Armed Services Committee on 5 February 1987 that his subcommittee on Military Construction had the previous year drawn a line in the sand in an effort comply with the limits in Gramm-Rudman-Hollings. "We are going to meet our ceilings," he said, and have no add-ons. "If it wasn't in the budget when it came over here, we will bite the bullet and take the heat and no add-ons." Dickinson called the resulting pressure "uncomfortable," but the line held, in both subcommittee and committee. That the committee even tried to hold the line in an area often known for distributive politics is impressive; that they succeeded at the committee level is even more impressive.

What happened after that, according to Dickinson, was that the Senate Appropriations Committee tried to pressure the authorizing committee to include some of the Appropriations Committee's pet projects. The authorizing committee had already denied their own members any special projects and did not want to go over the ceilings to provide special projects for the Senate Appropriations Committee members. This issue had reportedly come up in prior years as well, but the committee had caved in to pressure. Congressman David Martin added that the committee members were getting a little "suspect" that the Defense Department branches were intentionally leaving out items from the budget request that were legitimate projects in members' districts because Defense officials were confident that Congress would add the projects later. In other words, if the Department of Defense would include the projects that Congress was concerned about in their initial budget request, the committees would not look so bad by adding projects on to the president's proposal.

This story is significant not only because it reflects the real attempts of at least some congressional committees to curb pork-type requests in an effort to comply with Gramm-Rudman-Hollings and the resultant political heat but also the ability to shift the location of the political onus for adding pork projects between the executive and legislative branches without changing the amounts involved. Cutting something out of an executive budget proposal that everyone knows Congress will add back is not a real cut. It makes one branch look good at the other's expense. But the other issue that these committee members were raising was how they could exercise enough power to enforce their line in the sand inside Congress. The complicated committee structure that diffused power among four sets of committees was making it difficult for at least this committee to comply with budget constraints. The committee members were just waiting for a change in the chairmanship of the Senate Appropriations Committee; they were not sure they could develop enough power to do anything else.

Gramm-Rudman-Hollings was not particularly successful. It may have had some marginal effect in reducing the rate of growth of deficits, but deficits continued to grow. Both Congress and the president began "gaming" Gramm-Rudman requirements to reduce the apparent size of the deficit just before the calculation would be made on whether to invoke Gramm-Rudman cuts (called sequesters) to get down to the mandated deficit levels. Gimmicks included overly optimistic estimates of growth in the economy, pushing back spending from one fiscal year to the previous one, and keeping new spending "off budget." Gramm-Rudman's one-year focus encouraged "quick-hit" temporary revenue raisers that would do nothing to help balance the budget in future years.

Many legislators were reluctant to give up Gramm-Rudman because the symbolism was bad—it looked like they were giving up on deficit reduction. Hence they decided to overhaul the legislation, trying to close the loopholes that had appeared and eliminate some of its worst features. In the fall of 1990, after five months of summit negotiations between the administration and Congress, a new plan for deficit reduction was passed.[7]

The budget reforms of 1990 had a number of features. First, the social security surplus was taken out of the Gramm-Rudman-Hollings deficit calculations, so the true size of the deficit problem would be clear. Second, instead of trying to control the size of deficits, the new legislation tried to limit discretionary spending, raise taxes, and require "pay-as-you-go" provisions. The agreement sets separate spending ceilings for defense, domestic, and foreign discretionary spending, in an effort to keep spending down. The "pay-as-you-go" requirement meant that proposed increases in mandatory expenditures have to be balanced by a compensating increase in revenues or decrease in other entitlements, and proposed reductions in revenues must be balanced by a decrease in expenditures or an increase in some other revenue source.

The legislation addressed several problems that had arisen during Gramm-Rudman days. Congress had cut the defense budget, but had used much of the savings on domestic spending increases; the new process prohibited such transfers. Each area of the budget has to come in at or under ceiling, and savings in one area cannot be transferred to other areas. Those constraints may make it easier to achieve savings to reduce the deficit.

Another problem of Gramm-Rudman was that the target had to be reached only briefly; there were no sanctions if the deficit estimates increased later in the year. The new law added a feature called "look back," which allowed a check on conformity with the new limits later in the year. If the limits were breached in any of the three caps (defense, domestic, or international), then automatic across-the-board cuts would be invoked in the area that breached the limits. Sequestration, or automatic cuts, would also be invoked if pay-as-you-go provisions of the mandated portion of the budget were violated. If such breaches occur late in the year, the legislation provides that the amount of the breach be subtracted from the next year's ceiling.

A third problem with Gramm-Rudman was its one-year time span, which encouraged temporary revenue increases that did not solve the problem for future years. The Budget Enforcement Act included a five-year resolution that discouraged that kind of action.

The new budget process is less rigid than the previous one, because it provides for exemptions in emergencies and builds in flexibility related to changes in the economy. The rigid fixed-deficit targets are gone, but the mechanisms to help achieve balance are strengthened. The new process is easier to live with, and hence is more likely to be observed. The process is still laden with constraints, as Gramm-Rudman-Hollings was, and it explicitly regulates and redefines what programs must compete with what programs.[8] Evaluations of the Budget Enforcement Act suggest that it is working better than Gramm-Rudman-Hollings. One scholar observed, "A complete reckoning of what has happened since the rules were devised in 1990 would show that Congress has achieved substantial deficit reduction by increasing revenue and cutting direct spending under existing law while also offsetting any deficit increases resulting from new legislation."[9]

The Budget and Accounting Act of 1921, the Congressional Budget and Impoundment Control Act of 1974, Gramm-Rudman-Hollings in 1985, and the Budget Enforcement Act of 1990 mark the major formal changes in the federal budget process. In addition, there have been some informal changes.

One change has been toward summit bargaining between the president and leaders in Congress. In part because of the increased budgetary power of Congress after 1974 and in part because of a divided government in which the president and the majority in Congress were of different political parties, the authoritative nature of the president's budget proposal deteriorated to an initial bargaining position. During the 1980s, the president's proposals were often reported in the press as "dead on arrival," meaning that Congress basically had disregarded the proposal and had come up with its own instead. Congress's willingness to come up with its own detailed budget proposal was reinforced by the election of a Republican majority in Congress in 1994. The result was an increased use of presidential vetoes in 1995 and the protracted set of negotiations between the White House and congressional leadership described in the preface.

Unless Congress can muster a veto-proof majority on budget votes, it still requires the president to sign off on bills. Since neither the president nor Congress has been able to count on the support of the other, an informal system of bargaining has emerged. Throughout the 1980s and 1990s, at key points the president and leaders of Congress have met and worked out budget agreements, which have usually then been passed into law.[10] Each of these agreements has covered several years, creating a kind of de facto multi-year budget. Even though annual budgets are still produced, they are drawn up under the constraints of these longer-term negotiated settlements.

A second informal change may be under way. Vice-President Al Gore oversaw efforts to draw up a set of proposals to improve management at the federal level. The results were published, beginning in 1993, as a set of reports and supplements. A number of the proposals dealt with budgeting. The emphasis was on improving accountability through measuring performance and making management more output oriented and less concerned with input controls. Some of the proposals would require congressional action that may or may not take place, but other proposals can be implemented by the White House alone. The goal of these proposals is to give managers more discretion to manage. Individual proposals include reduced legislative earmarking and consolidation of some budgetary accounts, which require legislative approval, and more flexible controls over allocations and allotments and a general simplification of budget categories.[11]

In short, the history of the budget process at the federal level in the 1970s shows a president taking a disproportionate amount of policymaking power over the budget away from Congress, and Congress reacting by increasing its own policymaking power. By the 1980s, the budget process began to deteriorate, for a variety of reasons, including the split between a Republican president and Democratic Congress, and large and growing deficits reflecting a budget process poorly matched to a slow-growing economy. The breakdown in the budget process led to a series of ad hoc solutions, punctuated by budget reforms such as Gramm-Rudman-Hollings and the Budget Enforcement Act of 1990. As controlling the deficit became more urgent, consensus began to form on devising a process that would put the incentives in the right places to restore balance and reduce the level of gaming.

Changes in Budget Process at the State Level

After an initial period of strong legislatures in the 1700s, state legislatures declined in public trust and responsibility. Legislatures tended to be nonrepresentative of voters, and they were often overly large and overly responsive to interest-group and constituency demands. These flaws sometimes led to a series of structural characteristics intended to limit their influence, including short sessions, constitutional constraints on what they could do, and early awards of line-item veto to governors.

To compensate for legislative weakness in yielding to demands, the governor was strengthened in budget dealings with the legislature, but the executive branch, reflecting that same early distrust of state government, remained highly fragmented. Many key state officials were elected rather than appointed by the governor, so they had their own power bases and were not controlled by the governor. A governor and his lieutenant governor might be rivals rather than teammates, and the elected controller might be out to blame the governor for budget problems. In addition, legislatures tended to create many independent commissions. Departments were often headed by commissions that appointed their own heads. Thus the governor's control, even when he gained the power to present the executive budget, was often very limited. The history of the early evolution of the budget process in Illinois illustrates many of these themes.

MINICASE: EARLY BUDGET EVOLUTION IN ILLINOIS

Looking back to the 1800s, the Illinois constitution of 1848 greatly limited the power of the legislature. This was "both because Jacksonian democracy emphasized the executive as the embodiment of the best interests of the people and because excesses of the General Assembly had almost bankrupted the state through the creation of banks and internal improvements."[12] In response to the state's debt, debt was limited under the 1848 constitution to under $50,000.[13] As the power of the legislature was curtailed, the power of the governor was somewhat increased. The governor was given a veto, but only a simple majority was required to overturn.

The 1870 constitution gave a stronger veto power to the governor, requiring a two-thirds majority to overturn. Governor John Palmer was widely respected at the time, which helped him achieve this power, but more specifically, he tried to limit the private and special laws passed by the legislators, many of which were perceived as wasteful. "Palmer had vetoed seventy-two of the twelve hundred private laws passed at the [1869] session. The General Assembly repassed seventeen of these by a simple majority; most could not have been repassed if a two-thirds majority had been required."[14]

Early in the twentieth century, on Governor Edward Dunne's recommendation, the Illinois legislature appointed a Legislative Study Committee on Efficiency and Economy to prepare reform bills.[15] The committee issued over 1,000 pages of reports in 1915.[16] But the legislature did not take action on the proposals during Dunne's administration. Instead, it went in the opposite direction, creating several new boards and commissions.

Governor Frank Lowden, who followed Dunne, believed that industrialization had created new centers of power, such as banks and corporations, but that their growth had thrust on government the unfamiliar role of guardian of the commonweal against mighty and conflicting forces. Power alone could check power. He spoke of the need for more government action, surfacing roads for automobiles, serving the people in state hospitals, and encouraging soil conservation, farmers' cooperatives, and reforestation of wastelands. The governor should have ample discretion and funds to carry out this duty. His proposals provided more centralization, recommending departments headed by single persons rather than committees, and he included the executive budget as a cornerstone of reform. He proposed identical accounting systems for every department, a central purchasing agency, and competitive bidding. He wanted a constitutional convention to modernize the constitution and remove some of its restrictions.

Lowden decided that to maximize support for his more important proposals, he would not include references to the elected officials that kept the executive branch so fragmented; he kept his proposed legal code to departments and officers over which he had jurisdiction. His proposals were passed speedily by the legislature in 1917. They included administrative consolidation into nine departments. The key new position was the director of the Department of Finance. Lowden created cabinet government.

The reforms of 1917 were retained. They were advocated as a model outside Illinois, which contributed to their retention. They brought tax reduction and a virtual end to calls upon the legislature for extra appropriations to cover administrative deficits, both of which worked in favor of keeping the reforms.

Recent changes in budget process at the state level have been somewhat parallel to changes taking place at the national level, in that the extremes of executive budgeting are yielding to more shared power between the executive and legislature. As at the national level, the capacity of state legislatures to review the governor's budget and question the assumptions underlying it has improved. The difference at the state level is that the states had gone further in awarding the governors budget power, in part because the legislatures were less capable of making policy analyses. Forty states have given their governors line-item vetoes (more powerful than the veto power of the president) and sixteen states had an amendatory veto that allowed their governors to reject the language of the appropriations.[17] In the 1960s as a result of Supreme Court mandates of one-man, one-vote, the redrawing of electoral districts, and the election of more representative legislatures, state legislatures began to reform themselves and prepare themselves for a more active policy role, and the budget was a key focus of that increased capacity. Legislatures increased the length of their sessions, changed from meeting every two years to once a year, and added staff with expertise on fiscal and budgetary matters to advise them. These staff members routinely review the executive's budget proposal, make revenue projections, provide studies of current financial issues, and make "fiscal notes" or descriptions of the fiscal implications of pending legislation. In some states, the staff capacity is sufficient to help the legislature draw up its own competitive budget proposal.

Strong executive budgeting powers characterize most of the states. Nevertheless, in recent years, state legislatures began to insist on an auditor who reports to them and have expanded the scope of funds they appropriate.

The example of Illinois shows a continuing centralization of the executive branch, with the creation of the Bureau of the Budget and the limited reduction in the number of elected executive officers, and with the expanded veto power of the governor. The case also illustrates the legislature's parallel efforts to reform itself and to increase its budgetary powers. Although the executive is still dominant in Illinois, the tendency of the legislature—even in this strong governor state—to increase its policy capacity over the budget is apparent.

On the executive side, the first major change was the creation of the Bureau of the Budget. The Bureau of the Budget grew out of the Illinois Budgetary Commission, created in 1937 by Governor Henry Horner, to study revenue problems.[18] He created this committee when his proposed tax increase (3 percent on utility sales) was defeated. Though its initial charter did not include any budgeting functions, it came to review department requests and give informal advice to the governor. The committee included the governor and legislative elites, and hence became a liaison between the governor and the legislature. Its raison d'être was to give the governor advice on spending proposals. When governors chose not to use it, the commission had no legitimate source of power. If the governor accepted its recommendations, legislative-executive cooperation was established.

In the mid-1950s, a financial scandal resulted in more responsibility being put on the commission, with a staff and resources assigned to it. By 1969, however, the governor, with the reluctant consent of the legislature, abolished the commission and set up an executive Bureau of the Budget. The Bureau of the Budget has been strengthened considerably since its founding.

Under Governor Richard Ogilvie (1968–72), the Bureau of the Budget got to make some policy. "Ogilvie's BOB and the often intimidating 'whiz kids' who ran it were usually at the center of, and the source of, major controversies over State expenditures and their policy implications. For the first time, Illinois had an executive budget process and a staff to run it, which could accommodate serious analysis of issues, alternatives, spending levels and finances."[19]

Governor Dan Walker (1972–76) reined in BOB staff, arguing they should "help solve problems and achieve financial accountability but under no circumstances were they to speak for him or to make decisions on matters of program and policy."[20] Walker doubted the usefulness of the planning capacity built into BOB under Ogilvie, and largely dismantled it.[21] Under Governor James Thompson, the BOB continued to play some policy role in its reviews of the departmental budget proposals.

Parallel with these changes, in the mid-1960s the legislature began to reform itself. It created a bipartisan staffing system, and standing committees for policy development and oversight, and initiated annual and interim sessions. The period of reform culminated in the constitutional convention of 1970 and a new constitution for the state. The 1970 constitution gave the governor a reduction and an amendatory veto, greatly adding to the governor's power to reduce the budget and implement his own budget request. The constitution eliminated only one of the elected executive offices, but made the governor and lieutenant governor partners. The constitution tried to balance the powers of the governor by increasing somewhat the power of the legislature. The auditor of public accounts was replaced by the controller, who provided an alternative to the governor and his budget bureau. And the constitution gave post-audit powers to the legislature.

The legislature remains relatively weak in budget matters, with the governor exercising his veto power with considerable frequency.[22] There is no evidence that the increased powers of the governor have reduced spending or improved the balance in the budget. Recent governors have been concerned with distributive politics, and have often hidden the extent of continuing fiscal problems. The success of the reform in reducing expenditures and increasing efficiency depends on the existence of a legislature that is not overly responsive to interest groups and constituents, and on a reform-minded governor. When both pieces are not in place, giving more power to the governor does not have much visible impact on outcomes. Given the apparent incorrectness of the model that argues that more executive budget power is more financially healthy, there has been an increase in sentiment in recent years to curtail the governor's extremely strong veto. It is not clear when this change will happen, but even in Illinois, which is a very strong executive budget state, there is sentiment for a more balanced role for the legislature.

Two other examples of changes since the 1950s show the direction of change toward more legislative budget power more dramatically. In New Mexico the governor went along with the changes; in Florida, the executive branch saw the changes as more threatening to its position; but in both cases a formal executive budget process became more balanced between the executive and legislative branches.

The governor in New Mexico wrote in 1953 that the addition of budget staff for the legislature was a must. "The Legislature has the burden of appropriations and it is direct. Over the years they have relied completely on the executive to handle this job. Sometimes it was good and sometimes bad. But the legislature will never be able to do its job on appropriations without a budget officer and staff."[23] The legislature got its budget staff, which gradually increased its role.

In Florida, the changes began after reapportionment of the legislature in 1967. Until that time, Florida was a strong executive state. "... the executive had allowed the legislature to make only certain non-meaningful decisions from time to time."[24] By the early 1970s, the "role of the executive telling the legislature what it can or cannot do"[25] was gradually changing so that the legislature could function as a separate branch of government.

In the early 1980s, legislators felt that Governor Robert Graham was usurping their constitutional budget power.[26] In response, the legislature passed a law in 1983 mandating the budget format and content in considerable detail, and requiring the governor's staff and the legislative staff to jointly develop the budget instructions sent to the agencies. The new law directed agencies to "submit their independent judgment of their needs to the legislature."[27] The legislature also strengthened its budgetary oversight role, reviewing extensively budget changes initiated by the executive during the year.

Within the executive branch, the governor emphasized improved performance measurement and performance agreements between the governor and appointed agency heads. About half the heads of state agencies are independently elected or appointed by a majority of the elected executives and hence are independent of the governor's control. The governor's budget office is responsible for policy development as well as budget development and administration.[28]

With capable staffs in both the executive and legislative branches, some formal and informal means of negotiation between branches have developed. Consensus-based estimating conferences, combining legislative and executive staffs, develop the revenue, economic, and population estimates that underlie the budget. The revenue estimates become limits for spending. All parties agree to use the consensus estimates.[29]

Changes in Budget Process at the Local Level

The budget process in cities has taken on different characteristics over time, depending on whether budgeting was occurring during a time of economic and governmental expansion or contraction. But there has never been a simple one-to-one relationship between growth or cutback and budget processes.

The financial history of Cleveland, Ohio, illustrates the excesses of many cities in building railroads at public expense in the mid-1800s and the increase in state and local limits on taxing and spending. In the effort to control local spending, governmental structures were decentralized, power was fragmented, and any kind of concerted action or plan became difficult. By 1890, however, Cleveland had created a modern executive budget, centralizing budget power in the hands of the mayor.

MINICASE: CLEVELAND, OHIO

Cleveland was incorporated in 1814 and was granted limited taxing power.[30] Property tax rates were not to exceed 1 percent of the value of property and were to be in proportion to the value of the property. The treasurer collected taxes and paid out expenses on the order of the trustees. In 1833, there was some expansion of taxing powers for public works—there was a limited tax for some areas to protect against lake damage, use of a poll tax for roads, and a pro rata tax for benefits from sidewalks and streets. In the 1836 charter, the mayor and council were granted the right to tax more broadly. Borrowing for railroad projects became excessive, however, and in 1851 the state legislature stepped in and limited taxing and borrowing. Restrictions were tight, and the city had to apply for special grants to cover spending.

In line with the withdrawal of the right to borrow and raise revenues, the city's organization was decentralized between 1852 and 1891, to a series of commissions and boards. A board of improvements was supposed to check ill-considered plans for improvements. In response to the revenue constraints, this board developed a system of special assessments to relieve the stressed general fund. The board consisted of the mayor, a civil engineer, chairman of the council committee on streets, and one street commissioner elected for two years. Its power over public improvements became absolute after 1868.[31]

The municipal code of 1869 carried further the substitution of administrative boards for council committees. Four of eleven boards created were elected; four were approved by the mayor and council and one by the council alone; two were ex officio. The decentralized boards had no interest in the whole. The efficiency and economy of the board system were soon questioned, but it took another fifteen years to bring about change in it.

For the first half of the nineteenth century, the city had no modern budget. There was a specific property tax levy for most of the major departments. The departments, boards, and officers relied on probable income from levies. Before 1873, a large number of funds annually showed deficits, which were funded, and then the process was repeated the following year. The law forbade the practice, but the provision was constantly violated. No department knew what spending would be allowed, since it could go over its levy and have the difference made up later. The auditor borrowed from funds running a surplus to cover those running deficits.[32] The decentralized board system, with its lack of concern for the whole, fueled the problem.

In 1873, the auditor began the first budget when he sent the council a statement of estimated revenues and expenditures with an apportionment to different departments. Requests from the departments were gross and allocations were gross in this early budget form. By 1890, the city passed the requirement for a modern budget in which the council had to pass detailed and specific appropriations for the functions the city had to provide. Within three years, the mayor declared each fund balanced.

The budget pattern adopted in Cleveland in 1890 was distinctly oriented toward fiscal control. The departments were to make estimates to the auditor and the mayor, who were to present statements to the council, along with the previous year's expenses, and the previous five years' expenses. The mayor was to present the annual budget; the council was free to omit items or reduce them, but was not allowed to increase the total. Similarly, the mayor was given the power to alter requests coming from the departments, but was not allowed to increase the totals of those requests. The council's role was to examine and pass the budget, and to set the property tax levy. Its recommendations for taxes had then to be reviewed and approved by a tax board. If the board were to reject proposed tax levies, it would take a three-fourths vote for the council to override. The tax board routinely passed requests in the early 1900s.

Shortly after the budget was modernized, the city succeeded in reforming its extremely decentralized structure. The financial powers of the council were greatly increased. As part of the reform, spending bills, revenue bills, and contracts had to be introduced a week before passage to allow for examination and consideration of the measures. The council's responsibilities included setting salaries for police and fire chiefs, police officers, and firemen. They also set water rates. On the executive side, the reform set up a half dozen departments, each headed by a director, appointed by the mayor with the consent of the council. The mayor, with the department heads of the six departments, formed a board of control, which took over the functions of the old board of improvements and the commissioner of sewers. This form of government was declared unconstitutional in 1902, but it coincided with the period of the introduction of the budget, and the two together probably accounted for the improved financial integrity of the city.

The financial history of Cleveland in the 1800s was not unusual. The 1800s were characterized by initial grants of taxing authority, which were abused; in the rush to control the cities, the states limited their borrowing and taxing powers. Internally, the cities' organization shifted to an extreme decentralization, which was inefficient and lacking in financial control. Limitation of the power of taxation was accompanied by a fiscal demoralization. The early reform period at the end of the 1800s was characterized by reorganization for capacity, with budgeting and financial control as dual focuses.

Municipal budgets originated as a control mechanism after the Civil War, during a period of major spending growth. Early budgets were estimates of how much taxes would be required, based on detailed accounts of receipts and expenditures for preceding years. Officials submitted detailed requests. Typically, the head of the finance department, the controller, the auditor, or the mayor would receive and cut back these requests, or in smaller cities, the departments would forward their requests directly to the council or the budget committee.

To control nonapproved spending during the year some cities adopted annual appropriations, fixing expenditures for the year. Cleveland, Boston, Denver, Minneapolis, and Omaha all had appropriations budgets, and state law required appropriations in Illinois, Indiana, and New York.[33]

The 1870s and 1880s were years of sharp economic and governmental contraction for most cities. The focus of budgeting became one of keeping government small and inactive. Beginning in 1873 in New York City, a form of budgeting appeared in which budget estimates from the departments went to a board of estimate, variously composed, but generally consisting of the mayor, controller, president of the board of aldermen, and others. It is difficult to get a board of independently elected officials to agree to the same projects, which slows down spending.

The extent to which the boards of estimates were viewed as a way of curtailing tax levies is underscored by a description of how the Board of Estimates actually worked in New York City. In the early days of the board, aldermen would add to the recommended amounts. From 1873 to 1888, they added on average about $500,000 annually. But they were constantly overruled by the Board of Estimates. Over time, the aldermen added less and less. "Responding to consistent pressure for economy in government, particularly from middle-class groups experiencing the brunt of taxation, the Board of Estimates ignored the proposed increases of the council and continued to reduce the level of public expenditures."[34] By 1898, the charter granted the council some formal budget authority, but only to decrease the estimates. If the mayor vetoed any reductions made by the council, a five-sixths majority was required to overturn. There was to be no reconsideration by the Board of Estimates after council action.[35]

During the Progressive era expansion (from about 1895 to about 1920), the focus of budgeting shifted from keeping government small and ineffective to combining activism with efficiency and accountability. The result was a major push for a single executive responsible for the budget. Executive budget reform reflects the Progressive era sense of government as a necessary counterbalance to business and a major provider of services, but at the same time it reflected the perceived need to control government and provide accountability. The single executive reforms reflected as well the notion of government moving on a plan, of change in an agreed-on direction, rather than the random expenditures of a council and a pork-driven budget.

The massive expenditure increases that characterized the early 1900s through the early 1920s stimulated interest in cost accounting and additional techniques for public accountability, and the first tentative steps were taken toward performance measurement. The gradual adoption of the executive budget process in Boston, which culminated in the charter reform of 1909, illustrates the simultaneous increase of the budget power of the mayor, the weakening of the budget power of the council, and the increasing control (centralization) of the mayor over the executive departments. The timing of the major steps to Boston's executive budget reflects Boston's somewhat earlier adoption of Progressive era reforms and increased spending than occurred elsewhere.

The charter of 1854 gave the mayor a veto over all acts of the city council and all acts of either branch which involved the expenditure of money.[36] His veto could be overturned by a two-thirds vote. Despite this important grant of authority, in other ways the charter limited the mayor's powers. The city council "would not limit its executive power," and established "still more firmly government by committee."[37] By 1885, however, a new charter provided for separation of the executive and the legislative, and took detailed budget-making authority away from the council and gave it to the mayor. The mayor was given the power to hire and fire department heads and to approve any expenditure over $2000. The mayor's veto power was enhanced to include an item veto.[38] The charter of 1909 extended the role of the mayor from budget implementation and fiscal control to budget proposal. The council's power was limited to reducing or omitting items; they could no longer add new items. The mayor was given an absolute veto power over all acts of the city council—he could veto part of an item, not simply a whole item.[39]

To summarize, the early history of budgeting in cities began with broader grants of taxing powers to deal with rapid growth in the mid-1800s; these taxing powers were often abused, especially with such capital projects as the acquisition of railroads to promote economic development. The recession that began in 1873 ushered in a period of contraction in many cities, which was marked by tax limits, and by structural mechanisms to render budgeting difficult, slow, and inefficient. These budget processes indeed kept the costs of government down, but did not help cities solve the growing problems of urbanization. As the need for more activist and problem-solving government forged new political coalitions, new forms of budgeting emerged that combined cost controls with the potential for activism; they simultaneously provided accountability, activism, and cost control in the form of the strong mayor who presided over a more centralized bureaucracy and was responsible for the budget.

The themes of activism in problem solving and efficient and accountable government remained strong in succeeding periods when social and economic problems accumulated and became urgent. The city-manager form that began to gain popularity after World War I reflected those themes and added two new ones, the importance of hiring a technical expert (the city manager) to solve problems and the subordination of politics to problem solving.

The issue of accountability became more acute under this form because of its emphasis on eliminating political machines that linked people directly to government. Accountability was to be formally provided by the frequently exercised right of city councils to fire the manager if he (early managers were males, frequently engineers) did not do as they wished. But accountability was also provided by improved budget documents that demonstrated how well public money was being spent.

The major spurts in adoptions of the council-manager form occurred after the two world wars. From 1945 to 1959, the number of council-manager adoptions increased from 637 to almost 1,500.[40] One reason was that the infrastructure of the cities was in a state of neglect and technical problems seemed to require competent staff and an activist approach.

The modern history of budget processes in cities has been parallel in some ways to the state and federal governments, but it has been different in other ways. Cities responded to the same waves of reform that affected the federal and state governments, and adopted some of the same reforms. While there was a distinct flavor of efficiency and keeping costs and waste down, there was also a flavor about the city changes that emphasized capacity to respond to problems.

The executive budget reforms went even further in the cities than they went in the states, often limiting the ability of the councils to change the executive's budget recommendations. City councils still do not generally have much budget expertise or a separate professional staff to help them question executive budget proposals or formulate their own. There are still a few cities in which the council prepares the budget, but they are quite rare.

Even so, the direction of change is toward more participation by councils in budgetary decision making. A recent survey of cities over 100,000 population found that 44 percent of city budget or finance officers perceived that the influence of the municipal legislative body in the budgeting and appropriations process had increased in recent years; 8 percent indicated council influence had decreased. The reasons they gave included a more interested and involved and better qualified city council. They also argued that declining federal revenues and fiscal stress were factors.[41]

One reason for increased council participation is an increase in the number of council-manager cities since the end of World War II. More recently, the trend away from completely at-large to at least partly district elections to increase minority and neighborhood representation on city councils may have increased council participation. Neighborhood-based representatives might be more likely to fight for neighborhood capital projects and actively resist cutbacks that affect their territories.[42] Another possible reason for increased council participation is that municipal budgets have become much clearer and easier to follow, even for nontechnically trained elected officials.

The recent history of municipal budget formats begins in the 1950s. Cities began to adopt performance budgeting after the Hoover Commission report in 1949, which advised the federal government to adopt performance budgeting. Los Angeles was one of the early municipal adopters, beginning its performance budgeting in fiscal year 1953.[43] But performance measurement did not suit the needs of the time in the growth period of the 1950s and 1960s.

Performance budgeting focused on efficiency, being good at whatever the public organization does; it is not particularly useful in helping make decisions between competing ends, or deciding what the organization should be doing. It was to meet this need that PPBS (Planning Programming Budgeting Systems) was developed and implemented. During the period of rapid growth of the 1950s, 1960s, and early 1970s, the planning focus of PPB was more attractive, although in some cities, the planning and performance approaches merged.

As with performance measurement, the formal stimulus was from the federal government, which had experimented with PPB first. With the aid of a grant, an experimental program called the 5-5-5 program introduced PPB to five states, five counties, and five cities.[44] The experiment began in 1968. More than five cities became involved with the planning and analysis of PPB, however. In early evaluations, more than fifty local governments reported at least beginning steps on PPB. The George Washington University research team that evaluated early efforts at implementing PPB noted that the prospect that program analysis would be a requirement for receiving federal grants promoted cities' interest. "The cities, with Model City fund applications and approval by the U.S. Department of Housing and Urban Development still ahead, anticipated that a start on PPB would help them gain the federal agency funds."[45] Many of the cities that tried it did so with lukewarm commitment, however, to see how it would work. Some found it too cumbersome or too expensive, and dropped it when the recessions of the mid-1970s hit; others tried the system, but modified the parts they liked best and dropped the rest.

PPB's emphasis on planning worked best in an environment of growing resources, when choosing programs and defining city goals were immediate policy decisions. But by the middle of the 1970s the financial situation had changed, first with a deep recession and then, in the later 1970s, with the decline in federal aid dollars and taxpayer revolts and then, in the early 1980s, with a second deep recession. In this environment, some cities began to experiment with zero-based budgeting. For example, Oakland, California, drew up a zero-based budget to help it handle anticipated cuts resulting from California's Proposition 13, which was passed in 1978.[46]

Zero-based budgeting was very cumbersome. A number of officials worked out and used modifications of it called target-based budgets. The departments calculate a constant services budget—how much it would cost next year to provide this year's level of service. The budget office, based on its estimates of revenues, then gives each department a target which may be below the constant-services level. No department's request may exceed the target level. The departments then formulate lists of high-priority items that are unfunded, which include projects or programs that have been squeezed out of their base budgets by low targets as well as some new items. They rank their lists of high-priority unfunded items. Then city officials (which officials actually do this varies from city to city) merge and rerank the departments' priority lists until they can create a citywide list. Whatever money is available from new revenues or from service cuts or giving up low-priority programs is allocated down the priority list until the money gives out.

This system has proven well adapted to pressure to reduce property taxes. The targets are driven by estimates of revenues. Politicians can lower property tax rates and force cuts by reducing targets. This has proven a fairly common use of the system by mayors intent on taking the credit for lowering property taxes. Target-based budgeting also creates some discretion for policy making for political leaders within extremely constrained budgets, since mild cuts plus new revenues can be used to reallocate between departments for high-priority, citywide projects, such as economic development, housing, or crime control. The departments find their chances of getting funding over the targets much improved if they suggest projects high on the mayor's or manager's priority list.

Though the target system works reasonably well during growth as well, cities that have adopted it have often done so under the pressure of fiscal problems and with the desire to keep departmental requests to a moderate level. An interesting element of the system is that while it reserves policy decisions to top officials, it forces decisions between projects and expenditures as much as possible back on the departments. It thus offers a new balance between top-down and bottom-up budgeting.

Summary and Conclusions

In an overview of the main lines of evolution of budget processes, four themes appear:

□ First, when there is discontent with the current outcomes, in terms of level of spending or level of borrowing, and those outcomes cannot be altered in the usual ways, there is increasing pressure to change the budget process. That pressure can be in either direction, to increase expenditures and the scope of government or to decrease it.

□ A second theme is that legislators at both state and national levels have been willing to give up power when it seemed that their own discipline was inadequate to control debt or spending. While there is much jockeying to maximize power, there have been restraining forces in which political actors give up power to achieve what they perceive as the common good—in fiscal terms, a stable, balanced budget.

□ Third, the long-term trend toward more executive power and the withering away of legislative budget control may have ended, to be replaced with a period of more balanced power between the two. When the executive's budget power becomes too strong, some kind of balancing mechanism seems to come into play. When President Nixon took too much policy control over the budget away from Congress, Congress responded by taking back some budget control and strengthening its own capacity to make budget decisions. At the state level, when the chief executive has extremely strong veto powers that effectively prevent legislators from introducing expenditures that are higher than or even different from the governor's recommendations, then legislators sometimes seek, formally or informally, a greater role in determining the governor's budget recommendations. Alternatively, the legislatures seek professional staff to balance the executive branch staff, and enable them to examine the budget in some detail and make their own policy and draw up their own proposals when they wish. At the local level, strong executive budget powers have led to adaptations that allow the council to influence the policy in the budget while it is being prepared by the executive.

□ Fourth, at least on the executive side of the ledger, the long trend toward greater centralization may finally be abating. Cities in particular have markedly increased their use of target-based budgeting, which helps prevent micromanagement from the budget office and gives back many budgetary decisions to the departments. Vice-President Al Gore's National Performance Review reports included a number of recommendations for changing executive budgeting at the national level. Many of these changes argued for greater budgetary control at lower organizational levels.

Notes

1. Charles Stewart III, "Budget Reform and Its Consequences: Agencies, the Committees, and the House, 1865–1921" (paper presented at the 1987 American Political Science Association meeting, Chicago, 3–7 September). Also see Charles Stewart III, *Budget Reform Politics* (New York: Cambridge University Press, 1989).

2. For the state level, see ACIR, *The Question of State Government Capability* (Washington, D.C.: Government Printing Office, 1985), 146 ff.

3. Howard Shuman, *Politics and the Budget: The Struggle Between the President and the Congress* (Englewood Cliffs, N.J.: Prentice Hall, 1984), 27.

4. Ibid., 28.

5. Frederick Mosher, *A Tale of Two Agencies: A Comparative Analysis of the GAO and OMB* (Baton Rouge: Louisiana State University Press, 1984), 27.

6. Allen Schick, *Congress and Money* (Washington, D.C.: Urban Institute Press, 1980), chap. 2.

7. Congressional Budget Office, *The Economic and Fiscal Outlook: Fiscal Years, 1992–1996* (Washington, D.C.: Government Printing Office, January 1991), chap. 2.

8. Ibid., 57.

9. Allen Schick, *The Federal Budget: Politics, Policy, and Process* (Washington, D.C.: Brookings Institution, 1995), 41.

10. For a description of some of these summit negotiations, see Allen Schick, *The Capacity to Budget* (Washington, D.C.: Urban Institute Press, 1990), chap. 6; and Joseph White and Aaron Wildavsky, *The Deficit and the Public Interest: The Search for Responsible Government in the 1980s* (Berkeley: University of California Press, 1989), 235–41, 298, 319–22.

11. National Performance Review Staff, *From Red Tape to Results: Creating a Government That Works Better and Costs Less, Mission-Driven, Results-Oriented Budgeting* (Washington, D.C.: Government Printing Office, 1994), 27–47.

12. Janet Cornelius, *Constitution Making in Illinois, 1918–1970* (Urbana: University of Illinois Press, 1972), 33.

13. Ibid., 34.

14. Ibid., 68.

15. William T. Hutchinson, *Lowden of Illinois*, vol. 1 (Chicago: University of Chicago Press, 1957).

16. Ibid., 295.

17. ACIR, *Significant Features of Fiscal Federalism, 1989*, vol. 2, table 75.

18. The material through the 1950s is from Thomas Anton, *The Politics of State Expenditure in Illinois* (Urbana: University of Illinois Press, 1966).

19. Edgar Crane, "The Office of the Governor," in *Illinois: Political Process and Governmental Performance,* ed. Edgar Crane (Dubuque, Iowa: Kendall/Hunt, 1980), 74.

20. Ibid., 78.

21. Ibid., 77.

22. Irene Rubin, Jack King, Steven Wagner, and Ellen Dran, "Illinois: Executive Reform and Fiscal Conditions," in *Governors, Legislatures, and Budgets: Diversity across the American States,* ed. Edward Clynch and Thomas Lauth (Westport, Conn.: Greenwood, 1991).

23. Maralyn Budke, "The Legislative Fiscal Staff's Role in the Budgetary Process—New Mexico," in *The Political Pursestrings: The Role of the Legislature in the Budgetary Process,* ed. Alan P. Balutis and Daron K. Butler (New York: Wiley, 1975), 51.

24. Joseph Kyle, "Florida Legislative Budget Review Process" in Balutis and Butler, *Political Pursestrings,* 78.

25. Ibid.

26. Gloria Grizzle, "Florida: Miles to Go and Promises to Keep," in Clynch and Lauth, *Governors, Legislatures, and Budgets,* 98–99.

27. Ibid., 98.

28. Ibid., 94.

29. Ibid., 95.

30. This case is taken from Charles C. Williamson, *The Finances of Cleveland* in the series *Studies in History, Economics and Public Law* 25, no. 3, ed. Faculty of Political Science, Columbia University (New York: Columbia University Press, 1906–7).

31. Ibid., 22.

32. Ibid., 44.

33. Martin Schiesl, *The Politics of Efficiency: Municipal Administration and Reform in America, 1800–1920* (Berkeley: University of California Press, 1977), 90.

34. Ibid., 91.

35. Ibid., 92.

36. Charles Phillips Huse, *The Financial History of Boston, From May 1, 1822 to January 31, 1909* (Cambridge: Harvard University Press, 1916), 62.

37. Ibid.

38. Ibid., 177.

39. Ibid., 233–34.

40. Charles Glaab and A. Theodore Brown, *A History of Urban America,* 3d ed. (New York: Macmillan, 1983), 200.

41. Stanley Botner, "Trends and Developments in Budgeting and Financial Management in Large Cities in the United States," *Public Budgeting and Finance* 9, no. 3 (Autumn 1989): 41.

42. See Carolyn Adams, *The Politics of Capital Investment: The Case of Philadelphia* (Albany: State University of New York Press, 1988), chap. 5, for an illustration of the interaction between neighborhood loyalties, fiscal stress, and council participation in the capital budget process.

43. See George Terhune, *An Administrative Case Study of Performance Budgeting in the City of Los Angeles, California* (Chicago: Municipal Finance Officers Association, 1954); and Ali Eghetedari and Frank Sherwood, "Performance Budgeting in Los Angeles," in *Perspectives on Budgeting,* 2d ed., ed. Allen

Schick (Washington, D.C.: American Society for Public Administration, 1987).

44. Selma Mushkin et al., in cooperation with the Council of State Governments, the International City Managers Association, the National Governors Conference, the National League of Cities, and the U.S. Conference of Mayors, *Implementing PPB in State, City, and County: A Report on the 5-5-5 Project* (Washington, D.C.: State and Local Finances Project of George Washington University, June 1969).

45. Ibid., 13.

46. See Charles Levine, Irene Rubin, and George Wolohojian, *The Politics of Retrenchment: How Local Governments Manage Fiscal Stress* (Beverly Hills, Calif.: Sage, 1981), 76–77.

5. The Politics of Expenditures: Managing Competition, Accountability, and Acceptability

The politics of expenditures is the politics of choice. Some budget actors want one thing, some want something else, and there is not enough money to go around. Many budget claimants may get a little bit of what they want, some may get all or almost all of what they want, while others may get nothing or may actually lose benefits to provide others with what they ask for. The elderly may benefit from increased Medicare payments at the expense of reduced college loans to the young; the Defense Department may grow at the expense of housing programs.

The choices in the budget might be based on policies that imply trade-offs between areas of the budget. One such policy statement might be that the health of agriculture is essential to the economy, so benefit programs must be targeted specifically at farmers. Another example might be that crime suppression is more important than crime prevention, so police must be funded before social services or education. But the choices in the budget might be framed without obvious policy preferences and tradeoffs between areas. The choices might be between two weapons systems with different technical capabilities, or between two different street-improvement plans. The choice might depend only on which claimant has enough support or can negotiate enough support to succeed. The environment might favor some claims over others, exaggerating some needs and toning down others. Jobs programs have more appeal during a long and deep recession; drainage programs have more appeal after a period of serious flooding.

When revenue increases or budget cutbacks are allocated across the board—that is, the same percentage increase or decrease is given to all existing programs—there may not seem to be much choice in the budget. No one program expands faster than others, no program is cut back disproportionately to preserve others. There may be little change from year to year. Nevertheless, budgets make choices between expenditures even when priorities seem to remain the same from year to year. Each year (or each budget cycle) there is a choice of spending revenue increases the same way money was spent in the past, or doing something different with it. There is also a choice of reallocating funds among existing programs or from old to new programs. The decision to keep this year's expenditures the same as last year's is also a choice.

Because public budgeting involves a wide variety of actors with different spending goals, the necessity of choice in the budget leads to competition between actors, between programs, and between beneficiaries. How is this competition handled in the politics of expenditures?

One model prevalent in the 1960s and 1970s envisioned the politics of expenditures as bargaining between individuals, each with personal goals, to influence budget outcomes. This competition was constrained by shared understandings that developed over time, and by decision rules, often formulas, that created fairness in the distribution of resources. The result was that no one asked for too much and that new revenues were allocated in small amounts, pretty much in the same way that previous revenues had been allocated. Competition was minimized by mutual consent. This model may have been accurate at some times and in some places, but it has to be modified considerably to describe most of contemporary public spending.

One of the reasons that this model (called *incrementalism*) is inapplicable to contemporary budgeting is that norms of moderation in making budget requests and norms of fairness of allocating increases in revenues can only operate to limit claims on the budget and constrain allocations if every budget actor knows what every other actor gets from the budget process. An agency head is not likely to be constrained in asking for more if he or she feels that other agencies may have received more in the previous year. In recent years, especially at the national level, the variety of resources spent and the relative invisibility of some of those resources make it nearly impossible to compare budget outcomes; moreover, multiyear projects, cutbacks during the year, and supplemental appropriations may introduce changes during the year, making keeping up with others' funding levels very time-consuming if not impossible.

A second problem with the incremental model of moderation is that norms of fairness and moderation apply only to actors in the government who have to deal with one another year after year; they do not apply to interest-group representatives whose goal is to get as much as possible from the budget and have no interest whatsoever in what anyone else receives.

To the extent that internal actors cannot compare the increments they received to make sure they were fairly allocated, and to the extent that external actors such as interest groups are involved in making budgetary demands, competition may be intense and may not be regulated by shared understandings and decision rules. The result is more variability in budget proposals, more range of choice, and more competition between expenditures.

The model of restrained bargaining among actors is flawed in other ways as well. It underestimates the importance of the budget process in regulating competition; it underplays the fact that various budget actors have different capacities to mobilize support, which means that the playing field is not even to start with; and it underemphasizes the role of the environment in setting constraints on revenue totals, and on preferences for particular programs. Budgeting takes place in a political environment in which spending has to match public preferences at least roughly. Citizens may rebel against certain programs they do not want to fund or demand the continuation of existing programs. These preferences may become constraints that budget actors have to work around. Allocation of expenditures is not just a matter of bargaining between a limited set of internal actors.

The constraints of the environment and the budget process make the success of individuals' budget strategies conditional. A particular strategy might be successful at one time and fail at another time, or be successful in one budget process and fail in another. For example, an agency that tries to bypass the budget scrutiny of the executive budget office and make its presentation directly to the legislature might be successful in a legislatively dominated budget process and fail dismally in a centralized executive budget process. Even the best-conceived plans for program expansion will fail if the environment dictates cutbacks because of sharp revenue declines. The politics of expenditures is not an open competition of all against all, with the best strategists winning; it is bargaining among unequals, within a changing environment that shifts the goals and the level of discretion; it is also bargaining within a process that structures the level of competition and gives some interests a better chance than others.

The four characteristics of public budgeting outlined in chapter 1 help explain the politics of expenditures. These characteristics are: multiple actors with different goals; a budget process filled with constraints about what can and cannot be done; decision making that is open and vulnerable to the environment; and a separation between those who make spending decisions and those who pay taxes.

Multiple Actors Compete for Spending Preferences

All budget processes involve choice, but the number of actors involved in public spending decisions, their variety, and the variety of their spending preferences all contribute to a structurally high level of competition. The chief executive is likely to have a policy or a series of programs that he or she would like to support or terminate; legislators may support some of those programs but not others; agency heads are likely to support the narrower goals of their own programs, each agency head representing some potential demand on the budget. Interest groups typically request spending that favors that interest group, introducing a wide variety of possible requests. In a city, the animal protection league, the historical preservation society, the public housing board, the downtown business association, the library, the spouse-abuse center, the student association of the university, and supporters of the airport might all make spending proposals in a given year.

Groups can make narrow or broad demands. On the narrow end are demands such as providing shelter for the homeless or requesting sewer repairs in a given neighborhood. On the broad end, political parties or coalitions of interest groups of the political right or left may demand particular patterns of spending. Many Republicans, for example, favor increases in defense spending and oppose spending on regulatory agencies and many social services; many Democrats favor more social spending and less spending on defense. Party activists may try to implement these spending preferences through the political party organization.

Competition is keen because there are more demands than revenues, but it can be made keener when the competing interests are in some sense oppositional, so that the gains of one group may be seen as losses for another. Spending on agriculture and interstate highways is seen as spending for rural areas; spending for urban renewal or mass transit is viewed as spending for cities. These are viewed as oppositional. Spending for elderly, such as on social security or Medicare, is viewed as oppositional to spending on the young, as in programs for educational loans. Spending for the downtown area is often seen as antagonistic to spending for the neighborhoods. And spending for defense is seen as antagonistic to spending on social services.

How this competition is reflected in budgetary decision making depends a lot on the budget process and the budget format. If comparisons are framed between antagonistic programs, the amount of competition may be severe enough to slow down or even disrupt decision making. For example, when DeKalb, Illinois, had to deal with the loss of revenue sharing, decisions about what to cut were framed as basic services (police, fire, streets) versus social services (transportation for the elderly, counseling for abused spouses, and day care). The resulting controversy was emotional and held up approval of the rest of the budget pending the solution to this problem. Similarly, in 1995, at the national level, budgetary decisions were phrased in terms of health care for the elderly and poor versus tax breaks for the well-to-do. These and other emotionally laden comparisons derailed the budget process, actually closing down portions of the federal government twice because appropriation bills were delayed and the controversy prevented the passage of continuing resolutions.

If the comparisons are framed so that antagonistic programs are not in direct competition with one another, the level of conflict may be dampened. Thus, if there are multiple appropriation bills, one for defense and one for housing, and targets have been set for spending for each one based on the existing allocation plus inflation, housing programs compete with housing programs, and defense programs compete with defense programs, but individual housing programs do not compete with individual defense programs. Budgeters do not ask, Do you want to house the homeless or buy the navy a new helicopter?

No matter how decisions are grouped, there is likely to be competition within the categories for particular pots of money. For example, suppose a budget is divided into capital and operating expenses. (Capital items are goods purchased and/or built by governmental agencies that have a life expectancy of more than two or three years. Operating expenses recur regularly, such as salary, lighting bills, and postage.) If $500,000 is set aside for capital improvements, then all proposed capital improvements must compete with one another for that $500,000. Competition is likely to be acute within the capital budget. If $120,000 is set aside for all social services, then the social services have to compete with one another for the $120,000. When the budget process determines how much money will be set aside for what groupings of expenditures, it regulates who will compete with whom, and for how much money.

The capital budget can be used as an illustration of the responses of budget actors to high levels of competition. Examples of capital items are a firehouse (built by a city) and a ship (purchased by the navy). Capital items have particular characteristics that intensify the competition between them.

First, as long-term investments and one-time expenditures, capital items are in competition with operating expenditures, which are regular and recurring. Capital expenditures can be delayed, their exact timing is usually not important; operating expenditures, by their nature, have to be paid regularly. There is a tendency, especially when overall revenues are tight, to cut back on capital expenses and pay the operating expenses. As a result, the total amount of resources allocated to capital items may be both fluctuating and small with respect to demand, making the competition keener.

Second, when capital projects involve construction, they create temporary jobs. Any politician who creates jobs can claim an accomplishment due to his or her political skills and clout. Politicians vie for this kind of accomplishment. Since capital projects have to be built in a particular location, they introduce some geographic competition: Which council member or legislator or congressperson will be able to deliver a major project to his or her district?

Since most capital projects are carried out by private contractors, there is a third level of competition—between companies for the contracts. Companies do not necessarily wait until a project has been approved and then bid for it; they may press for the passage of particular projects because they know it will increase the possibilities of contracts. Estimates of what the contractors will charge for projects or equipment are presented in the budget. The more competition between contractors for business, the lower the cost is likely to be. Government agencies (theoretically) have an interest in keeping the competition high and the prices low, while contractors have the opposite interest, to keep competition low and prices high.

Since a capital budget groups together demands from competing agencies, and it taps geographical competition between legislators as well as competition between contractors, the capital budget is intensely competitive. How do budget actors deal with the competition? How do they compete? Or how do they reduce the competition?

One way of dealing with competition is to work at increasing the priority of one's proposals. Sometimes the environment may be kind and may provide an obvious example of overwhelming need that is underfunded. Relatively poor performance of fighter planes in a combat situation may be radical evidence of the need for a newly designed airplane; a Soviet victory in space may be deemed an outstanding reason for launching a U.S. space program. The need to compete with any well-known and dominant opponent can be used to raise the priority of particular expenditures. The environment itself does not bring about the change in priorities; rather it presents an opportunity that if seen by program supporters and documented, can strengthen their case and push their projects up on the priority list.

One way of increasing the priority of projects is to represent them as solutions to crises or emergencies. The emergency need not be imminent, only easily imaginable. Thus a fire department can make arguments for new equipment in terms of its capacity to save lives in a fire; the Defense Department can argue for new weapons systems because the Russians have more firepower, and what would happen if they attacked us. The possibility of such events may have to be exaggerated to make a powerful case. Supporters of the defense budget, for example, often gave different and sometimes exaggerated estimates of Soviet troop and armament strength in order to justify military buildups in the United States. The information was not blatantly false so much as misleading—saying we had fewer divisions of men under arms than the Soviets, for example, although the size of our divisions was much larger.[1] The tactic of selectively presenting a threatening portrait of the environment in order to justify budget increases can be called "The Russians Are Coming."

At the local level, at a recent budget presentation, a fire department official presented a film of a fire in a residence, with the blaze going from room to room; the film showed the temperatures in each room, the smoke and toxic fumes and the damage done, second by second. One had to conclude that the house could be one's own, and that the quicker the fire department's response time, the safer one's own house and family. The department requested an extra ambulance that year, complete with emergency equipment, and got it, although the justification was garbled and technically weak.

The threat of disastrous consequences if expenditures are not made is particularly common in defense. For example, in 1986, President Reagan argued for a real (above inflation) increase in Defense Department spending because failure to provide increases would risk a return to the problems of the 1970s, "a hollow army, ships that can't sail, and aircraft that can't fly." It would encourage adventurism on the part of the Soviets, and it would weaken the administration's ability to negotiate a satisfactory arms reduction agreement.[2]

The "just imagine what would happen if this purchase were not made" argument has widespread applicability. It requires an imagination and a word picture, or a film or photographs, or even props. A budget presentation at a state university library included a seat back, to illustrate that furniture purchased with the construction of the library was falling apart. The staff member went on to paint a verbal portrait of a crowded library where there were tables but no seats and the students had to sit on the floor. In another example, a director of water and sewer at City Hall argued that he had to have certain new equipment because if he did not, the city sewers would back up into peoples' homes, and council members would get angry complaints from citizens. His brief argument was very vivid and suggestive, both as to events and the probable political consequences.

Another way of reordering priorities is to imply that the current prioritization is too political or too ignorant and that technical scientific analysis indicates that whatever one is after is absolutely necessary and highly desirable. One instance of this argument occurred several years ago in a city that was considering its capital budget, when staff insisted on building a water tower rather than digging a well as was required by a grant the city had received. The staff recommendation tripled the estimated expense. The project was in an undeveloped portion of the city, and the project's intent was to create a visible sign of the available infrastructure to help lure in new business. A well that provided water alone could not provide the same symbol.

When a citizen advisory board member asked why a water tower was necessary when a new well would satisfy the conditions of the grant, the city manager angrily replied that the decision was a technical one and would be made by staff; it was beyond the citizen's competence.[3] The staff later came up with a technical reason for a water tower, to save costs in electricity. The argument then turned on whether there would be a rate increase, and how much it would be; city staff invited a representative of the power company to speak at the budget session, to convince the advisory board that the move to water towers would be cost effective. The project was approved, and the technical argument was the clincher.

An argument for increasing the priority of routine maintenance or construction of undramatic capital projects is that "it will cost more later." Maintenance projects may be routinely delayed because other needs seem more urgent. To push up the priority of routine tasks, proponents sometimes argue that the costs are inevitable and that doing the projects now will be cheaper than waiting, so the only logical choice is to do them now. Public works directors routinely argue that if roof repairs on public buildings are delayed, rain will cause structural damage and the eventual costs will be many times greater than if the work is done soon. If street maintenance and repair is delayed, the streets will fall apart and have to be rebuilt at much greater costs. Another version of this argument is that whatever project is being proposed is most cost effective—that is, a dollar spent here will have (by implication) more positive effect than a dollar spent elsewhere.[4] At the federal level, spending for children's programs is justified as an investment. For example, the Children's Defense Fund argued that research proved that such programs as prenatal care and immunization save more money than they cost.[5]

Yet another way of dealing with high levels of competition is to argue that the project will not cost much anyway. One can just slip it into a list of projects and not worry about the priorities because it will not cost much. Sometimes the programs really are not very expensive, but sometimes they are, and the budget strategy is to make them look less expensive than they are. One way to make programs or projects look cheap is to use "free" money, or money whose costs are not obvious. At the local level, grant money from the state or federal government often appears free. From the perspective of the federal government, loan programs often appear cheap or even free because they are usually paid back by the borrower.[6]

Many other techniques have been employed at all levels of government to make programs look inexpensive. Sometimes these techniques revolve around substituting leases for purchases, which shifts expenditures from highly visible capital budgets to much less visible operating budgets. Sometimes governments make costs of programs less visible by using tax breaks instead of outlays; in this manner, revenues are never collected or due, and hence they may never appear in the budget as an outlay, though the money is spent as surely as if the revenue were collected and then disbursed. Recent trends in tax expenditure reporting have made this strategy somewhat less effective in reducing the visibility of these expenditures, but there is very little tax expenditure reporting at the local level.

In general, taking something out of the budget makes it less visible. At the federal level, this strategy has led to the seeming surrealistic tactic of taking a program off budget. Congress took the Export-Import Bank off budget in 1971 and restored it to on-budget status in 1976; Section 202 Housing for the Elderly and Handicapped was taken off budget in 1974 and restored to budget status in 1978; the Strategic Petroleum Reserve program was declared off budget in 1981. The reason these programs were taken off budget was to protect them from cuts or impoundments, that is, presidential refusal to spend legally approved funds. More recently, social security was taken off budget to protect it, though it was probably not in real danger.[7]

Besides simply declaring a program off budget, politicians and staff can take an item out of the budget by arguing that it brings in revenue (or will bring in revenue at some future date) and therefore need not be reported. This practice may be quite common at the local level in economic development activities, where a city invests in extending water and services to an undeveloped parcel with the idea that it will recapture these outlays in the future when the land is developed and sold. The time lag between the initial outlays and the recapture may be many years, during which time the city has collected taxes and spent public money with no budgetary record. To a reader of the budget, it may be unclear how much was spent and how much is owed; moreover, the land may never be developed. The federal government has used fee income to offset spending, sometimes making spending appear lower than it is.[8]

Another cluster of budgetary strategies has arisen to deal with the intense competition in capital budgeting. Capital projects, especially construction projects, are by nature located in one spot or another, which leads to intense competition between states and cities and neighborhoods for the projects. Geographic competition may be handled by overtly touting the advantages of one's own location or by breaking projects into smaller parts and scattering them geographically to gain sufficient political support for passage. It can also be handled by norms of reciprocity.

An example of geographic competition occurred recently as states vied for a new federal physics project, the Superconducting Supercollider. States took out ads in newspapers, and some even took out ads on billboards, arguing their advantages as a site or trying to disarm opposition.

Being the best site or the most appropriate site for a capital project may help to put one's community on the list of possible sites, but there is more to getting a capital project than advertising the community's advantages. Local projects are supported by the communities that compete for them, and usually by the legislators who represent those communities. The trick is to turn that minimum level of support into enough political power to pass the legislation and designate the location. If the community's representatives are on the appropriate committees and are themselves powerful, that is helpful; in fact, one way to get support for capital programs is to locate them in the districts of powerful representatives. To get the support of other legislators the project may be divided, to give other representatives a stake, or the community's representatives may offer their support for future projects of other representatives.

The competition between potential bidders for contracts on the capital budget leads to a different set of tactics, not all of which are legitimate or even legal. These may include kickback schemes, or the dissemination of inside information to potential contractors to help them design their bids. Or an agency may legally designate some firm a sole-source bidder, implying that no other company has the capacity to build this product. In that case, competition is eliminated. Lowballing, or putting in a low estimate of what the contract will cost, is probably quite common, especially where government agencies are required to accept the low bid. If it turns out that the real expenses are higher than the contract, the agency is already dependent on the contractor and simply has to pay the cost overruns. If the agency refuses, then it has already paid money on the contract but has no product to show for it.

While competition may be especially keen inside the capital budget, there may also be competition between other, noncapital programs. Budget actors may use some similar tactics in the operating portion of the budget as they use in the capital budget, but they are more likely to emphasize policies as part of their strategies and try to show how their programs achieve current policies or are linked to other highly valued goals. In the extreme case, the strategy is to define the output of a program as so valuable and so politically untouchable that no tampering with revenues is possible. This strategy may be used by agencies, by the chief executive, by interest groups, or by legislators.

For example, the goal of paramedic service is lifesaving. Politicians are politically unwilling to estimate the dollar value of a life saved. Hence they may not be willing to calculate the cost of paramedic service or may not hold the program to the same standards of cost effectiveness as other programs. It is politically difficult to deny requests to the paramedic service when the implied consequence of not spending the money is loss of life.

At the national level, the Export-Import Bank has successfully used the strategy of linking the program to goals with unlimited value. Its function is to loan money, both to foreign countries and to U.S. companies to provide credit to purchasers abroad of U.S.-made goods. Supporters of the program do not describe it as serving the interest of a handful of major exporters (which it does) but as necessary to the strength of the national economy because it improves the balance of trade. The goal is of such value that the means have been difficult to question. The question whether it is cost effective compared to other possible programs has seldom been asked. For the paramedic example, the public may indeed be receiving a good that it values, but for the Export-Import Bank, the recipients of the program have managed to define their benefits as a nationally desirable good, and thus made their benefits politically difficult to reduce.[9]

A variant of this strategy is to create programs with symbolic outputs. To the extent that the outputs are symbolic, their worth cannot be priced and hence the programs seem to justify spending any amount of money. Putting a man on the moon was such a program. Its costs were not estimated or even estimatable at the time the program was announced. The outcome was symbolic. We were going to do it, no matter how much it cost. A positive climate for business is another of those symbolic goals that seem to justify a wide range of expenditures. How much is it worth? How much will it deliver in terms of economic expansion? No one knows, but a good climate is perceived as of value in itself.

For agencies that want to grow, but whose goals are not sufficiently valued to escape cost/benefit calculus, a frequently used strategy is to try to hook on to more highly valued goals. Thus a local airport serving private airplanes is running at a loss; it is providing a service valued by some but paid for by all. The ratio of costs to benefits will be a political and budgetary red flag unless the airport can be tied to a more valued (preferably an unlimitedly valued) goal, in this case economic development. Even if the case is weak for linking private airplanes and economic development, if the agency and its backers gain general acceptance for the argument, the airport's funding too can be treated as not requiring cost/benefit analysis. Similarly, at the state level, university funding had been fairly low on the priority ranking of state programs, but received a boost when higher education officials managed to redefine higher education as the nucleus of economic development. But not every agency or program can take advantage of the strategy of overvalued ends. For most programs, even with valued outputs, it still matters how much they cost. When costs get out of line, the result is embarrassment and a search for alternative programs that provide as good a service at less cost.

One of the key strategies that supporters of farm subsidies used over the years was to link their programs to the symbolic worth of protecting the family farm. But it gradually became clear that a substantial proportion of the funding was going to large, wealthy corporate owners, not to struggling family farmers. In the face of continuing pressure to reduce the deficit and continuing pressure to deregulate and increase the use of market forces, farm programs lost considerable support after the passage of Gramm-Rudman-Hollings. Funding for farm programs had been cut by roughly 60 percent between 1986 and 1995, from $26 billion to $9 billion, and it looked as if the reductions were going to continue over the next few years. The linkage to a valued goal has to be credible in order to work.

Another strategy to help gain backing for a proposal is to put forward proposals for spending that seem in line with stated policy objectives of the chief executive. Thus, at the federal level, some of the agencies whose programs were disapproved by President Reagan in 1981 tried to design new programs that were more in line with the president's goals. Sometimes the policy guidance may not be as clear as it was in 1981, leaving agencies to hunt for hints about what might be approved or desired.

To summarize, the variety of claimants on the budget and the variety of expenditures they ask for creates a situation of choice and competition between objects of expenditure and between programs. The budget process frames the comparisons between expenditures and can damp down or increase the level of competition. For those programs and projects that must compete, especially for those that perceive themselves low on a priority list, budget actors may devise a variety of strategies to help them compete successfully.

Budget Constraints Can Reduce Competition

The second element of public budgeting is that it is characterized by numerous constraints, rules about what can be done and how it can be done. In the context of expenditures, these constraints may be expressed in terms of "you must do this first" or "you cannot do that or cut that." Because competition can be fierce in parts of the budget, the participants sometimes strategize more about how to reduce competition than how to compete effectively. They seek to put constraints on budgeting that give their own programs automatic funding and/or make their programs untouchable. They seek to take their own programs out of the rough and tumble of policy-related tradeoffs.

Between 1987 and 1991 in San Francisco, spending for children's programs had declined 20 percent. Continuing budgetary shortfalls threatened to reduce the amount of funding each year. Advocates for children found they had to fight for funding each year, with limited success. While they would have liked to earmark new revenues for children, the antitax sentiment was so strong that supporters decided to try to earmark existing revenues instead and set a minimum level of funding for children's programs.

Supporters put a proposition on the ballot to amend the San Francisco charter and then actively campaigned for the proposal. Using the argument that spending money on children would save money for other programs later and using generously the symbolism of the importance of children, supporters won a major victory at the polls. They had managed to restructure the budget to reduce the level of competition for their program.[10]

Reducing competition hardly ever involves trying to destroy other programs that compete for funds or even trying to make them look bad. Instead, it often involves taking a program out of the portion of the budget in which departments and programs compete for money. Competition is likely to be keen inside the general fund, where many programs and projects compete for unearmarked revenues. To reduce competition, program supporters may try to get their program out of the general fund. This may mean setting up an independent fund with just that one program in it, and no direct competition. To work really well, the new fund should have its own earmarked revenues, and have legal restrictions forbidding anyone to transfer money out of the fund for expenses not related to the program. Trust funds and public enterprises reduce competition in this manner. Entitlement programs are a different way of reducing competition. These programs often have no ceilings on expenditures; the more people who are eligible for them, the more money must be spent. Money for entitlements has to come first because it is a legal obligation; what is left over goes to other, more discretionary programs. Entitlements are thus not in competition with other programs for revenues. Mandates involve getting someone else, usually another level of government or a professional association, to require a particular level of spending on particular items or programs. Budget processes can be altered to reduce competition in several ways. For example, resources can be allocated by predetermined formulas, which reduce competition dramatically; or budget processes can specify that only a limited amount of money will be allocated through competition; or the process can specify that certain programs will not be cut back, regardless of need.

PUBLIC ENTERPRISES

Public enterprises are governmental services that are run like businesses, in the sense that they sell the goods or services they produce on a fee-for-service basis. Public enterprises may be owned or operated by government agencies. They are intended to pay for themselves through the sale of what they do or make. To the extent that they succeed, they involve no direct expenditures and hence appear free. They are segregated from the rest of the budget, and the revenues they generate are supposed to go exclusively for the expenses they incur. They typically have great policy independence because of their own revenue base.

There are public enterprises at all levels of government. At the national level, the Tennessee Valley Authority (TVA), which provided electric power, is one example of a public enterprise; the postal service is operated as a public enterprise, as is Amtrak, the passenger rail company. States have historically run a number of enterprises, but currently the state university systems are probably the most widespread enterprises at the state level. At the local level, common public enterprises include water and sewer services, and parking. In Illinois, about 20 percent of local budgets are derived from such enterprises. This is a substantial share of government activity.

If a city is providing a service for which it charges a fee, and revenues are coming in from those fees, there may be enormous temptation to channel money from those fees to other services, to keep taxes down, or to charge extra for the fees and use the difference as a form of general revenue. The service may not have enough money left to run itself properly or it may be priced out of the market.[11] Enterprises may have to compete to retain their own revenues to keep functioning. In such circumstances, to reduce competition for revenues, program supporters may try to create a separate enterprise fund with legal constraints about spending all the revenues it generates on the services it produces. Or, in a more extreme case, supporters of the enterprise may work to remove it from the city's budget completely, to become a special district (a minigovernment with just one function), effectively preventing any competition with any other municipal program. Some states, such as California and Illinois, have a large number of special-purpose local governments, severely restricting the scope of general government and sharply limiting the ability to make tradeoffs within the budget, and seriously reducing the amount of competition between programs.

TRUSTS

Trusts are a second way of reducing competition. Many governments hold some money in trust funds. When the money is in trust, agency officials can spend the money only in accordance with the instructions laid down when the trust was established. Trust fund revenues (at least in theory) do not mix with other money in the budget. If government employees and interest groups can define their benefits as trusts, they can prevent the possibility of a future erosion of benefits resulting from tradeoffs with other expenditures that later seem more important.

The most common example of governmental trust funds is pension funds. Employers and employees may contribute money to an employee's retirement fund. Recipients of pensions feel deeply about previously earned, contractually guaranteed benefits. The money is supposed to be segregated from the rest of the budget with absolutely no tradeoffs with other expenditures. Pensions involve long-term commitments of funds with (almost) no possibility of cutback or retrenchment of already granted benefits.

Despite occasional marginal infringements, trust funds usually are inviolate, which means that to insulate a program from future tradeoffs with other items in the budget, a trust fund may be a perfect vehicle. Examples include social security, the federal highway trust fund, and the mass transit trust fund at the federal level. Program supporters specifically seek the trust fund structure in order to reduce competition.

EXAMPLE OF A TRUST FUND:
THE RECENT HISTORY OF SOCIAL SECURITY

Social security is an example at the federal level of a trust fund set up to ensure that money for the program is not spent on anything else. The recent history of social security has been tumultuous and suggests the difficulty of keeping trust funds truly apart from the rest of the budget and the long-term success of program supporters in maintaining the integrity of the fund.

Over the years, social security has had very little surplus. Unlike most pension funds, which try to build and invest a reserve against the time when larger numbers of people will retire, social security has been payout funded, that is, money paid in by those currently working has been spent on those currently retired. Payout funding has some serious problems. If the economy weakens and current workers earn less or many become unemployed, revenues going into the system fall. If more people than expected apply for disability benefits, expenditures rise, independent of income to the trust fund. Over the long haul, if more people reach retirement age than are currently working, either social security taxes will skyrocket or the system will go belly-up.

According to Gwendolyn King, commissioner of the Social Security System, in 1983 the system was near collapse. "Social Security Trust Fund reserves were nearly exhausted."[12] Senator Dave Durenburger reminded Senate Finance Committee members that in 1983 "things were so bad the government had to borrow from the Medicare Hospital Insurance Trust Fund."[13]

A Social Security Commission was established to work out a rescue plan and ensure the integrity of social security into the twenty-first century when it would have to deal with larger numbers of retirees and relatively smaller numbers of workers who were paying into the fund. As a result of the commission recommendations and the support of the president and the Speaker of the House, the problem was resolved, and social security taxes were increased.

When combined with other changes in the federal tax structure during the early 1980s, the increase in social security taxes made the federal tax structure considerably less progressive, that is, it shifted the burden of taxation more onto the poor. The reason is that everyone pays the same rate for social security up to a dollar limit; there is no social security tax on incomes over that limit. For people earning more than the cutoff point, the richer they are, the smaller the proportion of their income they pay for social security. That is a classic definition of a regressive tax.

The increased social security taxes contributed to rapidly growing surpluses. That should have been a good thing, but it turned out to be a difficulty of unanticipated proportions. Senator Daniel Patrick Moynihan accused social security of thievery; Senator John Heinz elevated the charge to embezzlement.[14] Other senators charged that the government was taking social security money and spending it on other things. These charges were intentionally flamboyant; they suggested that the sanctity of the trust fund had been violated, which was an exaggeration, but not completely without foundation.

What was happening was that the government was borrowing from the Social Security Trust Fund surplus to fund the deficit. That made some supporters of the trust fund nervous about how the government was going to repay the borrowing, and if the trust fund was going to be cheated in some way. The Social Security Trust Fund was required by law to invest its surplus in U.S. Treasury securities, so there was less of a conspiracy involved than the rhetoric implied.

A related problem was that the balances in the Social Security Trust Fund were being subtracted from the size of the deficit for the purposes of calculating how much needed to be cut from the budget to meet Gramm-Rudman-Hollings requirements for deficit reduction. The bigger the social security surplus, the smaller the deficit looked, even though it was actually growing. The rapidly growing social security surplus gave the illusion of progress toward deficit reduction, although the surplus could not in fact be spent to eliminate that deficit without violating the trust fund. If the social security surplus were removed from calculation of the deficit by taking social security "off budget," the deficit would take a large and disheartening leap, and possibly discourage efforts to reduce the deficit by creating the impression of an impossibly large problem.[15] The administration proposed to keep social security on budget until 1993, when Gramm-Rudman-Hollings should have attained a balanced budget, but skeptics argued that the proposal condoned massive deception until after the next election.

To address the issues of tax regressivity and the use of social security surpluses to obscure the size of the deficit, Senator Moynihan proposed to reduce social security taxes and return to a payout-based system. Such a change would put severe stress on the Social Security System, resulting in increased taxes in the near future, shifting the funding to other sources of revenue besides the payroll tax, or inability to meet spending requirements by 1998. Senator Moynihan's proposal did not pass Congress, but he successfully called attention to the problems. Most members of Congress preferred to address the issues he raised without threatening the financial future of social security.

The problems were addressed during the 1990 Omnibus Reconciliation. Social security was taken off budget for purposes of calculating the budget deficit, effective right away, not in 1993. It was to be excluded completely from the requirements of Gramm-Rudman-Hollings. Once social security was on its own, some senators feared that Congress might spend the reserves if there were not additional protections preventing such action.[16] Hence, the Omnibus Reconciliation contained a ("firewall") protection for social security. It was to be considered out of order in the House or Senate to propose changes in social security that would seriously deplete the surplus. In addition, some effort was made to make the tax burden lighter on poorer people, by increasing the Earned Income Tax Credit. And a major effort was made to overhaul the procedures to reduce the deficit. While this effort had impacts well beyond social security, it addressed the broader issue of the social security surplus funding, and hence encouraging, the deficit.

ENTITLEMENTS

Entitlements are "legal obligations created through legislation that require the payment of benefits to any person or unit of government that meets the eligibility requirements established by law."[17] They reduce competition because money must be found to pay for the program as long as there are eligibles making demands. It sets up a prior obligation.

Some entitlements are so rooted in the values of what government should do for citizens that they are treated as rights.[18] For example, people may have a right to basic protection or a roof over their head or a right not to starve or freeze to death in a society that can afford to feed and warm them. Basic health care may also be considered a right. Once an entitlement is treated as a right, it is virtually nonnegotiable in a budget. Entitlements, when they are treated as rights, represent an extreme form of the strategy of locking in benefits.

Part of the politics of entitlements relates to the changing social definition over time, sometimes over centuries, as to what constitutes a right-based demand on the budget. Some entitlements can be relatively weak for many years and gradually grow stronger, as public consensus grows that the benefit is a right. The actual beneficiaries may not be organized or may have little political power, such as the unemployed or the homeless. Their plight must catch the public imagination, and the public must define their situation as worthy of collective aid. Right-based programs may be terminated or reduced if popular belief in their necessity wanes, or if the need for the program is reduced.

For program advocates, trying to design programs as entitlements is a strategy to reduce competition. They may also try to change the social definition of the right underlying an entitlement, by bringing dramatic instances of socially caused suffering to the attention of the public and of politicians. Documenting need is an important part of this strategy, and the ability to rouse public sympathy may be crucial.

MANDATES

Mandates take a variety of forms. One is the "professional accreditation" model. The model occurs in universities, where accounting associations, journalism societies, bar associations, planning associations, and public administration associations set standards for academic programs. In many cases, the accreditors set restrictions on transferring money out of the program (as in law schools) and set staffing as well as academic standards. These standards become mandatory minimum levels for funding because if the program (or the whole school) loses its accreditation its ability to attract students seriously diminishes. The accreditation model also applies to some other public-sector agencies. For example, cities are rated on their capacity to handle major fires, and fire departments use these ratings as arguments for what they must have in the way of staffing and equipment.

While the accreditation process may be presented as an outside force, subject to no internal control, agency heads and interest groups can help form professional societies and urge them to set up standards in order to reduce the competition they face in the budget. Professional societies can play the role of accreditor or help to set standards that are set into law.

Another kind of mandate is established by the perception of what financial markets will "require" in order to provide capital or operating loans. If we do not do what is required, the market will not buy our bonds, or the banks will stop issuing us credit. Sometimes a budget officer in a city will alert an auditor to a particular management problem, hoping that the auditor, with external clout and high visibility, can successfully call attention to problems. Then the budget officer can say, "The auditor said (whatever)," so we must do it.

Mandates may also come from the federal government to the state and local governments and from the state governments to their local governments. The federal government can pass a law requiring states to implement laws on clean air or water or require state and local governments to provide equal transit services for the handicapped. Carrying out such laws can cost state and local governments hundreds of millions of dollars. State governments often make laws with spending implications for local governments, which the local governments have to carry out. Thus if the state passes a law requiring municipalities to dispose of toxic wastes in a certain way, the cities must comply; if the state also passes the money along, fine, if not, the cities must pick up the burden themselves. State governments can require a certain level of salary for police or a particular increase in pension contributions; they can mandate collective bargaining, too, which may have major implications for spending.

Spending mandates from the states are constraints on budgeting that reduce competition. Internal actors can try to use this process to reduce the competition they face. For example, public employee unions can form a statewide coalition and lobby the capital for mandated increases in salaries. This creates a kind of end run around the entire local political and administrative system. When the costs are mandated, there is no competition with other requests for spending.

BUDGET PROCESSES

A budget process can tone down competition. One way of doing that is through formula allocations. Formulas include simple across-the-board increases or decreases, where the same percentage increase is given to each department or program, and more elaborate distribution schemes that include measures of need, such as size, case loads, enrollment, or age of housing stock. Many grants from federal and state governments are based on formulas; recipients do not have to apply for them, and once the formula has been established, there is no competition between recipients. They get their money automatically. There may be intense competition between potential recipients as the formula is being designed, because some will lose and others will gain from the actual formula used, but once the formula is in place, competition is eliminated.

A second way of using the budget process to tone down competition is to limit the portion of the budget that departments and programs can compete for. If most of the budget is treated as fixed and only a small portion as potentially variable, the scope of competition is limited. Incremental budgeting, which is said to concentrate mainly on the difference between last year's actual budget and this year's proposed, is one way of limiting the scope of competition. Or, in the more extreme case, this year's budget is basically the same as last year's, and most new money is allocated in proportion to last year's allocation; only a tiny bit may be held out to respond to changing priorities or emergency demands. Target-based budgeting allows a bit more competition but still limits its scope. The budget office may assign each department only a large percentage of its last year's budget, but not the whole amount; the difference is set aside in a pool that all the departments have to compete for.

Another way of using the budget process to tone down competition is to provide a list in priority order of the programs that will be cut in case revenues are less than projected. In this situation, some programs are more at risk, but some are relatively less at risk; for the latter, the level of competition is markedly reduced. Some state governments use this kind of process. In a more extreme model, some programs are exempted completely from cuts. For example, Gramm-Rudman-Hollings, which revised the federal budget process, specified that if deficit reduction targets were not met, there would be across-the-board cuts in defense and domestic spending, but some programs would be completely exempt. The minicase of the Children's Amendment in San Francisco illustrates a related strategy of establishing a floor of funding below which a program cannot be cut.

Clearly, there are a variety of ways of eliminating or damping down competition, and the effort to reduce competition explains a substantial amount of the politics of expenditures. There are three things to keep in mind about the tendency to handle competition by reducing or eliminating it. First, not all agencies or programs feel the need to do it. If they are competing successfully, they may not try to reduce the level of competition. Second, for those who do try, the techniques chosen may vary substantially and have different implications for budgeting. The different techniques are not equally available to all budget actors. For example, to make a program an enterprise fund requires the ability to charge fees for service, fees large enough to cover or almost cover expenditures. To make a program an entitlement, especially a right-based entitlement, implies a public perception of the need for and worthiness of the program. Third, these techniques have varying degrees of reversibility. Even trust funds, which are almost inviolate, may end up sharing their funding with unrelated expenditures. There is a counterpressure to break down the rigidity and increase the amount of competition, and hence flexibility and responsiveness, in the budget.

For example, there have been major efforts in recent years by state and local governments to curtail unfunded mandates. After years of state efforts and legislation, the federal government finally passed antimandate legislation in 1995. It is not clear how effective this legislation is going to be, but both state and national legislators are clearly far more aware than in the past of how much burden they are shifting to other levels of government.[19]

MINICASE: STATES TRY TO CONTROL MANDATES

In the 1960s and 1970s, states increased the number of mandates they imposed on local governments. By 1981, there were an overwhelming number of state mandates and they were expanding rapidly in quantity, range, and scope.[20] As long as state aid more or less kept up with state mandates for increased or improved service delivery, stress was kept in limits, but during the 1970s, a deep recession hit the cities, the federal government began to cut back on aid, and the states began to reduce the rate of growth in their aid to cities. These trends combined with a new round of tax and expenditure limits during the 1970s to put real pressure on cities' finances. Cities' long and loud complaints about unfunded mandates pressured the states to curtail or control them.

States responded to the need to curtail unfunded mandates. For example, Rhode Island passed the Property Tax and Disclosure Act in 1979, responding simultaneously to the pressures to hold down taxes, help prevent deficits, and reduce unfunded mandates.[21] The most common state response was to add to proposed mandating legislation a fiscal note estimating the costs to local governments. By the end of 1979, twenty-five states had adopted some form of fiscal noting.[22] By 1991, the number had increased to twenty-eight.[23] The idea behind fiscal noting is that state policymakers, forced to calculate the costs they were imposing on local governments (by a note to the bill), might be more restrained in imposing unfunded mandates. The real costs of mandating, which had appeared to be free, would be clearer. In addition to fiscal notes, fourteen states adopted some form of reimbursement to local governments for mandated costs.

Neither fiscal noting nor reimbursement legislation has been completely successful in curtailing state mandates. The legislation is too easy to ignore and bypass, and estimates of costs are difficult to measure accurately, especially before legislation has passed. Florida's constitutional amendment to control unfunded mandating, a strong provision passed in 1990, is still relatively easy to evade by declaring an important state interest in the provision.[24] It has been difficult to track down the financial impact of many bills. In 1993, of forty-five laws passed that had mandates on cities and counties, the state ACIR was able to find estimates of impacts for six of them. The state also passed twenty-one laws with new or expanded revenue opportunities for cities and counties. The Florida ACIR was able to track estimates of impacts for seven of them.[25]

Regardless of the effectiveness of particular measures, it is clear that states are trying to improve relations with local governments, have increased their awareness of the impacts of unfunded mandates, and are changing the legislative process to include more consultation with local governments before regulatory actions are proposed.[26]

The Environment Can Affect Spending Priorities

The third characteristic of public budgeting is its openness to the environment. Spending strategies are framed not only by the budget process but also by the environment. A change in the environment can overwhelm all strategies, temporarily reducing the scope of activity of individual actors. Or it can create a situation in which policy mandates are clear and urgent.

The environment can change in a variety of ways. There can be tornadoes or floods, natural disasters of many sorts; there can be wars, cold or hot, and arms races; there can be elections and changes of policy resulting from the change in the composition of the elected officials; and there can be a change in popular opinion, elevating some benefit programs to rights and demoting others from rights to formula funded grants. These changes may occur once in a while or gradually over a long period of time. In addition, the environment continually affects the politics of spending because it influences the level of resources and rate of growth of revenues, and because it influences the certainty that revenues will appear.

One major change in the environment that affects budget strategies is the difference between relative abundance and continuing growth, on the one hand, and ragged stability or revenue decline, on the other. During growth, budget actors may argue for minimum staffing levels and high levels of specialization; during decline, they may work to undo minimum staffing levels and hire for flexibility. During decline, general skills, overlapping capacity, and redundancy may be more important. You can add new people or equipment during growth; during decline, the existing staff and equipment have to do more different kinds of jobs.

Even more important, the model of incremental growth, with a line-item budget, allocation of revenue increases by fair shares, and general suppression of conflict, is premised on moderate, gradual, but continuous growth. If growth is more rapid or if there is no growth, this pattern is likely to be disrupted. Rapid growth in revenues may lead to a burst of planning and search for new missions and programs; there may be an outreach to new potential interest groups or service beneficiaries; new needs may be documented and new programs designed. Outsiders might be involved in the budget process and in weighing alternative new programs—none of these things is supposed to occur when the margin for growth is small and divided up proportionately among existing actors.

A change in the environment from rich to lean may mean the elimination of the increase in revenues from last year to this that is the focus of the internal actors' bargaining in the incremental model of politics. The set of strategies associated with this model may become less relevant during decline. Budget processes are likely to become more centralized, making the competition between individual actors subordinate to the achievement of collective goals. If there is a need to cut back departments and programs, then each department's budget may be at some risk, vastly increasing the scope of competition. Agency heads are more likely to use defensive strategies, such as linking current programs to politically valued ends, distorting program goals to make them look like they are within an approved policy set, and trying to reduce competition and lock in current spending levels.

Even governments that are reasonably well off financially may not be able to count on their revenues—the environment may be unstable, or revenue sources unpredictable. At all levels of government, there may be reductions in the level of budget during the year if revenues were overestimated or if the economy declines unpredictably during the year. Uncertainty can be introduced for state and local governments by changes in tax laws at other levels of government. Taxpayer revolts may change the amount of revenue that can be collected, or redefine taxable wealth. As national economies are increasingly open to the world economy, changes in the price of oil or droughts in the former Soviet Union can have an impact on spending programs. If the price of fuel suddenly increases, then operating costs go up; if other countries purchase unforeseeably large amounts of grain, the cost of agricultural subsidies may suddenly go down.

When revenues become uncertain, spending behavior may change. Planning assumes long-term stability; with continual disruption and reallocation from project to project, planning makes little sense. The idea of being patient and giving up current programs or capital projects to someone else with the assurance that you will succeed in the future, vanishes. Being on top of the current list is all that counts. This pattern makes it difficult to save money for a large project or allocate one large project in one area one year and another large project somewhere else another year. Instead, the emphasis is likely to be on a number of smaller projects each year, even if none of them can solve real problems because they are too small. Also, one is not likely to break a larger project or program into parts, assuming that one part can be achieved this year, and another next year; the later parts may never arrive, and the project may remain incomplete and useless.

Uncertain revenues also affect spending by encouraging higher-level executives to hold back on the budget, allocating a little at a time so that there is uncommitted money to eliminate from the budget if cuts come suddenly. The result may be more money and fewer commitments. Requests for spending may pile up, awaiting release during the year, generating a continuing competition between agencies to get portions of their budgets released.

In short, changes in the environment provide an overriding consideration. They may directly impose policy mandates that cancel out other kinds of politics; thus a war, or warlike peace, may impose defense spending. Or they may simply make policy directions clearer, as in a major shift in the political party in power or a major shift in public opinion. Such a shift may be the result of urban uprisings in the ghetto, which supported increases in police spending, or the result of changes in the balance of trade, which may generate a variety of policies. Changes in the environment may alter the budget process and thereby alter appropriate budget strategies. Changes in revenue levels are likely to affect the politics of spending as well.

The Separation between Payer and Spender Requires Public Approval of Spending Choices

The fourth characteristic of public budgeting is the separation between those who pay taxes and those who make decisions about how those revenues will be spent. This separation introduces the concepts of accountability and acceptability. *Accountability* means transparency to the taxpayers about what budget decisions have been made; *acceptability* means that whatever decisions are made should not stir up too much public opposition. In some circumstances, accountability and acceptability go together; in others they are clashing opposites.

For example, if elected officials' spending decisions agree with the opinions of the majority of citizens, as when a service clearly benefits everyone, currently or in the future, then accountability and acceptability go together; the decision is acceptable and can be openly arrived at and be highly visible.

But if spending decisions favor only one small group and the majority of citizens would not approve the expenditures if given the choice, then accountability and acceptability may be opposites—to gain acceptability may mean obscuring or making less clear what the decisions were or how much they cost.

Spending decisions at some level have to gain public support, or at least acquiescence. That may mean providing services that nearly everyone wants, and no others; or it may mean trying to deliver programs to smaller or more targeted groups and either convincing the whole public to go along or offering other programs to the people who do not directly benefit from particular programs. When neither of these options seems to work, then supporters may represent the costs as low or free, and hence not important, or obscure the costs in a variety of ways so that they do not rouse too much opposition.

PROVIDING SERVICES NEARLY EVERYONE WANTS

Direct service delivery means using public employees or using tax money to hire someone to accomplish a public goal, such as providing road and street repair or snow plowing. Governmental services normally benefit many citizens at some point in their lives. Fires can occur in any neighborhood and can spread from one house to another, so almost everyone can perceive that he or she receives benefits from the fire department. Most people use public streets and are sensitive to their level of repair. Everyone benefits from an effective national defense and from inspection of meats for cleanliness. Because services generally benefit wide sections of the population, they are not particularly controversial, and expenditures for them need not be obscured. The services portion of the budget is the most open one. The costs are the clearest and most meaningful, the numbers typically are the most accurate, and the departments are the most accountable for what they are doing.

When they are threatened with cuts, budget actors often defend direct services by describing the negative consequences of reduction in services. For example, a director of public works may argue that it will take more time to clear the roads of snow if the council cuts his staffing levels. It is clear that the public wants this service to work well and speedily and that the council will get citizen complaints if this service is cut back. But agency heads have to pick services that are really popular, or decision makers are likely to say, "OK, go ahead and cut." In its extreme form, this strategy is called the Washington Monument ploy because, at one time, in response to threatened cuts, the National Park Service offered to cut staffing of the very popular national monument in Washington, D.C., forcing a closing of the monument or reduction in the hours it was available to visitors. Congress, knowing the public outcry that would have resulted, restored the cut.

Even with popular services, the Washington Monument ploy does not always work. It depends on a fairly decentralized budget process in which the departments and agencies have considerable power. In a more centralized process, the executive budget office will catch such ploys and simply force the agency to make cuts elsewhere. The particular service that is so popular will not get cut, but the agency's other, less popular programs remain vulnerable.

Given the nature of direct services, such as their general popularity and the relative openness with which they are treated because of their popularity, it is interesting to note that services are more often provided by state and local governments than by the federal government. The federal government provides defense services directly, and some regulatory services, such as inspections of meatpacking plants for cleanliness and places of work for employee safety. State governments often provide mental health services, some police and highway services, and higher education. Local governments typically provide police, fire, street repair, public schools, and water and sewer services.

Services like police and fire are characterized by broad distribution of benefits across groups and little geographic specificity. They tend to generate little public conflict and little specific interest-group support. When the services are targeted to particular groups or neighborhoods, or are allocated unevenly, more citizen and neighborhood group involvement may result. Thus, if a recreation department closes services in a particular neighborhood, or a branch library reduces its hours, or a fire station in a particular neighborhood is closed, then those benefiting specifically from those services may organize and protest. If street repair is neglected in some neighborhoods and carried out routinely in others, neighborhood activism may develop.

The general sense of approval that clings to direct service delivery also applies to some entitlement programs. After a long and painful depression in which many people lose their jobs and suffer downward mobility, there is likely to be a general awareness that unemployment and need can happen to good people, hardworking people, as well as the shiftless. Citizens can see welfare and food programs as available to all, and feel some security that the programs are there for them if they are needed. But after years of continuous high employment and increasing incomes, they may come to feel that they are succeeding because they deserve to succeed, that the economy has little to do with it, and that others are failing because of personal or moral flaws. They no longer see welfare as a safety net for everyone, but a dole or gift from the many hardworking to the few and lazy. The safety net may lose its general public support.

EXPENDITURES THAT DO NOT HELP EVERYONE

Not every program or service gives benefit to every taxpayer in even measure. Leaf pickup may benefit disproportionately the wealthy, who have large wooded lots on tree-lined streets; municipal airports may benefit the owners of private aircraft; various federal programs benefit middle-class students or underprivileged youngsters or owners of private boats. How do these programs get the approval they need?

Geographic Dispersion. One way is to spread out the benefits so that even a narrowly conceived program acquires a number of different beneficiaries. A program for repairing naval ships may be divided into ten parts, when location in a single city might make more sense; a program for helping cities recover from economic problems may be expanded to affect a larger number of cities in more states. The support base is expanded to get more geographically diversified backing for the program.

Positive Spillovers. Another approach is to convince people that there are positive spillovers, that is, people in general benefit from a program even if they do not use the service directly and never intend to. Public subsidies to mass transit are often justified in terms of positive spillovers. It is not just the transit riders who benefit from mass transit. The users of automobiles also benefit because if all riders on mass transit took their cars, there would be traffic jams of immense proportions, and the costs of road repairs would be much higher, a cost paid in part by automobile users through their gasoline taxes. Downtown businesses and mall owners also benefit from mass transit because buses and trains bring in customers during the day and increase the pool of available employees, increasing the quality and reducing the price for workers. Mass transit is more fuel efficient, slowing down the need for imported oil and the depletion of nonrenewable resources and keeping gas prices down for everyone. In addition, some elderly or handicapped people can become economically self-sufficient through the use of mass transit, reducing the public cost of supporting them.

Programs can be sold in terms of advertising their actual positive spillover effects or by exaggerating potential spillover effects. An example of an exaggerated positive spillover effect is the claim that local airports should be subsidized by general taxpayers because they aid economic development. The argument is that small airports, which directly serve only wealthy owners of private planes, contribute to economic development because businesses will not locate in the city unless it has an airport. Every taxpayer presumably benefits from economic development because there will be more taxpayers sharing the burden, and so taxes for each resident will presumably drop. The impact of the airport on economic development may never be measured or questioned. The supposed impact on economic development becomes a rationale for public support of a program with a narrow group of beneficiaries.

Balancing Benefits to a Variety of Groups. If a program benefits a particular group, and there are not clear positive spillovers to help rationalize public expenditures, then several other strategies may be employed. One is to see that everyone gets a little something from different programs. Thus there may be rent subsidies for the poor and low-cost loans for education to the middle class and a coast guard fleet to maintain the safety of pleasure boaters among the wealthy. There may be water subsidies to farmers in the Southwest and dairy subsidies to farmers in Wisconsin and New England. The interstate highway system that served primarily rural areas may be balanced by the public transit program that serves primarily urban areas.

In order to make this model work, not only must the key interests each get something but the benefits should be roughly even to each group or else those receiving less are likely to protest. For example, a recent program to provide long-term home health care for the elderly was defeated in the House, at least in part because the elderly had just been given an expensive new program to protect them from the costs of catastrophic illness. Critics of the proposed home health care measure argued that the elderly were being greedy, that they had just had a turn, and now other needy groups should get their turn.[27] Opposition to the home health care bill was framed in terms of intergenerational splits: The elderly were getting more benefits, while the young were actually losing theirs. Lobbyists for the elderly tried to redefine the situation and create the perception that care for the elderly helped the entire family (positive spillovers to everyone), not just the elderly. They argued that if family funds went to take care of the elderly, families would have less money to send young people to college.[28]

In the case of the elderly, less money for them does not automatically translate into more money for the young and middle classes; there is not an explicit agreement among supporters of these programs to balance the spending. Since the elderly have been so politically powerful, they have been able to get much of what they want without forming any coalitions. But among some competing interests, such informal agreements to balance expenditures may emerge.

One example involves urban and rural interests concerned with subsidies for agriculture. Agricultural subsidies have been both expensive and in some cases quite visible. The agriculture program was created during the depression of the 1930s when 25 percent of the population or more was on the farms and poor. Subsidies to agriculture were not considered payments to a small, undeserving minority; farmers were a substantial part of the population, and the extent of their need was widely known and accepted. Since then fewer and fewer people own farms; farming has become more productive; there are more big industrialized farms, and fewer poor family farmers. The logic of paying huge subsidies to so few large businesses has come under attack. The agriculture lobbies have had to work for continued legislative support.

The politics of farm support has a geographic bias, since rural states are more likely to benefit directly, and more urban states are likely to pay the bill in terms of higher food costs as well as higher tax bills. To offset this potential urban opposition to agricultural subsidies, advocates of agricultural subsidies have supported programs like food stamps, school lunch programs, and mass transit, which aid the poor and big cities.

When farm subsidies were being reconsidered by the budget committees in Congress in 1990, advocates of continued subsidies testified at the hearings. Charles Rose, chairman of the Agriculture Subcommittee on Tobacco and Peanuts, argued not very subtly that he expected loyalty from representatives of large northern cities who had received his votes before.

> Mr. Downey had a good time poking fun at wool and mohair and laughing about that and about the honey bee program. I would like for you and him to know that a lot of people I represent do not think subsidies for New York City and the Long Island Railroad and mass transportation up north are very funny, either, but we continue to vote for them and we continue to support them. . . .
>
> I remember when Eddie Koch [later mayor of New York City] was here and he led the whole Congress against the farm bill. I believe he even beat major farm legislation . . . and then he turned right around and said everybody has to sign on in the bailout of New York City. I wrote Eddie Koch a letter, and I said I believe that must be what you call "chutzpah," Mr. Koch. I think that you need to know that the problems of this country extend beyond the Hudson River and the Long Island Railway. Do not ask us who represent the farms of America to come to your aid when you take cheap shots at us in the farm bill.[29]

Dan Glickman, representative from Kansas and chair of the subcommittee on wheat, soybeans, and feed grains of the Agriculture Committee, made a similar argument that sounded just short of a threat. "I have supported food stamps, urban programs ... as have most of us.... I would hate to see a lot of programs jeopardized because of an attempt to drive a train through agriculture programs. That could happen. I am serious about that."[30]

In fact, as these farm state representatives suggested would happen, the tight linkage between farm supports and food to the poor appeared to have broken down by 1995. The Senate's version of the budget resolution for 1996 cut heavily into spending for school lunches, Women, Infants, and Children (WIC) food support, and food stamps. These programs represented the support for urban poor that farm state legislators had used to build their coalitions of support for farm spending.

Agriculture has not represented a single interest but a range of interests, from apple growers to dairy farmers, to sugar and peanut farmers. The interests of the different agricultural lobbies have sometimes been antagonistic, which has weakened their lobbying power. To compensate for these differing demands, representatives from farm states and agricultural supporters in Congress have tended to trade off support for different agricultural products, the same way they do on pet capital projects. As long as the amount of money to be allocated was allowed to increase, this arrangement stood, but the threatened reductions during the Reagan administration broke this coalition apart and increased competition between the lobby groups. "In 1981 budget pressures created such bitter conflicts among commodity groups involved in omnibus farm legislation that Congress came close to killing target prices—a major crop price support—and the federal tobacco and peanut programs. The legislation finally passed the House by a scant two-vote margin, with a significant number of farm state members voting against it."[31]

Making Program Costs Look Cheap. Pairing antagonistic interests is one way to broaden support for programs aimed at narrow groups. Such pairing is not always possible, however. Another technique for funding narrow interests is to make the costs small or even free. As long as the public does not feel that it is funding the costs, their objections to programs they do not benefit from should be limited. Three ways to make programs look cheap or free are grants, loans, and insurance programs.

Grants are transfers of money from one level of government to another or from a governmental unit to an outside agency to accomplish some particular program goal. The national government often awards grants to the states and sometimes directly to local governments as incentives for compliance with national policies. States may pass on federal grants to their local governments, and add some further aid.

Grants may seem free to the state and local governments that receive them. To the extent that money comes from another level of government to accomplish some purpose, the provision of that desired good or service by local governments may be noncontroversial. If the local government has to put up some of its own money in order to get the grant, however, applying for or accepting the grant may be much more controversial.

In the case of DeKalb, Illinois, and its response to revenue sharing, described in chapter 1, as long as services for the elderly and poor were provided from federal revenue sharing, and not from local taxes, there was little opposition to the program. When there was a question of paying for the social services with local taxation, a brouhaha ensued, and comparisons were made between basic services, economic development, and social services. Once the programs were paid for from local money, they had to compete with other programs, especially programs targeted to larger groups or the whole community. The support for the social services survived the transition, but at a lower level of funding. The reduced costs lowered the level of controversy.

Grants sometimes require a local match of money. One level of government offers a grant to another level of government, with the requirement that the recipient also put up some money. Every 75 cents of federal money may require 25 cents of local match. The local match may be in dollars or in labor or even from other grants. When the local match can be taken out of nontax revenues, it may seem like magic, and the project may seem free or nearly free. Such projects are likely to go to the top of the priority list, even if the beneficiaries are a narrow group. If the city has to put in some of its own money, or an increasing portion of its own revenues over a period of time, more thought may go into the priority of the project. Still, a project with a state or federal match is cheaper to undertake than one without any grant support, and hence there may be a bias in its favor even if everyone does not clearly benefit.

Government loan programs often charge less than market rates for interest. Below-market rates for interest on loans is often the least visible form of subsidy. The difference between the government rate and the market rate is the rate of the subsidy. Typically, no one has bothered to calculate what it would have cost a farmer or a student to borrow without the government loan; hence the degree of subsidy is often not recorded or known. Since the government should get its money back plus interest to keep the loan pool going and cover defaults, it has been difficult to perceive these subsidies as expenditures.

Direct loans from the federal government have been primarily for agriculture and secondarily for foreign aid, aid to companies to help boost exports, housing and urban development, and small business assistance. Some of this aid is targeted to specific companies, such as the Boeing and

Westinghouse corporations. Approximately two-thirds of the lending activity of the Export-Import Bank in 1981 benefited seven large commercial exporters.[32]

Sometimes the costs of a loan program exceed what has been set aside to cover costs, and the capital for loans is depleted. Sometimes the loans are forgiven, or perhaps it was never intended that they be repaid. In one agricultural program, farmers deposited their grains in special storage facilities and then could borrow from the government (usually at subsidized rates) up to the agreed value of the crop. If the farmer could not get that price for his crop, he did not have to pay back the loan; the government got the crop instead, which was not worth the loan amount. While loans may appear "free," they may actually cost a substantial amount of money.

Loan guarantees are a form of insurance. When loans are considered too risky by commercial bankers, but the demand for loans seems to reflect larger social problems, the government may guarantee the loan, that is, agree to cover the debt if the borrower is unable to pay it back. From the bank's perspective, the loans are almost risk free. If the loan is guaranteed, the borrower can pay less interest, since interest is to some extent proportional to risk. Such loan guarantees are a form of subsidy to the borrower, who pays less than market price for interest, and to the lenders, who gain interest with virtually no risk.

The cost to government agencies of loan guarantees is typically low, since costs occur only if the borrower fails to pay back the loan. For most of its life, the guarantee is an obligation, but not an expenditure. It is difficult to estimate outlays for guarantees in advance, but if and when they come due, they must be paid. Such obligations are called contingent liabilities. Since the government only gets involved when there is high risk, the costs are not totally negligible. There was $588 billion in outstanding federal loan guarantees in 1989,[33] and some unknown proportion of that contingent liability will turn into expenditures.

Many loan guarantee programs involve particular narrow groups. Some are for college students, some are for private businesses developing alternative fuels, some are for farmers, and some are for housing. Major loan guarantees have been issued to specific businesses that were in financial trouble, such as Lockheed and Chrysler, and to industries, such as steel. Despite the targeted nature of the guarantees, with the exception of the Chrysler guarantees, these programs generated little public opposition, since they seem virtually free. In recent years, however, the high costs of defaults in the Higher Education Loan Guarantee program made that program politically vulnerable. When the costs become more apparent, opposition to the program increases.

In addition to grants, loans, and loan guarantees, government provides some forms of insurance. Because insurance is based on the collection of premiums from those who buy the insurance, it should cost taxpayers little money. The government offers insurance at times when there seems to be a national need or when private insurers find the risk too great. The federal government often charges much less than the actual risk might warrant. The federal government offers insurance to farmers, in case weather conditions wipe out a crop. The program goal is to prevent farmers from going out of business and hence to ensure a continuing supply of food without extremes of price fluctuations. The national government also provides flood insurance that commercial dealers do not handle. Another insurance program that is both national and state is the unemployment insurance program.

Federal medical insurance programs—Medicare, Medicaid, and disability insurance—have generated controversy in part because they turned out to be very expensive and hence very visible, threatening deficits in the trust funds. The possibility of subsidizing these insurance programs with general revenue has been controversial. A second controversy has concerned social security. As the number of elderly on social security increases, the problem of younger people being disproportionately burdened to pay for the elderly increases, creating a tension between age groups. As with any user-fee-funded expenditures, beneficiaries are concerned about whether their benefits are proportional to their expenditures and whether they are unwillingly subsidizing someone else. Third, the nonvoluntary aspect of some of the insurance programs has roused some opposition, especially from people who feel that they could do better for themselves with private investments, and will never need the public insurance.

Insurance programs became visible and controversial when the federal government discovered that it had to pay out large sums on insured accounts for failed savings and loans. Other programs that look low in cost, such as loans and loan guarantees, may also turn out to be expensive. When the costs become apparent and burdensome, the political dynamics change.

MINICASE: FEDERAL CREDIT REFORM

At the federal level, loans, loan guarantees, and insurance grew enormously from 1970 to 1989, at least in part because they seemed cheap or free. Total credit and insurance outstanding was $861 billion in 1970; that figure had increased to $5.7 trillion by 1989 (see table 5.1). This amount represents total exposure; only a small portion of the amount is likely to be translated into actual governmental outlays. Nevertheless, recent experience with rising rates of default on student loans, massive expenditures for failed savings and loans, and scary experiences with government-sponsored enterprises such as

TABLE 5.1

FEDERAL CREDIT AND INSURANCE OUTSTANDING

(IN BILLIONS)

Program	1970	1975	1980	1985	1989	Percentage increase 1970–89
Direct loans	$ 51	$ 74	$ 164	$ 257	$ 207	306
Guarantees	125	189	299	410	588	370
GSE^a loans	24	49	151	370	763	3096
Deposit insurance	445	837	1465	2227	2927	558
Other insurance	216	187	831	1021	1286	495
Total	$861	$1337	$2909	$4285	$5771	570

SOURCE: *Budget of the United States Government, FY 1991*, 229.
a. Government Sponsored Enterprises.

the Federal Housing Administration convinced many officials that the contingent liabilities were real and needed to be controlled. In 1982, loan defaults and writeoffs were $3.7 billion; by 1989, the figure had increased to $14.4 billion. These numbers, although sobering, were dwarfed by the savings-and-loan crisis. According to the 1991 budget, insurance losses in 1989 were $67.2 billion, 96 percent of which was for 400 insolvent savings and loans. In 1982, insurance losses had been only $4.6 billion. The Congressional Budget Office, writing in early 1991, estimated that outlays for insurance losses for 1989–96 would total $155 billion, more than three times the amount estimated in 1989 legislation.[34] Continual upward revisions of costs contributed to the impression that matters were out of control.

These numbers created widespread pressure in Washington for credit reform. Congressman Charles Schumer summarized the case for credit reform:

> Too many of our credit programs have spun out of control. Our perverse budgetary accounting procedures have led us to dish out credit as if it were cost free. As a result of this painless overindulgence, we have placed ourselves at the brink of financial disaster. If we don't apply the brakes now, we will speed off a trillion dollar cliff.[35]

Schumer explained that the cash-flow accounting of the federal budget obscured the true costs of lending and insurance programs. Loan guarantees and insurance involved no immediate cash outlays, and because guarantee fees and insurance premiums are recorded as income, new loan guarantees and expanded deposit insurance coverage appeared to reduce the deficit in the short run. When direct loans slowed down, loan guarantees actually increased after the passage of Gramm-Rudman-Hollings. Schumer argued that there should be some reported costs at the time the loan and guarantee programs are approved so that Congress would be more aware of what it was doing and make better decisions.

The hearings on credit reform reveal the concerns and intent of the backers of the reform. Congressman Bill Gradison argued that failure to control the credit programs resulted in spending that absorbed limited funds for other activities and reduced capacity to expand social service expenditures. And Congressman Schumer argued that the separate ceiling on credit should be eliminated, and credit included in one massive ceiling, so that tradeoffs between grants, loans, guarantees, and direct expenditures could be made.[36] Without their agreeing explicitly to it, their priorities had been reordered by massive obligatory spending, and what might be a loan or insurance program of lesser importance was driving out what might be more important expenditures made through grants, entitlements, or direct services. Part of the goal of credit reform was to enable Congress to recover its capacity to define priorities.

In the fall of 1990, Congress included credit reform in the Omnibus Reconciliation. One feature of the reform is that the cost to the government of the loan or guarantee over its life is to be estimated, appropriated, and included in the spending ceilings required by the Budget Enforcement Act of 1990. The older notion of a separate spending ceiling for credit was dropped. These changes make the real costs of loans and guarantees clear at the time of approval and treat loans and guarantees like any other expenditures, allowing for both comparability and tradeoffs. The reform was limited in its scope. It omitted several key programs and did not address the issue of insurance, but it effectively eliminated the perverse incentives that resulted from Gramm-Rudman-Hollings and the cash accounting system.

HAS CREDIT REFORM BEEN EFFECTIVE?

Credit reform was to be implemented beginning in 1991. To evaluate how effective it has been requires the answers to several questions. First, how well have the federal agencies that provide credit complied with the law? Second, how well has the law succeeded enabling Congress to make tradeoffs and choices between direct loans and loan guarantees? Third, what have been the incentives built into the new scoring system? Has scoring under credit reform led to a new kind of gaming and overestimates of future savings or underestimates of costs? Has credit reform led to a more realistic evaluation of costs of guaranteed and direct loans?

How well have agencies complied with credit reform? Initially, not well, not because they were unwilling to comply but because they had inadequate historical data on which to estimate what their loss rates were likely to be over the life of loans and inadequate staff and skills to redo the books for prior years' loans in order to get more adequate figures.[37] It will take time to redo the accounting systems of those agencies with large loan portfolios to get accurate numbers. As of 1995, four years after the beginning of the credit reform requirements, major lenders, including the FHA, the Export-Import Bank, and Veteran's Affairs credit programs, still had not complied with the requirements of credit reform.[38]

Despite some compliance problems, comparability between credit and noncredit programs has increased, and legislators have actually made some tradeoffs between the credit budget and the noncredit budget. Tradeoffs are required under the Budget Enforcement Act's spending caps; if one program is to be increased, another has to be cut to pay for it. Congress increased the enforcement provisions of the Student Guaranteed Loans to reduce the number of loan defaults, decreasing the long-term costs to the government. Congress then used the estimated savings from this loan guarantee program to extend unemployment benefits for people who had been out of work a long time. The action generated some controversy, since how much money would be saved through the new procedures for collecting loan repayments was not known with certainty.[39] Nevertheless, a real tradeoff did occur as intended by the supporters of credit reform.

Part of the intent of the legislation was to be able to compare credit and noncredit programs, but the legislation also made it more feasible to compare credit programs. President Clinton supported a program, passed by Congress, in which a federal agency would offer student loans to supplement the bank-administered student loan guarantee program. The direct service was estimated under credit reform to be cheaper. The new Republican-dominated Congress elected in 1994 opposed any expansion of direct federal services and argued that under credit reform administrative costs were excluded from the subsidy costs, making direct federal delivery look more cost effective than it was. Their goal was to return this program to the banks, for whom the program was profitable. The result was an imbroglio over how to count administrative costs and how to evaluate which program delivery mechanism was really more cost effective. While the issue may have been motivated by an attempt to increase the profits of bankers, the argument took place in the context of figuring out how to compare costs of two different service delivery vehicles.[40] That this debate took place in this way should probably be scored as a plus for credit reform.

As for the incentives built into credit reform and how Congress is responding to them, it is too early to tell, but one incident is suggestive. In 1993 Congress proposed and the president signed a reduction in the subsidy cost of loans guaranteed in the Small Business Administration. This reduction was achieved by reducing the proportion of large loans that the federal government guaranteed from 85 percent to 75 percent. "In the summer of 1993, legislation from our committee was enacted and signed by President Clinton, reducing the subsidy cost of 7(a) loans from 5.4 percent to 2.2 percent and more than doubling the 7(a) program level with the same amount of appropriated dollars."[41] In 1995, legislation was passed to reduce further SBA subsidy costs. As the chairman of the Small Business Committee described the proposal, which further reduced the guaranteed portion of loans and increased the loan guarantee fee, in 1996 only $133 million needs to be approved to support $10.5 billion in loans, a reduction of 39 percent with a 35 percent increase in loan volume.[42]

Under credit reform, by reducing the proportion of each loan that the government guaranteed, Congress would have to appropriate less money to cover likely losses. Congress took some of the freed-up money for new loan guarantees. Banks were probably going to make the loans anyhow, whether 85 percent or 75 percent of the loan was guaranteed. As long as loan guarantees were considered free, as in pre-credit-reform days, such a tradeoff between percentage of each loan guaranteed and total dollar amount of all loans guaranteed would not have been made. There would have been no motivation to do so.

What do the numbers say about tradeoffs between direct loans and loan guarantees? First let us look at the volume of credit by category before and after credit reform.

The figures in table 5.2 suggest a number of conclusions. The level of direct loans outstanding went down, and the level of guarantees went up, and then the numbers stabilized, neither one increasing very much. The awareness that new loans and new loan guarantees cost money that has to come out of some other expense seems to have frozen both of them after credit reform. Equally important, the amount of GSE loans continued to grow; these continue even after credit reform to appear free and do not impinge on the rest of the budget. Insurance levels drop.

When one looks not at the size of lending and insurance programs but the costs of this activity in federal government expenditures after credit reform, these figures, too, were generally coming down (see table 5.3). These trends were harder to see because many agencies were still struggling with estimated future costs of the programs, and as the numbers improved, the estimates of future losses increased. Subsidy costs also increased without additional legislation, when interest rates in the market increased above the maximum allowed on the government loans. The declining estimates of subsidy costs for direct loans suggest that credit reform, as clumsy and difficult as it has been to get up and running, may be helping make Congress more aware of the costs of these programs. A new, more conservative Congress is also campaigning against a direct role for government in areas where banks could make a profit, so it is not clear how much of the credit belongs to credit reform.

TABLE 5.2

FEDERAL CREDIT AND INSURANCE OUTSTANDING, BEFORE
AND AFTER CREDIT REFORM MAJOR PROGRAMS
(IN BILLIONS)

Program	Year		
	1989	*1993*	*1994*
Direct loans	$ 207	$ 151	$ 155
Guarantees	588	693	699
GSE loans	763	1,255	1,502
Deposit insurance	2,927	2,833	2,829
Other insurance	1,286	511	484
Total	$5,771	$7,115	$7,342

SOURCES: *Budget of the United States Government, FY 1991, and 1996.*

Obscuring Costs. While there are a variety of ways of getting public support for spending programs that do not benefit large groups of taxpayers, sometimes, perhaps only occasionally, decision makers go ahead and spend money on something that the taxpayers would probably disapprove of if they knew about it or understood its impact. At the least, the expenditures would rouse controversy. On these occasions, the costs of programs may be intentionally distorted downward or even hidden. The intention of budget actors to obscure costs is difficult to prove, but the level of invisibility is clearer. Unpopular costs may be hidden in the budget; subsidies may be virtually invisible; expenditures may be made with relatively hard to trace money; and costs may be systematically underestimated.

For example, if a particular project is likely to arouse controversy, or even has been forbidden by the legislature or by higher levels of government, administrators may shift the costs of the program into other programs or simply not break out costs in a way that shows how the money was spent.

TABLE 5.3
ESTIMATED SUBSIDY OUTLAY COSTS OF FEDERAL CREDIT,
1995, 1996, AND ESTIMATES FOR 1995–2000
(IN BILLIONS OF DOLLARS)

Program	1995	1996	1995–2000
Direct loans			
Farm Service Agency (w/o CCC)			
Rural Development and Rural Housing	18–24	15–21	3–5
Rural Electrification Administration and			
Rural Telephone Bank	3–5	2–4	1–4
Federal Direct Student Loan Program	7–10	11–15	6–7
Export-Import Bank	3–5	3–5	0–1
Agency for International Development	5–7	0–1	0–1
Public Law 480	7–9	2–3	1–2
Foreign Military Financing	0–2	0–1	0–1
Small Business	2–3	2–3	0–2
Other direct loans	2–4	2–4	0–1
Total direct loans	47–69	37–57	11–24
Guaranteed loans			
FHA Single-Family	(18)–0	(13)–0	(10)–0
VA Mortgage	3–6	4–6	2–3
FHA Multifamily	4–6	5–6	0–1
Federal Family Education Loan Program	8–11	13–23	17–18
Small Business	2–4	4–5	1–3
Farm Service Agency/Rural Housing	1–4	1–2	0–1
Export-Import Bank	4–5	6–8	2–3
CCC Export Credits	4–5	4–5	2–3
Other guaranteed loans	1–3	2–3	2–3
Total guaranteed loans	9–44	26–58	16–35

SOURCE: *Budget of the United States Government, FY 1996.*

The Illinois Board of Higher Education forbade all but one of the state's universities from doing research at public expense. To appear to comply with the state board, administrators at one of the universities not approved for research buried the costs of doing research. The library budget was presented, but the costs to the library of serving faculty and students doing research was not broken out; the cost of faculty salaries was reported, but the extra expense of hiring a research (as opposed to a teaching) faculty was not described. Travel lines were reported, but the amount of travel related to research (as opposed to teaching or administration) was not summarized.

Some forms of subsidy are difficult to see and estimate. For example, some public enterprises sell their services at differential rates, charging some groups less and others more. The cost of the subsidy to those paying less may be completely invisible. Sometimes price reductions to large users are justified as based on economies of scale, that is, it is cheaper per unit to produce and deliver large amounts to a single address. But the size of the economies of scale may never be calculated or documented, so any amount of reduction may be "justified" in this way. One would have to know the real costs of producing and delivering the service in order to compute the level of subsidy, an impossible task without the enterprise's cooperation. In these cases, where a service is provided at less than the cost to produce it, an expensive and almost invisible subsidy is being provided to narrow groups of beneficiaries.

Most public enterprises do not break even and are subsidized by general taxation. Sometimes these subsidies are clearly labeled in the budget, but sometimes they are not. The postal service, for example, is subsidized by tax dollars, to keep rates low. Postal subsidies to newspapers and news magazines are direct and widely known, but postal service personnel costs have been subsidized in a less visible way. The postal service has paid two-thirds of the pension and health benefits of employees, while the U.S. Treasury has paid the rest. The subsidy in 1984 was $.8 billion, and was projected to increase to $4.4 billion by 1989.[43] By the end of 1987, however, the level of subsidy was reduced.

The subsidies may be intentionally secret if the level of subsidy is politically controversial. Subsidies at the local level may involve unrepaid (possibly unrecorded) interfund transfers or transfers in kind. A city government may provide an enterprise with free space or subsidized rent; the true market value and hence the amount of the subsidy is not calculated. "Free" snow plowing of the municipal airport or "free" engineering services are additional examples. People who want to increase the political acceptability of an airport enterprise by making it look cheap (if it pays for itself, how can anyone object?) may try to hide subsidies or minimize their amounts.

When subsidies to public enterprises are not hidden, they may be highly controversial. Not all subsidized enterprises benefit the poor or handicapped; some benefit farmers (with subsidized electricity) or rural residents (with subsidized train services)[44] or other particular target groups. What makes subsidies so controversial is that ultimately all taxpayers, most of whom do not benefit from the service, are paying to reduce the cost of selected services for others. In the case of airports, it is often the owners of private airplanes whose costs are being subsidized, a group that is certainly not poor.

Another kind of subsidy that can be difficult to see and count is a reduction in competition that allows businesses to charge higher prices. Farmers may receive such indirect subsidies to keep competition low.[45] The actual mechanism of delivering the subsidies has varied enormously over the years. One approach has been to limit the amount of land planted to certain crops, to reduce the total yield and thereby improve prices. Another regulatory approach has been to limit foreign imports of some crops so that U.S. farmers will not have to compete with less expensive crops from abroad. U.S. consumers pay for these market interventions when they pay routinely higher prices for their food. Taxpayers directly bear the costs of paying farmers for not planting certain crops; they indirectly pay for the subsidy in higher food prices at the supermarket.

Another example of a subsidy that is difficult to estimate is called a land writedown. Its intent is to be an economic development tool, to help attract new businesses to an area and hence generate local jobs. The city or other jurisdiction acquires land, possibly through its legal right of eminent domain, which allows it to purchase land against the owners' will for a public purpose, presumably at a fair market price. Since a private developer would have to deal with holdouts—those who refuse to sell, and those who pretend to refuse to sell to bid up the price—the government's action in putting together a large plot of land for development is a benefit to the private sector. The land may then be sold to the developer for considerably less than the parcel would now go for on the market. The difference between the worth of the land and the cost of the sale to the developer is called a writedown. The amount of the writedown may never be calculated, because it depends on estimates of the current value of the land for its intended use. How much money state and local governments spend on such incentives is difficult, if not impossible, to ascertain.

Land writedowns are an example of using almost invisible money to make an expenditure for a single company that might otherwise arouse controversy. The expenditure is rationalized in terms of positive spillovers, that is, the resulting economic development. But the amount of future development and the distribution of benefits from that development are highly uncertain. The company may not hire many local residents; or it may take the subsidies, make profits for a few years, and then leave the city and the state. Current costs should be weighed against potential future gains. If the costs of the development are high and visible, and there are many competing projects, some of which may have more certain return, such subsidies may generate much discussion and possibly opposition. Businesses already located in the city are likely to wonder why the city spends so much on a company that has yet returned nothing to the city, while they pay their taxes, generate jobs, and get nothing back from the city. Homeowners may question why they pay taxes that go for single companies to lower their costs when there are a variety of needs in the city, such as street, water system, and sewer improvements.

Using invisible or nearly invisible money can head off controversy. Another example is the use of pensions to increase the total compensation package for public employees. Little public information is distributed about how pension funds are run. While perhaps not intentionally hidden, they tend to be secret on a secret-open continuum. Their relatively secret nature combined with the fact that they generally involve future rather than current expenses make them ideal salary incentives in governments where salary increases to local employees would be looked at askance by taxpayers. For example, mayors can give raises to employees through pension funds while seeming in public to be holding the line on salaries, being tough with employee demands and easy on the taxpayers' pocketbooks. Labor is kept content, presumably avoiding embarrassing strikes. The cost of this strategy is ballooning future obligations. Although later officials will be stuck with the tab, current politicians will be long gone by the time the consequences are felt.

The practice of spreading costs over time and putting fewer costs in the present and more as the years go by is called the "nose in the tent" technique and has applications to many kinds of program and project spending. The idea is that when you see a camel's nose in your tent, there is probably a camel behind it, coming in. By only showing the nose, that is, by making the project appear less expensive in its first year or two, opposition to the program may be moderated. One way of doing this is to propose the beginning of a new program in the middle or toward the end of a budget year, so the first "year's" expense is really only for a few months. This tactic seems a bit transparent, as camels' noses are usually followed by camels, but it may in fact be difficult to estimate the future costs of current projects. It is not so much that political decision makers are unlikely to realize that there will be future costs as that future costs have much less political impact than current ones. The public, on the other hand, may be stuck with a program that is much more expensive than any they envisioned, and that they might have objected to if they had understood the real costs over time.

Perhaps the epitome of intentional secrecy in budgeting is the Defense Department's "black budget," the portion of defense spending that has been classified and is not subject to public discussion or debate. It includes most of the Central Intelligence Agency and all of the National Security Agency and the National Reconnaissance Office. It pays for secret wars and secret police, at the discretion of the president. While there are undoubtedly some legitimate national secrets in the black budget, during the 1980s it expanded to include controversial weapons systems, and by extension, the policies that drive their invention and intended deployment. None of these policies may be discussed, and some of the projects cannot even be named in public. By 1989, the black budget peaked at about $36 billion a year. The declassification of the Stealth bomber and MILSTAR, a complex computerized communication and coordination project to run a nuclear war, brought the black budget down to $34 billion by 1991.[46]

From 1981, at the very beginning of the Reagan administration, to 1985, the Pentagon budget doubled, but the secret portion for weapons increased eightfold.[47] During that period, there was no outside scrutiny of secret spending, not by the General Accounting Office and not by the Pentagon's own auditors.

After the GAO was allowed in, it discovered that the air force and navy refused to tell "their civilian overseers about new black programs they … created."[48] The military had created hundreds of unauthorized programs during the 1980s. The lack of oversight suggested not only that civilians had lost control of the military but also that the quality of management might be worse in the secret portion of the defense budget than it was in the overt part. Secrecy made it possible to hide mistakes and made economizing unnecessary.

Congress began to try to take control of the black budget in 1986. Procurement horror stories in the regular Defense Department budget roused Congress and made many wonder about the waste that might be occurring out of sight. Congressman John Dingell, who chaired the Subcommittee on Oversight and Investigations of the House Committee on Energy and Commerce, spearheaded the effort; also important was Les Aspin, who took over the House Armed Services Committee and was the first chair in many years who was willing to question what the generals asked for. Dingell asked the secretary of defense for a list of air force black programs over $10 million; the secretary ignored the request. Then Les Aspin and the ranking minority member of the House Armed Services Committee, writing for the committee, argued with the secretary that too many defense programs were being put into the black budget and that the budget numbers for the Stealth bomber and the advanced Cruise missile should be released. The secretary did not release the figures. In the face of this intransigiency, Congress passed a law the following year, requiring the Defense Department to reveal the information. The information was not revealed until 1989, by which time much of the weapons research had been completed.[49] In 1992 the secret satellite program was made visible; its budget was about $6 billion.[50] Though technically still part of the secret budget, the satellite program has been opened to financial oversight. That oversight further erodes the sanctity of the black budget. By 1995, newspapers were estimating the size of the black budget at about $28 billion.[51]

MINICASE: THE IMPACT OF BEING IN A SECRET BUDGET

The spy satellite program, in the National Reconnaissance Office, was made public in 1992 after operating for more than thirty years as a supersecret agency. While it was secret, the satellite program got into the habit of ignoring the bottom line. In some cases, spending estimates for the expensive satellites were too low by about half, but Congress approved the overruns "because the technology was essential for monitoring the Soviets."[52] With the collapse of the Soviet Union, the agency's rationale disappeared, and with it, its cloak of secrecy. Pressure to make the agency public was intertwined with the need to make budget cuts. The agency's mission was scrutinized and its budget deeply cut.

After the agency went public, the level of scrutiny of its budget increased, calling attention to a series of peculiar financial maneuvers. The agency had developed a certain laxness about budgetary responsiveness and accountability. In 1993 the agency had signed a multi-billion dollar contract for ocean surveillance satellites, in direct contradiction to congressional instructions. Then the agency built a $347 million building for itself, without telling Congress that it was doing so, drawing from accounts that were not labeled for construction. In 1995 financial overseers discovered that the agency had built up a contingency fund of $1.5 billion, a substantial proportion of its total budget, ignoring congressional directives to reduce the size of the fund. Reportedly the contingency fund began because the agency did not want to compromise its secrecy by asking Congress for supplemental appropriations to keep production lines going. The fund was allowed to grow from year to year, however. Congress cut back the discretionary fund in 1995 when it discovered the size to which the fund had grown.[53]

Congress has not yet developed general controls over the black budget, but after a period of expansion in the 1980s, the size of the secret budget has begun to come down. The collapse of the Soviet Union has taken away a major excuse for secrecy at the same time that efforts to control the deficit have made it imperative to control agency spending and eliminate waste. Especially when agencies flout congressional will, they may lose their secret status and some of their discretion. The Department of Defense may actually find this loss of secrecy advantageous because it both allows and requires the department to gain public and congressional support for weapons and surveillance programs earlier in their development instead of presenting such programs as done deals later on. At the least, greater openness allows the Defense Department to demonstrate managerial improvements and reduced waste in procurement; at best, greater openness suggests that the Defense Department, and especially its spy agencies, is controllable by elected officials.

Summary and Conclusions

In the public sector, because of the wide variety of budget actors and the variety of their preferences, the amount of competition underlying the budget is necessarily high. The chief executive and his or her staff, the department heads, and legislators and their staffs all play a role in formulating or approving proposals for expenditures. A variety of interest groups may lobby for particular expenditures, and the public at large may have marked preferences about what government should and should not spend money on. The level of competition may be exaggerated or reduced by changes in the environment and in the budget process. The budget process frames choices and hence determines what expenditure proposals compete with one another.

When programs or departments are forced to compete with one another for resources, they develop a variety of strategies to improve the priority of their spending goals. In the capital budget, project supporters may argue that the technical requirements for some project absolutely require this expense immediately; or they may argue that delay will only cost more. In the operating budget program supporters may argue the political consequences of failure to provide a popular service, or they may try to link their programs to widely accepted policy goals.

Competition in some parts of the budget and under some budget processes may be so keen that the actors, rather than try to compete successfully, switch to strategies to reduce the level of conflict. They do this in a variety of ways. In the capital budget, competition can be defused through the use of a long-term plan; projects not funded this year can be kept alive and possibly funded later. There are winners, but no absolute losers. In the service portion of the budget, competition may be defused by norms forbidding sudden termination or deep cutbacks in one program to build another. Change occurs in small amounts at the margins, limiting the scope of competition. In trust funds and enterprises, competition is defused by taking revenues and expenditures out of the general fund, isolating them from potential tradeoffs. For some program expenditures, competition is defused by setting them up as entitlements, distributing funds by formula, or by imposing particular expenditures by mandates. One cannot understand these adaptations and the direction of change without appreciating the intensity of competition that underlies them.

The direction of change over the past fifty years has been to lock up more and more of the budget, to take out programs and projects from the competitive parts of the budget. There has been an increase in the use of trust funds and, even more dramatically at the national level, in the use of entitlements. At the local level, services that charged fees have been increasingly segregated from the municipal budget, and in some states have been set up as special, single-purpose governmental units. Contractors may push for long-term sole-source contracts, to lock in particular spending for capital projects; coalitions of interest groups, legislators, and bureaucrats may, when the environment favors them, push to lock their programs into the budget for as long a period as they can manage.

The result of the changing composition of the budget is that budgets may now look more interest-group dominated, and it may be difficult to perceive competition over the short term. But trying to lock in expenditures at the peak of one's power is part of budgetary politics; if anything, it underscores the waxing and waning of interest-group influence and the responsiveness of expenditures to outside contingencies. Coalitions of support for a particular program may peak at some point, and at that point supporters try to lock in their programs through a trust fund structure or an entitlement. The coalition may not be able to stay together after that, or the environmental conditions that made their program seem desirable may disappear. If they were successful in locking in their program or project, their programs will survive future changes in environmental conditions.

The process of locking up expenditure decisions and reducing budgetary competition is not permanent and one-directional. There are major pressures in the opposite direction, to reduce or weaken entitlements, to borrow from public enterprises or use their revenues for other purposes, to use trust funds for other purposes or use general funds to pay for programs funded by trust funds. But the time frame for unlocking expenditures may be relatively long. Politicians find it extremely difficult to terminate entitlements that are popular with a broad segment of the public. If, over a long period of time, that support erodes, politicians may be able to change programs from entitlements to block grants, making them easier to cut. It took many years and a massive reduction in the number of family farms before cuts in the agriculture support programs became acceptable. Efforts to break into trust funds may take years, but have sometimes been successful, as in the Highway Trust Fund.

MINICASE: THE HIGHWAY TRUST FUND

Congress created the Highway Trust Fund in 1956, relying on user fees from gasoline taxes to fund highway construction and later highway repair. The purpose of the trust fund from the point of view of highway supporters was to insulate the highway lobby from budgetary competition.

That the congressional motivation in creating the Highway Trust Fund was to protect highway spending from competition was immediately apparent. The House Committee on Ways and Means stated when it set up the trust fund that "the existence of this Fund will insure that receipts from the taxes levied to finance this program will not be diverted to other purposes."[54] That motivation was even clearer when, years later, President Ford proposed to return much of the trust fund revenues to the general fund and turn another portion back to the states to spend as they wished. Representative Robert Edgar of Pennsylvania, from the Public Works Committee, declared, "I am concerned about protecting a transportation trust fund so that we do not have to compete with the B-1 Bombers for highway and mass transit moneys...."[55]

For many years, efforts by the general fund to raid the trust fund failed. The Ford administration, for example, proposed returning some of the money to the general fund and returning one cent of the tax to the states to spend as they wished. Supporters of the trust fund fought back this effort. More recently, mass transit managed to get defined as an eligible expenditure from the Highway Trust Fund, but this incursion was beaten back by setting up mass transit with its own trust fund. Finally, however, in 1990, the general fund managed to earmark a portion of new gas tax revenues for deficit reduction. While this change did not reduce trust fund revenues, it did create the notion that not all gas tax revenues belonged automatically to the Highway Trust Fund.

Handling competition is one key theme in the politics of expenditures; the second one is managing accountability and acceptability to the taxpaying public. The budget choices do not depend only on what the budget actors want and can get from one another; they are constrained by the preferences of the public that pays the taxes. Accountability and acceptability are handled differently depending on how popular particular expenditures are, and what techniques are used to gain support for less popular programs.

The delivery of services that benefit citizens broadly is generally publicly acceptable, and the costs are open and clear. In situations in which the benefits are targeted at a narrower group, and costs can be pinpointed, program supporters may offer their support to other groups to help them get their programs, in order to widen the support base. Thus supporters of agricultural subsidies to rural areas supported school lunch programs for the urban poor. Coalitions of support may be engineered between various interests. Spending under these conditions may occasionally be controversial, but the strategy generally works. In areas of spending where individual groups or geographic areas benefit without any apparent trades of support, such as many public enterprises, the costs are deeply submerged, often made invisible. Controversial issues may be kept off the policy agenda.

The politics of expenditures is not dominated by the motives and strategies of a limited set of actors. Instead, varying groups of actors, with strategies framed by the budget process and the environment, strive to achieve their goals. But it is not only their goals that count; they are ultimately accountable to the public, and the degree of acceptability of spending decisions to the public influences the pattern of politics, including the openness of spending, the geographic distribution of beneficiaries of spending, the formation of coalitions among rivals for spending, and the kind of resources allocated by the budget. The result is simultaneously highly competitive and highly constrained, open to the environment, and accountable, more or less, to the public.

Notes

1. See Richard Stubbing, "The Defense Budget," in *Federal Budget Policy in the 1980s*, ed. G. Mills and J. Palmer (Washington, D.C.: Urban Institute Press, 1984), 81–110.

2. Office of Management and Budget, "Major Policy Initiatives," FY 1987 budget, 12, quoted in Roy T. Meyer, "Microbudgetary Strategies and Competition" (Ph.D. dissertation, University of Michigan, 1988), 305.

3. This occurred while I was doing participant observation on the Finance Advisory Board of DeKalb, Illinois. I was the citizen involved, and the event left me chagrined.

4. These arguments were all used in the 1986 and 1987 hearings before the Finance Advisory Board in DeKalb.

5. Meyer, "Microbudgetary Strategies," 284.

6. Ibid., esp. chap. 4. Meyer discusses a wide variety of strategies to make federal programs look less expensive than they are.

7. Roy Meyers, *Strategic Budgeting* (Ann Arbor: University of Michigan Press, 1994), 70, 71.

8. Ibid., 85 ff.

9. On the Export-Import Bank, see Jordan Jay Hillman, *The Export-Import Bank at Work: Promotional Financing in the Public Sector* (Westport, Conn.: Quorum Books, 1982), xiv–xv.

10. Genie Stowers, "Earmarking as a Strategy Against Budgetary Constraints: San Francisco's Children Amendment," *Public Budgeting and Finance* 15, no. 4 (Winter 1995): 68–85.

11. Irene Rubin, *Running in the Red* (Albany: State University of New York Press, 1982).

12. U.S. Congress, Senate, *Social Security Tax Cut: Hearings Before the Committee on Finance on S. 2016*, 101st Cong., 2d sess., 5, 8, and 27 February 1990, 14.

13. Ibid., 8.

14. Ibid., 5.

15. Allen Schick, *The Capacity to Budget* (Washington, D.C.: Urban Institute Press, 1990), 200.

16. U.S. Congress, Senate, *Social Security Preservation Act, Report 101–426 of the Committee on the Budget, to Accompany S. 2999, to Exclude the Social Security Trust Funds from the Deficit Calculation*, 4 August 1990, 29.

17. Aaron Wildavsky, *The New Politics of the Budgetary Process* (Glenview, Ill.: Scott, Foresman, 1988), 259.

18. Jeffrey Straussman, "Rights-Based Budgeting," in *New Directions in Budget Theory*, ed. Irene Rubin (Albany: State University of New York Press, 1988).

19. While the federal government has passed legislation to curtail new unfunded mandates, the legislation is weak concerning elimination of existing mandates. Moreover, many current proposals to balance the federal budget require changing entitlement programs into block grants and turning them over to the states. This change is likely to increase the financial responsibilities of the states without increasing their revenues proportionately. Finally, efforts to balance the federal budget will necessarily result in cutbacks in federal funding to the states. The states still have to perform the functions formerly funded by the grants.

20. Catherine Lovell and Charles Tobin, "The Mandate Issue," *Public Administration Review* 41, no. 3 (May/June 1981): 318.

21. John Petersen, Catherine Spain, and Wayne Stallings, "From Monitoring to Mandating: State Roles in Local Government Finance," *Governmental Finance* 8 (December 1979): 7.

22. Maurice White, "ACIR's Model State Legislation for Strengthening Local Government Financial Management" *Governmental Finance* 8 (December 1979): 23.

23. Janet Kelly, *State Mandates: Fiscal Notes, Reimbursements, and Anti-Mandate Strategies* (Washington D.C.: National League of Cities, 1992), 22.

24. For information on Florida's amendment and how it is working, see

Florida ACIR, *1991 Report on Mandates and Measures Affecting Local Government Fiscal Capacity,* Tallahassee, Florida, September 1991, and the same agency's *1993 Intergovernmental Impact Report, Mandates and Measures Affecting Local Government Fiscal Capacity* (Tallahassee, 28 September 1993), and *1995 Intergovernmental Impact Report, Mandates and Measures Affecting Local Government Fiscal Capacity* (Tallahassee, September 1995).

25. Florida ACIR, 1993, 27.

26. Irene Rubin, *Class, Money, and Politics: Municipal Budgeting in the United States* (Chatham, N.J.: Chatham House, forthcoming).

27. "Aid to Elderly Divides Young, Old and Politicians," *New York Times,* 23 June 1988.

28. Ibid.

29. U.S. House of Representatives, Committee on the Budget, *Hearing Before the Task Force on Urgent Fiscal Issues, U.S. Farm Policy: Proposals for Budget Savings,* 101st Cong., 2d sess., 28 June 1990, 11.

30. Ibid., 16.

31. Nancy Blanpied, ed., *Farm Policy: The Politics of Soil, Surpluses, and Subsidies* (Washington, D.C.: CQ Press, 1984), 80.

32. Dennis Ippolito, *Hidden Spending: The Politics of Federal Credit Programs* (Chapel Hill: University of North Carolina Press, 1984), 37.

33. *The Budget of the United States Government, 1991* (Washington, D.C.: Government Printing Office, 1990), 229.

34. Congressional Budget Office, *The Economic and Fiscal Outlook: Fiscal Years 1992–96* (Washington, D.C.: Government Printing Office, January 1991), 100.

35. U.S. Congress, House, *Federal Credit Reform: Hearings Before the Task Force on Urgent Fiscal Issues of the Committee on the Budget,* 101st Cong., 2d sess., 11 April 1990, 1.

36. Ibid., 3.

37. General Accounting Office, *Federal Credit Programs: Agencies Had Serious Problems Meeting Credit Reform Accounting Requirements,* no. AFMD-93-17 (Washington, D.C.: GAO, January 1993).

38. Marvin Phaup, "Conceptual Dissonance and Utility of the New Credit Accounts in the Budget: FHA under Credit Reform," *Public Budgeting and Finance* 16, no. 1 (Spring 1996): 23–36.

39. General Accounting Office, *Credit Reform: Speculative Savings Used to Offset Current Spending Increase Budget Uncertainty,* no. AIMD-94-46 (Washington, D.C.: GAO, March 1994).

40. For a summary of the arguments about how to treat administrative costs, see Phil Joyce, *Budgeting for Administrative Costs under Credit Reform* (Washington, D.C.: Congressional Budget Office, January 1992).

41. Senator Bumpers, *Congressional Record,* 11 August 1995, S. 12516.

42. Senator Bond, *Congressional Record,* 11 August 1995, S. 12515.

43. Congressional Budget Office, *Curtailing Indirect Federal Subsidies to the U.S. Postal Service* (Washington, D.C.: Government Printing Office, August

1984), ix.

44. See Congressional Budget Office, *Federal Subsidies for Rail Passenger Service: An Assessment of Amtrak* (Washington, D.C.: Government Printing Office, July 1982).

45. See Blanpied, *Farm Policy,* for a good summary of various kinds of agricultural subsidies through 1984.

46. Tim Weiner, *Blank Check* (New York: Warner Books, 1990), 5.

47. Ibid., 10.

48. Ibid.

49. Ibid., summarized from chapter 4.

50. "Spy Satellite Unit Facing a New Life in Daylight," *New York Times,* 3 November 1992.

51. "House Approves Intelligence Funds," *Chicago Tribune,* 22 December 1995.

52. "Spy Satellite Unit."

53. "Disclosure of Spy Agency's $1.5 Billion Fund Leads to Shake-up," *New York Times,* 25 September 1995.

54. House Document 1899, 84th Cong., 2d sess., March 1956, 45. Cited in *The Highway Trust Fund, A Historical Review of 11 Years of Operation, 1956–67* (Washington, D.C.: National Highway Users Conference, August 1967), 2.

55. U.S. Congress, House, *Hearings Before the Subcommittee on Surface Transportation of the Committee on Public Works and Transportation,* on H.R. 8235, H.R. 8430, H.R. 9544, and related bills, 94th Cong., 1st sess., 31 July 1975 and 30 September 1975.

6. The Politics of Balancing the Budget

We still need to constrain the deficit. We still need ways to impose budgetary discipline.... Yet ... Gramm-Rudman has accomplished neither reduction nor restraint.... the time has come for something more effective.

— Senator Jim Sasser

The most important constraint on budgeting is the requirement for balance: Revenues must equal or exceed expenditures. The constraint of balance means that revenues and spending decisions must be linked. The revenue limits pose constraints on spending, forcing choices among possible claims on the budget. Necessary expenditures put claims on revenues, requiring tax levies and periodic tax increases, despite their unpopularity. A reduction in tax revenues creates pressure to reduce spending by a proportionate amount. The constraint of balance forces discipline on budget actors. Generally, they cannot simultaneously give away expenditures and reduce taxes without facing the painful consequences of deficits, which include initial embarrassment and, later, difficult and unpleasant choices between increasing taxes and decreasing program and project expenses.

Balancing the budget is a routine part of budgetary decision making. The process of achieving balance is often iterative, that is, it goes back and forth between revenue and expenditure estimates, trying to stretch revenues and shrink expenditures until balance is achieved in the proposed budget. Sometimes, revenue estimates are quite rigid because decision makers have concluded that any increase in taxes that year is impossible; in that event, proposed expenditures have to be cut back to fit revenue estimates. Sometimes, the need for expenditures is considered so pressing that new tax proposals are put forward to cover them. Budgets can be balanced by increasing revenues, decreasing expenditures, or a combination of both.

Budgets may be balanced several times during budget preparation. The first time may be in the executive budget; the second time may be in the leg-islatively approved budget; the third time may be in the finally approved budget.

In an executive budget process, the central budget office may give de-partments and agencies targets for their budget proposals. If the proposals, when they are received by the budget office, add up to more than the esti-mates of available revenues, the budget office and/or the chief executive offi-cer may send them back to the departments or may themselves trim down the proposals until the sum of the proposals matches the estimated revenues. The budget as presented to the legislature should be balanced, but it may be balanced by proposed revenue increases or proposed spending decreases that the legislature may disapprove of. Consequently, budget balance is tentative at this point.

When the executive's budget proposal reaches the legislature, the legis-lature may be formally or informally forbidden to unbalance it; if they vote against revenue increases built into the proposal, they may also need to cut expenditures to match the revenue reduction; if they reject some proposed spending cuts, they may need to increase revenues or make alternative cuts to preserve balance. If the legislature ignores the executive's proposal and draws up its own alternative, the alternative proposal too needs to be bal-anced. If the budget as approved by the legislature is not balanced, the exec-utive may veto it. At the state level, where the governor often has a line-item veto, and in some cases a reduction veto, the governor can simply cut back on legislative spending that unbalances the budget, and unless the legislature can gather enough votes to override the governor's veto, the governor's veto stands and the budget is rewritten to balance.

Balancing is a key part of budgetary decision making, but it is not al-ways successful. Budgets may look balanced but not be really balanced. Even if budgets are truly balanced at the beginning of the budget year, they may become unbalanced during the year. This may occur by accident, if rev-enue projections were not good enough or if some expenditures were unin-tentionally underestimated. But governments sometimes run deficits inten-tionally. There may be an emergency—a war, a diplomatic initiative, or a natural disaster—that requires spending whether budgeted or not. Or gov-ernment can run deficits to moderate negative trends in the economy (at the national level) or to maintain spending for unemployment benefits and wel-fare during a recession. Government can also run deficits because the budget actors are unwilling to make difficult choices.

When deficits are caused by emergencies or by declines in the economy, the borrowing required to cover the deficits is temporary and is not usually particularly harmful. Budgets have to be flexible and responsive to the environment, and some borrowing may be necessary to that end. But sometimes deficits occur because revenues are growing more slowly than expenditures and decision makers are unwilling to make the politically difficult choices of cutting expenditures and increasing revenues. This kind of imbalance may be chronic rather than temporary and is more serious than deficits that occur briefly during economic downturns.

The most serious deficits occur when decision makers ignore the constraints of balance or treat them as more flexible than they are. They may choose to cut taxes without cutting back spending proportionately; or they may increase the rate of spending beyond the rate of growth in revenues, causing potential deficits down the road, especially if the increases in spending are in entitlements or other hard-to-cut areas of spending. This kind of deficit spending is attributed to a lack of discipline or a lack of will; the proposed solution is often more rigid constraints, embodied in constitutional amendments, new statutes, or new budget processes.

While decisions that have to be made to avoid deficits may be politically unpopular, the solution of ignoring hard decisions and running deficits is not popular either. Both the public and the financial community oppose deficits. Since the 1940s, opinion polls have shown that the public favors balanced budgets by approximately 2 to 1. The Harris survey in 1982 found that Americans agreed by more than a 2 to 1 margin that a constitutional amendment to balance the federal budget would be "an effective way to keep federal spending under control."[1] Financial markets that loan governments money also insist on balanced budgets.

Because deficits are embarrassing, when governments run chronic deficits, those responsible for them tend to deny them or minimize their size and importance. The quality of the budget numbers suffers under these circumstances, and it can be extremely difficult to figure out the real size of the deficits. Once the numbers are obscured, pressures to reduce the deficit are also diminished, making it more difficult to gather the necessary political support to return to balanced budgets.

By the time budget actors decide to eliminate deficits, those deficits may be very large and proportionately difficult to cut back. Whose programs should be cut back, and by how much? Where can cuts legally be made? How can resistance from interest groups be minimized? Whose taxes should be raised, and by how much? Can expenditures be shifted to other levels of government to reduce the size of the deficit? How can the appropriate actions be taken while maintaining accountability and acceptability to the public? How can politicians make such unpopular choices and still maintain their support base?

The politics of budget balance revolves less around the routine decisions made in most budgets to make them balance than it does around how and why budgets get unbalanced, and how to rebalance them when they get out of balance. This kind of budgetary politics can be explored by returning to the characteristics of public budgeting: It is marked by constraints, it involves multiple actors with different budgetary goals, it is open to the environment, and it has to resolve the separation of taxpayer and budget decision maker through techniques of accountability and acceptability.

Balance as a Constraint

The politics of budgetary balance is fundamentally a politics of constraints. Balance is itself a budget constraint; and when a budget gets out of balance, that constraint may have to be strengthened in a variety of ways. Governments may define or redefine what the constraint of balance means. They may make the constraint looser or tighter, depending on conditions. There are a variety of ways of making the balance constraint looser or tighter.

One way to have constraints that are simultaneously stringent and easily avoidable is to require that budgets balance, but not require governments to submit budgets. This is true, for example, in Illinois, at the local level. Local governments may submit what is called an *appropriation ordinance,* which lists approved expenditures without specifically matching them to projected revenues. Theoretically local governments do not spend money until it is in hand, which prevents deficits, but such jurisdictions do not have to propose a balanced budget at the beginning of the year. Local governments get to choose whether they wish to be bound by the constraint of balance in their proposal for spending.

The scope of balance requirements may vary. For example, balance may be narrowly defined in terms of operations: The government must receive more in income than it spends on routine operating items. Or balance may cover all money, including savings from previous years. A city can be running operating deficits, routinely spending more than it is taking in revenues, but still be in compliance with the law requiring balance because the city has some money tucked away from previous years that it can draw on.

Scope of balance may also be defined in terms of separate funds. Government spending is often divided into segregated accounts for the purposes of accountability—to check that earmarked revenues are actually spent as required, for example. Those segregated accounts may each be required to balance separately, or there may be a looser definition of balance that allows surpluses from one fund to be applied to deficits in other funds, to come out with one aggregated balance. The latter is a looser definition of balance than the former and is usually easier to achieve.

The balance requirement may include or exclude borrowing. That is, a budget may have to be in balance without any borrowing, or the government may borrow and still be in balance. Because state governments segregate capital from operating expenditures, they normally require balance in the operating budget and define the capital budget as balanced if income from borrowing and transfers from the operating budget equal or exceed expenditures. This means that states can borrow millions of dollars for capital purposes and still be in compliance with balanced budget laws. There is a continuing tension at state and local levels concerning how to define operating and capital expenses, because an expense defined as operating must be covered by current revenues, and can cause an imbalance; the same expenditure defined as capital can be borrowed for, and thus escape from the requirement of having revenues on hand to cover it. This problem may push up the level of borrowing.

The issue of borrowing is a central one to comparing how stringent balanced budget requirements are, and it is a central one to understanding the politics of budget balance. In some states, even the operating budget may be balanced with borrowed money, which weakens the requirements of balance to the point of ineffectiveness. This can happen if the basis of accounting is cash. In a cash accounting system, to calculate the balance, all cash on hand is counted. Since the cash total can be swelled by borrowing, and the bill for the borrowing does not show up until it is due, the balance is always positive.

Another way that the constraint of balance can be loosened or tightened is to adjust when the budget must be balanced. For example, in some states, such as California, New York, and New Hampshire, the governor is required only to present a balanced budget to the legislature; after that, anything can happen. In Alaska, the legislature has only to pass a balanced budget, but there are no features describing what happens after the budget is passed. In some states, any deficit that occurs after the budget is passed must be eliminated within that fiscal year; in others, it may be carried over into the next fiscal year or biennium.[2]

The size of the margin required for balance also varies. In some states, revenues are expected to exceed or equal expenditures in order to have balance; other states require that revenues exceed expenditures by a specified margin. This excess becomes part of a balance that can be used to apply against revenue shortfalls when they occur. Requiring revenues to exceed expenditures by a specified percentage is a more difficult constraint than requiring revenues just to cover expenditures.

When governments run deficits, public officials have a tendency to increase the number and severity of constraints as a way to restore balance.

The additional constraints can vary from a moderate change in the budget process that makes the linkage between revenue and expenditure decisions tighter and more authoritative, to a change in statutes making the requirements for balance more inclusive and more difficult to get around, to a change in the constitution, narrowly specifying the conditions under which deficits may be run, or generally forbidding deficits.

To summarize, the politics of budget balance illustrates the characteristic of public budgeting that emphasizes constraints because balance is itself one of the key constraints in budgeting. But the definition of balance is highly variable, and to some extent manipulable. Governments may choose more or less restrictive definitions. When governments find themselves running deficits of more than temporary nature, they may choose to strengthen the balance constraint to help restore balance and create the discipline to cut spending or raise revenues.

Multiple Actors, Ideologies, and Deficits

Who gets involved in the politics of balance, and how do these actors come down on a variety of policy issues involved in budget balancing?

The public plays an indirect role, putting pressure on elected officials to balance the budget. Citizens seem to feel that their personal budgets have to balance and hence governmental budgets should also balance. When the public simultaneously plays the role of investor, buying government bonds (enabling government to borrow), then its role becomes more direct, and its demands for balance can be translated into the costs of borrowing.

Interest groups may contribute to deficits by making it difficult to raise taxes or cut programs. When cuts are being proposed, interest groups may be vociferous in protecting programs that benefit them. But interest groups that represent narrow constituencies do not generally have distinct policies toward deficits (as opposed to policies toward maintaining the programs that benefit them) or play much of a policy role in the politics of deficits.

Because many of the policy issues surrounding balance of the budget affect broad social classes, broad coalitions of interest groups that come close to representing social classes may play a more active policy role. A coalition of labor unions may oppose a coalition of business groups or a farmers' alliance may oppose an urban coalition. Politicians sometimes use the requirement for balance as a vehicle for arguing about the appropriate size of government and level of taxation. These are issues that affect the rich and the poor differently and thus class-based coalitions often take a side in debates on budgetary balance.

Officials at different levels of government also become actors in the politics of deficits because of the possibility of one level of government balancing its budget at the expense of other levels of government. There are at least four major policy issues in the politics of balance that these actors take sides on.

THE APPROPRIATE SIZE OF GOVERNMENT

[handwritten annotation: liberal position — Increase revenues / conservative " — cut programs]

Budgets may be balanced by allowing revenues to increase, by freezing revenues at current levels and cutting expenditures to match, or by reducing revenues and cutting expenditures deeply to create a new level of balance. Allowing revenues to increase to reduce deficits is a fiscally conservative but socially more liberal position, without major implications for current program spending. Achieving budget balance by deeply cutting programs is a more politically conservative position. Some conservatives press for cuts in taxes, to force cuts in expenditures, using the requirement of balance as a vehicle to reduce the scope of government.

THE ROLE OF THE BUDGET IN THE ECONOMY

Should the budget be a tool of control over the economy to dampen economic swings, to control inflation and unemployment levels? Political liberals have accepted the need for deficits during recessions because the need to increase unemployment benefits and welfare spending occurs at the same time that government receipts decline as a result of falling incomes. Some conservatives oppose deficit spending as a technique to help stimulate the economy when it is weak, possibly because such spending has had a bias toward the poor and the unemployed. They prefer that the budget not be responsive to economic cycles at all, and argue that expenditures should be cut back when revenues fall during recessions. Other political conservatives will tolerate deficits during recessions if the deficit is caused by tax reductions to businesses and the wealthy. This policy is supposed to increase the supply of capital and thus stimulate the economy. Not only conservatives and liberals line up on this issue, but also aggregates of interest groups that represent business and labor.

THE ROLE OF EACH LEVEL OF GOVERNMENT

Where should the burden for providing services and benefits be placed? If balancing the budget becomes a valued goal at the federal level, there may be a strong temptation to balance it at the expense of other levels of government, cutting back grants and passing on program responsibilities. The states may do the same with local governments. Local governments may try to give service responsibility back to the state government or to townships, counties, or special districts, or the private sector. In theory, each level of government has an interest in passing on expenditures to other levels of government and preventing expenditures from being passed to themselves.

THE CHOICE OF OUTCOMES

Which functions should continue to be performed? Whose benefits and programs should be maintained or cut? The politics of balance may lightly veil a bitter politics of outcomes with protection or termination of particular programs or benefits as the goal. Interest groups, service recipients, and agency heads may take sides on this issue to protect their programs.

These four issues summarize what many of the actors in this portion of the budgetary decision-making process are trying to achieve. Liberals are trying to maintain the scope of government, while conservatives are trying to shrink it; working people and their representatives want the budget to be used to keep the level of employment high, while business people and their representatives prefer that the budget be used to keep taxes low; each level of government wants to balance its budget, possibly by shifting the burdens of programs and projects elsewhere, so that the tough decisions of what to cut or how to increase taxes do not have to be made; and interest groups, legislators, beneficiaries of programs, and agency heads are trying to protect their programs from cuts that are made to balance the budget.

The Environment, Unpredictability, and Deficits

Deficits occur in part because budgets are open to the environment, which can challenge the budget in a variety of ways. The courts may declare that mental patients cannot be committed to a mental hospital without treatment or that overcrowding of prisons is cruel and unusual punishment, so governments have to increase treatments in mental hospitals and build more prisons and hire more guards. State or federal governments may mandate expenditures, requiring local governments to list all their toxic materials or provide higher pensions for the police. Or natural events can provoke increases in expenditures, for example, hurricanes, floods, blizzards, or exceptionally cold weather. Violence, such as riots, crime waves, or political demonstrations, can require extra staff hours, increased communication equipment, improved training or better public relations, more jobs, new programs, and additional housing. War, with its overriding urgency, can increase expenditures without reference to current revenues.

Unexpected losses of revenues can result from courts declaring some tax unconstitutional, which may require the restoration of the revenues to the taxpayers. Or sudden declines in tax revenues can result from changes in state laws that affect local governments. There may be a sudden change in the type of bonds that cities may legally issue, or some forms of borrowing may become unexpectedly expensive or hard to get when a government is planning to borrow for a large project. A sudden downturn in the economy can shrink revenues below expectations. At the local level, a business may close unexpectedly, or move to another state, causing a decline in property taxes and leaving employees without jobs and without income, reducing sales tax revenues.

The intergovernmental revenue system introduces considerable uncertainty for state and local governments. Some grants are competitive, and so the potential recipients do not know in advance if they will receive the money. Sometimes intergovernmental aid is phrased as an entitlement so that all those cities, for example, who have over 6 percent of their population unemployed for longer than a certain number of months are eligible for particular kinds of aid. Those paying for the program cannot estimate its cost; those who might receive the aid do not have any way of knowing in advance whether they will be eligible. They may find out in the middle of a fiscal year that they will get the aid.

When state governments give aid to local governments in the form of entitlements, the problem is exaggerated because the state governments themselves have to balance their budgets. To meet unexpected increases in costs, they have to set aside contingency funds. Some states at times incur obligations to their local governments that they in turn do not have the money to fund. Local governments that planned on revenues from the state and included them in their budgets have to guess how much they will receive of what they were "entitled" to.

Another, related problem with intergovernmental revenues is that when the donor-level government is in financial trouble, it may hang on to the money it is supposed to give to the recipient for weeks or even months, so it can earn interest on the money to solve its own financial problems. Or it can simply delay payments into the next fiscal year, forcing those who needed the money and planned to use it at the normal time to borrow in anticipation of receiving the money later.

Some expenditures are demand driven rather than revenue driven. That means that the cost depends on the demand; the supply of the service is not determined by how much money is budgeted. For example, fire departments are to some extent demand driven; they respond to calls, and the calls are not limited to or even related to the supply. One response to such a situation from the budgetary perspective is to create an overcapacity and budget for it so that no matter what the demand, it is budgeted for. But that is a very expensive solution. Ambulance calls are demand driven; social service agencies that deal with battered spouses or abused children are demand driven. You cannot turn someone away in the middle of a crisis in which they are in physical danger, yet costs are proportional to the number of clients. Environmental changes may push such costs up beyond plans or expectations. For example, the increasing use of crack, an addictive form of cocaine, seems to increase the number of abandoned children and the incidence of spouse abuse, but it is hard to predict when it will hit a particular community or with what force. A poor economy in other parts of the world may set the jobless migrating, and an influx of non-English-speaking immigrants may tax the capacity of the Immigration and Naturalization Service and all the social agencies that deal with poor immigrants.

The problem of demand-driven costs is particularly acute at the federal level because so much of federal spending is now composed of entitlements, many of which are open ended. That means that if there is an increase in the number of people eligible for a given benefit, the money must be found to pay them, regardless of what is happening on the revenue side. Entitlements decouple revenue and expenditure decisions, and hence contribute to deficits.

Long and severe recessions contribute most directly to budgetary imbalance because they simultaneously increase expenditures for unemployment relief and welfare and reduce revenues because so many people are out of work or earning less. It is politically very difficult to raise taxes when many people are unemployed, and perhaps equally difficult to reduce the benefits of people who are desperate for them because they have been thrown out of work. Moreover, reducing public spending in order to balance the budget may have the effect of worsening the recession because people have even less money to spend to keep the economy going.

The environment may also contribute to deficits when the economy of a whole region is gradually declining and the amount of taxable wealth is stable or declining. The costs of delivering programs and projects may continue to increase, since costs are often not proportionate to the size of the population but to the number of lane miles, or the number of square miles of area. There may be a long-term disequilibrium between the cost of government and the availability of revenues. Either governments must continue to raise tax rates, taking a higher and higher share of people's income, against which the public will eventually rebel, or continue to cut back the level of programs and projects, potentially exaggerating the decline. In the face of such continuing negative choices, officials may from time to time run deficits. Such deficits are not inevitable and not acceptable to the public or the financial community, but they are perhaps understandable.

In short, many deficits, perhaps most of them, stem from changes in the environment. These changes may require more flexibility than the budget can deliver. Despite the best of intentions, deficits happen. Forbidding deficits, which is one response to them, seems futile in the face of the openness of the budget to the environment. The budget can be made less open to the environment, and it can be made more flexible, so that it can adapt without deficits. But the most common response seems to be to run the deficits, and then worry about how to eliminate them in a timely and fair manner.

Increasing Stress between Payer and Decider

The potential difficulties created by the separation of payer and decider may become acute when governments run deficits. The public wants balance, but it simultaneously wants to maintain services and programs that it likes, and does not want to increase its tax burden. Decision makers are faced with what appears to be a series of impossible choices from the perspective of political acceptability. Citizens may argue to tax someone else, and cut someone else's programs, but for the decision maker, there may not be many legal options that satisfy those conditions. The result in these cases may be a reduction in accountability.

On the simplest level, in cities, cuts may be taken where they are least visible, in order to prevent citizens' complaints. Such cuts break the visible link between taxes paid and services produced; it appears as if cuts can be made without reducing services. The costs of such a strategy, besides the long-term decline in trust of the taxpayers, include the increased costs of delayed maintenance, of capital projects deferred, and the inability to downsize in a logical way.

The unpopularity of deficits when combined with the unpleasant options to reduce them may lead to a tendency to hide or minimize them, and to pretend they are not there. The budget in this case loses much of its capacity to act as an instrument of accountability, transparently telling the citizens how their money is being spent. Balance may be redefined, the system of accounting may be changed to a cash basis to hide deficits, long-term capital borrowing may be used to cover operating deficits, expenditures may be pushed off into the next year, funds may be borrowed between accounts inappropriately and possibly without record (presumably with intent to repay). Revenues may be overestimated or expenditures underestimated to make the budget, as passed, look more balanced than it is. The longer this hiding goes on, the more convoluted and uninformative the budget becomes. The worse the situation looks, the more unwilling those responsible for it may be to have the situation revealed.

How, then, can the deficit situation ever be fixed? What kinds of pressures are there to reveal the problem and restore balance? Actually there are a number of such pressures. For example, if there has been a lot of internal borrowing, those agency heads whose budget is being borrowed may become desperate enough to complain, especially if they are not being left with enough money to run their programs and they are being publicly criticized for poor management. Second, the problems of internal borrowing may become so tangled that auditors can no longer certify the honesty and integrity of the financial records, a sure warning sign of trouble that may begin unraveling the situation and bringing it to public attention. Third, if the problem goes on long enough, there is likely to be an election, and if there is competition, the rival for chief executive is likely to be more than willing to discover his or her opponent's financial misdoings. If and when new politicians are elected they have the incentive to reveal as much as they can attribute to their predecessor, and make a highly publicized effort to clean it up, casting the blame on the previous incumbent. Fourth, the amounts involved may become so large that they are impossible to keep quiet. If these amounts grow large enough, they necessitate public borrowing, which means turning to a public market for funds. Banks and other investors normally require evidence of sound financial practice. The more desperate a government is to borrow, the more it needs to restore its fiscal integrity to be able to do so. The cost of borrowing may become so substantial that it interferes with the ability of the government to carry on its routine activities, adding to the pressure to restore balance.

Once the need is recognized, the difficult task of restoring balance remains. When many programs are entitlements and difficult to cut back or trim, and other programs have intense interest-group support, it may be difficult to know where and how to cut expenses while maintaining acceptability to the public. These problems have been particularly intense at the federal level, where the size of the deficit became astronomical before serious efforts were taken to reduce it.

The four characteristics of public budgeting, constraints, variety of actors and goals, openness to the environment, and the separation of payer and decider, provide some common themes for the politics of deficits at different levels of government. Nevertheless, some important differences between federal, state, and local budgeting give different emphasis and different interpretation of deficit reduction efforts at different levels of government.

One difference between levels of government is that state and local governments are required to balance their budgets; the federal government is not. When changes in the environment push up the costs of entitlement programs at the federal level, the increased costs show up as increased deficits; at the state level, the costs have to come out of a contingency fund or reduced spending for other budgeted expenses. Alternatively, the state may try to delay payments or push more of the burden for the entitlements on to local governments. At state and local levels, budgetary surpluses are sometimes built up to guard against deficits. Another aspect of the state and local requirement for balance is that efforts to hide deficits may be more intense.

A second difference between the levels of government is that the role of deficit spending in regulating the economy is most salient at the federal level of government. State governments are only marginally involved in efforts to control the economy, and local governments are generally too minor a part of the economy to control it no matter how they spend their money.

A third difference has to do with overall size. At the federal level, the tremendous size of budget deficits and their chronic nature create a noisy and stubborn problem with potentially major impacts on the national economy. Deficits are more rare and more tractable at state and local levels. The state requirements for balance make rebalancing the budget during the year a frequent activity, so that it is more difficult for large deficits to accumulate from year to year.

The Politics of Deficits: The Federal Level

Deficits have been a fact of life at the federal level for many years, but they have become particularly large over the past decade. Deficit spending has historically been of three types: borrowing for wars, borrowing to deal with economic recessions, and borrowing to cover a long-term imbalance between revenues and spending.

From the beginning of the republic to the 1930s, deficits were associated primarily with wars, and debts were paid off after the wars were over. During the Great Depression of the 1930s, politicians responded to falling revenues and the urgent need for aid for the poor by allowing deficit spending. The depression forged a new role for the federal government, to help minimize swings in the economy and the attendant social and economic distress. After the depression, an economic theory (Keynesianism) emerged, arguing that deficits for this purpose were not necessarily harmful to the economy, that spending during recession actually helped stimulate the economy. Deficits incurred to offset recessions and stimulate the economy are supposed to be temporary. Since the middle of the 1970s, deficits have occurred regardless of the state of the economy.

Politicians who promised to eliminate deficits have dramatically failed to do so, creating the impression that deficits are out of control. Whatever acceptance there was of moderate-size and occasional deficits began to evaporate when the deficits became huge. In 1974, the federal government had a deficit of $6.1 billion, which was .4 of 1 percent of the gross national product (GNP). By 1992, the deficit had reached a peak of $290 billion, or $340 billion if the social security surplus is subtracted.[3]

David Stockman, in a candid speech in spring 1985 just before his resignation as director of OMB, summarized the reasons for these deficits. He argued that the first cause of the deficits had to do with demobilization after the Vietnam war. Instead of reducing expenditures, the newly freed-up money was absorbed in increased income-support programs. Outlays for defense were reduced, allowing the massive inventories created by the war to be drawn down. But lower defense spending could not continue; the hostage situation in Iran highlighted U.S. military weakness, contributing to a consensus for increases in military spending, beginning with President Jimmy Carter in the late 1970s and continuing well into the Reagan administration. The rate of inflation increased, contributing to higher interest rates. The result was a major increase in interest payments on the federal debt. The Reagan administration's policy of tax reductions added one more major factor to the increased deficits. When these tax reductions were combined with the recession of 1981–82, the deficits soared.[4]

Stockman pointed out that the Reagan administration strategy of cutting back discretionary programs (while maintaining support for defense, social security, and tax cuts) could not possibly reduce the deficits because there was not enough money in these discretionary programs. "We argue with Congress over $80 or $90 billion of nondefense appropriation, but those that are truly discretionary amount to only a few billion dollars a year—not enough to fix a $200 billion problem."[5] Taxes had to be raised, or entitlement programs reduced, and defense curtailed. Thus deficit reduction was framed in terms of major policy priorities. There was no easy way or even relatively easy way to cut the deficits.

Citizens favored balanced budgets and increasingly supported efforts to control or limit the level of taxation. This sentiment spawned a number of revenue and expenditure limitation movements in states across the country. Many of them were not successful, but some, such as Proposition 13 in California and Proposition 2½ in Massachusetts, were very successful, and convinced politicians across the country that public desire to limit growth of public revenues was real and deeply felt. Moreover, taxpayer groups (those that opposed higher taxes) were organized and began to press the state legislatures to vote for federal balanced budget amendments. Under pressure from national taxpayer associations, many states did pass calls for a constitutional convention to add a balanced budget amendment to the constitution.

President Reagan was interested in reducing the scope of government activities and wanted to reduce taxes. He advocated a balanced budget in his election speeches, but there is considerable evidence that his administration was not terribly interested in reducing deficits, in comparison to achieving other policy goals.

> The Reagan administration, while it does not like deficit spending, has opted for this course of action because deficits facilitate the achievement of some of its other policy objectives. Deficits have enabled it (1) to preserve the 1981 tax cuts; (2) to blame Congress for fiscal irresponsibility; (3) to pressure for cutbacks in domestic programs; and—at least in its first years—to finance additional defense spending.[6]

At least one of President Reagan's entourage admitted that the tax cuts of 1981 would increase deficits. He confided: "Reagan's main goal is not to balance the budget—it is to reduce the role of government ... if we don't cut taxes and generate big deficits, spending will never come down ... with huge deficits, their choices are tougher, ... they'll have to cut spending."[7]

Having been pressed by its own policy goals to accept a growing deficit, the Reagan administration attempted to minimize its size and importance. The Reagan administration purposely underestimated the size of the deficit by overestimating revenues. Those giving him financial advice knew that he was underestimating the deficit.

David Stockman, director of OMB in the Reagan administration, was reported in the *New York Times* as stating, "The economics of Mr. Reagan's successful drive to cut taxes and restrain government spending in his first year in office ... was predicated upon an economic forecast for 1981 that its authors, Mr. Stockman and the president's chief economist then, Murray Weidenbaum, knew to be false but a politically expedient device."[8]

According to Stockman, the administration used accounting gimmicks to make the deficit look smaller. In 1981, he reported, a series of spending reductions and revenue measures was inadequate to close the gap opened by tax cuts. "Bookkeeping began its wondrous works. We invented the magic asterisk: If we couldn't find the savings in time—and we couldn't—we would issue an I.O.U. We would call it 'future savings to be identified.'"[9]

The administration also minimized the importance of deficits. In hearings before the Ways and Means Committee in 1983, after Chairman Dan Rostenkowski described the size of the deficits in the $200 billion range, he asked Secretary of the Treasury Donald Regan if he still opposed new taxes. Regan responded that he did. "We think that to have tax increases over the next two years would be folly, because it is not needed at this point. The deficits can be handled."[10]

President Reagan pressed for spending cuts in Congress, with considerable success in the first year of his administration. As his ability to dictate cuts to Congress waned, he threw more of his support to the movement for a constitutional amendment that would combine a balanced budget with spending limitations. Such an amendment would accomplish more of the president's goal of cutting back the size of government than the balanced budget amendment alone.

The balanced budget/revenue limitation amendment was only one of several approaches circulating in Congress from 1979 to 1986. Other proposals included statutory requirements for budget balance, changes in procedures for drawing up and passing budgets, and tax reform. Tax reform received the least attention as a technique to balance the budget.

PROPOSED CONSTITUTIONAL AMENDMENTS

The U.S. Constitution can be amended in two ways: Congress can adopt an amendment by a two-thirds vote in each house and then put the matter before the states to ratify by a three-fourths majority, or two-thirds of the states can vote for a constitutional convention, at which an amendment would presumably be discussed. Then three-fourths of the states need to ratify the proposed amendment. Partly because of the legal ambiguities in the second route (it is not clear that the constitutional convention could be limited to consideration of the balanced budget amendment), there was mounting pressure in Congress to head off the states and present a carefully considered congressional proposal.

As early as 1939, states began petitioning Congress to propose an amendment limiting federal taxing power. The movement continued on and off until 1963, when thirty-four states had passed it, but some of the resolutions were fifteen to twenty years old. Twelve states had withdrawn their applications, so the convention was never called.[11] The current budget-balancing calls began in 1975 and received impetus from the success of Proposition 13 in California. The National Taxpayers Union and the American Farm Bureau Federation were active in starting this movement.[12] By 1985, thirty-two of the required thirty-four states had passed a resolution calling for a constitutional convention.

As the pressure mounted in the states for a constitutional amendment, Congress began considering its own proposals. The Senate passed a proposed constitutional amendment in August 1982; the House of Representatives voted down the measure in October 1982. A budget-balancing amendment was voted on in the Senate in March 1986, where it narrowly failed because a competing form of limitation had been passed several months earlier, draining away some of the support for the constitutional amendment.

Proposals for a balanced budget amendment to the Constitution gained much support in 1992, 1994, and 1995 but did not pass both houses by the required two-thirds majority. In 1990 Congress had passed the Budget Enforcement Act, closing many of the loopholes in prior legislative efforts to balance the budget, but the deficit got worse in 1991 and 1992. Legislators kept telling each other that a balanced budget amendment was the only remaining possibility, that nothing else could possibly work.

Robert Reischauer, who was then director of the Congressional Budget Office, explained in the fall of 1993 why Congress felt so disempowered with respect to its ability to control the deficit. "That agreement [the 1990 budget accord] was billed as the largest deficit reduction in American history, yet it was followed by back to back record deficits in Fiscal Year 1991 and 1992."[13] Reischauer explained the anomaly as resulting in part from a misunderstanding about when the deficit reduction would show up in the deficit numbers, and in part from a slower than expected recovery from the recession. In addition, a lot of technical factors went in the wrong direction, including better-than-average farm weather, large crops, and below-average prices, requiring high federal payments to farmers. By the end of 1993, the deficit was finally headed downward, reflecting the 1990 spending caps and more technical factors going the right, rather than the wrong, way.

The version of the amendment that came up before the House in 1992 included a requirement of a two-thirds majority to increase the debt limit, in addition to the requirement of a two-thirds majority to suspend the requirement that outlays not exceed estimated receipts. An alternate proposal that would also limit revenue increases to the rate of increase in national income died in committee. The proposal that was voted on (H.J. Resolution 290, the Stenholm proposal) was inclusive in terms of covering all revenues and expenditures, including social security, and did not deal with the possibility of shifting the burden of spending to the states. This particular version of the proposal reportedly earned the opposition of the Chamber of Commerce, because it suggested to them that taxes might increase to balance the budget; organized labor and the American Association of Retired Persons also lobbied against the measure, fearing that cutbacks in social security and Medicare would be the result.[14] The measure was defeated in the House.

Although the deficit situation did improve as the economy recovered from recession and the effects of the 1990 spending caps were felt, the prospect of large deficits resuming later in the decade, as a result of entitlement spending, remained in the foreground. When the elections of fall 1994 created a Republican majority in both the House and the Senate, an ideological passion for change swept over the House in particular. New energy was expended to get a balanced budget amendment passed, and other legislation to reduce taxes and give the president a line-item veto or accelerated rescission powers was introduced within the first few months of the new Congress.

The question on whom the burden would fall if a constitutional amendment was passed was partly resolved with the passage of a limitation on unfunded mandates in 1995. Although this legislation does not protect states from cutbacks in grants, it should help prevent the federal government from setting standards and requirements that states have to implement at great cost. With new and enthusiastic Republican majorities, and the problem of state opposition out of the way, it seemed more likely than ever that the constitutional amendment would pass Congress and go on to the states for ratification. The measure did pass the House of Representatives, but failed in the Senate by one vote. The closeness of the vote suggested that legislators were trying to maximize their popularity by taking a public stance in favor of a balanced budget amendment as long as the measure did not actually pass. In fact, legislators charged each other with taking symbolic stances.

The issue of giving the president greater budgetary power was addressed in separate legislation, as Congress passed a version of the line-item veto (P.L. 104-130) and it was signed into law in April 1996. The measure enhances the president's ability to rescind an appropriation, an expansion of entitlements, or an increase in tax breaks granted to a small number of beneficiaries. Although this legislation does shift considerable budgetary power to the president, it may not have a major impact on deficits.[15]

The main political debates on the balanced budget amendment dealt with the concrete lists of cuts that would have to be made to balance the budget. Opponents of the balanced budget amendment were disturbed by the idea of passing a balanced budget amendment requiring deep cuts in spending while proposing massive tax reductions. The proposed tax reductions exaggerated the difficulty of finding acceptable places to cut. Moreover, if opponents of the balanced budget amendment could elicit a list of specific cuts, they could rally support against the measure. Unable to elicit much of a list before the vote, opponents argued that Congress would be no more able to come up with the list after the passage than before and the result would be a fraud and widespread evasion, analogous to the evasion that occurred with Gramm-Rudman-Hollings, a legislative approach to balancing the budget in the mid 1980s.

Each time that the balanced budget amendment came up, fairly standard arguments were made for and against it. The arguments on the positive side included the following:

1. Deficit spending is detrimental to the economy, it increases inflation, and it crowds out other uses of capital.

2. The need for flexible economic policy is overstated. Keynesian politics doesn't work, and monetary policies (controlling the economy by regulating the amount of money in circulation and influencing interest rates) are sufficient to influence economic cycles.
3. Growth of government should be checked.
4. Congress, if let alone, will not act or cannot take effective action.

The arguments against a constitutional amendment requiring a balanced budget included the following:

1. There is little relationship between either deficits or the size of government and inflation, and a balanced budget/revenue limitation is likely to have major negative economic impacts.
2. Constitutional budget constraints will impede the government's ability to respond to economic and other crises.
3. A constitutional requirement for a supermajority to allow an unbalanced budget will have the effect of magnifying the power of a small minority of congressmen who could demand a high (and unrelated) price for their votes.
4. A constitutional amendment is unenforceable.
5. Spending cuts are likely to fall on social services and aid to state and local governments.
6. A constitutional amendment will shift budget-making power to the courts (because of enforcement issues).
7. This is not a proper subject for a constitutional amendment.
8. The same result can be achieved through legislation.

These arguments highlight three sets of issues. The first includes the size and role of government and its distribution of benefits. The second set of issues involves the shifting of power as a result of such an amendment. The third issue involves the potential shifting of the deficit from one level of government to another.

On the issue of the size and role of government, two sides lined up predictably, with one side pressing for smaller government and fewer programs and fewer dollars for the poor, and the other trying to maintain the size of government and especially to maintain the services for the poor.

Jamie Whitten, chair of the House Appropriations Committee, typified the arguments of those who wanted to maintain current spending levels. He was not generally in favor of revenue restraints and balanced budget requirements, but his position on them was that if they were going to be adopted, they should not require sharp cuts in existing programs.

We have to balance the budget at a high level. We have to keep income up. If we don't keep income up, we will crack up right there. So in leveling off, cutting out all federal expenditures wouldn't solve our problem. You would be cutting all the things you have to have, but it would be equally bad and probably more sudden if we let income fall. So we have to level off where it is. We can't hope to turn back without cracking up in my opinion.[16]

The measure that the Senate rejected in March 1986 maintained the requirement of a three-fifths vote of both houses to allow a deficit, and to raise the debt ceiling, but required only a simple majority to raise revenues. One argument was over how much money could be raised. Senator Paul Simon, a Democrat from Illinois, managed to liberalize the proposal slightly in exchange for his vote. In his proposal, there was no limit to the amount of revenue growth that would be allowed as a result of real growth in the economy. The effect of his amendment would have been to restrict the future growth of government to the rate of growth in the economy, but not to require the government to shrink with respect to the economy.[17]

The issue of where power would be shifted was more complicated. A constitutional amendment would reduce congressional power by reducing congressional discretion. The power of the Federal Reserve Board would be enhanced because it controls monetary policy, and monetary policy would be the only remaining public tool to dampen cycles of the economy once fiscal power of the budget was reduced or stripped away. The version of the amendment that passed the Senate in 1982 tried to curb the increased power of the president over the budget that was implicit in many of the bills circulating, but it is not clear how the Senate version was expected to work. Some of the bills tacitly assumed the president would have enhanced powers to withhold spending in order to balance the budget. The role of the courts would be enhanced by the amendment because the courts would be called upon to settle questions of enforcement and to handle lawsuits from people who believed some particular tax or spending bill was illegal. Finally, the requirements for supermajorities (three-fifths) to allow deficit spending enhanced the power of minorities in Congress who opposed spending or who were willing to hold the budget hostage, that is, prevent passage of the budget until they got something else they wanted.

The third issue that came up in arguments against a constitutional amendment was that the effect would be to shift the burden of services and taxes to state and local governments without shifting revenues to match. The 1982 version of the amendment that passed the Senate contained no language (although it had been extensively discussed) to prevent the federal government from shifting financial responsibility for programs to state and local governments. To the extent that such a shift occurred under the amendment, programs would increasingly be funded from the more regressive tax structures characteristic of state and local governments. Since some states and many local governments have inadequate tax bases for current services and are wrestling with reduced federal aid, further program burdens would exacerbate existing fiscal stress. Legislation was passed in 1995, however, to limit additional unfunded mandates from the federal government to state and local governments.

STATUTORY APPROACHES TO BUDGET BALANCING

Some members of Congress supported measures to balance the budget and/or limit spending whether those measures were constitutional or statutory. But others tended to favor one approach or the other, arguing either that statutory means were easily ignored and nothing less than a constitutional amendment would do or that a constitutional amendment was too inflexible and was unnecessary because Congress already had the legal power to impose constraints. Some of the proposals for legislative solutions were more oriented toward revenue constraints and constraints on the growth of government; others were more exclusively directed toward balancing the budget and eliminating the deficit.

The proposals to limit spending growth varied not only in technical mechanism but also in scope. Some included loans, some included tax expenditures, and some both of these; others pointedly excluded loans and tax expenditures. Some of the limitations were much more severe in the level of cuts required than others.

One of the proposals seriously considered by the House was Congressman Robert Giaimo's proposal (H.R. 6021) to limit spending to a percentage of the GNP. In Giaimo's proposal, the limit could be breached by a simple majority of both houses if economic circumstances warranted. This proposal allowed for much easier adaptation to economic cycles than constitutional amendments that required a two-thirds majority to allow a deficit in an economic downturn. Giaimo's proposal included tax expenditures and loan guarantees to prevent increased spending in these areas to bypass controls on program spending. Congresswoman Marjorie Holt introduced a bill that included loans in the controls on spending but ignored the issue of tax expenditures; and Congressman James Jones introduced a spending limit as percentage of GNP without spending limits on either tax expenditures or loan guarantees. The issue of whose programs would be cut back—those of business and the wealthy or cities and the poor—was debated under the guise of how inclusive spending limits should be.

Business groups testifying on congressional proposals to limit spending and balance the budget uniformly approved the general idea, but opposed Giaimo's proposal to curb tax expenditures. For example, the National Association of Manufacturers (NAM) offered its support for spending limitations and a balanced budget, but specifically excluded tax expenditures from controls.

> Balancing the budget is essential to reduce and then eliminate inflation. This policy goal should be implemented by forcing down spending levels rather than allowing tax levels to rise ... NAM strongly endorses the approach in H.R. 5371 to limit fiscal 1981 spending to 21 percent of the estimated GNP and subsequent years to 20 percent. We oppose including "tax expenditures" in a higher percentage.[18]

NAM piously argued that Congress should have the strength to sacrifice some legislative sacred cows while arguing to maintain its own tax breaks.

Congressman Richard Bolling opposed any new formal procedures to limit expenditures or balance the budget, but he was more sympathetic to Giaimo's proposal, which included tax expenditures in the limitation, than to those of Holt or Jones which excluded tax expenditures from controls. Bolling was sarcastic about the Business Roundtable (a lobbying group of chief executive officers of big businesses), which was calling for congressmen to curb their requests for special projects while businessmen were trying to protect their tax breaks.

> I think the best case that can be made for a gimmick like this [a spending limitation that includes tax expenditures] is that the business community comes in through the Business Roundtable and tells us what an outrage it would be to include tax expenditures, but of course, these [tax expenditures] are different in kind [from other expenditures], and I honor their view. It's about as unselfish as the view of those of us who are for our own water projects.[19]

The issue of legislative approaches to budgetary balance and spending limitations was also discussed on the grounds of whether such ceilings were necessary or workable. Congressman Richard Gephardt, for example, argued that new limits were not necessary because strengthening the existing budget process would achieve the same goals, with the greatest degree of flexibility. Strengthening the existing process maintained congressional budgeting power, instead of giving it away or constraining it, but it also gave more power to the budget committees in Congress, as opposed to the appropriations, authorizing, and tax committees.

The debate as to whether a ceiling was necessary was phrased by some congressmen and interest groups in terms of the need for discipline and the need to provide an excuse to constituents when congressmen said no to requests. The opponents of ceilings argued that constraints were artificial and could not substitute for will. Congressman Bolling argued, for example, that fiscal decisions were "a whole lot more a matter of will than procedure."[20] Jamie Whitten, chairman of the Appropriations Committee, agreed with Congressman Bolling.

> Let us not kid ourselves that some artificial gimmick will ever substitute for the real will of Congress. Congress by its very nature is unlikely to lock itself into a room without keeping a key. And when the confinement begins to pain us, we tend to be all too willing to use the key.[21]

Whitten, as chair of the House Appropriations Committee, stood to lose a lot of power if Congress hamstrung itself with limits or gave the budget committees more enforcement power. Thus, while his description of congressional behavior is undoubtedly true, his argument against additional controls on spending probably also reflected his desire to maintain his power.

The proposals made by Giaimo, Jones, and Holt were aimed primarily at limitations on spending, and though their proposals aimed at balanced budgets, they did not guarantee them. Some other proposals discussed in the House were focused more on the balance aspect, assuming that revenue raising has its own natural political limits. James Wright, majority leader in the House in 1980, and Phil Gramm, both of Texas, offered a proposal to require a three-month review, after the budget year began, to project deficits for the remainder of the year. "If the deficit were to represent 5 percent of the controllable expenditures for the remainder of the fiscal year, then the president would be instructed to reduce every such item by that same 5 percentage points."[22] Gramm explained that to avoid such cuts Congress would pass balanced budgets.

In the Wright-Gramm proposal, the budget could be unbalanced if both houses voted to approve a deficit resulting from unforeseen circumstances or overriding concerns. The bill was thus fairly flexible in terms of adaptation to the economy, requiring no supermajority, but it did require positive congressional action to unbalance the budget. Gramm noted in the hearings that although Wright's and his proposal addressed budgetary balance, they were willing to consider adding Jones's proposal to limit spending as a percentage of GNP and Giaimo's proposal to limit tax expenditures and loans.

Among the proposals to balance the budget and limit revenues or expenditures were a number of suggestions for strengthening the existing congressional budget act. One recommendation was to use the existing reconciliation procedures. This process allowed Congress to make cuts in any spending that was over the targets formulated by the budget committees. This proposal was the first major one to be adopted. Reconciliation was used a little in 1980 and in a major way in 1981, and the result was major budget reductions. Because Congress also passed the president's tax reduction package, however, little progress was made in closing the deficit gap.

The use of the reconciliation process gives somewhat more power to the budget committees because it allows them to set targets for the appropriation and authorizing committees and gives the budget committees a procedure for gaining compliance. If the targets set are lower than their own preference, the appropriations and authorizing committees can pare down their requests in whatever way they see fit. Reconciliation thus shifts power away from the appropriations and authorization committees, but not drastically so. In 1981, however, President Reagan and OMB director David Stockman were not content with the House reconciliation. OMB drew up an alternative version and had two representatives, Phil Gramm and Delbert Latta, introduce the administration's version as an amendment; and the Gramm-Latta amendment passed the House. The OMB version became the Omnibus Reconciliation Act of 1981. The work of the appropriations and authorization committees in attempting to comply with the reconciliation instructions was bypassed, creating considerable resentment against using the process again.

In December 1985, the Balanced Budget and Emergency Deficit Control Act of 1985, popularly called Gramm-Rudman-Hollings, was passed. Gramm-Rudman-Hollings was oriented toward deficit reduction and budget balance rather than expenditure or revenue limitations. It allowed some rise in revenues to balance the budget, rather than rigid limitations on revenues. It protected entitlement programs such as social security. It reduced the shock of cutting back the deficit by phasing in balanced budgets over a five-year period. The law stipulated that Congress could vote to allow deficits in excess of targets in case of economic recession. The requirements for balance were to lapse during a war.

The goal of Gramm-Rudman-Hollings was to achieve budgetary balance by 1991 by reducing the size of the deficit by specified amounts each year from 1986 to 1991. If the deficit in any year was larger than the target for that year, an automatic provision would take over, cutting programs across the board after certain special rules had been considered. The cuts were to be divided evenly between defense and nondefense expenditures. The threat of cutting all programs, on the one hand, was supposed to be more fair, and on the other hand, was supposed to be so distasteful that it would force Congress to eliminate the excess deficit before the automatic cuts could take effect.

The cuts were to be taken across the board, to offend both liberals and conservatives, but several major entitlement programs were exempted from cuts, including social security, Aid to Families with Dependent Children (AFDC), veterans' compensation and pension, food stamps, and Medicaid, among others. Other programs, such as Medicare and veterans' health care were limited in the percentage they could be cut. Thus the issue of scope of program cuts was resolved in favor of protecting major entitlements and sharing the pain between defense and other spending. For the purposes of balance, the budget was defined broadly.

For fiscal year 1986, the first year of Gramm-Rudman-Hollings, $11.7 billion in cuts were targeted. The cuts were equivalent to 4.3 percent across the board for nondefense categories, and 4.9 percent in defense.[23] In February 1986, two months after Gramm-Rudman-Hollings was passed, a three-judge federal panel ruled that the role of the General Accounting Office (GAO) in designating the automatic cuts was an unconstitutional violation of separation of powers because the controller general (the head of the GAO) has to answer to Congress. The decision went to the Supreme Court where, in July 1986, that portion of the law was declared unconstitutional.

President Reagan's 1987 budget proposal had to be presented before the Supreme Court could act, and thus his budget assumed that Gramm-Rudman-Hollings would be in effect for 1987. The administration estimated a $182 billion deficit, with a gap of $38 billion to get down to the deficit level required by Gramm-Rudman-Hollings. The president's proposed budget included a mix of program cuts, fee increases, and asset sales totaling $38.2 billion to close the gap.

In April 1986, while the Senate was trying to come to some agreement with the president on the 1987 budget, Budget Director James Miller urged the Senate to use more optimistic economic forecasts. Such a change would bring the budget resolution within reach of the deficit target set by Gramm-Rudman-Hollings. Miller reportedly argued that if the Senate would use more optimistic assumptions about the economy, they could reduce the deficit estimate by up to $29 billion. Senator Pete Domenici argued back that the administration was "cooking up" assumptions and that its proposals overestimated revenues by a probable $14 billion.[24]

In its efforts to close the Gramm-Rudman-Hollings gap, it appears that the administration also froze billions of dollars of transportation project funding in 1986. These funds are earmarked user fees and can be spent for no other purpose, but if the projects' expenditures are deferred, the cash balance in the Treasury is increased, apparently lowering the deficit. Although this had been done in previous administrations, reportedly the dimensions of the problem increased under President Reagan and Gramm-Rudman-Hollings. "By reducing the official deficit through the trust fund balances, the administration has contended in recent weeks that it is able to ease the spending cuts for other agencies."[25] The two trust funds (highway and airport) had cash balances of $16 billion in March 1986.

In short, Gramm-Rudman-Hollings contained incentives to make the budget look more balanced than it was, to reduce the size of the amount that had to be cut across the board. Selling assets to balance the budget makes the budget appear more balanced than it is; since the revenues from the sale of assets occur only once, the problem of finding additional revenues or cutting expenditures is delayed only a year. The use of surpluses in one earmarked fund—surpluses created by preventing the funds from being spent as intended—to apply against deficits elsewhere in the budget would be considered illegal in local governments, which are required by law to balance their budgets. The practice depends on the estimation of the deficit in terms of cash on hand, as if revenues in trust funds were not earmarked. The cash balance is notoriously manipulable. Finally, Gramm-Rudman-Hollings encouraged optimistic estimates of the economy, so revenues might be overestimated and expenditures underestimated.

Gramm-Rudman-Hollings had a fallback procedure in case some part of it was declared unconstitutional, requiring Congress itself to do the automatic cutbacks. But from the time when a part of the law was declared unconstitutional, it was unclear what its status was and whether Congress would really enforce it. By September 1987 Congress had passed and a reluctant president signed a new Gramm-Rudman-Hollings, which used OMB rather than the GAO to make cuts. The new law made some other changes as well, including a slowing down of the time to eliminate deficits and a generally more gradual approach.

Gramm-Rudman-Hollings was not successful, in either its original or its revised form. It encouraged stopgap measures and overestimates of economic growth, and created incentives to take existing programs off budget and create new off-budget enterprises. Senator Herbert Kohl observed, "Since we enacted Gramm-Rudman, we have created five off-budget government sponsored enterprises. Only one was created in the previous thirteen years."[26]

Senator Nancy Kassebaum summed up a lot of accumulated congressional frustration with the budget process in 1989 when she decried the use of such emergency devices as continuing resolutions as a substitute for the budget. She claimed that Congress had routinely failed to make timely fiscal decisions. "In doing so," she argued, "we lose the power to allot money among programs of greater or less merit. We lose the chance to weigh revenue options thoughtfully. In fact, we lose the ability to do anything other than affirm the aggregate spending, taxing—and borrowing—decisions of earlier years. That is not policy making."[27]

Pressure increased to reform the budget process as deficits grew beyond the ability of Gramm-Rudman sequesters to cure without doing unacceptable damage. The Budget Enforcement Act was passed in the fall of 1990. Like Gramm-Rudman, the Budget Enforcement Act of 1990 picked from and blended a large number of different proposals. As a result, it was a complex measure. But its essential feature was that it strengthened the constraints for balance, rather than tried to reduce the size of the deficit.

One portion of the measure focused on limiting spending on domestic "controllables," those programs that regularly go through the congressional appropriations process. Another portion of the reform focused on entitlements and other mandatory spending. The goal for entitlements was less on keeping spending down than on maintaining balance; pay-as-you-go (often called PAY-GO) provisions required compensating increases in revenues or decreases in other noncontrollables to pay for any increases in entitlements. Similarly, revenue reductions were to be controlled by strict requirements that they be offset with either increases in revenue or spending reductions. The linkage between revenues and expenditures was intentionally tightened in two key areas, entitlements and tax expenditures.

Part of the thrust of the reforms was to make the real costs of spending apparent when decisions were being made in order to restructure the incentives more toward balance. For example, credit reforms included in the budget reforms of 1990 make the costs of loans and loan guarantees more visible at the time when the programs are being approved. Before the reform, approval was separated by many years from the actual costs, which were routinely underestimated.

The removal of the social security surplus from the calculation of the deficit also had the effect of making the costs of current spending and revenue decisions more apparent at the time the decisions were being made. When social security balances were included in the deficit calculation, the deficit looked like it was decreasing even when it was growing, which encouraged a lack of fiscal discipline. With social security surpluses subtracted out, each action that increased the deficit would have an immediate, visible, and negative consequence.

The budget reforms of 1990 were especially significant because they show the budget process starting to adapt to a slower-growing economy. The reform discourages increases in expenditures and reductions in revenues and strengthens the expectations for balance. It helps make costs clearer and raises revenues. It is of broad scope in the sense of including regular appropriations, entitlements, loans, and loan guarantees, and it is more inclusive of time, requiring enforcement at several points during a year and over several years. Instead of a rigid series of goals intended to last only until the problem goes away, the new process is much more flexible, leaving room for choices among programs, for adaptation to the economy, and for emergencies. The Budget Enforcement Act does not set a specific date for the elimination of deficits; it links revenues and expenditures more tightly and restructures the incentives to make it easier to achieve balance over the long haul.

The Budget Enforcement Act of 1990 has been the most successful of the statutory approaches taken to deficit reduction, especially in terms of capping discretionary outlays. Its more flexible approach to deficit reduction and its explicit closing of the loopholes in prior legislation have markedly reduced the manipulations that marked the Gramm-Rudman-Hollings period. After 1992, for a combination of reasons including the budget caps in the Budget Enforcement Act, the deficit actually began to fall. From its peak of $290 billion in 1992, the deficit dropped to an estimated $192 billion in 1995.[28] Because of the continued growth in entitlement costs, however, especially in health care, the deficits were predicted to go up again after 1995 unless more drastic action was taken. The Congressional Budget Office estimated the 1995 deficit at only $176 billion, but projected the deficit to rise continuously after that, to an estimated $421 billion in 2005.[29]

Controls over entitlements in the 1990 reforms were less successful than controls over discretionary spending, at least in part because they were aimed exclusively at new rather than existing legislation. The PAY-GO provisions for revenues and entitlements have been useful in curtailing new legislation that would unbalance the budget, but the costs of existing provisions in both entitlements and tax expenditures have continued to rise, threatening the budget process with large deficits, despite tax increases and spending reductions. Failure to adopt a health-care package in 1994 to help control federal spending on health exaggerated the problem. Pressures remained high to adopt further reforms. In 1995 Congress attacked existing entitlements, with proposed major reductions in the rate of growth in Medicare and Medicaid expenditures. Many other changes in entitlements were proposed, including narrowing the base of those eligible for entitlements, shortening the period of eligibility, and putting caps on spending, essentially transforming entitlements into grants. The depth of the proposed cuts aroused the opposition of the president, creating a confrontation between the branches that closed down the government for four days in November and for three weeks in December 1995 and January 1996.

To summarize, there has been extensive political activity surrounding efforts to balance the federal budget. One aspect of the politics of balance has been the competition between different approaches to the problem. These approaches have varied from the unpredictable and possibly uncontrollable constitutional convention called by the states, to a rigid constitutional amendment, controlled by Congress, to legislative restrictions and ceilings, to modifications of the existing congressional budget process. Pressure from the states for a constitutional convention helped press Congress to take its own action on a constitutional amendment, and that activity stimulated action on a legislative solution to the deficit. A moderate approach was tried first, using the existing budget process. When the more moderate and flexible procedural approach (reconciliation) failed, the somewhat more radical legislative solution of Gramm-Rudman-Hollings was passed. This legislative "solution" drained away some of the pressure for a constitutional amendment.

When the Gramm-Rudman-Hollings solution proved unworkable, Congress, working with the president, worked out a new set of controls that would not only reduce the deficit but also make it easier to balance the budget. A budget process adapted to a rapidly growing economy was gradually being changed to match a more slowly growing economy.

Because the idea of a balanced budget is so popular, it has been difficult for legislators to take stances that are directly opposed to a balanced budget. As a result, traditional splits between liberals and conservatives have played themselves out in support for various features of balanced budget or revenue/expenditure limitation proposals. These features include protecting various portions of the budget from cuts. In addition to questions about how the cuts will be made and who will be affected by them, the question of who will exercise increased budgetary control has colored the politics of budget balance. Also important is the question of who will bear the brunt of program costs dropped by the federal government. The relationships between federal, state, and local governments are being realigned.

Deficits in the States

When they are facing deficits, the states, like the federal government, have to decide whether and how much to raise revenues or cut expenditures, with similar implications for the scope of government. Just as at the federal level, there are problems of defining what constitutes a deficit and problems of measuring the size and importance of deficits. Just as the federal government has to decide how much of a financial burden it can shift to the states or the private sector, states have to decide how much expense to absorb from or pass on to local governments, and how much of a service burden they can unload on local governments. Nevertheless, the requirement, variously interpreted, of annual balance at the state level normally prevents the buildup of large, long-term deficits, and makes rebalancing the budget both more routine and somewhat easier.

Although there is considerable variation between states in who has power to make reductions in spending to restore balance after the beginning of the fiscal year, the responsibility is generally given to the governor. In 1989, twenty states reported that the governor had unlimited rights to cut the budget during the year to avoid an impending deficit. Ten states reported that the governor could make cuts during the year but that they could be only across-the-board cuts. Seven states reported that the governor must consult with the legislature before making midyear cuts.[30]

The issue of which interests will be protected and which will be cut back has been less salient at the state level because deficits, when they have occurred, have usually been caused by recessions and hence been relatively short term. Because the deficits are considered temporary, states can adopt temporary measures to handle them, including temporary taxes or surtaxes. They can tighten belts and make across-the-board cuts. They can often avoid making difficult choices between programs or types of programs.

For example, Michigan has responded to recent recessions with budget cuts rather than tax increases, but these cuts have tended to be across the board. "It is clear that there is a tendency to accommodate budget reductions by cutting across the board, and that further reductions would lead (at least initially) to cutbacks in all services, and not in any particular targeted programs."[31]

There are some exceptions to the tendency to cut across the board. For example, Arkansas has a preset series of priorities that go into effect if there is a revenue shortfall. Expenditures are grouped into three categories. Category 3 is cut across the board until it is eliminated; then, if further cuts are necessary, category 2 programs are cut across the board until they are eliminated. Only if all category 3 and all category 2 programs are eliminated will category 1 expenses be reduced. West Virginia has a similar system.[32] The tendency to cut across the board or make cuts according to preset priorities takes some of the bitterness out of allocational battles concerning the elimination of sizable deficits.

When financial problems occur that cannot be categorized as moderate in severity and short term (e.g., when the bottom fell out of the oil market), they are likely to provoke much argumentation about priorities as well as tradeoffs between additional taxation and additional cuts.

MINICASE:
CONNECTICUT CUTS BACK TO BALANCE THE BUDGET

Connecticut was particularly hard hit during the recession of the early 1990s, and when the recession was combined with the effects of growth in entitlement spending, the result was a deficit of a billion dollars in an $8 billion budget.[33] The enormous size of the deficit combined with continuing growth in entitlements that outstripped revenue growth meant that ordinary across-the-board cuts and delaying action were not viable options. The unusual depth of the recession also suggested that the economy might not snap back in a short period of time. Fears about long-term economic growth helped shape the response to deficits.

Over a two-year period, the governor increased taxes (in a highly unpopular move) and then cut $1.1 billion in services to slow down the rate of increase in spending. Governor Lowell Weicker argued that the budget had to be not only cut but restructured because annual uncontrollable increases were outstripping revenue increases. His restructuring included tightening eligibility standards for welfare and reducing the increasing costs of long-term health care, reducing employee benefits, downsizing the state workforce, and changing the relationship between the state and local governments. Forced to cut back on a variety of support programs to local governments, the state tried to compensate somewhat for the damage it was causing by reducing the burden of state mandates on local governments.

The reductions in state aid included lowering the funds for public schools, eliminating or reducing various kinds of property tax relief, cutting back on general assistance (a form of welfare) funding, and reducing benefits for the teachers' retirement fund. Among the more burdensome mandates the state proposed to reduce were those that required all heart disease and hypertension among police and firefighters to be considered work related, and the state recommended a modified set of binding arbitration rules for municipalities.

Although the governor argued that the cuts would be spread evenly across the public, responses to the recession and to the deficits included major new and expanded tax breaks for business to facilitate economic recovery. The cost of these tax breaks was expected to increase from approximately $100 million in 1992 to over $350 million in 1995.[34]

Although states sometimes face long-term fiscal stress, most of their experience with deficits results from handling downturns in the economy that simultaneously reduce revenues and increase social services expenditures such as welfare and unemployment payments. Because deficits incurred for this purpose tend to be temporary, and because deficits are almost always illegal at the state level, states have frequently engaged in temporizing, stalling cuts and hiding deficits until the economy improves.

OBSCURING THE DEFICIT

States wrestling with balanced budget requirements frequently try to obscure or minimize the size of the deficits they are running. For example, Representative David Obey from Wisconsin reported, "I come from a state with a balanced budget requirement. In the six years that I served in the legislature, Wisconsin's indebtedness doubled, because they engaged in all kinds of phoney-baloney devices, off-budget accounting, dummy building corporations, all the rest, that simply defined out of the budget all kinds of spending that was really governmental. And they are still doing it today."[35]

Another gimmick to make a budget look balanced is to accelerate tax collections, which produces a one-time windfall for the state. For example, if a state changes from a quarterly to a monthly collection schedule, it can collect fifteen months' revenues in twelve months. On a quarterly basis, it could collect taxes the first of the year, for the preceding three months; the second payment would be at month 3 for the preceding three months; the third payment would be at month 6 for the preceding three months; and the final payment for the year would be at month 9 for the preceding three months. But if the state goes to monthly collections at that point, it can collect the taxes for months 10, 11, and 12 that they would normally have to wait for until the next fiscal year.[36]

A similar gimmick is to delay some expenditures so that they occur in the next fiscal year. That increases the next year's expenditures, but the hope is that by then the recession will have ended and increased revenues will cover the extra expenditures. A way to push expenditures into the following year is to change the basis of accounting from modified accrual to cash. Under cash accounting, expenditures that are incurred this year, but not paid until next year, are officially counted as next year's expenditures. Under accrual accounting, they would be counted as part of *this* year's expenditures. By switching the basis of accounting, some items that would have been counted as expenditures this year get carried over into next year.

In Illinois, the governor changed the accounting system from modified accrual to cash in 1978. He made the budget look more balanced in that year because the cash accounting system pushed off some expenditures into the next year's budget.[37] In addition, the cash budget changed the definition of a deficit. A cash budget measures deficits by looking at the available cash balance at the end of the year rather than matching revenues and expenditures during the year. The result is an easily manipulable deficit.

The available cash balance is eminently suited for manipulation: Any cash on hand goes into the available balance, even if its source is a loan. The available balance is also affected by speedups in revenue collections or delays in paying vendors or by manipulating the timing of drawdowns of federal funds. "When an administration commits itself to a specific end of year available balance, it can manipulate the revenue processing system to bring about an available balance consistent with its prediction."[38] Perhaps most important, the cash balance is always positive and hence makes it look as if the state is always running a surplus, whether or not it is in deficit.

Other common gimmicks include borrowing between funds to make the general fund look more balanced than it is, and using one-time revenues to make the budget look more balanced than it is. For example, California, in order to address an incipient deficit in FY 1981–82, began its deficit-reduction plan mainly with one-time revenues. These included financing capital outlays previously funded from the general fund with one-time use of tidelands oil revenues; anticipation of increased federal funding for Supplemental Security Income/State Supplemental Income; and temporary elimination of the state bailout for local governments required to replace revenues lost by Proposition 13. One-time revenue increases totaled nearly $514 million; one-time expenditure reductions totaled $208 million.[39]

Taking expenditures off budget, manipulating the cash balance by borrowing or moving expenditures forward or revenues backward, closing the gap with one-time revenues, and internal borrowing are all techniques to reduce the amount of cuts or tax increases that might otherwise be necessary. They are part of a politics of avoidance and delay to help avert hard political choices, the kind that make enemies. These techniques are not necessarily bad; it makes sense to avoid deep cuts and expensive restructuring to eliminate a deficit that will disappear on its own within a year or two as the economy recovers. If state laws allowed more time to recover from a deficit resulting from a downturn in the economy, less effort would be taken to hide such deficits.

CREATING BUFFERS

While some states temporize to get past the worst of a recession without deep cuts in service levels, the routines of handling deficits require action during the year, when the deficits are discovered. It is often the governor's responsibility to make those cuts, which are perceived as a political liability. The governor may try to avoid them by creating buffer funds through underestimating revenue.

The politics of balance is intimately related to the politics of revenue estimation. In Illinois, for example, the governor and the state Office of Management and Budget have a tendency to underestimate revenues, to build in a buffer in case some revenues do not show up. Such a buffer prevents deficits, and hence the politically awkward cuts the governor would otherwise have to make in the middle of the year. The legislature has pressed for higher estimations of revenues, knowing that if a deficit occurs during the year, the governor, not the legislature, will have to cut back expenditures.[40] The higher estimates of revenues allow legislators to make a more generous budget and satisfy more claims.

In Michigan, a different dynamic has emerged. Michigan had for many years met recessions with tax increases, but in the late 1970s began to respond to recessions with expenditure reductions. The prior history of growth of expenditures was reversed in the early 1980s. The governor proposed budgets with high estimates of revenue for 1980, 1981, and 1982. The legislature passed the budget pretty much as proposed, but then, in each of the three years, the economy did not grow as expected, "forcing" the governor (with the approval of the legislative appropriations committees) to cut expenditures, reduce state employment, and cut programs.[41] The projected deficits provide apparently irresistible pressure to make cuts while reducing the level of blame. Presumably if the governor had just recommended the cuts initially, he would have run into more opposition. One observer remarked, "Fiscal crises have been an important agent through which the majority of state political officials have chosen to shield their aim of reducing the scope and level of government programs in the state."[42]

In the Michigan case, the politics of balance became linked to the politics of government size. Cutting back on expenditures became the option of choice for dealing with deficits—so much so that the deficits may have been created for the purpose of forcing cuts and gaining political legitimacy for doing so. Of course, the state need not have depended on a cutback strategy; it could instead have chosen to raise revenues. But, since the mid-1970s, there has been increasing pressure in the states to limit revenues and expenditures.

By 1992, twenty-three states had some kind of revenue or expenditure limitation.[43] The earliest of these was New Jersey's in 1976. The bulk of the limitations were passed in 1978, 1979, and 1980. Eleven of the limitations were written into state constitutions.[44] While there was a marked trend toward limitations of revenues in the late 1970s and early 1980s, by 1983 and 1984, the effort seems to have faded. State and local tax revenues in relation to state personal income dropped from 1978 to 1982 from 12.75 percent to 10.96 percent, but by 1984 they were back at 11.71 percent.[45] By 1986, they had dropped again to 11.27 percent.[46] In 1991, in the middle of a recession, four states passed new spending or revenue limitations: Colorado, Connecticut, Louisiana, and North Carolina.[47] State (and local) governments have been cautious about increasing revenues more quickly than income.

Rather than raise taxes during a recession, which may exaggerate the economic downturn and will almost certainly raise a public outcry because taxes will take a bigger bite out of people's shrinking income, or cut expenditures, which are needed more acutely during recessions, some states in recent years have tried to create special funds to tide them through a recession. The idea is to put more money in during periods of economic growth, and to take more money out when the economy is in a slump, without running deficits. Such funds are called "rainy-day funds."

As of the end of 1983, nineteen states had rainy-day funds, most of which had been set up in the early 1980s. ACIR, using a looser definition, estimated that thirty-five states had some kind of stabilization fund in 1988.[48] By 1992, ACIR reported that forty-four states had some kind of fiscal stabilization fund.[49] Some of these funds were tiny or even had a zero balance, however, so their impact during a recession would be minimal, especially if the recession lasted for more than a year.

It is not easy for a state to maintain a high level of annual balance without stimulating demands to either reduce the level of taxation or spend down the surplus. The very large balance held by the state of California before Proposition 13—$4 billion—is said to have contributed to the passage of Proposition 13. If the state was running that large a surplus, then it must have been collecting too much tax money. The farther away politicians get from the last recession and its painful cuts, the greater the temptation to spend down the year-end balance.

Separate rainy-day accounts with automatic provisions for buildup and spenddown may lessen this temptation somewhat. Rainy-day funds, as differentiated from an annual positive balance, set aside money for a specific purpose under state statutes. They are somewhat easier to defend than unearmarked year-end balances that look as if the state collected more revenues than it needed. The formula for funding the rainy-day account is decided first; then the money is set aside each year, generally in a special fund, and is drawn down when economic conditions cause a decline in revenues.[50]

Passing the Buck to Local Governments

For states without effective rainy-day funds, there may be great temptation to balance the budget without cutting expenditures or raising revenues. Since local governments are the subordinates of the states, and have to take orders from state governments, the states can decide to pass the burden of paying for programs and projects to their local governments. Richard Lamm, governor of Colorado, described the politics of passing the buck:

The Gramm-Rudman bill is the result of Washington's inability to deal rationally with its mounting deficit. My hope is that this bill will be a catalyst for more careful analysis of Federal programs. My fear is that it will be an excuse for fiscal federalism at the point of a budgetary bayonet. I would be more critical of the Federal Government but for the fact that Colorado state government plays the same tricks on its cities and counties. Every election year, legislators brag that Colorado ranks forty-eighth nationally in the level of state taxes based on personal income. What they don't tell the public is, local governments are having to shoulder the tax burdens that the state passes along.[51]

When Michigan passed a constitutional amendment in 1977 to limit expenditures, it wrote into its constitution that the state had to maintain the current proportion of expenditures on local governments. The state was forbidden to economize by disproportionately cutting intergovernmental transfers to local governments.

In California, after Proposition 13, the state government provided aid to local governments to make up the losses in revenues. To protect its own finances, however, it passed a law providing that if the state's fiscal condition deteriorated, the aid to local governments would be reduced.

These three examples—Colorado, Michigan, and California—illustrate the three possibilities of passing the burden on to local governments, protecting local governments from increased burdens, and absorbing some of the burden and passing on the rest. To get some idea of which pattern is dominant, one can look at the laws states have passed requiring them to absorb costs resulting from mandates they impose on local governments and at the proportion of state and local spending that the states have picked up over time.

By 1988, fifteen states had passed laws and constitutional amendments requiring state reimbursement for imposed costs. Those laws and amendments overestimate local ability to resist state imposition of costs since half the laws are statutory, and they may be overlooked in practice.[52]

More direct evidence is provided by looking at the state proportion of state and local expenditures (excluding federal aid) over time. If the state proportion is going up or is constant, then the state is not passing on any burden to the local governments. The proportion of state and local expenditures picked up by the state governments increased continuously from 44 percent in 1942 to 58 percent in 1982, but in 1983 and 1984 it began to decline, to 57 percent in 1983 and 56 percent in 1984, rising slightly to 57 percent in 1986. In welfare, the state share increased to a peak of 89 percent in 1982 and then declined to 82 percent in 1984, rising to 83 percent in 1986.

In other areas, such as education, highways, and health and hospitals, the proportion of state aid has remained fairly constant.[53]

These figures are averages derived from all the states and do not specifically deal with the years of recession or with those states that were most fiscally stressed. During 1982, half the states had to make reductions during the year; and during 1983, two-thirds of the states had to make such cuts. In states that had to make cuts, aid to local government was not cut back disproportionately. "Aid did not escape the budget axe, but it was not cut as much as spending on state-operated programs was."[54] Seven states cut across the board, and twenty-two cut aid less than other programs. While the level of aid was generally maintained, there was a marked tendency for states to slow down welfare payments to local governments, making the local governments either sacrifice interest payments or have to borrow in anticipation of state payments.[55]

Fiscal stress in the states became worse in the early 1990s, raising the question again of the extent to which the states would balance their own budgets on the backs of the local governments. These fiscal problems included a recession in 1990–91, explosive growth in Medicaid expenditures, increased enrollments in public schools, and tougher sentencing laws and higher numbers of people imprisoned. General end-of-year balances and rainy-day funds that had averaged 8 or 9 percent of general fund expenditures in the late 1970s and early 1980s dropped as low as 1.1 percent in 1991 and had only risen to about 2.6 percent by 1994.[56]

Since the mid- to late 1980s, the states seemed either more willing to shift the burden to local governments or had less flexibility to do anything but cut higher education and aid to local governments. More of the tax burden is being borne at the local level. "In every year since 1985, local taxes have risen faster than state taxes."[57] Aid to local government generally lost out in comparison to other state spending priorities. From 1990 to 1992, aid to local governments became a smaller percentage of state spending in forty states.[58] California shifted some of the property tax from local governments to the school districts, and then cut the state payments to the schools. It only partially compensated the local governments for this loss. Thus the state reduced its own payments while increasing the financial stress of the local governments.[59] In Minnesota, state aid to local governments dropped from 26 to 18 percent of general fund spending between 1990 and 1995.[60] As fiscal stress intensified at the state level, local governments took a disproportionate hit.

The realignment of the federal, state, and local governments is not yet complete. Deficits continue to squeeze federal spending at the national level, and it is not clear how much of the burden for currently provided programs will fall to the states, or how much of that increased burden the states will put on the local governments. Even with the federal anti–unfunded mandates law, the intensifying crisis at the national level may spill more burdens on to the states. If the states' fiscal picture does not improve, they may continue to pass the burden on to the local governments, with major implications for health, education, and welfare.

The Politics of Balance in Cities

Cities, like states, are required to balance their budgets. But, unlike the federal government, local governments have virtually no role in influencing cycles of the economy with their budgets. Generally, their budgets are too small and their economies too open for local governments to be able to have an impact on the economy. The result is that cities do not have to worry about whether they should run deficits. They try to maintain year-end balances to tide them over when recession hits, but they are often unable to predict downturns in the economy and have to reduce expenditures during the year to balance the budget.

At the local level, as at the state level, considerable effort may be spent to hide or minimize the size of deficits, especially those that are not the result of immediate environmental exigencies. Many of the same tactics used at the state level are employed, including "borrowing" between funds (sometimes invisibly and without intent to repay), changing the basis of accounting so that some expenditures are counted in the next year's budget, delaying paying bills and "borrowing" from pension funds by not putting in the required amount of employer contribution. Cities may also hide deficits by borrowing outside the city for operating expenditures, pretending they are borrowing for capital. Cities sometimes shift expenditures from a fund that is poorer into other funds that are richer.

Depending on the definition of deficit used, cities can make the budget look balanced by drawing down reserves, which is usually technically legal but obscures the fact that the city is running an operating deficit. Or the budget can be balanced with one-time revenues, resulting from the sale of property or grants or other one-time income. Overestimating revenues also makes the budget look more balanced than it is.

When deficits occur unintentionally during the year, the normal response is to gather unspent money and defer spending it until the crisis is over or the council has had a chance to act on priorities. The result may be heavier cuts in some areas than in others; the intent is not to choose program areas but to find money that is as yet unspent. Capital projects are often delayed because the money is not yet spent or irrevocably committed.

When a deficit is imminent in the following year's budget, or when a deficit is carried over from one year to the next, then the manager or mayor makes recommendations for how the deficit gap is to be closed, and the council must approve or disapprove the recommendations. In this situation, program priorities must be decided, revenue increase and expenditure decrease weighed, and scope of services reevaluated. Formally, the council has the power to make these decisions, but in fact the distribution of power between the mayor, manager, or administrator on the one hand and the council, on the other, is highly variable.

The council may give the chief executive officer general policy for the upcoming budget, such as balance the budget without tax increases this year or figure in a 1 percent increase in local sales taxes. The manager or administrator may make recommendations for the figure to use for inflation and give estimates of yield for revenue sources. Council members may accept or reject these estimates, or give alternate estimates. The council may give general guidelines about what services may be cut, and which ones sustained, or it may get involved in the details of line-by-line, program-by-program cuts. Whatever balance of power exists in one year may change the next as council members lose interest or the manager or mayor restructures the budget process and asks for a different kind of input or asks for input at a different stage of the process.

The issue of scope of services is unlikely to arise in response to a midyear revenue decline, but it can arise as local governments wrestle with what appears to be an impending imbalance in the next year's operating budget. For example, in the 1970s when cities were dealing with recessions, economic base erosion, and the effects of the leveling out and decline of federal revenues, if the cities were responsible for a range of functions they often tried to shift some of those functions to other levels of government. Services such as courts, city universities, and museums were either shifted to other levels of government or to the private sector. Some cities gave their planning functions to the county. In some states, cities were able to shift some or all of their share of welfare to the state, and some of the cost of police.[61] More recently, one city wrestling with slow growth in property tax revenues and termination of revenue sharing tried to give a city sewer to the sanitary district, the city bus system to the local state university, the dog pound and animal-control function to the county, and the airport and economic development office to regional authorities.

The option of solving local financial problems by shifting burdens of service delivery elsewhere and begging more revenues from state and national governments may have been cut off by the 1980s. The shift in burden may actually go the other way, toward the cities. If states can build and maintain their rainy-day funds, they may be able to buffer themselves from the worst of the financial pressures and hence not place additional burdens on local governments during recessions. But the states still have to deal with diminished federal aid. How far the federal government will cut back on aid to states and local governments is not clear, but the continuing federal struggle with deficits suggests that the financial pressure on state and local governments will continue. The ability of the states to absorb the fiscal problems of the local governments has diminished in recent years.

The issue of scope arises not only in terms of shifting the level of government at which some services are performed but also in the question of what services will be cut back or eliminated. During the 1970s, when the public seemed determined to hold the line on revenues, cities perceived they had little choice but to cut back services. They chose to do this, insofar as they could, in ways that would not overly affect the public. They cut back in invisible ways, such as delaying maintenance and deferring capital projects. When deep service cuts appeared necessary, their choice was to find some other unit of government to perform the task.

The following example of a city running deficits illustrates several themes about how city budgets get unbalanced, the tendency to obscure deficits when they occur, and the kinds of pressure necessary to force a city to rebalance its budget. The case also illustrates how difficult it can be to cut spending when every expenditure seems to have a political protector or be exempt from cuts. A change in structure was required, with an increase in constraints, in order to force a linkage between revenues and expenditures and create enough central authority to cut back spending proposals. The example occurred in the 1970s, when the option of increasing federal aid was still open. The same story told in the 1980s might have a different ending.

THE POLITICS OF DEFICITS: AN URBAN EXAMPLE

The city of Southside (a fictional name given to protect the anonymity of those involved) ran deficits that were hidden in the budget from 1972 to 1976.[62] During the later part of this period, there was no recession to blame. The initial causes of the deficit include hiring at the same time a young and inexperienced city manager and an inexperienced budget officer. But the city's problems went well beyond hiring a few inexperienced people. It was suffering from a long-term economic base erosion as heavy industry in the region declined and left behind many unemployed and a reduced demand for housing. The result was frozen or slow growing revenues from both sales and property taxes. Department heads and elected officials seemed unwilling or unable to cut back expenditures proportionately. Elected officials at one point actually reduced property tax rates despite increasing costs. The young city manager did not have enough power to force the elected officials and department heads to cut expenditures, so he tried to reduce labor costs instead, aggravating the city's employee unions and actually increasing labor costs.

The young manager initially hid the deficits, then tried to publicize them as a tool to force the council to make the requisite cuts. He used his budget message to warn council members about emerging deficits, but council members later argued that they did not understand that the budget had to balance fund by fund; they said they were looking at the bottom line, in effect, a cash balance. Cash balances are nearly always positive at the end of the year, and are misleading indicators of deficits. The council in effect chose a loose definition of balance.

The deficits were kept secret in part by inappropriate, secret internal borrowing, especially from the cash flow of the water fund. The director of the water department worried that he could no longer do his job properly. He pleaded his case at a budget hearing in an emotional tone. When auditors came to examine the financial records of the city, they refused to audit the water fund, because the records were not complete—the first public acknowledgment of serious financial trouble.

The second key event in forcing the deficits into the public view occurred as the council and manager struggled to deal with the long-term decline of the economic base of the city. They helped promote a new regional shopping center on the edge of the city. To carry out their end of the bargain required annexations, property acquisitions, and capital outlay for water, roads, traffic signals, and a new police substation. The city had to borrow, issuing a bond. The bond issue meant that Moody's, one of the major bond evaluators, would have to examine and certify the city's creditworthiness, or potential bond buyers would not risk their money. The evaluation of the city's creditworthiness was a disaster; the staff had to struggle to retain any rating at all. The problem was now public, and the city had to take action to avoid complete humiliation, as well as to maintain the marketability of its bonds.

The manager tried to cut back expenditures of the departments but was hampered by the independence of the department heads. The police and fire chiefs were hired and fired by a police and fire board, appointed by the mayor, and so were not directly responsible to the city manager and felt free to ignore his budget advice. The fire department was spending more than its budgeted allocation; police department expenditures had grown rapidly in response to urban riots a number of years earlier, and the manager seemed unable to cut them back. He requested cuts from the department heads, which they refused to make. The manager also tried to cut out council members' pet capital projects, but found that he did not have the power to do that either. In frustration, the manager tried to cut some of the union agreements and restructure the unions so that they would be easier to deal with, but ended up with some very expensive arbitration settlements that further unbalanced his budget. The manager was fired, and replaced with a more senior manager.

The new manager froze departmental budgets and increased revenue by increasing federal aid, an option still open in the late 1970s. Perhaps more important, he changed the budget process. He had control over the street department head who was responsible to him, and fired him. The manager forbade department heads to communicate directly to the council without going through him, to prevent end runs in which department heads got protection for expenditures from the council before they put them in the budget request. The new manager insisted on the right to hire the police and fire chiefs, and was successful, so they reported to him. The fire department was broken out of the general fund and set up with its own earmarked taxes, so the temptation to overspend by borrowing from other departments was reduced. These changes vastly increased the manager's ability to control budget requests and spending of the departments. The departments and the council were burdened with more constraints, but the manager had more authority to enforce balance.

The case study of Southside indicates that despite balanced budget requirements, cities sometimes do run deficits, but because of the balance constraint, the size of the deficits may be obscured. When that happens, the size of the deficit can grow to a substantial portion of all spending and make remedies politically difficult. Because many of the actors shared a belief that the property tax could not be increased because the public would not tolerate it, the expenditure decrease option was explored. But the political coalitions that supported expenditures were stronger than the young manager, and he failed to make significant cuts. When the manager was finally fired, and the city resolved to handle its deficit problems, they chose budget process reform as a key to the solution. Give the manager more power to make cuts and balance the budget; centralize the executive budget process. The deficits seemed to result as much from failure of structure as from economic circumstances, so a reform of structure seemed a logical response.

Summary and Conclusions

Budget balancing is a lot more than a technical activity that readjusts spending and revenue decisions. It is structurally linked to issues about the scope of government because balance depends on decisions to raise taxes and maintain scope, or cut spending and reduce scope. Balance is also linked to spending priorities because when cutbacks in expenditures are used, some programs will be protected and others cut back disproportionately, or all programs will be cut across the board. Balance is linked to federalism because the scope of responsibilities and the relationship between revenue capacity and spending responsibilities can easily be changed as one level of government seeks to balance its budget at the expense of others. Finally, the politics of balance is linked to the politics of process, as governments shift budget-making power in an attempt to increase discipline, control expenditures, and systematically and authoritatively link revenues and expenditures.

Many of the issues involved in budget balance are not immediate distributional questions, but questions of the structure and size of government, questions on the level of taxation, and sometimes even questions on the form of government. These questions bring out ideological differences between people, between Democrats and Republicans, liberals and conservatives, farmers and city people, business and labor. Even the public at large may be involved, in terms of preferences for taxation levels or insistence on the constraint of balance.

Those who want to limit the size of government have striven to link spending caps with balanced budget requirements and have sought to reduce flexibility to a minimum, striving to place simply worded amendments in the constitution. Business groups have sought to limit the size of government while maintaining their own tax breaks by excluding tax expenditures from controls. Those who want government to continue to provide existing programs or even expand them have sought to maintain balance without constraints on revenues.

More specialized interest groups and department heads may become involved in the politics of balance if particular programs are threatened by cuts; they increase the constraints on cutting the budget, making the political choices more difficult, and hence encourage options that do not rely on deep budget cuts. One consequence of the political difficulty of making cuts is delay, minimizing the size and importance of the problem, hoping it will go away. When governments resort to delay, at state and local levels where they are normally required by law to provide balance, the result has been the use of gimmicks that make the budget appear balanced.

The politics of balance is closely linked to the politics of budget implementation. A budget can become unbalanced during the year because of environmental changes. Also, some of the gimmicks used to make the budget look balanced cause problems during the budget year. Budgeters may overestimate revenues and underestimate expenditures so that the budget as submitted looks balanced, but it will become unbalanced during the year. At the state and local levels, the budget may have to be changed during the year to rebalance it. At any level of government, departments may request supplemental appropriations if their initial estimates of expenditures were too low. Requirements for balance also encourage interfund transfers during the year, to make the budget look more balanced than it is. The importance of changes that occur during the budget year is discussed in the next chapter.

Notes

1. Alan Blinder and Douglas Holtz-Eakin, "Public Opinion and the Balanced Budget," *American Economic Review* 74 (May 1984): 144–49.

2. Advisory Commission on Intergovernmental Relations, *Significant Features of Fiscal Federalism,* vol. 1, *Budget Processes and Tax Systems, 1992* (Washington, D.C.: ACIR, 1992), table 3.

3. Congressional Budget Office, *Historical Tables of the United States Budget* (Washington, D.C.: Government Printing Office, January 1996), table 1.1.

4. David Stockman, "The Crisis in Federal Budgeting," in *Crisis in the Budget Process: Exercising Political Choice,* ed. Allen Schick (Washington, D.C.: AEI Press, 1986).

5. Ibid., 65.

6. Allen Schick, "The Evolution of Congressional Budgeting," in Schick, *Crisis in the Budget Process,* 53.

7. Norman Ornstein, "The Politics of the Deficit," in *Essays in Contemporary Economic Problems,* ed. Phillip Cagan (Washington, D.C.: AEI Press, 1985), 311.

8. "Stockman Book Offers An Inside View," *New York Times,* 13 April 1986, sect. 1.

9. David Stockman, *Triumph of Politics* (New York: Harper & Row, 1986), 124.

10. U.S. Congress, House, *Hearings before the Ways and Means Committee, Administration's Views on the Deficit and Possible Revenue Increases for the Next Three Fiscal Years,* 14 June 1983, 15.

11. U.S. Congress, House, Subcommittee on Monopolies and Commercial Law of the Judiciary Committee, *Hearings, Constitutional Amendments Seeking to Balance the Budget and Limit Federal Spending,* 97th Cong., 3 August 1982, 351–64.

12. U.S. Senate, *Balanced Budget—Tax Limitation Constitutional Amendment,* Senate Report 98–628, 1984, 13.

13. From speech given to the Association for Budgeting and Financial Management, Washington D.C., 15 October 1993.

14. Jeffrey Birnbaum, "House Rejects Bid to Require Balanced Budget," *Wall Street Journal,* 12 June 1992, A2.

15. Philip G. Joyce and Robert Reischauer, "The Federal Line-Item Veto: It's Now the Law, But What Effect Will It Have?" July 1996. Photocopied.

16. U.S. Congress, House, *Hearings of the Task Force on Federal Spending Limitation Proposals of the Committee on Rules, on Legislative Measures to*

Amend the Congressional Budget and Impoundment Control Act of 1974, 96th Cong., 2d sess., 1980, 127.

17. "Budget Balancing Change for Constitution Loses," *New York Times,* March 1986, 11.

18. Statement submitted to the Task Force on Spending Limitations, Committee on Rules, U.S. House of Representatives, 20 March 1980.

19. *Hearings on Federal Spending Limitation Proposals,* 133.

20. Ibid., 127.

21. Ibid., 123.

22. Ibid., 193.

23. Harry S. Havens, "Gramm-Rudman-Hollings: Origins and Implementation," *Public Budgeting and Finance* 6, no. 3 (Autumn 1986): 15–19.

24. Dorothy Collins, "'87 Budget Optimism Urged," *Chicago Tribune,* 23 April 1986.

25. "Freezing of Transport Funds Debated," *New York Times,* 25 March 1986, 11.

26. U.S. Congress, Senate, *Budget Reform Proposals, Joint Hearings before the Committee on Governmental Affairs and the Committee on the Budget,* 101st Congress, 1st sess., 18 and 26 October 1989, 167. Roy Meyers, *Strategic Budgeting* (Ann Arbor: University of Michigan Press, 1994), 75, lists the government sponsored enterprises that were proposed in 1986–1987: the Corporation for Small Business Investments, the Airways Corporation, the National Public Works Corporation, the National Long-Term Care Corporation, and several GSE-style corporations to carry out uranium enrichment.

27. *Budget Reform Proposals,* 147.

28. *Historical Tables of the United States,* 1996.

29. Congressional Budget Office, *Reducing the Deficit: Spending and Revenue Options,* (Washington, D.C.: Government Printing Office, February 1995), 3.

30. Tony Hutchison and Kathy James, *Legislative Budget Procedures in the Fifty States: A Guide to Appropriations and Budget Processes* (Denver: National Conference of State Legislatures, 1988), 92–93.

31. John G. Cross, "Michigan State Expenditures and the Provision of Public Services," in *Michigan's Fiscal and Economic Structure,* ed. Harvey Brazer and Deborah Laren (Ann Arbor: University of Michigan Press, 1982), 379.

32. Steven Gold, "Preparing for the Next Recession: Rainy Day Funds and Other Tools for States," Legislative Finance Paper no. 41, National Conference of State Legislatures, Denver, Colo., 30 December 1983, 12.

33. Statement of Lowell Weicker, 13 May 1992. U.S. Congress, House, *Hearings before the Committee on the Budget,* 102d Cong., 2d sess., 12, 13, 19 May and 3 June 1992, 216.

34. State of Connecticut, *Governor's Budget Summary, 1992–1993.*

35. U.S. Congress, House, *Hearings Before Committee on the Budget,* 12 May 1992, 8.

36. Example modified from ibid., 14.

37. Robert Albritton and Ellen Dran, "Balanced Budgets and State Surpluses: The Politics of Budgeting in Illinois," *Public Administration Review* 47, no. 2 (March/April 1987): 135–42.

38. Illinois Economic and Fiscal Commission, *Revenue Estimate and Economic Outlook for FY 1978*, (Springfield, Ill.: June 1977), 17; cited in Albritton and Dran, "Balanced Budgets," 144.

39. Naomi Caiden and Jeffrey Chapman, "Constraint and Uncertainty: Budgeting in California," *Public Budgeting and Finance* 2, no. 4 (Winter 1982): 114–15.

40. Albritton and Dran, "Balanced Budgets," 145.

41. Harvey Brazer, "The Anatomy of a Fiscal Crisis: The Michigan Case," *Public Budgeting and Finance* 2, no. 4 (Winter 1982): 140.

42. Ibid., 140.

43. ACIR, *Significant Features of Fiscal Federalism, 1994*, 14–15.

44. Ibid., table 6.

45. ACIR, *Significant Features of Fiscal Federalism, 1985–1986*, 52.

46. ACIR, *Significant Features of Fiscal Federalism, 1988*, 72.

47. ACIR, *Significant Features of Fiscal Federalism, 1994*, table 6.

48. Gold, "Preparing for the Next Recession," 2; ACIR, *Significant Features of Fiscal Federalism, 1989*, table 74.

49. ACIR, *Significant Features of Fiscal Federalism 1994*, vol. 1, table 4.

50. Gold, "Preparing for the Next Recession," 7–8.

51. "Learning to Live in an Age of Strict Limits," *New York Times*, 13 April 1986, "The Week in Review," 5.

52. ACIR, *Significant Features of Fiscal Federalism, 1985–1986*, 163. See also Janet Kelly, *State Mandated Local Government Expenditures and Revenue Limitations in South Carolina* (Columbia: South Carolina ACIR, June 1988).

53. ACIR, *Significant Features of Fiscal Federalism, 1988*, 48–59.

54. Steven Gold, *State and Local Fiscal Relations in the Early 1980's* (Washington, D.C.: Urban Institute Press, 1983), 29.

55. Ibid., 33.

56. Steven Gold, "State Fiscal Problems and Policies," in *The Fiscal Crisis of the States*, ed. Steven Gold (Washington, D.C.: Georgetown University Press, 1995), 14.

57. Ibid, 33.

58. Ibid.

59. Jeffrey Chapman, "California: The Enduring Crisis," in Gold, *Fiscal Crisis of the States*, 125–26.

60. Thomas Luce, Jr., "Innovation in an Era of Constraint," in Gold, *Fiscal Crisis of the States*, 338.

61. Charles Levine, Irene Rubin, and George Wolohojian, *The Politics of Retrenchment* (Beverly Hills, Calif.: Sage, 1981).

62. Irene Rubin, *Running in the Red: The Political Dynamics of Urban Fiscal Stress* (Albany: State University of New York Press, 1982).

7. Budget Execution: The Politics of Adaptation

Budget execution is the fun part of budgeting, and the most important part. You get to see how good your estimates were, and whether it all works. You can't just put a budget on the shelf and expect it to work.
— Neil Neilson, City Manager

Budgets are passed at the end of a long period of analysis, debate, disagreement, and compromise. As a result, they often seem to be the outcome and end point of the budgetary process. But budgeting does not stop completely once the budget becomes law. Because of a changing economy, poor predictions of revenues and expenditures, continuing political battles, changed leadership, and the altered salience of public problems, the budget may change after it is passed. Whether or not the budget changes, it must be implemented, to ensure that the amounts budgeted are actually spent in the manner outlined. Every budget goes through an implementation stage.

The implementation stage often involves formulas for disbursements and rules about how much money can be shifted from one item or program to another after the budget has been passed. The emphasis in budget execution is on carrying out the budget exactly as it was enacted, which makes budget execution seem highly technical, the proper sphere of administrators and accountants, devoid of political content. In reality, budget execution is also political because it regulates the degree of public accountability in the budget, because it involves battles for policy control between the executive and the legislature, and because even the most technical of issues, such as the elimination of waste, fraud, and abuse, may become part of political campaigns.

The people who draw up a budget have to make predictions about revenues and expenditures, predictions based on guesses about the future performance of the economy, the rate of inflation, and even the weather. When the economy improves, revenues increase, and outlays for programs such as unemployment compensation and welfare go down. When the economy slows down, revenues drop off, and expenditures for unemployment compensation and welfare go up. Inflation affects the price of goods and services purchased during the year, as well as the payout for pensions that rise with the cost of living. Weather conditions affect the cost of heating bills, street repairs, and cleanups after hurricanes, tornadoes, or floods. If the guesses underlying the budget are wrong, the budget may be adjusted in midyear to reflect the real revenues and expenditures. If budgets are required to balance before the end of the fiscal year, environmental changes may force budget changes.

Budgets may change during the year because the budget process was not complete before the beginning of the fiscal year. The budget year may begin under one set of figures but continue under a different set after the decision making is completed. Budget actors may tentatively resolve an issue, expressing the result in the budget, but later back off from the agreement, bringing about a new set of negotiations. Sometimes actors distort information in order to get an agreement that will pass, but end up with an unworkable budget and have to modify it later.

A budget may represent the best thinking and compromises of actors involved during budget preparation, in reaction to situations that were pressing at the time, but the salience of problems and the composition of the actors may change by the time the budget is executed, requiring changes in the budget itself. When leadership changes, which often occurs during a budget year, the new insiders may be eager to implement their policies and hence may make changes in the existing budget.

For all these reasons—a changing economy, continuing political battles, a changed leadership, and the altered salience of public problems—the budget implemented may not be the same as the budget passed. A certain amount of flexibility and change during the budget year may be both necessary and desirable. But changing the budget during the fiscal year raises potential problems.

Granting the executive branch wide discretion to implement the budget and make such changes as may be necessary may give agency heads or chief executives a disproportionate amount of decision-making power not allowed during the regular budget process. If agency heads or the chief executive use that discretionary power to reverse the intent of the legislature, the result may be a major battle between the executive and legislative branches. And changes in the budget during the year, if they are extensive or clearly policy related, may create a shadowy second budget process, outside public scrutiny, threatening the ability of the budget as originally passed to represent government decisions to the public.

The need for flexibility in the budget, to adapt to changing conditions, conflicts with the need to implement the budget as it was passed. Public accountability requires that the budget passed in full public view, with public and interest-group participation, be the budget implemented.

How is this dilemma resolved? First, budgets are generally implemented as passed. The requirement to do so is taken seriously, so that consideration of important policy issues that arise during the year is often delayed until the next full budget process. Second, flexibility is allowed and discretion is granted by the legislatures to the executive branch to make necessary minor or technical changes during the year. These technical adjustments may be carefully monitored (constrained) to ensure that more important policy decisions are not slipped in among the more routine adaptations without due consideration and participation.

Policy-laden budget decisions may be allowed during the year under particular conditions. When a new president is elected, he may be given fairly broad rein in reshaping the existing budget to fit his policies. Or Congress may design and implement new programs for relief of farmers in the middle of a drought or to help the unemployed during a deep recession. These decisions are made in the normal way, by the usual committees; what is unusual about them is that they feed into the budget in the middle of the year, and they may be made in haste. In these cases, the changes have high visibility and widespread public acceptability. Consequently, they do not threaten public acceptability or accountability.

Despite the care with which budgets are normally implemented, deviations from the budget that are not routine and minor sometimes occur. These deviations may be of two kinds. The first is a violation of fiscal control, resulting in overspending or waste, fraud, or abuse. The second is a violation of policy control, in which some budget actor makes policy changes in the budget without going through the whole formal, public business of lawmaking. If the consequences are serious enough, or irritating enough, or embarrassing enough, the chief executive or the legislature may increase control over budget implementation. The legislature may increase its control over the executive, the chief executive may increase his or her control over the agencies. The result may be an increase in the number and severity of constraints over budget implementation—the third characteristic of public budgeting.

Adapting to Economic Changes

Budgets can be affected by declining economies either through decreases in revenues or increases in program expenditures triggered by increased unemployment and poverty. At the federal level, the pattern has been to increase supplemental expenditures when the economy declines in order to cover increased program costs. The result is to add to the size of the deficit during the year. (The data in table 7.1, p. 233, show how supplemental expenditures increased during the recession of the mid-1970s.)

The Congressional Budget Office estimated that for 1970 to 1980 about 28 percent of supplemental appropriations was for expenditures that were underestimated as a result of changing economic conditions.[1] Of supplemental money spent in the mid-1970s because of recession, a substantial proportion was caused by new programs enacted during the year, such as the extension of unemployment benefits in 1975 and the enactment of antirecession fiscal assistance to cities in 1976. A similar story could be told of the 1980s, when supplemental appropriations jumped up during the deep recession of 1982–83. Not only were costs increased for unemployment benefits—the total cost of unemployment compensation was reported at $32 billion in 1983[2]—but a new jobs program was enacted (P.L. 98-8). The cost of the Emergency Jobs Appropriations Supplemental Appropriation was over $16 billion, or about two-thirds of the entire supplemental appropriations for the year. The extension of benefits through new legislation is by no means automatic; it is a political choice made possible by changing economic and hence changing political conditions. During a deep recession, political pressure for relief creates increased political salience for new legislation.

At the state and local levels, because deficits are formally forbidden, supplementals are rarely used to adapt to negative changes in the economy. Midyear adaptations to economic declines are more likely to include budget cuts, tax increases, and reductions in reserve accounts. Because these adaptations are so much more politically painful than supplemental appropriations, more effort is taken to prevent or delay such midyear action. The tough political decisions are likely to be postponed at least until the next budget cycle when they can be considered at length as part of the normal budget preparation process. If the recession is brief, the economy may have recovered by the next budget cycle, preventing the necessity for tax increases or deep service cuts.

The adaptation of states to recessions implies that if politicians delay, they will not have to make serious budgetary changes. But for some states, a downturn in the economy may be of long duration rather than temporary. For example, states affected by long-term economic declines in farming and energy prices found themselves faced with midyear reductions in expenditures in 1986. Mississippi reduced its budget midyear by 4.67 percent; Oklahoma, by 4.5 percent; Arkansas by 4.3 percent.[3] Texas led the way, with midyear budget cuts totaling 13 percent of the budget. Texas is dependent for about one-third of its state revenues on taxation of gas and oil production. The drop in oil prices that occurred in 1986 created a severe midyear decline in revenues, and a shortfall of $1.3 billion. The initial state response was to delay, to belt tighten, and to borrow cash from other funds to put into the general fund, until the issue could be addressed as part of a full budget discussion.[4] It takes a long time to build a consensus for new policies in response to a long-term decline. Texas was still wrestling with these revenue problems in 1991, with an estimated budget gap of $4.6 billion in a two-year budget of $53 billion.[5]

At the state level, the cost of delaying a response to economic decline is often short-term budget manipulation and a reduction in the usefulness of the budget as an instrument of accountability.[6] The long-run effect, however, is to ensure that policy decisions reflected in the budget are made in the open, during the regular budget process by the authorized and appropriate budget actors. The slow building of consensus for radical changes in spending or revenue structure encourages public participation. The public nature of the decisions guarantees substantial public accountability.

The response of cities to apparently temporary downturns in the economy is similar to that of the states, that is, there is a general belt tightening during the year and a delay of consideration of major changes in taxation or program levels until the following budget cycle. Two ministudies of city-manager cities illustrate the responses to temporary revenue shortfalls. The first case, of Rock Island, Illinois, illustrates the belt tightening phenomenon and the delay of policy decisions until the following year. The city avoided major cuts at the expense of running deficits briefly. The second case, De-Kalb, Illinois, illustrates a response in which deficits were avoided by making fairly severe cuts, but the cuts were taken in such a way as to avoid major policy choices. The DeKalb case also shows the efforts cities take to avoid policy decisions in revising the budget during the year, even when revenues are unexpectedly large, as opposed to when they are unexpectedly small.

MINICASE I : ROCK ISLAND, ILLINOIS

Rock Island is a council-manager city that was seriously affected by the deep recession of the early 1980s. The city manager described it: "We had about a $300,000 deficit that one year [1983]. The personal property replacement tax failed [this is a payment from the state] and sales and income tax revenues declined." The city addressed these problems the following year; but during 1983, the city did not make hasty policy changes in the budget; the major response was belt tightening. The result was that the city ran a deficit in 1983.

The manager described the process of belt tightening that goes on when a revenue shortfall is detected during the year. "You get the department heads together, and tell them you need help. Where can you give me money? They know I'm fair. They will help. Someone may say to me, 'We can delay our purchases of new radios until next year.' Sometimes you freeze capital improvements, but there are some projects you can't stop. Then you try to coast it out for the rest of the year."

The actions taken often assumed either the economy would improve or the council would increase taxes and make appropriate cuts for the following year. But the manager had to be prepared for the possibility that the council would not raise taxes. To prevent deeper cuts and reduce the size of the deficit, he tried to build up the size of the year-end balance, despite the deficits. The year-end balance is carried over to the following year. In order to build up the balance, "The departments will underspend. You need 'cash carry forward.' If the council won't increase taxes, you try to make savings this year [for next year]. If you overstated the cost of something [this year], don't spend the difference."

The Rock Island case indicates several points. First, during the year in which revenues dropped, there was no major rebudgeting, that is, no deep targeted cuts that changed program priorities. The budget was carried out pretty much as passed, despite the looming deficits. Responses included new procedures to respond more quickly to falling revenues, deferral of capital expenditures, job freezes, and delays in refilling positions. The departments cooperated with the cuts, the content of which was not centrally dictated. The city staff worked on creating a buffer/contingency fund for deficit reduction, carrying a small amount of one year's money into the next year.

Getting the departments to go along with the deferrals required the political credit of the manager. His modest statement about their reason for cooperating was that "they know I'm fair." In other cities, such trust may not be there. If the departments are not cooperative, it can be very difficult to make cuts during the year. The degree of authority of the mayor or manager is an important part of these informal "voluntary" cuts.

MINICASE 2 : DEKALB, ILLINOIS

The DeKalb case illustrates the budgetary adaptation both to a revenue shortfall and to a revenue windfall, and shows exactly where the money was cut during the shortfall.

In 1980–81, DeKalb experienced a revenue shortfall in the general fund. They had planned to receive $5,637,472 in revenues, and to use some of the year-end balance from 1980 for 1981 expenses. Actual revenues were only $5,420,793, and the year-end balance never materialized. To avoid deficits in 1981, the city had to cut $635,936 (about 10.4 percent of the budget) in midyear. Then it had to find what funds it could to build a year-end balance to carry over into the following year. (No balance at all is considered very risky. Cities and states normally keep year-end balances of about 5 percent of the budget.) The city managed to cut expenditures by $654,332, avoiding a deficit, but was not able to contribute much to the fund balance.

What expenditures were reduced in the middle of the year? An amount totaling $282,005 came from Public Works (overtime, repairs to traffic signals, sidewalk repair, snow and ice control, vehicle maintenance, and labor for storm sewers); $255,000 came from general fund support, including $175,000 budgeted for storm sewers and $80,000 for contingency. About $50,000 came from the legislative section, from underspending by the Economic Development Commission. About $40,000 came from police (travel, training, and office equipment); $30,000 came from fire (training, vehicle maintenance, training overtime, and personal services); $18,000 came from code enforcement. Slight increases from other departments reduced the savings from $680,000 to $654,332.

These cuts were in no sense across the board. The bulk of the cuts came from public works. Some of it came from delayable projects, such as storm sewers and sidewalk repairs. Some of it came from small earmarked contingency funds, such as for snow removal and traffic-signal accidents. The next largest amount was from general fund support, which was primarily for the capital portion of the sewer project, and from a small contingency fund. Other departmental savings were minor—from travel, training, vehicle maintenance, and office equipment. In short, the process of cutting and postponing picks up money wherever it is available—from large capital projects with low immediate need and from contingency funds.

Interestingly, in 1983-84, as the city was pulling out of the recession, it found that it had underestimated revenue. Did it then allocate the surplus during the year? No. Instead, it replenished the year-end balance.

To summarize, budgets at all levels adapted to economic declines during the year. There was a tendency to treat the changes as minor (even when the dollar amounts were major) and without political content, to delay the policy decision making until the next budget cycle. At the state and local levels, spending was often trimmed during the year, mostly by absorbing whatever money was loose, that is, not yet absolutely committed. Some programs were hurt more than others because they depended more on contingency funds and their budgets were heavy with capital projects or equipment purchases that could be delayed. Agencies with relatively high turnover were more likely to be hurt by hiring freezes and delays. Implicit in these responses to economic conditions is the policy that providing services or transfer payments at stable or increasing levels is sometimes more important than balancing the budget in a given year.

THE POLITICS OF PUBLIC BUDGETING

Budgeting has to be adaptive not only to economic declines, but also to economic recovery and growth. When the economy first begins to improve after a recession or a slowdown in growth, revenues often come in higher than budgeted. The typical response is to use the extra revenues to build back reserves depleted during the recession, without changing expenditures. But what happens if revenue growth continues after fund balances are replenished and revenues are continuously underestimated? What happens to the surplus of uncommitted revenues that appears during the year?

A case study of the state of Georgia for the period 1977 to 1986 is suggestive about how such uncommitted revenues may be used. Under conditions of continuing economic growth and systematic underestimation of revenue, Georgia made midyear appropriations a standard feature of the budget.[7] While the average increase over the general appropriation was only 2.9 percent, in some years 5 percent or more over the general appropriation was allocated midyear.

The money was allocated differently from the general appropriation. "Legislators view the midyear budget amendment as an opportunity to fund local projects that do not compete very well with statewide projects when the General Appropriation Act is initially approved ... there is generally much more pork in the midyear amendment."[8] Some agencies are able to do much better in the midyear allocation than in the normal annual budget, but not because priorities are redetermined or changed in the middle of the year. Fiscal conservativeness leads "legislative leaders and the governor to prefer capital construction projects which will not have recurring obligations in years when the surplus may not be available."[9] Similarly, they prefer projects that have a potential of producing revenue.[10] The result is that departments having appropriate projects get more of the midyear revenues, which are treated (properly) as one-time revenues.

Georgia's budget behavior may or may not be typical of other states, but it suggests an underlying principle. When increases in revenues are seen as resulting from unpredictable growth in the economy, the money is appropriately treated as one-time revenues to be spent primarily on one-time expenditures. Just as cuts during a recession come disproportionately from departments with major projects that can be delayed, some departments will do better during economy-induced windfalls because they have the right kind of projects to absorb temporary money. Over the long term, and as part of routine budget decision making, politicians may alter the emphasis on one program or another,[11] but during the year, there was little reprioritizing. While there were midyear changes in response to change in the economy, the budgeting process was not repeated on a smaller scale during the year, either by bureaucrats or by elected officials.

Budgetary Changes for Noneconomic Reasons

There are many other reasons for changing the budget in midyear besides adapting to the ups and downs of the economy. Programs may become obsolete, making expenditures unnecessary; a new president may come into office eager to make a policy impact on his predecessor's budget; agencies may not accept decisions made during the budget approval stage and may request changes; contingencies such as weather conditions or changing political situations may require increases in state or foreign aid or in emergency services. Some of the changes that occur in the budget are for technical and relatively nonpolitical reasons, but some are more policy related. This section describes the kinds of budgetary changes and explores the relative policy content of each kind of change. Changes include supplemental appropriations, rescissions and deferrals, reprogrammings, building and depleting contingency and reserve funds, and interfund transfers. In all instances, the proportion of the budget involved in these adjustments is small; the proportion of these changes that is policy related is also small.

SUPPLEMENTAL APPROPRIATIONS

Supplemental appropriations are laws passed to add to the budget after it is passed. They are used primarily at the national level because the federal budget may run deficits, so an increase in spending during the year (the supplemental) just adds to the size of the deficit. At the state level, supplementals are sometimes used, but the funding has to come from fund balances, which operate like savings accounts. The amount is limited by the size of the savings accounts. At the local level, supplementals are seldom used, except to pay for collective bargaining agreements reached after the budget has been passed. Supplemental appropriations fit the model of a separate budget process after the major and well-publicized budget process is over, so the content, size, and purpose of supplementals is important in determining the level of accountability in the budget.

At the federal level, agencies request supplementals. The OMB must approve the request before it is transmitted to Congress. Congress collects most of the requests to consider as one or two omnibus supplemental bills, but a few bills are usually passed separately, outside the omnibus bills.

According to a Congressional Budget Office study,[12] supplemental appropriations at the federal level varied between 2.8 percent and 7.8 percent of budget authority from 1970 to 1980. In dollar terms, the lowest amount was $5.994 billion and the highest for the decade was $36.724 billion. By any standard, these are substantial amounts of money. As discussed earlier, less than a third of all supplementals during the 1970s was spent in adapting to changes in the economy. What about the rest of the supplementals?

Some 36 percent of the supplementals reflected delayed authorizations or new legislation during the year. If the authorizing legislation specified increased dollar amounts of spending ceilings for programs, late authorizations might result in supplemental appropriations. Also, new legislation completed during the year might require start-up funding not provided for in the budget. While legislation can be late for a variety of reasons, much of the delay is because legislators are still exploring issues and working out compromises.[13] New legislation during the budget year is often in response to changing political priorities. Hence, many of these supplementals are both explicitly political and policy related. They follow the normal legislative process, however, and represent agreements worked out by all parties. There is nothing invisible about them, and they do not distort the official distribution of power in the budget process or represent stress between branches of government.

About 15 percent of the supplementals were for salary increases. The regular appropriations bills exclude salary increases, so agencies have to request supplemental appropriations during the year to cover them. The omission of salary increases from the appropriations bills makes the cost of programs look smaller than they are, which may be one reason for this practice. The justification for using supplementals for salary increases is quite different, however. There is pressure from both OMB and Congress for agencies to use unspent money to fund salary increases. The logic is that if agencies have money lying around unspent, they will spend it on something unnecessary rather than return it to the Treasury, so the money would be better spent by contributing toward the salary increase. Agencies have to wait until part of the year has passed and they know the amount of unspent money before they can request a supplemental appropriation for the rest of the salary increase.

Some of the supplemental appropriations have occurred because a new president wanted to put his imprimatur on an existing budget by raising appropriations for some agencies and lowering the appropriations for others. The first year of the Carter administration saw supplemental appropriations for social service programs that had been reduced by his predecessors. The first year of the Reagan administration saw supplementals for the Defense Department. The request for the supplemental in defense was for $12.3 billion, an amount much larger than most supplemental requests.

The rather dramatic increase in the amount of supplementals in the early years of a new president is demonstrated by the peak in 1977, the first Carter year, and by a second peak in the first years of the Reagan administration. Tables 7.1, 7.2, and 7.3 show the amounts of supplementals from 1970 through 1989 net of rescissions. Since there were many rescissions in 1981 as Reagan reshaped the budget, the figure looks low for 1981. Without

TABLE 7.1

SUPPLEMENTAL APPROPRIATIONS, 1970–89

NET OF RESCISSIONS

Year	Budget authority		Year	Budget authority	
	Amount (in millions)	Percentage of total budget authority		Amount (in millions)	Percentage of total budget authority
1970	$ 5,994	2.8	1980	$19,461	2.9
1971	9,871	4.2	1981	6,923	.9
1972	11,599	4.7	1982	21,020	2.6
1973	11,371	4.1	1983	21,123	2.4
1974	14,796	4.7	1984	16,222	1.7
1975	27,588	6.7	1985	14,804	1.4
1976	24,636	5.9	1986	2,249	.2
1977	36,724	7.8	1987	9,370	.9
1978	16,054	3.1	1988	1,302	.1
1979	13,845	2.5	1989	5,615	.5

SOURCE: Congressional Budget Office, *Supplemental Appropriations in the 1980s,* x.

subtracting the rescissions, however, there were $21.7 billion in supplementals in 1981 and $27.0 billion in 1982.[14]

The use of supplemental appropriations has declined at the federal level. In the 1970s, net supplementals averaged about 4.6 percent of total budget authority; from 1980 to 1989, they averaged 1.3 percent of budget authority, and the trend was down—from 1985 to 1989, net supplementals accounted for an average of .6 percent of budget authority. To some extent, this decline in supplementals has resulted from a long period of economic growth, which has reduced the need for supplementals to handle entitlement spending that increases during recessions. But to some extent, the reduction has been intentional. In the Bipartisan Budget Agreements of 1987 and 1989, Congress said that it would consider supplementals only for "dire emergencies." Supplemental spending for defense seems to have been especially sharply curtailed.[15]

The number of dire emergencies increased in the early 1990s, with an earthquake in California; Hurricanes Bob, Andrew, and Iniki; and Mississippi flooding throughout the Midwest. The need for increased supplemental spending for defense jumped with the Desert Shield, Desert Storm expenses. Hurricanes cost nearly $4.4 billion in supplemental budget authority in 1992; Midwest flood relief was almost $4.1 billion in 1993; and the Califor-

TABLE 7.2
SUPPLEMENTAL APPROPRIATIONS, 1990–95
NET OF RESCISSIONS

	Budget authority	
Year	Amount (in millions)	Percentage of total budget authority
1990	$ 2,253	.16
1991	45,771	3.30
1992	16,107	1.09
1993	7,345	.49
1994	8,229	.53
1995	−889[a]	n.a.

SOURCE: Cost of Supplementals through 17 May 1995 provided by the Congressional Budget Office, Scorekeeping Unit; calculations of percentage of budget authority based on U.S. Budget Historical Tables.

a. This figure represents only two of the three major supplementals for the year. The third one, which occurred after 17 May, had about $7.4 billion in supplementals but about $15.5 billion in rescissions. A net figure for supplementals for 1995 would add this negative $8 billion ($7.4 billion supplemental minus $15.5 billion rescission) to the negative $889 million from the first two supplementals, for a whopping negative number of about $8.8 billion.

TABLE 7.3
SUPPLEMENTAL APPROPRIATIONS, 1990–95
EMERGENCY AND NONEMERGENCY

	Budget authority (in millions)		
Year	Emergency	Nonemergency	Total
1990	$ 0	$4,297	$ 4,297
1991	44,846	1,256	46,102
1992	22,008	2,526	24,534
1993	5,248	4,594	9,842
1994	11,398	2	11,400
1995	≈6,865[a]	≈595[a]	7,460

SOURCE: Cost of Supplementals through 17 May 1995 provided by the Congressional Budget Office, Scorekeeping Unit; remainder of 1995 calculated by the author from P.L. 104-19.

a. These numbers are approximate because of the large amount of unaggregated data and the difficulty of figuring out what constitutes an addition to budget authority. I have included contract authority in budget authority. The division into emergency and nonemergency is taken directly from the law.

nia earthquake alone resulted in $9.6 billion of supplemental budget authority in 1994. Desert Storm and Desert Shield added about $43 billion in supplemental budget authority in 1991 and about $14 billion in 1992.[16]

Short of real emergencies, the constraint requiring that cuts be made elsewhere or revenues increased to fund supplementals limited the number and size of supplementals. A military readiness supplemental passed in April 1995, for example, was funded by rescissions in the Department of Defense and foreign aid.

Supplementals have not disappeared completely but they have become more restricted to genuine emergencies. From 1990 through May of 1995 there were $12.5 billion in nonemergency supplementals and $85.9 billion in emergency supplementals. This balance resulted in part from the timing of the Gulf War, but may have also resulted from the passage of the 1990 Budget Enforcement Act with its strict spending ceilings, with exceptions for genuine emergencies. The use of supplementals more exclusively for emergencies signals a decline in their policy content and policy contentiousness. Nevertheless, because of their association with rescissions, supplementals have continued to provoke controversy. *cutback*

Because supplementals and rescissions often appear together in the same legislation, one may be held hostage to the other. For example, in 1995 the Republican-dominated Congress proposed rescissions in many programs that the president found objectionable, but because the legislation was paired with supplementals that would provide relief to Oklahoma City after the bombing of the federal building in that city, congressional Republicans expected the president to accept the whole package. But the president threatened to veto the bill. Republicans responded by accusing the Democratic president of holding emergency relief hostage to his political preferences and charged him with being against balancing the budget. The president countercharged that Congress could pass a relief measure that afternoon, and that it should. He placed the burden for not funding the emergency relief back on to Congress. To avoid the charge that he was against balancing the budget, he proposed his own package of rescissions.[17]

Because supplemental appropriations increase the size of the deficit, which is politically embarrassing, there is a politics of "blame shifting" that sometimes accompanies the supplementals. The president complained in 1987 that in order to get the spending he sought for farmers, he was forced to accept $1.7 billion in unrequested funds.[18] And in the same year, he claimed that he had balanced his request for new budget authority with proposed spending reductions, almost all of which Congress rejected. According to the president, Congress missed the goal of deficit neutrality by more than $6.4 billion.[19] Congress rejected this interpretation, arguing that it had lowered the president's requests for supplemental spending and that the president's requests for offsetting reductions, which he called negative supplementals, were bogus. They were for loan programs in agriculture that Congress had restored in the FY 1987 appropriations act. The House report on H.R. 1827 indicated that the committee rejected about $1.5 billion of such negative supplementals.[20] In short, the president was requesting cuts that he knew would be unacceptable to Congress, and then he blamed Congress for unbalancing the budget.

State and local governments use supplementals less than the federal government because they are bound by balanced budget amendments and are not supposed to spend money they do not have. They can use supplementals if they experience windfall revenue growth or if they have underestimated revenues. They can use supplemental appropriations for emergencies by drawing down reserves. Not much is known about how state and local governments use supplementals. Fortunately, a recent study[21] provides some information on supplementals in cities. The study is based on a survey with responses from forty-nine central cities with an average of 159,000 population in the United States. The study found that supplementals were used extensively, averaging just under 10 percent of the budget.

Budgets do not necessarily increase by 10 percent during the year, however. The largest portion of the supplementals comes from the fund balance, a kind of emergency savings account; the second largest portion comes from transfers; the third, and smallest source, is from new revenues. When the supplementals come from transfers, each increase to one department or program requires an offsetting decrease somewhere else in the budget.

Despite the blurring between transfers and increases, the 10 percent figure gives some idea of the extent and importance of supplementals in cities. The budget process for allocating these supplementals is different from the allocation of the original budget; public hearings are much less common on supplementals, and the public role is generally much reduced compared to the adoption of the annual budget. It becomes important to know, then, how much of this activity is routine and technical, and how much is policy related.

According to the key actors in the forty-nine responding cities, supplementals are generally considered to be routine. Some of the supplementals are technical in the sense that they result from changes in the economy or mandated expenditures by the state. Sometimes supplementals result from misestimates of revenues, especially intergovernmental revenues. Most of the time, those misestimates are the result of environmental changes over which cities have no control. Supplementals are most prevalent for capital projects, public safety functions, and streets and highways. Important additions also occur in parks and recreation and in administration. Legislatively initiated supplementals follow the same pattern as administratively proposed priorities, but with more emphasis on housing and community development.

Additional midyear spending on capital projects is a predominantly technical issue. It is difficult to estimate accurately how much projects will cost, and underestimates require supplemental appropriations later. Unless the costs of a project are intentionally underestimated, this is a technical problem. Emergencies may also occur, requiring unanticipated capital outlays during the year.

The frequency of supplementals for public safety is more difficult to explain. Respondents in the survey explained that these additions to the budget were made in part because of the difficulty of estimating overtime in these departments, a technical issue. Also, large departments, such as police and public works, can absorb freezes when revenues drop, and act as reserves "in the event of reduced discretion and environmental pressures in other functions."[22] This function suggests they are built up and depleted as revenues expand and contract, still primarily a technical rather than a policy decision, based on the size and complexity of these departmental budgets.

While midyear increases in spending for capital projects and overtime are primarily technical issues, midyear spending can be policy related. Lower-priority capital projects may be funded during the year when they do not compete with other citywide projects. For example, in one city this author studied, the city manager and the council routinely added large capital projects to the airport during the middle of the year. The exact amounts required for projects such as land acquisition could not be known in advance (a technical reason for a supplemental). Nevertheless, the expectation that there would be capital projects at the airport was clear at the time the annual budget was put together. Not even an estimate of these expenditures was included in the budget. During the year, the money was transferred from the fund balance to pay for the projects. Airport expenditures did not compete with other capital projects, and they were not subjected to the kind of scrutiny the rest of the budget endured.

The forty-nine cities survey also revealed some clearly political and policy-related factors in police, housing and community development, neighborhood capital and recreation projects, human services, streets, public safety, and hospitals. Some of these projects are subject to community lobbying or lobbying by community service organizations. In particular, "public safety services are involved due to the high levels of public support for the services provided and a conception (in some cities) that they are generally 'under budgeted.' "[23]

Available evidence suggests that some effort is made to include popular projects and programs during the year that have been left out of the annual budget or have received less funding than supporters wish. The general annual budget pays less attention to these specifically political projects, and the midyear budget, with limited amounts, pays more attention to them. Research has not yet been done to reveal what proportion of the supplementals are policy related; that proportion will probably vary substantially from city to city.

In short, many supplementals have some policy implications, although they may be primarily technical. The use of supplementals at the federal level is declining, at least in part as the result of pressure exerted by the budget deficit and the need to hold down new budget authority. At the local level, supplementals still seem to be a substantial portion of the budget, but there is no evidence as yet whether this practice is increasing, decreasing, or remaining the same. Since cities' supplementals do not contribute to deficits, there is no pressure from this source to keep the levels down. The financial community frowns on major changes between the annual budget and final expenditures because of the implication of poor management and lack of control over spending. But current accounting practice allows these differences during the year to be obscured because auditors compare revised budgets with actuals, not original budget estimates with actuals. Including a comparison of the original budget with the actual revenues and expenditures in the comprehensive annual financial report would put some pressure on cities to keep the amount of midyear changes down.

RESCISSIONS

A rescission is a legislatively approved midyear reduction in previously appropriated funds. Rescissions are used at the federal level, and to some extent at the state level. At the federal level, rescissions were less important than supplementals during the last half of the 1970s. Rescissions ranged from a low of about $148 million to a little under $1 billion between 1976 and 1979 (see table 7.4); supplementals ranged from about $13.8 billion to about $37 billion over the same time period (see table 7.1).

Rescissions were used more extensively in the early Reagan administration (see table 7.4). With the exception of a few particular years, the amounts of rescissions have been moderate, especially when viewed as a percentage of total budget authority. If anything, rescissions as a percentage of total outlays declined modestly over the period.

While rescissions have generally been modest in size, the $24.5 billion figure for 1992 is suggestive of the possibility of using rescissions to balance the budget. In 1995 Congress actively sought to use rescissions to cut the size of government, proposing a set of rescissions reflecting its own priorities.

TABLE 7.4

FEDERAL GOVERNMENT RESCISSIONS,

FISCAL YEARS 1976–93

Year	Budget authority rescinded	Percentage of total budget	Year	Budget authority rescinded	Percentage of total budget
1976	$ 148,331,000	.035	1986	$ 5,552,620,000	.517
1977	986,412,943	.208	1987	12,395,390,675	1.120
1978	585,819,000	.114	1988	3,888,663,000	.327
1979	771,109,000	.135	1989	327,966,000	.025
1980	4,015,902,546	.590	1990	2,304,986,000	.168
1981	14,617,426,150	1.900	1991	1,706,886,000	.123
1982	4,413,918,000	.540	1992	24,594,499,054	1.670
1983	310,605,000	.034	1993 est.	2,400,000,000	.162
1984	2,224,064,000	.23	1995 est.	19,000,000,000	
1985	5,632,320,000	.524			

SOURCES: Total rescissions, except for 1993 and 1995, come from the General Accounting Office, *Summary of Proposed and Enacted Rescissions, Fiscal Years 1974 through 1993* (Washington, D.C.: Government Printing Office, 3 February 1993). The annual budget authority totals used for calculating the percent of budget authority is from the 1996 *Budget of the United States,* Historical Tables, table 5.2.

NOTE: The figure for 1993 is my own rounded estimate. The figure for 1995 is derived from CBO files on supplementals (that also contained rescissions) through 1 May 1995 and my own estimates of the amount of rescissions after 1 May in P.L. 104-19, P.L. 104-32, and P.L. 104-59.

The president was determined to take rescissions where he thought they would do the least harm, threatening to veto the congressional proposal for rescissions and offering alternative rescissions that reflected his policy preferences.[24] The result was another large set of rescissions.

After the large 1992 rescissions, there was great excitement on Capitol Hill about the possibility of enhancing the president's ability to rescind spending in order to help control the deficit. The underlying argument was that the president often proposes rescissions that Congress does not approve and so the budget deficit grows. There is an element of truth to this picture, but also an element of distortion. The president does propose rescissions that Congress does not approve: from 1974 to the end of 1992, the president had proposed rescissions of $69.2 billion, of which Congress approved only $21.3 billion. At the same time, however, Congress initiated more rescission requests than the president. Moreover, while Congress rescinded spending in areas it chose rather than in areas the president recommended, it cut more than the president requested. Over the period from 1974 to 1993, the president requested $69.2 billion while Congress rescinded $86.5 billion.[25] These figures suggest a scenario other than an irresponsible Congress unbalancing the budget; it further suggests that shifting more budget power to the president will probably not do much to solve the deficit, although it may give the president a greater ability to impress his or her values on the budget in lieu of Congress's values.

DEFERRALS

Under the 1974 Congressional Budget Reform Act, the president had to propose deferrals to Congress, and if Congress did not disapprove, the spending was deferred. Some or all of the money for a particular project or program could be delayed for some specified period of time. Deferrals are common at all levels of government, but they were perhaps most formalized at the federal level. The amounts of money deferred at the federal level were substantially greater than the amounts involved in rescissions from 1975 to 1979, (see table 7.5). Rescissions were more permanent than deferrals and required positive approval from both houses of Congress; deferrals were easier to get because they involved only a temporary delay in spending, and unless Congress actively disapproved, spending was deferred.

Deferrals are generally classed as routine and technical or as policy related. In policy-related deferrals, the president disapproves of some spending that Congress approves and recommends that the spending be delayed. Congress normally accedes to the president's requests on routine deferrals, which averaged about $8 billion a year from 1981 to 1988. But Congress gets very

TABLE 7.5
FEDERAL DEFERRALS, 1975–79

Year	Amount deferred (in thousands)	Amount disapproved (in thousands)
1975	$24,574,236	$9,318,217
1976	9,209,780	393,081
1977	6,831,194	25,600
1978	4,910,114	69,531
1979	4,393,328	13,852

SOURCE: Adapted from Allen Schick, *Congress and Money* (Washington, D.C.: Urban Institute Press, 1980), 404.

touchy when the president refuses to spend money that has been legally appropriated and that represents Congress's preferences. In 1981 and 1982, Congress allowed almost all the president's requested policy deferrals; he was a very popular new president with an apparent mandate to reshape the budget quickly, and Congress went along with his initiatives. From 1983 to 1988, Congress got more balky about approving the president's proposals to defer spending for policy purposes. Although Congress had approved $6.1 billion of policy deferrals in 1981 and 1982, it approved only $7.7 billion in policy deferrals for the next six years.[26]

The timing of the change was probably related in part to the two difficult years of 1981 and 1982, during which Congress had acceded to many cuts it might have preferred to have opposed, but felt that the political risks of opposing the president were too formidable. During those years, the president not only invoked the reconciliation procedures of the 1974 budget reform act but also bypassed those procedures by substituting his own amendment for the work of the congressional committees. Reportedly, the president used a lot of pressure tactics to get support on these measures and amassed considerable resentment for his seeming lack of respect for congressional ways. When the Supreme Court nullified Congress's ability to veto presidential requests for deferrals in 1983 (*Immigration and Naturalization Service* v. *Chadha*),[27] it must have seemed one more powerful blow to congressional power. In fact, however, the congressional veto of deferrals was declared unconstitutional because it required only one house to take action and therefore did not have the force of law.

Congress responded to the elimination of its veto powers over deferrals by putting its rejection of deferrals into supplemental appropriations, and passing them as they would other laws. In 1986, when Reagan deferred some $10 billion that he did not want spent, "Congress's response was to insert a provision in that year's supplemental appropriation bill nullifying most of the policy deferrals."[28] In 1987, the Senate report on the supplementals rejected the president's request for deferrals, arguing that the president was using them for policy purposes, not programmatic technicalities. The report questioned the president's legal ability to defer the funds.[29] Indeed, in 1987, the U.S. Court of Appeals for the District of Columbia barred any kind of policy-based deferral.[30] On 1 April 1987, the controller general advised Congress that twenty-five policy deferrals submitted by the president after the decision by the court of appeals were illegal. The administration decided not to appeal the decision to the Supreme Court. Consequently, it is currently illegal to defer spending for policy purposes, although spending may still be deferred for technical reasons.

At state and local levels deferrals have never been clearly policy related.

Projects are deferred when there is no cash to pay for them. Because governors often have line-item vetoes, and sometimes have amendatory vetoes, it is not necessary for them to withhold spending on projects when the legislature increases their budget requests.

To summarize, at the national level, rescissions and deferrals, like supplementals, often have policy implications, and like supplementals their most dramatic role is in reshaping the existing budget when a new president is elected. Deferrals for policy-related reasons became illegal in 1987. Rescissions and deferrals are used less at the state level, and for more technical reasons, primarily because governors have more initial power over the budget and do not need to make midyear changes for policy reasons.

REPROGRAMMING

Reprogramming means transferring some or all of the money budgeted to one program to another in the same appropriation account or fund. Public budgets are approved and administered not in terms of one whole budget but in terms of funds or appropriation accounts for specified purposes. The reason is to ensure financial control, so expenditures will be spent as intended. But sometimes these funds or appropriation accounts are so large that discretion to move funds around within them amounts to the ability to change the priorities in the budget. Within one huge defense appropriation account, money can be shifted from any defense program to any other defense program at the discretion of the secretary. At the local level, a manager or mayor can transfer money from any program within a fund (such as the general fund) to any other program in that fund. Since police and fire are often both in the general fund, money can technically be reprogrammed from police to fire. The city council does not usually intend such transfers to occur, but there is freedom in budget execution to do so.

Reprogramming is potentially important because it can thwart the intent of the legislature. But because such transfers are discretionary and legal, there is seldom a written record of them. There is, however, some information about them. At the state level during the 1970s, reprogramming revolved around federal funding, which created a great deal of midyear discretion for administrators because the money was often late.

> State governments frequently face uncertain or late federal notification of assistance ... when federal dollars do arrive, administrators, not legislators adjust budgets and transfer funds. Programs expand or contract without legislative approval as administrators transfer funds from program to program.[31]

Until recently, governors retained control over most federal grants and used their discretion to reprogram funds. The amount of executive discretion to reprogram was thus considerable. As the Reagan administration turned over more explicit policymaking to the states on how federal money should be spent, state legislatures became more active in appropriating and controlling federal money.[32] Thus this major source of executive discretion in budget execution was curtailed.

At the federal level, the number of formal reprogrammings, those reported to Congress, are typically under a thousand a year.[33] Congress has been monitoring the reprogrammings of the Department of Defense for years, and the amount of reprogramming has not been increasing. More broadly, in situations in which Congress has been most concerned about the content of reprogrammings, it has taken an increased role in monitoring those budget changes to make sure they conform to congressional policy. The amount of reprogramming in the Defense Department from 1980 to 1985 is reproduced in table 7.6.

The Department of Defense reprogrammed an average of $3.3 billion a year or 1.3 percent of obligational authority during the five years ending 30 September 1987. In 1987, Congress reviewed 69 reprogrammings, involving about $1.6 billion, or about .5 percent of the DoD's obligational authority.[34] During most of the 1980s, then, the amount of formal reprogramming was limited to a small proportion of the Defense Department's budget.

In the last few years, however, financial pressure to reduce the deficit has resulted in tight budgets and smaller supplemental appropriations, putting pressure on agencies to increase the amount of reprogramming. This relationship between overall cuts and increased pressure for reprogramming has been particularly clear in the Defense Department, although the overall amounts are still not a large percentage of defense funding.

During the hearings on the 1990 Department of Defense appropriations, committee members questioned the air force's requests for reprogramming of 1989 funding, mentioning that the source of the reprogrammings was not savings or unspent appropriations from the cancellation or shrinkage of projects but other programs that also needed money. Seventy percent of the reprogrammed money would have to be restored later and hence represented a sort of borrowing from the future. When committee members questioned the air force's choices, air force spokesmen responded that there was no slush fund from which they could draw.[35]

The department elaborated for the record:

Over the past several years the Air Force has been forced to live within an increasingly constrained fiscal environment. At the same time, we have also

[been] forced into major reprogramming actions due to fact-of-life problems and urgent unfunded requirements. In the acquisition area we have reprogrammed for fiscal year 1988 almost $2 billion (about 5.4 percent of acquisition total obligation authority).... So far in fiscal year 1989 [eight months into the fiscal year] we have reprogrammed almost $1.5 billion dollars with over $250 million going out of the investment accounts in support of similar serious unfunded requirements in fiscal year 1989 for the O & M [operations and maintenance] appropriation.[36]

TABLE 7.6

REPROGRAMMING ACTIONS FOR THE DEPARTMENT
OF DEFENSE, 1980–85

	Number of actions	Amount (in billions)
1980		
Requiring congressional action	69	$1.161
Not requiring congressional action	973	1.004
1981		
Requiring congressional action	47	.788
Not requiring congressional action	1300	1.400
1982		
Requiring congressional action	60	1.303
Not requiring congressional action	1597	2.399
1983		
Requiring congressional action	85	2.275
Not requiring congressional action	1020	1.706
1984		
Requiring congressional action	87	1.335
Not requiring congressional action	1112	1.791
1985		
Requiring congressional action	69	1.711
Not requiring congressional action	876	2.081

SOURCE: House Report 99-793 on the Department of Defense Appropriation Bill 1987, to accompany H.R. 5438.

The navy reported a similar situation, in the sense that in 1988, their operations and maintenance portion of the budget was reduced $2.2 billion, and they ended up reprogramming $471.5 million back into Operations and Maintenance. They were requesting $398 million for 1989 reprogrammings for the same purpose.[37]

Congress has watched reprogrammings carefully because of the possible use of such transfers to get around congressional policies. In the 1950s, Congress limited allowable reprogrammings by the Army Corps of Engineers and the Bureau of Reclamation to 15 percent of their budgets. Also, in the late 1950s, Congress objected to "deobligation" from one project and "reobligation" on another project in the Agency for International Development (AID), which provides foreign aid programs. A GAO study of AID from 1968 to 1972 concluded that the amount of AID deobligations (also called *recoveries*) came to $435 million. Congressman Otto Passman estimated in 1960 that "It might very well be that perhaps one-half or more of the projects now funded were never approved in the beginning, by any committee of the Congress."[38] Instead, they were funded from informal reprogrammings.

By 1978, the Appropriations Subcommittee on Interior and Related Agencies (which has jurisdiction over the Bureau of Reclamation) had extended reporting requirements on reprogramming to all agencies in its jurisdiction and had made reporting requirements more stringent.[39] The only explanation given for the codified requirements was that the House Committee on Appropriations for many years had an informal agreement with the various agencies and bureaus funded in the Department of the Interior and Related Agencies Appropriations bill with respect to guidelines and procedures for reprogramming, and that the practice of requesting approval for reprogramming or notifying the committee about reprogramming actions was not uniformly understood by the twenty-nine agencies funded in this bill. The committee acknowledged the need for some reprogramming but argued that the integrity of the appropriations process required the committee to be fully apprised of all proposed reprogrammings. The Senate report added that the reprogramming procedures had been developed piecemeal to deal with specific situations, and the 1978 action was a clarification to get uniform guidelines.[40]

These guidelines require that reprogramming occur only when an unforeseen event takes place, and then only if postponement of the project or the activity until the next appropriation year would result in actual loss or damage. Convenience and desire were considered inadequate reasons for reprogrammings. Reprogramming to initiate new programs or change allocations specifically denied, limited, or increased by Congress was forbidden.

Reprogrammings in excess of $250,000 or resulting in an increase or decrease of more than 10 percent annually in affected programs were to be submitted to the committee in writing before implementation.

Similarly, the Appropriations Subcommittee on the Departments of Commerce, Justice, State, and Judiciary and Related Agencies (which has jurisdiction over AID) included in its reports a section concerning the reprogramming of funds between programs or activities.[41] As had happened at the Committee on Interior, these restrictions were broadened to include more agencies, and emphasized timely notice rather than blanket prohibitions. The subcommittee required advanced notice on reprogrammings, whether temporary or permanent, in excess of $250,000 or 10 percent, whichever is less, or on reprogrammings even smaller if the effect was to commit the agency to future significant funding requirements. Any increase in funds or personnel, by any means, for projects or activities for which funds had already been denied must be reported in advance, regardless of amounts. It is clear from these requirements that the intent was not to limit flexibility in the budget, but to give Congress the right to review in advance any reprogrammings that have policy implications.

Generally, the requirements to notify Congress before carrying out a reprogramming were observed. Occasionally, however, a problem arose. For example, in 1989, the Immigration and Naturalization Service (in the Department of Justice) informed Congress of a $30 million reprogramming, but the agency did not give Congress the required fifteen days' advance notice. Moreover, even though the General Accounting Office ruled the reprogramming legal, both the committee and the agency knew that the intent of the law had been sidestepped. The problem occurred because a congressional committee had not set up tight enough controls over earmarked money. The Immigration and Naturalization Service took the surplus from a fund earmarked for adjudication and transferred it legally into an adjudication account that was not earmarked and then transferred money from this second account to other purposes that were not related to adjudication. The second account was depleted to pay for detention of Latin American immigrants in south Texas.

From the agency's perspective, the two-step transfer was justified. Congress had just cut the agency's budget by $59 million, supplementals had become very difficult to get, the agency was required to absorb substantial costs for its mandated salary increase, and the number of immigrants had recently surged.

From the perspective of the Subcommittee on Immigration, Refugees, and International Law of the House Committee on the Judiciary, the agency administrators had agreed to spend the earmarked fund exclusively on adju-

dication as a condition of legislative approval of the fund; agency administrators had asked for the fund and appeared pleased to get it, and then, once
they had it, they misspent it. Some committee members also observed that it
was administration policy to detain, and hence pay for the detention of the
new immigrants, rather than disperse them to immigration offices around
the country. The situation was less an uncontrollable event than the result of
policy choices. The administration gave higher priority to law enforcement
than to services to law-abiding citizens, such as those awaiting permission
for spouses to enter the country. From the subcommittee's perspective, routine services that members of Congress try to provide for constituents were
systematically slighted.[42]

The Appropriations Subcommittee had a different perspective on the
situation. Their concern was "the overall constraint on new funding authority."[43] The committee approved reprogramming the earmarked fund because
it meant the agency would not need a supplemental appropriation. The reprogramming would help keep down new funding authority. Nevertheless,
when requested by the chairman of the immigration subcommittee to insert
some legislation in the appropriation to strengthen the earmarking, the Appropriations Committee tried to oblige.

The former structure required the first $50 million of the earmarked fee
to be transferred to the Treasury for the general fund, and amounts in excess
of that amount to be available to the attorney general to reimburse any expenditures on adjudication and naturalization. The new language eliminated
the transfer to the general fund of $50 million, making the entire amount of
the earmarked fund available for adjudication and naturalization. This language did not close the legal loophole of allowing accounts that had something to do with adjudication and naturalization to have money transferred
out and then be reimbursed by the earmarked fee, as had already been done.

The intent of the committee to control reprogramming was spelled out
in the committee report rather than in the legislation, a milder form of control. Its intent was to provide funding "for ongoing operations plus necessary enhancements to the Adjudication and Naturalization program."

> It is the committee's intent that only those costs directly attributable to the
> adjudication of applications and petitions submitted for benefits and the
> processing of naturalization and citizenship petitions and applications shall
> be funded from this fee account.[44]

Moreover, the Senate Appropriations Committee "expected" the attorney
general to report to the committee plans for spending any additional revenues from the fund on new or expanded services and expected "the Attorney

General to promptly notify the Committee on Appropriations of any proposed uses of the fund other than for costs directly associated with" unplanned adjudication or naturalization activities or program expansion.[45]

This was a rather mild step in additional control. Rather than forbid any reprogramming of the funds, the Appropriations Committee asked for a more detailed planning and notification system, while reiterating the intent of the committee to earmark the funds for adjudication and naturalization. This result left the attorney general and the Appropriations Committee with considerable discretion and may or may not resolve the issue of whether adjudication and naturalization will receive more of its earmarked money.

The level of reprogramming in defiance of Congress seems to be moderate in recent years. There have been few major imbroglios, and most of the constraints in place seem to be working. Efforts to cut back the deficit and control spending, however, have put contradictory pressures on Congress concerning reprogramming. On the one hand, more reprogramming discretion granted to the agencies may give the added incentive to save money; on the other hand, more discretion granted to agencies during a time of cutback may mean that Congress's priorities may be seriously violated. Moreover, the granting of greater discretion over reprogramming may run into determined opposition from those who remember prior abuses. The minicase of the Defense Modernization Account illustrates some of these tensions.

MINICASE: THE DEFENSE MODERNIZATION ACCOUNT

The Defense Authorization Act of 1996 contained a proposal for a Defense Modernization Account. This new account would allow the secretary of defense to take funds that were saved from construction or procurement appropriations and put them in a special account that could be spent for modernization projects. The money could come initially from virtually any part of the budget and, as initially proposed, would turn appropriations with expiration dates into no-year appropriations that would be good indefinitely. While some expenditures from the fund would come under reprogramming controls and hence have to be reported to congressional committees, other mechanisms could bypass these controls.

Especially because of Congress's recent experiences in controlling the M funds, watchdogs in Congress were concerned that the Defense Department would not be able to account for the expenditures from the new fund. The M funds, a pool of lapsed accounts, had amounted to over $50 billion, $5 billion of which were never accounted for. Senators wanted to be able to encourage the Defense Department to save money on purchases and equipment, but did not want the new fund to become a slush fund used to purchase weapons beyond the number approved by Congress or to develop weapons without congressional approval. Nor did they want the money spent without properly accounting for it.

Senator John Glenn proposed an amendment to the proposal that passed both houses. The amendment prevented the Defense Department from changing fixed-year appropriations into no-year or permanent appropriations and made it clear that the money could not be spent on items of which Congress disapproved or on purchases beyond those approved by Congress. A dollar limit of $1 billion on the total size of the fund was included in the amendment. Glenn proposed also that the money spent out of the modernization fund not be spent on agencies or programs that would not ordinarily have access to the original source of money. The result was a proposal that would encourage savings and more efficient purchasing without giving the Defense Department a license to spend money any way it chose.

Senator Grassley supported Senator Glenn's proposed amendment:

> When I was first told about the Defense Modernization Account, I was very concerned. The alarm bells went off. Right away, I thought I could see another slush fund like the infamous $50 billion M accounts in the making. Subsection (B)(3) is what really set me off. This is what it says: Amounts credited to the Defense Modernization Account shall remain available until expended. To me that sounds like a permit to open a laundry operation to break down the integrity of appropriations. That sounds like another honey pot where unlimited amounts of no-year money could be stashed for a rainy day. Like the M accounts, I fear this money could be used to cover cost overruns and other unauthorized projects beyond the purview of Congress. Clearly, this is not the intended purpose of section 1003. But in my mind, it is a potential problem.[46]

The senators' response to the Defense Modernization Account illustrates the effects of prior negative experiences. These senators were suspicious about how the account would be used because of their past experiences with the M funds and because the Defense Department had been unable to show how it spent large amounts of money leaking through poor accounting systems. The discussion on the Senate floor also illustrates the tension between the desire to grant agencies more discretion over reprogramming as an incentive to increase savings and the felt need for more policy and financial controls.

How are these tensions working out on balance? The minicase suggests that Congress is willing to grant greater freedom to agencies but is cautious about granting more reprogramming authority to agencies that have abused their freedom in the past.

On the side of increasing agency discretion over reprogramming, Congress created the $80 billion Defense Business Operating Fund (DBOF) in 1991, a revolving fund to consolidate management and accounting for business-type activities by combining a number of existing accounts and funds.[47] By combining existing funds, the DBOF dramatically increased spending flexibility in Defense Department spending. One informant called the DBOF the biggest laundering facility this side of Colombia, a reference to the ability to take money from one account to another until the original purpose of that money is obscured. And in 1995, Congress created the Defense Modernization Account, also with the intent of increasing flexibility in spending. Some agency budget officers reported that appropriations committees were being more forgiving and lenient, especially toward operating budgets, as the annual budget process became more difficult.

Also on the side of increased flexibility, OMB has changed the way it apportions money to agencies, moving toward granting the agencies their full allotment at the beginning of the year rather than in four quarterly installments. This change gives the agencies much greater flexibility, reducing the need for reprogramming requests. As one observer noted, bigger buckets mean that you have more flexibility to stir the contents as you see fit.

On the side of tighter controls over reprogramming, Congress has put strictures on the use of the Defense Modernization Account and watchdogs are closely observing how the DBOF is functioning. A recent survey of agencies by the National Performance Review staff concluded that, overall, congressional constraints on reprogramming have become somewhat more restrictive between 1983 and 1993. The reason suggested is that budgetary pressure to cut appropriations "has put a premium on preserving particular programs, projects, and activities from executive branch as well as congressional action."[48]

MINICASE:
WATCHING THE DEFENSE BUSINESS OPERATING FUND

The Defense Business Operating Fund was created in 1991 as a revolving fund to support the business activities of defense agencies, especially in purchasing. It combined a number of existing funds and accounts, creating greater flexibility in spending. The DBOF was responsible for items as disparate as toilet paper and ship replacement parts. The DBOF was to set prices and the defense agencies were to buy what they needed from the DBOF. The hope was that the DBOF would be able to set up one accounting system to replace the many that preexisted it and that it would be able to establish incentives for the agencies to reduce purchases and unnecessarily high inventories. Though touted as a management reform, the DBOF got off to a rocky start because policies for using it were not devised and put in place, pricing was erratic, accounting did not improve, and the fund, as large as it was, was unauditable.

Senator Grassley was predictably upset at the lack of financial controls on the DBOF.

> DBOF is a $77 billion-a-year operation. DBOF purchases everything from fuel to repair parts to toilet paper and light bulbs. Much of what is bought by DBOF is needed to train the Armed Forces and keep them ready for combat. Unfortunately, DBOF's books are a mess. DBOF's books are in such bad shape that the Inspector General had to issue a disclaimer of opinion for the second year in a row. In the language of accountants, that means the IG could not audit DBOF's books. If you cannot audit the books, you do not know how much money is being spent. We know how much money is being pumped into DBOF, but we do not have any idea what is coming out the other end. . . . The breakdown of fiscal connections within DBOF alone means that there are no controls or accountability over about 30 percent of the defense budget.[49]

Among the problems that the DBOF ran into were that although it was supposed to be self-sustaining, it sometimes ran out of money, requiring additional supplements from Congress. Part of the difficulty appeared to be that Congress cut the Operations and Maintenance (O&M) budget of the defense agencies with the idea that the agencies would take excessive inventory and return it to the DBOF for a credit. The DBOF was then supposed to transfer money to spend on O&M to those agencies. Senator Grassley argued that Congress cut some $5.5 billion from the O&M budget of the defense agencies in the 1993 appropriation, with the expectation that the amount would eventually be made up, because those amounts were needed. The $5.5 billion was scored as a cut, but it was not really a cut because the agencies expected it back from the DBOF, which was, according to Grassley, overcharging for purchases and making a profit on the sales. That profit was supposed to be transferred to the agencies to make up for congressional cuts. Somehow, only part of the $5.5 billion was ever paid to the agencies. Grassley wondered where the rest of the money went, and GAO confirmed that the cash management of the DBOF was faulty. Grassley argued:

> . . . if the concerns about force readiness are genuine and if the services have a legitimate need for more O&M money, then why are we providing more

O&M money to DBOF? DBOF is the problem. The money should go directly to the military services through the front door where it is needed. There is no need to give legitimate O&M moneys a preliminary flush through the DBOF plumbing works. Why are we doing that? Air Force Maj. Joe Lokey, a former assistant comptroller at MacDill AFB, FL, knows why. I quote: There are fewer than a handful of people who understand the complex and convoluted way DOD washes money into and out of these funds. They are, however, useful in subverting the intent of Congress who will no longer appropriate for specific purposes but simply ensure that the DOD K-mart is adequately capitalized. It serves no value added purpose to warfighting capabilities as it simply moves money on paper from our right pocket to our left pocket.[50]

Grassley argued that the DBOF should be terminated within a relatively short period of time if the Defense Department could not prepare auditable records. His colleagues thought this excessively harsh, but recognized the problems. Instead, they required the secretary of defense to come up with a plan that would handle all the financial management problems the DBOF was running into, and required the secretary to report to Congress and the comptroller general on the plan. Reauthorization legislation for the DBOF also required the General Accounting Office to examine the Defense Department's plan to see if it covered all the bases and to examine whether the department was achieving the plan in a timely manner. Another feature of reauthorization legislation was to require the secretary of defense to come up with controls on pricing for the DBOF that would ensure that the fund paid for itself but did not make a profit.

The General Accounting Office found that the secretary had produced a plan that, if reliably implemented, would solve all the outstanding problems, but expressed pessimism that the Defense Department would implement the plan on time. By the third month of the plan, Defense was already behind on twenty-six of the planned tasks due at that point.[51] A year later, GAO still found the Defense Department had not put major reforms in place.[52]

How long congressional tolerance of such lax fiscal practice will last is not clear. If Defense does not make considerably more progress toward financial accountability, additional controls may be forthcoming. Though Senator Grassley thought he saw the hallmarks of intentional evasion of congressional will, most observers attributed the DBOF's problems to plain (and uninteresting) poor financial management. Congress tends not to get as excited about poor financial management as policy disobedience, and so has contented itself so far with a milder level of regulation and a wait-and-see attitude, while continuing to monitor the situation closely.

CONTINGENCY FUNDS

Contingency funds are sums of money budgeted for unknown or unstated purposes. There are some contingency funds, or discretionary funds, at the federal level, but they are less important at the federal level than at state and local levels. At the national level, contingencies are generally funded by sup-plementals, which usually increase the size of the deficit; at state and local levels, it is illegal to run deficits, so a variety of special funds are set aside for different contingencies. In addition, at the local level, departmental budget justifications are normally included in the budget, so a detailed plan of how the money is to be spent is part of the budget legislation. Most city agencies thus do not have much flexibility regarding how budgeted money will be spent. To create discretion during the year, administrators have to build it into the budget in terms of pools of uncommitted revenues, to be allocated during the year.

Cities normally aim for year-end balances between 5 and 10 percent of their budgets. In any given year, the amount may be lower, and the amount in the year-end balance traded off against the amounts in contingency funds. The more money there is in contingency funds, the less needed in the year-end balance, and vice versa. The money for salary increases is normally placed in one or more contingency accounts and transferred from the con-tingency funds to the departmental accounts after labor negotiations. Often a city with a very large year-end balance is planning some capital project and saving up for it.

Most of the uses of formal contingency funds are technical, but the in-formal creation of funds may be a way of rebudgeting during the year. In a study of Cincinnati during a period of fiscal stress, the city cut back expendi-tures in line with a worst-case revenue scenario. The process of worst-case planning created moderate amounts of slack in the retrenchment budget. The council used the slack to add police and fire personnel after the 1976 cuts. In 1980, the manager elicited supplemental requests from departments to use revenues that exceeded the somewhat pessimistic predictions in the budget. The manager then selected from these supplemental requests those that dealt with the managerial problem he saw as high priority, deferred maintenance.[53] How such "savings" will be used, and who will control their expenditure are policy-laden issues.

The use of funds built up through conscious overestimation of expendi-tures and/or underestimation of revenues occurs in cities not experiencing cutbacks. The following excerpt from an interview with a city manager indi-cates that he believes some other cities use their balances to make minor but policy-related changes during the year.

Q. What about year-end balances, how are they used?

A. They are strictly an accounting device. We don't play any games at all with the statements. I could, because most people don't read accounting statements. Some managers do use it. They purposely underestimate revenues and overestimate expenditures, so that will happen. The council may ask the manager to find money to fund a project during the year. The manager then can do it. The council thinks it's magic.

The project for which the council is asking midyear support may be one for which the need developed during the year, or it may be a pet project with political payoff, that could not be funded as part of the regular budget but could be funded midyear without much budget scrutiny or comparison to other projects.

While the need for contingency funds at the local level is substantial, year-end balances combined with contingency funds seldom exceed 8 to 10 percent of the budget. One of their major purposes is to fund labor agreements, which represent no policy change. The level of the contingency funds will normally remain constant from year to year, unless it is drawn down to fund a particular capital project or tide the city over a recession. In some cities, at some times, a portion of the contingency funds may be spent for special council projects, with explicit council approval. The budget may thus change somewhat during the year, with negative impact on public accountability, but the amounts involved are normally quite small, maybe 2 percent of the total budget.

INTERFUND TRANSFERS

Interfund transfers are shifts of money between appropriation accounts or funds. At the federal level, because the amounts of the individual appropriation accounts can be very large, most of the need for transfers can be accommodated within accounts, and without fanfare. Why go between accounts, which requires legislative approval, when there is sufficient discretion within accounts, which requires no approval? In cities, however, individual funds (the local analog to federal appropriation accounts) are sometimes narrow, covering only one function and having only a limited number of dollars. Some of these funds may be related in function, so interfund transfers may be planned and budgeted in advance. Formal transfers occurring during the year are treated as budget amendments and need to be approved by the council. Hence they are neither secret nor do they bypass the regular budget process, although they occur during the budget year.

There should be little reason for unanticipated transfers, and normally there are few of them. Sometimes, however, there is some informal borrowing, especially from cash-rich to cash-poor funds. If the borrowing is not approved by the council or becomes a long-term loan, or if a loan is not fully repaid, the implications are policy laden rather than technical.

For example, if a general fund borrows from a water fund and does not repay the loan, the water fund may develop deficits.[54] The fund showing the deficit will have to cut services or increase user fees or taxes to eliminate the deficit. The result may be to raise water fees to pay for police services, a result that is not only inequitable but secret. If the deficits are not eliminated, bond costs may go up, costing the city unnecessary interest charges on future water projects. This practice is probably not common, but it does sometimes occur, and when it does, there are policy implications.

Summary and Conclusions

For the purposes of accountability to the public and for managerial predictability, most of the budget is implemented as passed. Nevertheless, some flexibility has to be built into budget implementation because budgets are open to the environment. Rivers flood, countries invade each other, hurricanes knock down trees and houses. The economy waxes and wanes, reducing or increasing revenues beyond expectations, and reducing or increasing the number of those eligible for entitlements. If more people commit crimes and are caught and sentenced to prison, there has to be some way to pay for their imprisonment, even if the numbers were not correctly predicted when the budget was put together. Budgets also adapt to the priorities of newly elected officials, who must initially work within the framework of budgets put together by their predecessors.

Budgets adapt through a variety of techniques, including supplemental appropriations, rescissions, deferrals, reprogramming, contingency funds, and interfund transfers. Some techniques are more common at one level of government than another. The federal government can run deficits, so it can respond to an emergency with a supplemental appropriation; state and local governments cannot generally run legal deficits, and so have to build up various reserve and contingency funds to draw down in case of emergency, and often hold back on spending during the year in case revenues do not materialize. Contingency funds and deferrals of this sort are common at state and local levels, but supplementals are relatively rare. Interfund transfers are fairly common at the local level; reprogramming within accounts is more important at the national level because accounts are so large that moving money around inside them usually provides sufficient flexibility.

Most of the changes in the budget during implementation are the result of technical changes and adaptation to the environment, but the flexibility that is absolutely necessary to budgeting also allows for some changes due to policy considerations. If Congress adds on to the president's budget, the president may try to rescind or defer that unwanted spending; if Congress disapproves of some spending program the president favors, it may try to re-scind that spending by packaging it with supplementals that the president wants. Revenues may be intentionally underestimated and then put into a pool for allocation to council members' favorite programs or projects. Agen-cies may reprogram money approved by the legislature and the executive to spend on priorities they prefer. In general, the amount of money spent on policy-motivated changes during the year is quite limited and in some cases, as in the policy-related deferrals at the national level, has been reduced to near zero. Supplemental appropriations at the national level for policy rea-sons have been controlled, and reprogramming is under legislative control.

Once in a while, though, issues of budget implementation take front stage. For example, there has been a renewal of interest in rescissions as a possible technique for helping to control the deficit, and calls for greater flexibility in administration to save money have contended with the desire to control reprogramming. Tighter controls over reprogramming result in part from deficits and cutback and congressional efforts to see that their choices of cuts, rather than agency choices, prevail. But tighter controls also reflect a past history of the abuse of discretion.

Notes

1. Congressional Budget Office, *Supplemental Appropriations in the 1970s* (Washington, D.C.: Government Printing Office, July 1981).

2. P.L. 98–8, 96 stat. 13.

3. "Hard Times Lead to Budget Cuts in Seventeen States," *New York Times,* 16 March 1986.

4. Peter Applebome, "Officials Report Texas Is Falling Short on Budget," *New York Times,* 15 February 1986.

5. Robert Suro, "Texas Governor Is Elusive on Taxes," *New York Times,* April 1991, 13.

6. Kenneth Kirkland, "'Creative Accounting' and Short Term Debt: State Responses to the Deficit Threat," *National Tax Journal* 36, no. 3 (September 1983).

7. Thomas Lauth, "Midyear Appropriations in Georgia: Allocating the 'Surplus,'" *International Journal of Public Administration* 11, no. 5 (1988): 531–50.

8. Ibid., 538.

9. Ibid., 542.

10. Ibid.

11. Alan Saltzstein, "Changing City Policies in Times of Fiscal Uncertainty" (paper presented at the meetings of the American Political Science Association, Washington, D.C., 1986).

12. Congressional Budget Office, *Supplemental Appropriations in the 1980s* (Washington, D.C.: Government Printing Office, February 1990), x.

13. For examples of reasons why authorizations can be late, see Irene Rubin, "Reauthorizations: Implications for Budget Theory," in *New Directions in Budget Theory*, ed. Irene Rubin (Albany: State University of New York Press, 1988).

14. Congressional Budget Office, *Supplemental Appropriations in the 1980s*, 10. Rescissions mean withdrawing or reducing the right to spend previously approved spending authority. Supplementals net of rescissions measure net increased spending authority that occurs during the year.

15. Ibid., 28.

16. Dale Oak, "An Overview of Adjustments to the Budget Enforcement Act Discretionary Spending Caps," *Public Budgeting and Finance*, forthcoming.

17. Todd S. Purdom, "Clinton Vows to Veto Cuts in '95 Budget," *New York Times*, 18 May 1995.

18. "Presidential Comments on Supplemental Appropriations Act, 1987," *Weekly Compilation of Presidential Documents* 23, no. 28 (20 July 1987): 700–826.

19. Ibid.

20. House Report 100–28, to accompany H.R. 1987.

21. John Forrester and Daniel Mullins, "Rebudgeting: The Serial Nature of Local Government Processes." A revised version of this manuscript appears in *Public Administration Review* 52, no. 5 (September/October 1992): 467–73. It only partially overlaps the material in the manuscript version cited here.

22. Ibid., 20.

23. Ibid., 22.

24. Purdom, "Clinton Vows to Veto Cuts."

25. General Accounting Office, *Summary of Proposed and Enacted Rescissions, Fiscal Years 1974–93* (Washington, D.C.: Government Printing Office, February 1993), 3.

26. Figures are taken from Schick, *Capacity to Budget*, table 4.4, p. 112, based on OMB data.

27. For a fascinating discussion of this case, see Barbara Hinkson Craig, *Chadha: The Story of an Epic Constitutional Struggle* (Berkeley: University of California Press, 1990).

28. Schick, *Capacity to Budget*, 113.

29. Senate Report 100–48 on the 1987 Supplementals, to accompany H.R. 1827, 4–5.

30. *City of New Haven, Connecticut v. United States of America*, slip opinion 86–5319, DC Circuit (1987). See also Walter Oleszek, *Congressional Procedures and the Policy Process*, 3d ed. (Washington, D.C.: CQ Press, 1989), 65.

31. George Hale, "State Budget Execution: The Legislature's Role," *Na-*

tional Civic Review 66, no. 6 (June 1977): 288.

32. Advisory Commission on Intergovernmental Relations, *The Question of State Government Capability* (Washington, D.C.: Government Printing Office, 1985).

33. Allen Schick, *The Federal Budget: Politics, Policy, and Process* (Washington D.C.: Brookings Institution, 1995), 170.

34. General Accounting Office, *Budget Reprogramming: Opportunities to Improve DoD's Reprogramming Process* (Washington, D.C.: Government Printing Office, July 1989), 2.

35. U.S. Congress, House, Subcommittee on the Department of Defense, *Department of Defense Appropriations for 1990: Hearings Before a Subcommittee of the Committee on Appropriations,* 101st Cong., 1st sess., pt. 6.

36. Ibid., 887.

37. Ibid., 853.

38. Louis Fisher, *Presidential Spending Power* (Princeton: Princeton University Press, 1975), 80.

39. Its new requirements for reprogramming were listed in the committee report to accompany H.R. 12932, House Report 95–1251.

40. Senate Report 95–1063, to accompany H.R. 12932, 6.

41. House Report 99–669, Department of Commerce, Justice, and State, the Judiciary and Related Agencies Appropriations Bill, FY 1987, to accompany H.R. 5161.

42. U.S. Congress, House, *Immigration and Naturalization Service Budget and Reprogramming Hearings Before the Subcommittee on Immigration, Refugees, and International Law of the Committee on the Judiciary,* 101st Cong., 2d sess., 29 June 1989.

43. U.S. Senate, *Dire Emergency Supplemental Appropriations and Transfers, Urgent Supplementals and Correcting Enrollment Errors Bill,* Report 101–41, to accompany H.R. 2072, 101st Cong., 1st sess., 1989.

44. U.S. Senate, Report 101–44, to accompany H.R. 2991, 27 September 1989, Departments of Commerce, Justice, and State, the Judiciary and Related Agencies Appropriations Bill, 1990, 49.

45. Ibid.

46. *Congressional Record,* 7 August 1995, S.11735.

47. Fred Thompson and L.R. Jones, *Reinventing the Pentagon: How the New Public Management Can Bring Institutional Renewal* (San Francisco: Jossey-Bass, 1994), 86.

48. National Performance Review (supervised by Vice-President Al Gore), *From Red Tape to Results: Creating a Government That Works Better and Costs Less* (Washington, D.C.: Government Printing Office, 1993), 42.

49. *Congressional Record,* 22 March 1995, S.4312.

50. *Congressional Record,* 17 June 1993, S.7490.

51. General Accounting Office, *Financial Management: Status of the Defense Business Operations Fund,* AIMD 94–80 (Washington, D.C.: Government Printing Office, March 1994).

52. General Accounting Office, *Defense Business Operating Fund: Management Issues Challenge Fund Implementation, AIMD 95–70,* (Washington, D.C.: Government Printing Office, March 1995).

53. Charles Levine, Irene Rubin, and George Wolohojian, "Resource Scarcity and the Reform Model: The Management of Reform in Cincinnati and Oakland," *Public Administration Review* 41, no. 6 (November/December 1981): 619–28.

54. See Irene Rubin, *Running in the Red* (Albany: State University of New York Press, 1982), for an example of a general fund borrowing from the water fund and causing deficits in the water fund.

8. Budget Implementation and Control

The budget is generally implemented almost exactly as passed. Most of the changes that occur are for widely accepted reasons, and very little rebudgeting takes place out of public view or outside regular budget processes. Nevertheless, the discretion granted to the executive to carry out the budget is sometimes used for political and policy purposes during the year. Not all of this policy-related activity is unacceptable or threatening to democratic values. But sometimes changes in the budget during the year have the effect of rendering the publicly circulated budget document obsolete. Sometimes the discretion to adapt the budget to changing circumstances is abused or is perceived as a perversion of legislative intent. If there is some indication of overspending or underspending, or of corruption, fraud, or purposeful thwarting of the policies and priorities in the budget, the elected officials are likely to increase the level of their control over budget execution.

The Discretion, Abuse, Control Cycle

Senator Edmund Muskie described the impulse to increase control over implementation when agencies defy congressional will. In 1973, when he learned that the Environmental Protection Agency (EPA) had abused its discretion to implement the budget, Muskie said, "The clear language and debate was what we were giving you, in what we understood to be legitimate administrative discretion to spend the money, not defeat the purposes. Then to have you twist it as you have, is a temptation to this Senator to really handcuff you the next time."[1] "Handcuffing" involves writing detailed constraints into legislation and thereby reducing the agency's discretion over budget implementation.

The dynamics of control tends to follow a pattern over time: (1) an initial grant of broad discretion to the agencies; (2) a perception of abuse; (3) increased budgetary control, in the form of increased supervision and oversight, increased reporting responsibilities, and additional constraints written into committee reports and statutes; and (4) agency reaction to reduced flexibility. If reduced flexibility sufficiently hampers management, or if politicians become overburdened with politically irrelevant decisions about budget execution, there may be (5) a gradual reduction in the level of implementation of budgetary controls. The relationship between steps 1, 2, and 3 is well documented in the literature.

THE NATIONAL LEVEL

At the federal level, for the most part, Congress's control of agencies' budget execution is informal. There is an initial broad grant of discretion to the agencies and to the executive branch over budget execution. There are conversations between legislators and agency heads during budget hearings, or suggestions for restrictions on spending in committee reports, neither of which has the status of law. Congressional committees request and agencies prepare detailed budget justifications, but these justifications are not part of the appropriations; they are just part of the informal understanding between agency officials and members of Congress. But if the agency does not adhere to informal advice, congressional committees may increase their controls and put restrictions or advice into the appropriations act, giving them the force of law. "Usually when restrictive provisions are written into appropriations acts, it is because the agency has failed to comply with these less formal types of guidance or the Congress is not satisfied with how a particular agency is progressing toward some congressionally desired goal."[2]

One example of a broad grant of discretion, followed by a perception of abuse and a threatened and actual increase in controls over budget implementation has occurred in response to reprogrammings. Departments have sometimes taken money intended for one approved program and spent it on another program expressly disapproved by Congress. The problem of controlling reprogrammings accelerated after 1949 when Congress began to consolidate a number of appropriation accounts.[3] Reprogramming can occur only within a single appropriation account, so the move toward more lump-sum appropriations with many programs in a single appropriation increased the amount of discretion and the amount of reprogramming that could be done.

One department that has used reprogramming in ways that have sometimes provoked congressional ire is the Department of Defense. The ability to reprogram was abused during the Vietnam war. For example, the Pentagon used other appropriated funds to pay for projects Congress had disapproved. Congress took control of this particular reprogramming in 1974, with legislation prohibiting the Defense Department from reprogramming funds to any items previously denied by Congress. As a further discouragement of reprogramming, Congress took a more active stance in recommending rescissions of unspent money so there would be less temptation to repro-gram.[4]

Although Congress tried to increase controls over Defense Department spending in most areas, some problems remained in the late 1970s and early 1980s, provoking congressional threats of still more detailed control over spending. Congressman Joseph Addabbo complained in 1981 hearings that the Department of Defense had avoided specific congressional instructions and threatened detailed, line-item control in the operations and maintenance section of the Defense Department budget. Addabbo asked whether Congress had come to the point "when we should get the Congressional Budget Office to prepare a computer printout and we line item. When we cut, say, 'this is it' and the money will be spent in all of the other items."[5]

Addabbo charged that the Defense Department was funding a number of items during the year that were not even in the budget request and for which funds had not been appropriated.[6] Addabbo also complained that Defense Department officials were reprogramming in such a way as to try to force Congress to pass supplementals to restore the lines from which the reprogramming funds were taken. Addabbo described this ploy in the following terms:

> Well, take the Indian Ocean operation, moving the task force in there, you proceed to do that and within that category, the same category, you have a ship overhaul. You take the money from ship overhaul, which is a high priority item, and use it for this. I am willing to venture a guess that within that same category there are many items which we discussed and which there should have been a more careful look at .... You don't grab where it's easiest to grab and say we are going to get that back anyway. That is what we have seen.[7]

Defense Department officials, according to this description, transferred money (reprogramming) out of top-priority rather than low-priority programs, because they knew that Congress would have to pass a supplemental appropriation to replenish the funds for the high-priority programs. Congressman Addabbo, in particular, was not pleased by this maneuver and threatened to reduce Defense Department autonomy over spending even further. Departmental representatives vigorously resisted the imposition of further controls.

Congressman Addabbo also argued that the Defense Department used appropriations for ammunition (which Congress thought very important) as a source of reprogramming funds. Congress would appropriate the money for ammunition, the Defense Department would reprogram the funds into other areas, and then come back to Congress with an emergency request for additional funds for ammunition.[8]

The Defense Department did indeed come back later with requests for supplemental appropriations. During the hearings on the supplemental request, Congressman Addabbo pointedly argued that the Defense Department had tried to avoid cuts specifically recommended by Congress through reprogramming.

> Last year in R.D. and T.E. [the research and development programs] the Congress said you had too much budgeted for inflation. We cut, and all we got back was a lot of nonsense, a lot of wording that we cut so dramatically that many things are going to go wrong. You decided to teach Congress a lesson. You took the reductions out of add-ons by the Congress and we had to hold action on reprogrammings. Because action was required on the supplemental, you started taking it out of where you should be taking it out.[9]

The reprogramming Congressman Addabbo was describing represented not only an agency attempt to avoid specific congressional cuts but also an attempt to implement the president's budget over congressional preferences. That is, the Defense Department chose to take the cuts in those areas where Congress had added to the president's request. The usurpation of congressional prerogatives by the executive branch was not lost on the appropriations subcommittees, which held up the supplementals until the cuts were taken as specified.

MINICASE:
ABUSE AND CONTROLS AT THE DEPARTMENT OF DEFENSE

At the end of September 1985, the House Armed Services Committee took the deputy secretary of defense to task for what many committee members perceived as a violation of the reprogramming procedures.[10] Apparently, the Defense Department had proceeded with a contract bid even though the committee had denied the reprogramming approval necessary for funding the contract. There was some discussion on the committee as to whether the congressional interest stemmed from narrow concerns about who the low bidder was or broader concerns about cost effectiveness of the bid itself, but in any case the result of Defense's bypassing the committee's controls was considerable anger.

The first step was to bring the deputy secretary before the committee to explain what had happened and to reaffirm his understanding of the informal agreements between the committee and the department about the rules of reprogramming. The deputy secretary shifted the blame to a number of other locations and promised to try to do better in the future. He did reiterate a clear understanding of what the rules were.

Some committee members were not content with what they called "wrist slapping." The second step was to call in the General Accounting Office to review the Department of Defense's procedures on reprogramming and to have that office review all the Defense requests for reprogramming to see if they complied with the committee's rules. If not, the committee was determined to reject the request.[11] Then GAO was instructed by the Senate Armed Services Committee to evaluate reprogramming in the Defense Department and suggest improvements. The GAO found that the Defense Department was doing a reasonable job complying with the committee's rules but that the reporting procedure was such that the department did not sort out by fiscal years the reprogramming requests and did not highlight the items of interest to congressional committees. Nor did the department tell the committees of other pending requests that might give congressional committees a clue about what policies were being pursued. The GAO also found that there was considerable reprogramming that went on below the limits required for reporting.

Part of Congress's concern was where the money for reprogramming was coming from, not just where it was going to and whether the object was one Congress had forbidden. As a GAO report described, the Defense Department had proposed a $60.8 million reprogramming from a single program, the Small Intercontinental Ballistic Missile program, without indicating that this request was part of a $330 million sum that it had or was in process of reprogramming out of that program. When Congress understood the full impact of the proposed reprogramming, it denied use of the Small Intercontinental Missile program as a source of most of the requested reprogramming funds. Then it rescinded $266 million of the program's funds, eliminating it as a source of reprogramming.[12] In 1989, the Defense appropriations conference report included language requiring Congress to review decreases in spending resulting from reprogrammings, not just increases.

The ongoing battle between the Armed Services Committees and the Department of Defense continued, when a new controversy broke out over a request to reprogram "M" account funds. "M" accounts are a merged pool of lapsed appropriations.

According to a Senate Armed Services Committee report in 1989, the committee was "disturbed to discover that the Air Force was planning to use the so-called 'M account' to fund approximately $944 million in major corrections to the B-1 bomber."[13] The committee reported that the air force was using the funds in a manner totally inconsistent with usage over the past fifteen years. The issue highlighted for committee members a broader problem of controlling lapsed appropriations.

The House Armed Services report on the authorizing legislation claimed there was even more money involved; the committee was faced with a $1.5 billion recovery plan for the B-1B's electronic countermeasure system. The committee recommended a measure to restrict the way the air force could fund the work.[14] The plan they set up limited the amounts and controlled the manner in which unobligated balances could be restored after they had been withdrawn from availability for obligation. Any amounts over $4 million had to be approved by the secretary of defense or his designee. If the amounts were greater than $25 million, the secretary of defense had to notify, thirty days in advance, both the armed services committees and the appropriation committees, and provide a description of the proposed action, the legal basis, and the policy implications.[15]

The story did not end there.[16] The conference report on 1990 appropriations for the Defense Department specified that use of the M funds for funding changes in the B-1B should be handled by the secretary as a normal reprogramming requiring advance notice. In January 1990, the secretary informed the Appropriations Committee of its intent to use the M funds but did not use normal reprogramming procedures, as he had been directed to do.

House Appropriations Subcommittee chair John Murtha was only partly mollified by the explanation that the money was coming from accounts approved for the same purposes as the money was now being spent for, and so did not require formal reprogramming, and that the department had not in fact committed the funds yet. Murtha began to pressure the department, saying that the committee had been working on reducing the constraints that appear in the Defense Department appropriation,[17] implying that this effort could be suspended if the Defense Department did not cooperate.[18] Even more bluntly, Murtha told the Defense Department representative, "I hope you will take my message back. We can go one step further to putting it into the law and then you will have no leeway."[19]

The authorizing committee (Armed Services) did indeed go one step further and changed the law.[20] These changes eliminated merged M accounts five years after the ending date of an appropriation account. If further obligations resulted from an expenditure more than five years earlier, they were to be paid from some other account set up for similar purposes.

The House Armed Services Committee explained its action in its report on the 1991 National Defense Authorization Act. It described the origin of M accounts in 1956 and the intent to provide a way of paying obligations for which no current unexpired appropriation exists. They argued that generally the M accounts had been well used, but that they had occasionally been abused by the Department of Defense. There was currently nearly $50 billion in the Defense Department M accounts, some of which was truly for paying bills incurred but not yet paid out, and some of which consisted of excess funds that were no longer needed. The M funds had not been audited in recent memory, and no one knew if all the claims on the fund were valid. The committee called for an audit that would determine the legitimate claims on the funds and would terminate the unobligated balance. They estimated that about $38 billion of old spending authority would be eliminated.

The authorizing legislation amended the statutes to eliminate all M funding and require extensive reporting of all obligated and unobligated balances, regardless of agency. Though the M funds were technically eliminated at that point, the Department of Defense seems to have used them one more time, but in this case not to reprogram funds but to cover up overspending that violated the antideficiency act. The episode illustrates the continuing battles between Congress and the Department of Defense over legitimate financial management issues and the need, from Congress's point of view, to reduce the discretion of the Department of Defense.

MINICASE: THE LAST USE OF THE M FUNDS?

Senator Grassley of Iowa, a self-designated Defense Department watchdog, flagged an inspector general's report noting that the air force was asking for $649 million in supplemental appropriations to cover expenditures already made. Grassley threatened to cut out the $649 million from the supplemental appropriation bill; the threat got the attention of the Defense Department and the chair of the Senate Appropriations Subcommittee on Defense. The story came out in pieces. It seems that the air force had no way of reconciling bills coming in with orders it had made and often paid for bills it did not owe or overpaid, and sometimes overspent its budget for lack of basic accounting. More peculiarly, in 1993 the air force took money from the moribund M accounts that had theoretically been closed ten months before to make up for a $649 million gap. The negotiated solution between Senator Grassley, the gadfly, and Senator Inoue, who was defending the air force, was to ask the inspector general to examine the apparent inappropriate use of the M funds and the lack of adequate documentation on what the money was spent on.[21] Grassley wanted the specificity of illegal acts and culprits, not only to show the public that the problem was being taken care of, but to remind the Defense Department not to try this again and to keep working on getting an accounting system that worked.

The tension between the Defense Department and the congressional committees over reprogramming was not resolved with the dissolution of the M funds. Eventually the committees did resort to what Muskie had called handcuffing the agencies. Specific constraints were written into the appropriations, forbidding the agency from reprogramming money for specific purposes. For example, the 1994 Defense Department appropriation suggests a prior conflict without satisfactory resolution. The 1994 appropriation states that during the current fiscal year and thereafter, there shall be no reprogramming or transfer or shift of money by other means between the CIA and the Defense Department for any intelligence or specific activity different from that previously justified to the Congress unless the director of the CIA or the secretary of defense has notified the House and Senate Appropriations Committees of their intent to do so and described the project. The legislation also included a series of rescissions, which would prevent the accumulation of funds that could be used for reprogramming. Moreover, the appropriation legislation specified where money could be transferred from and where it could go for particular purposes.

Reading the 1994 Department of Defense appropriation would initially make one sympathetic to the complaint of the Department of Defense that Congress is micromanaging the Defense Department, especially because so many of the prohibitions seem narrowly political—don't move the 116th Fighter Wing of the National Guard from Dobbins Air Reserve Base to Robins Air Force base—but in the light of prior history of Congress trying to get compliance in gentler ways and persistent Defense Department defiance, the degree of detail and control seems more understandable, if not ideal. Moreover, some of the controls do seem to have clear policy implications, such as forbidding transfers between the CIA and the Department of Defense for unapproved projects.

Part of the congressional effort to respond to apparent abuses of accountability was to eliminate or reduce the discretionary funds that misbehaving agencies controlled. In addition to the M funds, Congress also went after carry-forward funds, intended to tide an agency over the beginning of the fiscal year in case appropriations did not come through on time. The effort to control this type of fund only occurred after an agency had flouted congressional controls. For example, the formerly secret National Reconnaissance Office, after defying congressional oversight, was discovered to have accumulated a carryover fund of $1.5 billion (on a budget of about $6 billion). Congress trimmed back the fund to one month of the agency's budget (about $500 million), forbidding the agency to allow the fund to grow any larger, and inviting the inspector generals of the CIA and Defense to examine the agency's spending controls and recent financial history.[22]

Earmarking is another common congressional response to agencies that evade congressional priorities through extensive reprogrammings, and it is also a constraint that may be written into the law and last for many years. Congress may specify in legislation that so much money or such a percentage of the appropriation be spent on a particular program. The earmarking may be less formal, if it appears in committee reports instead of laws. For example, the judiciary committees of both houses initially granted wide discretion over spending to the Department of Justice, but some committee members were concerned that some programs in the Justice Department were not being funded because the Justice Department's priorities were different from those of the committee. One program the committee supported that they felt was being obliterated was the program to catch and deport Nazi war criminals. The committee proceeded to earmark money for that specific purpose.

Another example of the broad grant of discretion followed by abuse and tightened congressional control occurred over the use of impoundments—the president's unilateral withholding of funds authorized by Congress for expenditures. Historically, Congress allowed the president to withhold some authorized spending for technical reasons. But under President Nixon, such withholding was used to increase the president's power over the budget and defy congressional intent.

> Executive officials seized on discretionary language in statutes to suspend or cancel programs. Through strained legal analyses, administrative officials contended that permissive language in authorization and appropriation bills allowed the president to terminate programs. Also the Nixon administration treated the president's budget as a ceiling on Congress. Any funds that Congress added to the president's budget could be set aside and left unobligated.[23]

The Nixon administration was also fairly free about reprogramming funds to get around congressional opposition to the administration's policy in Vietnam.

President Nixon's abuse of his discretion over budget implementation led to increased congressional control of budget execution, especially on the issue of whether the president could withhold spending that Congress had authorized. In 1974, Congress passed the Congressional Budget and Impoundment Control Act, part of the intent of which was to control presidential impoundments. The act divided withholding of funds into two categories, rescissions and deferrals. The law required the president to propose rescissions, and Congress to approve them. For deferrals, the president had to propose them, but as long as Congress took no specific action to deny, the deferral, or temporary delay in spending, would take place. The law also set up the GAO as watchdog, to make sure that the administration was not withholding funds from agencies without reporting the withholding to Congress.

After 1974, rescissions were still often used for programmatic and policy purposes. "President Ford tried to cancel billions of dollars added by Congress for social programs; President Carter persuaded Congress to rescind funds it had appropriated for military weapons."[24] More than 90 percent of the rescissions during the Carter years were in defense.[25] And under President Reagan, the rescissions were again in social programs. These policy-related rescissions had to be approved by Congress before they could take effect.

President Reagan was still submitting policy deferrals in 1986 and 1987, but Congress was no longer able to overturn such deferrals with one-house vetoes because the Supreme Court, in *Immigration and Naturalization Service* v. *Chadha,* had ruled such one-house vetoes unconstitutional. Congress then took the offensive to prevent the president from submitting such policy deferrals at all, and was successful in getting the courts to rule such deferrals illegal. Thus by 1988, Congress had good control over policy- related rescissions and had virtually eliminated policy-related deferrals.

As the determination of Congress to control impoundments (now called rescissions and deferrals) shows, Congress can be brought to the boiling point when the executive branch simply cuts out any additions to the budget that Congress makes. Such action implies that Congress is just a rubber stamp, and whatever the executive wants is what the budget should be. Treatment of pay raises further illustrates what Congress perceives as an abuse of discretion, and its determination to respond by tightening controls.

Salary increases have for years been determined government wide, without giving agencies enough money to cover the mandated salary increases. The logic was to force agencies to take money that had been unspent in other accounts to contribute to the salary increase. The intent is to reduce the need for, and the size of, supplemental appropriations to cover mandated salary increases. The process sounds like a technical and routine matter, but it has a definite political implication. First, Congress often sets targets for how much of the salary increase the agencies should aim to absorb. This amount has been in the range of 30 percent. Agencies do not necessarily have that much unspent money in personnel lines. OMB has encouraged agencies to transfer surplus funds from other accounts to salary. This practice raises the questions as to what is surplus, and whether program funds are being used to absorb salary increases, and if so, which programs are being cut to fund the salary supplemental.

The agencies sometimes have to guess at how large or small a supplemental appropriation OMB will approve, and create the surplus to make up the balance. That may mean leaving positions purposely unfilled or even increasing the size of a reduction in force, or using a furlough (mandatory, unpaid leave of absence) to save money in the salary lines. In short, OMB can force an agency to cut its personnel budget to absorb some portion—not necessarily the congressional target—of the salary increase costs. The issue becomes less one of efficiency improvements and using unspent money and more one of forcing unpublicized cuts on an agency midyear, without explicit congressional approval.

In the late 1970s OMB used salary absorption to discriminate against congressional add-ons.[26] OMB placed an inordinate burden on those agencies with salary and expense lines increased by Congress above the level of the president's request. "Administration officials were using their powers of implementation to frustrate congressional priorities."[27]

Congress responded to this arrogation of power with the threat of increased legislative controls and in some cases with a requirement that the agency seek supplementals for salary increases rather than try to absorb the costs from existing lines. Senator Lawton Chiles warned in 1979 that "continuation of this practice might prompt Congress to write into the appropriation bill the instruction that absorption cuts be made on a pro rata basis."[28] That restraint would eliminate discretion to cut some programs and leave others alone to fund the salary increase. The Senate Committee on the Judiciary added a section to the annual authorization bill stipulating that the Department of Justice would not be required to absorb any salary increases.[29]

THE STATE LEVEL

The cycle of broad discretion, abuse, and tighter control also applies at the state level. Traditional line-item controls (restrictions on spending according to the object of the expenditures, such as personal service, travel, or contractual services) became less effective as the level of state expenditures grew from $27.6 billion in 1964 to over $100 billion in 1976. Not only is there a lot of money in each line, which creates a lot of discretion, but funds appropriated for a line item can be disbursed legally for a wide variety of purposes. "Moreover, expanded federal grants in aid—from $1.6 billion in 1948 to $16 billion in 1969 to over $40 billion in 1976—vitiate legislative oversight by creating opportunities for state administrators to initiate new programs or to transfer funds among activities during budget execution."[30]

The list of techniques widely used at the state level to change the budget during the year is suggestive of the possibility of abuse of discretion, at least as perceived by the state legislatures. Techniques included padded requests, artificial accounting balances, and improper interfund transfers. Transfer authority also allowed funds to be shifted between line items and appropriation accounts.

In a survey in 1976, 62 percent of 324 state agency directors in eight states responded that they transferred money between line items; 66 percent of the directors reported that they engaged in reprogramming within appropriation accounts. These reprogrammings were used to compensate for cuts in priority items, to engineer expansions in programs, and to initiate programs that lacked legislative support. The more different federal programs the agencies received funding from, the more likely the agencies were to report that they were reprogramming funds.[31]

State legislatures gradually reacted to what they perceived as an abuse of discretion. One report noted in 1975 that "legislatures are paying increased attention to expressing their intent more clearly as a means of exercising policy control." The report continued, "... executive agencies' fun and games with the enacted budget are the cause of much of this concern."[32]

By 1984, major changes had been made in legislative control over state budget execution.[33] In the 1960s, legislatures began to assume the postauditing function that had been independent of the legislatures. By 1980, four out of five state legislatures selected a postauditor responsible to the legislature. The activities of these auditors expanded to include program and performance auditing. In addition, "Legislatures began to appropriate federal grant in aid monies in an effort to assure legislative rather than executive priorities in the spending of state funds, to guard against commitment of future state dollars for matching programs without legislative approval, to avoid pursuit of programs the legislature had disallowed through use of substitute money, and to guarantee effective delivery of services."[34] As of 1988, thirty-six state legislatures made specific appropriations of federal funds, and seventeen controlled appropriations of federally funded staffing levels. Another six states controlled the federally funded staffing in some cases.[35]

THE LOCAL LEVEL

At the local level, the discretion, abuse, control cycle is even clearer than at state and federal levels, although it is primarily state control over local governments, rather than the legislature controlling the executive. Local governments are creatures of the states, and when their finances get out of hand, the state governments step in to increase control levels. Two historical examples illustrate, in addition to the abuse and control cycle, managerial problems resulting from too-tight control and gradual relaxation of control under changing conditions.

MINICASE: MASSACHUSETTS
OVERCONTROLS THE CITIES, 1875–1933

After the Civil War, local debt grew enormously in Massachusetts.[36] The growth was in response to rapid urbanization and the need for infrastructure, but it also reflected the desire to keep property taxes low. Some of the borrowing was for current expenses and for railroads. The growth in borrowing was accompanied by increased assessed valuations until the fiscal crisis of 1873, but during the following recession the burden of debt was keenly felt, and taxes had to go up to cover debt payments when people could least afford the increased taxes.

By 1875, the state had stepped in to curtail and regulate local debt, and in 1876, the state limited cities' investments in railroads. The debt limit was lowered in 1885, from 3 percent of assessed valuation to 2.5 percent and then 2 percent. Also, in 1885, municipal tax levies were curtailed in an effort to control municipal expenditures, which were increasing rapidly. Debt declined from 1875 to 1882, then climbed slowly until 1890. But from 1890 to 1905, net debt more than doubled, and the annual tax levy increased 80 percent. The increases continued after 1905.

Increase in population and changes in social and economic conditions created new administrative problems for local governments, and a rising standard of public consumption pressed on the tax and debt limits. Cities had begun to petition the legislature for exemptions almost immediately after the 1875 legislation. More than 1500 special exemption acts were passed between 1875 and 1911. These exemptions allowed about $73 million in debt outside the limits.

In addition, cities got around the limits on long-term indebtedness by borrowing more short term, in excess of anticipated revenues, and through demand notes. They refunded these notes without appeal to the legislature, rolling over short-term debt for ten, twenty or even fifty years. Cities also borrowed for operating purposes for periods of less than ten years, another loophole in the law. Taxes that remained uncollected for long periods also contributed to the buildup of debt. Cities also borrowed from their trust funds.

Part of the cause of the buildup of debt was the limitation on property taxes. Because cities could not tax legitimately to cover their expenses, they resorted more frequently to borrowing. State mandates for spending also added pressure to local governments to bypass restrictions. The tax limit, like the debt limit, was loosened in application by legislative exemptions.

By 1913, the state had passed a new law attempting to fix some of the problems with the previous legislation. Tax limits were taken off all cities except Boston; debt limits were raised somewhat, and the state tried to improve recordkeeping and data presentation so that the legislature would have some independent basis on which to evaluate requests for borrowing outside the limits. Short-term debt was controlled.

Borrowing for current purposes was reduced by this legislation until the depression of the 1930s increased welfare expenditures and reduced revenues. From 1913 to 1920, debt increased only moderately, partly because of World War I, and the suspension of improvement projects. From 1920 to 1926, aggregate debt grew by 41 percent, then the rate of growth tapered off until 1930. In the early depression years, debt grew rapidly. The state responded to the depression-caused financial problems of the cities by loosening debt limits and loaning cities money.

To summarize, the state stepped in when debt got out of hand and popular pressure against increased taxes provided a base of support for state intervention and control. For a time, the controls had their intended effect, but they also had unintended effects; the tax and borrowing limits increased short-term borrowing beyond expected revenues. When controls are too tight, there is enormous pressure to evade them, and some of the evasions cause additional abuses that invite a new round of controls. Over time, the circumstances that brought about the original control may disappear, and changing circumstances, such as the depression of the 1930s, may require a loosening of controls.

MINICASE: OHIO'S ONE PERCENT LAW

Ohio imposed tax limitations from 1859 to 1911, but they were not restrictive, and there was no machinery for enforcement.[37] But in 1910 and 1911, the Smith 1 percent law was enacted, and it was stringent and enforceable. The context of the increased control was the Progressive era expansion of expenditures and the growth in the functions of government, combined with a very poor system of assessment for real estate and personal property taxes. Assessment reform could not take place without some kind of guarantee that taxes would not increase as assessments went up to 100 percent. Also, a lowering of rates was thought to encourage the reporting of personal property. The 1 percent limit was the total for all local governments, including cities, school districts, counties, and townships.

Before long, most cities were taxing at or near their limits. When a state law reducing liquor revenues was factored in, many cities received less revenues in 1914 than they had in 1910. By the end of 1914, there had developed an epidemic of floating debt. Cities were reportedly not being profligate, but were not receiving enough revenues to handle state mandated expenditures, inflation, and the growing demands of increased population. The legislature exempted the principal levies of counties and townships from the Smith 1 percent law, but kept the limits on cities.

As inflation continued to rise, floating debt increased to the point that in places it could no longer be carried. Bonds had to be authorized for their retirement. Efforts to educate the public to pass these bonds helped build pressure to revise the tax system. As inflation continued, cities had to raise salaries of employees, and the floating debt levels continued to rise.

By 1919, the legislature began to make serious adjustments. First, they authorized new and expanded nonproperty taxes that would help pay local bills. Then the legislature loosened the limits somewhat for school districts. Then all levies for existing indebtedness were excluded from the limit, if public support could be garnered. Since the cities had such a heavy debt load, this was a major relief. During the next session of the legislature, citizens were empowered to overrule the Smith law for up to three years by a 60 percent vote. The Smith law was repealed in 1923.

The 1 percent law was too strict. It did not allow for rapid population growth or make provision for very rapid inflation. The result was an accumulation of short-term debt to balance the budget, some of which was funded by deficiency bonds. The legislature made adjustments gradually, but not before considerable damage had been done.

The control cycle does not necessarily end with ever tighter effective controls. At the federal level, for example, the consolidation of appropriation accounts represented a lessening of legislative controls on expenditures. The result was increased agency discretion over reprogramming. The cycle of control began with a lessening of control from the previous cycle. At the state level, it was clear that line-item controls were weakened by both increases in total dollars and increased complexity resulting from federal grants. At the local level, overly harsh state controls have generally loosened over time.

When controls are tight, they make routine management problematic and adaptation difficult. Managers under these circumstances will often try to re-create flexibility within the existing constraints. For example, managers dealing with tight line-item controls have generated a system of invisible swaps between line items. Legislative controls on impoundment spawned ways of getting around the controls, such as executive reduction in staff. It can be difficult to devise a system of controls that will not be evaded and simultaneously will not be so rigid as to make good management impossible.

Sometimes legislatures may, in moments of pique, set up rigid oversight of implementation, and then gradually lose interest in maintaining the oversight. The initial issues that seemed such an affront to legislative power may have receded, or the amount of detailed work involved may not be paying much in the way of political dividends, and other issues press to the fore.

Under these circumstances, the laws are likely to remain on the books, but the level of surveillance is likely to ease. An understanding may emerge that the agencies need no longer conform to the letter of the law.

Implementation and Control: The Politics of Finding Waste, Fraud, and Abuse

Efforts to control waste, fraud, and abuse illustrate a second strategy for maintaining budgetary accountability. Here it is not policy divergence from the budget that threatens accountability, but accounting systems that do not work, programs that are poorly designed, and excessive claims for funding. Intentional fraud and just plain waste both interfere with carrying out the intent of the budget. These campaigns may seem technical, managed by accountants who work out improved techniques for financial control. But as elsewhere in this book, what is technical may also be highly political.

There are at least three ways in which efforts to control waste, fraud, and abuse may be political. First, the cycle of broad initial grants of discretion, perception of abuse, and then increased control is political in the sense of a shifting balance of power between the executive and legislative branches and between state power and local government autonomy. Second, whoever is chosen to be the auditor must have enough independence to be credible, but enough cooperation to get reliable information and to carry out recommendations for improvements. Gaining that independence and negotiating for cooperation are themselves political efforts. Third, the effort to reduce waste, fraud, and abuse may become a highly visible political campaign, one with a large number of pitfalls.

THE CASE OF THE INSPECTORS GENERAL

The Inspector General system at the national level is a good example of efforts to control waste, fraud, and abuse, and to increase the overall accountability of the budget. Inspectors General are auditors, who work with a team, within specific departments or agencies. The first Inspector General was appointed in the Agriculture Department in 1961, but the idea gradually spread to other departments and agencies. The Inspector General Act (P.L. 95-452) was passed in 1978, establishing Inspectors General in twelve federal departments and agencies. The system has gradually expanded; in 1993 there were sixty Inspectors General with a staff of 15,000.[38]

Like other forms of financial control described in this chapter, the Inspector General system was created in response to perceived abuses. "It was a series of scandals and abuses within government as well as a renewed em-

phasis on prevention and detection that led to congressional realization of
the need for an I.G. concept within the federal government and subsequent
passage of the act."[39] Congressional intent was to create a powerful instrument to root out fraud, waste, and abuse in government by creating a semi-
independent, centralized auditing and investigatory team for each major department. The intent of Congress was to create a dual structure of reporting,
to see that the Inspectors General reported to Congress as well as to the executive branch.

Almost every increase in the coverage of the Inspector General system occurred as a response to a perceived abuse and widely publicized scandal. The
first one, in the Department of Agriculture, was established as a response to
the Billy Sol Estes scandal. "Estes had been revealed to have parlayed fraud-
ulent warehouse receipts, mortgages, and financial statements into a fortune
from the Department of Agriculture despite the fact that his activities were
suspected by three different audit units within the Department."[40]

After 1969, Congress began to lose interest in the Inspectors General.[41]
But in 1974, reports of widespread cheating in Medicare and student loans
in the Department of Health, Education, and Welfare reinvigorated congressional interest. Reports of doctors overbilling and overtesting Medicaid patients further stimulated Congress; the HEW Inspector General Act was
passed in 1976.[42] By the time the Inspector General model was extended to
many other departments in 1978, Congress had come to accept that "government programs were rotten with massive fraud, waste, and abuse and
that neither the political executives nor the career civil servants who managed the programs could be relied on to root it out."[43]

The Inspector General system was designed by Congress to increase and
improve controls over implementation of the budget when signs of waste,
fraud, or abuse were observed. But the ability of the system to work as
planned was questionable because of its odd structure and its need for independence in order to function.

Legislators felt that other kinds of investigations lacked independence,
and put into the 1978 law features they felt would enhance the independence
of the Inspectors General.[44] To ensure independence, the Inspectors General
would be appointed by the president and report both to the department
head and to Congress. This dual reporting system is supposed to make them
more independent, but it also inevitably makes them somewhat more political.

The independence of the Inspectors General is necessary to carry out an
investigative role, but the independence is compromised by political appoint-
ment, and by responsibility to both Congress and the departmental secretaries. The early Inspectors General in the Department of Agriculture were

especially politicized because the two top positions were presidential appointees subject to Senate confirmation; and in addition, two assistant Inspectors General were presidential appointees not subject to Senate confirmation, in an office that never exceeded forty-seven employees.[45] That is a very high proportion of political appointees in one office.

The Inspectors General can get caught between departments and Congress and can be rendered useless. The GAO evaluated the first Inspector General in the Department of Agriculture negatively. There was "limited use of the office as a management tool, partly because of concern over external disclosure of inspection findings through routine distribution of reports to congressional committees and others."[46] Reported one observer of the Inspector General system, "In my opinion, the IG's independence will not be any better defined than it has been and will always be a subject of dispute. IGs are 'straddling a barbed wire fence.' "[47]

Because the Inspectors General are located in departments and do not always have their own appropriation accounts (only six had a separate budget appropriation in the FY 1984 budget), they come under departmental personnel ceilings. Thus if a secretary is threatened by the activities of an Inspector General, he or she may reduce the staffing levels of the Inspector General's office. Presumably, the knowledge that secretaries can do this curtails the Inspector General's independence.

The issue of independence of the Inspectors General became even more salient when President Reagan fired all sitting Inspectors General in 1981 and began to replace them with his own appointees.[48] Presumably the president wanted to make sure the Inspectors General were not going to embarrass the administration, but in doing so he harmed the appearance of neutrality necessary for any kind of waste/fraud investigator. Some congressmen were very upset by this action.

> The Reagan massacre established for all time in the minds of many on the hill ... when a position is created as a presidential appointment, a president is going to appoint the kind of people he wants ... Congress can add all the provisos it wants about being notified for reasons for removal—the fact remains that appointed incumbents serve at the president's pleasure. The unnecessary rubbing of people's faces in this fact was the costly aspect of the massacre.[49]

Once skepticism had been raised about the objectivity of the Inspectors General, future pronouncements by them were treated as campaign stances rather than statements of fact. The Inspectors General reported at the end of 1981 a savings of $2.1 billion, a figure that Congressman John Dingell and the GAO took apart as grossly exaggerated. In a subsequent report, the Inspectors General restated the $2.1 billion figure as $5.4 billion, by adding in savings from the Defense Contract Audit Agency—not a part of the Inspector General system. The DCAA's role is in preaward audits, preventing misclaims later. These were not dollars of money misspent and recovered, but the operation of routine controls. How much money one saves by preventing false claims through good contract management is no more than a wild guess.

The political will of department secretaries has clashed with the autonomy of the Inspectors General. Congress expanded the Inspector General system in 1988 to include several more cabinet departments, one of which was the Department of Justice. Like many other departments that had been subject to Inspector General programs, the Department of Justice firmly opposed having an Inspector General. The major reason given was that the attorney general (the political appointee of the president who heads the Department of Justice) would be unable to direct or stop investigations. That was indeed part of the intent of establishing the program—that Inspectors General could carry out investigations without departmental obstruction. Nevertheless, Congress, in recognition of the sensitive matters dealt with by the Department of Justice, gave the attorney general permission to halt some cases if he gave Congress warning that he was about to do so.

MINICASE: TENSION AT THE CIA

Congress created an Office of the Inspector General at the Central Intelligence Agency in 1989; the first Inspector General took office in 1990. As might be expected, the CIA did not want an Inspector General looking over its shoulder, and the agency's displeasure was frequently expressed in terms of criticism of Fred Hitz, the IG. As Senator Bob Kerrey put it, "The CIA has a proud but insular culture which tends to resist the scrutiny of an independent examiner."[50] But precisely because of the agency's secret missions, Congress felt the need for an independent Inspector General.

The IG was not only thrust between an agency that did not want it and Congress, which wanted good audit information in a secret environment; he also had to wrestle with the possible consequences of overcontrol. This possibility, that IGs would intimidate public officials into not taking risks, was mentioned for all agencies in the National Performance Review organized by Vice-President Gore in 1993 and 1994. Kerrey described the dilemma for the IG at the CIA:

> . . . an independent IG must not contribute to a climate in which the CIA is afraid to take risks when vital U.S. interests are at stake. An independent IG

must not create an internal empire of inspectors which has the same chilling effect on creative action in Government that excessive regulation has on business. Like the congressional oversight committees, a good IG must ensure that the Agency acts in accordance with U.S. law and U.S. values without inhibiting the Agency's ability to act boldly.[51]

Successfully negotiating this kind of environment with these kinds of constraints requires more than good accounting and auditing skills. The difficulty of getting information and the sensitivity of each possible report make political skills essential.

When the solicitor at the Department of Labor tried to stop an investigation by the Inspectors General at that department, the matter came to the Department of Justice for resolution. Did the Inspectors General have authority to make the kind of investigation they were making? The Department of Justice not only said no, they did not, but made a general statement applying to all Inspectors General, limiting the scope of their investigations.

The crux of the matter seemed to lie in the kind of investigation, which the Office of Legal Counsel of the Department of Justice called "regulatory." What they specifically opposed was when the Inspectors General, finding that a department had not deployed resources to investigate some regulatory compliance issue, took it upon themselves to do it. The Inspectors General claimed they had the authority to investigate fraud in federal programs; the Office of Legal Counsel said they had the authority to investigate only if the matter involved fraud or corruption of public officials and the expenditure of federal funds.[52]

The Legal Counsel opinion was based on a selective reading of the history of the Inspectors General law and ignored other specific delegation of authority in laws after 1978.[53] Still more disturbing, individual Inspectors General stated that the Department of Justice was threatening them and that it would not defend them in case of lawsuit if they pursued cases beyond Department of Justice's judgment of appropriate scope. Said Senator John Glenn, chairman of the Committee on Governmental Affairs: "As I understand it, your people have been told that if they don't get prior approval in particular areas, you were told by the head of the DOJ Office of Consumer Litigation that continued investigation of FDA cases by Inspector General employees would place your special agents in jeopardy of personal tort liability. In other words, if there is a suit filed against you, they would not defend you, as would be the normal case; is that correct?" Mr. Richard P. Kusserow, Inspector General, Department of Health and Human Services, answered: "That's correct, sir."[54] The implication was that the Inspectors

General had better clear every dubious case with the Department of Justice. Such action would have given the Department of Justice enormous power to cut off any investigation of regulatory matters.

The intent of the Department of Justice in this matter became clear when the name and policy position of Elliott Levitas was taken as evidence of the intent of Congress in passing the Inspectors General legislation. Levitas in a brief congressional career made a name for himself as a defender of the regulated against the regulators.[55] He argued on the floor of Congress that the Inspectors General should be engaged in watching government officials, not in finding noncompliance and fraud in business people subject to government regulations.[56]

After the Department of Justice memo limiting the scope of their investigations, Inspectors General from different departments found that subjects of some of their investigations were claiming the inspectors had no authority in the matter. The inspectors were forced in a number of instances to drop investigations in progress. They reported difficulty in interpreting what they were obliged to do under the law and what they were forbidden from doing. Collectively, they tried to negotiate the matter with the Department of Justice, but reported no progress. They then came to the Senate Governmental Affairs Committee, to suggest that Congress strengthen and clarify the law to make their jurisdiction clearer. The committee called a hearing, with both sides present.

During the hearings, Chairman Glenn managed to get Department of Justice spokesmen to back down verbally from the threat to force inspectors to hire their own attorneys if sued on a case where the Department of Justice disapproved of the appropriateness of the investigation. The Department of Justice spokesmen took a somewhat conciliatory view. They would meet with the Inspectors General at any time; many of the investigations questioned by inspectors after the DOJ policy statement were judged to be legitimate. But the Department of Justice spokesmen did not budge on the issue of preventing Inspectors General from investigating regulatory matters that the agencies were supposed to investigate themselves, even when the agencies lacked the resources or skills or determination to do the investigations. The Governmental Affairs Committee recommended additional time to work out a negotiated settlement.

The problem of proper scope of Inspectors General investigations was ultimately determined in favor of the IGs and a broad scope of investigations. Symbolic of this resolution was the public call of President Clinton for a crackdown on Medicaid and Medicare fraud in May 1995. The major sources of fraud in these programs are unscrupulous doctors and nursing homes who prescribe unnecessary tests or overbill. The campaign was spearheaded by the Inspector General of Health and Human Services and clearly established the idea that Inspectors General could and should investigate fraud perpetrated on the government.

The tension between policy control over investigations by appointed officials and the independence of the Inspectors General is endemic to the structure of the Inspector General system and adds a political dimension to budget implementation. A second source of political infusion in a technical process occurs when the effort to reduce waste, fraud, and abuse becomes a political campaign. During his first term, President Reagan, like his immediate predecessors, launched a national campaign to reduce the amount of waste, fraud, and abuse in the federal government. Not only did his campaign make headlines, but examples of fraud and waste kept hitting the newspapers, making the issue particularly salient. Military purchases of $2000 toilet seats, $600 hammers, and $7600 coffeepots became public knowledge; military procurement became the subject of congressional hearings. During Reagan's second term, military procurement became a widely publicized scandal.

A public effort to reduce waste, fraud, and abuse seems like an ideal political campaign issue, because it fits the public conception of waste in government, promises to clean it up, and offers to reduce tax burdens by cutting fat and leaving services alone. If done properly, it also helps cover over currently occurring scandals or abuses. On closer examination, however, such a campaign is fraught with difficulties both political and technical.

Campaigns against waste, fraud, and abuse often make the naive assumptions that there is fat in the public budget and that the fat is easily recognizable and surgically removable. In fact, the amount of fat is not easily determined, and it is almost always attached to something of value. For example, trying to get able-bodied people off the handicapped rolls requires tightening eligibility requirements. Inevitably, some people who are both eligible and needy will also be taken off the rolls. Should their plight become public knowledge, the result is likely to be worse publicity than if some undeserving person got public aid. There is a very real tradeoff between denying some people aid who need it and preventing the undeserving from getting it.

Second, waste, fraud, and abuse keep recurring, no matter how much is reported eliminated, because a small number of mistakes is inevitable in any large and complex operation.[57] Thus a campaign to eliminate waste, fraud, and abuse can be embarrassing, because the more you "save" the more you demonstrate how much more waste, fraud, and abuse exist. "No matter which administration is blamed, constant harping on fraud and abuse goes beyond its necessity as a deterrent to the point of further weakening an already dangerously tottering image of the governmental process."[58]

Moreover, much of the source of waste is systemic, which means that really getting to the basis of the problem may mean major revelations of structural problems, and major reorganizations. To eliminate wasteful purchasing in the military would require a drastic overhaul of the military. Such a change is a long-term proposition, not a short-term political campaign with highly publicized results and then silence.

Campaigns against waste, fraud, and abuse are useful political tools to bring down an opponent or discredit a predecessor, but they can boomerang and be used against one's own administration. Hence such campaigns are inherently political, regardless of their technical components.

To summarize, campaigns to reduce waste, fraud, and abuse combine the technical skills of the auditor with the politics of budgetary control. What appears to be technical is also political for a number of reasons. First, some waste, fraud, and abuse is inevitable in complex programs, so continual efforts to remove them only reinforce their existence in the public mind, and can undermine governmental legitimacy. Second, political campaigns to reduce waste, fraud, and abuse can boomerang, making the current administration look riddled with scandal. That possibility creates the desire to control the auditors politically, and underscores the need for independence of the auditors. To be effective, Inspectors General have to work with department administrators, but still be independent; and to serve the purposes of control, they must also be responsible to Congress. The Inspectors General have to struggle continuously to maintain independence and effectiveness in this environment.

Summary and Conclusions

Budget execution is not just a technical activity carried out by administrators; it is also a part of the politics of budgeting. Budgets have to remain flexible in order to adapt to changing economic conditions, but in doing so, they also allow for budget changes that reflect political policy. Only a limited portion of the budget is likely to change during the year, but for some agencies, those changes may be important. Moreover, in some years, midyear changes are substantial. Periodically the flexibility in the budget is abused, and legislative will is thwarted. Legislators may become angry and increase controls over an agency or program. Such controls may accumulate over time and remain in place long after they are needed. A morass of controls invites efforts to evade them, and even the legislature may gradually lose interest in enforcing outdated overcontrols.

When the legislature gets frustrated with poor budget implementation or intentional thwarting of its will, it has a range of techniques at its disposal, from threats and informal, unwritten agreements, through increased reporting and supervision, and finally to requirements for budget implementation written directly into law. In the case of the Defense Business Operations Fund, where Congress considered the problems to be simply poor management, Congress wrote into the law an increased level of supervision and reporting. In the case of the M funds, where the Defense Department was taking funds from lapsed accounts and spending them in a way that Congress disapproved of, Congress eliminated the M funds completely.

Legislative bodies tend to get excited when they think their will has been thwarted. They do not tend to get as excited about poor financial management, but the General Accounting Office and the Inspectors General at the national level and Inspectors General and auditors at the state level get upset about poor financial management, especially when it leads to major losses of money. Unlike the legislatures, auditors do not have line authority to make improvements. At the national level, the Inspectors General have to persuade the management of their agencies to make improvements. They have to develop a working relationship with the managers whom they are observing, while maintaining their independence and while reporting to Congress.

Improving financial management is not a neutral and technical topic even when it is handled quietly, but when mismanagement involves millions or billions of dollars and makes government look bad, those who report it become unwelcome presences. Efforts to control the auditors or put a particular spin on their findings have sometimes marred the independence of the Inspectors General.

The National Performance Review put some of the blame on auditors for creating an atmosphere of fear and overcontrol, but generally all they do is call attention to violations of rules and in some cases suggest new ones. The source of overcontrol is occasional intentional abuses of discretion that generate increasing controls. Not enough attention is paid to moderating and eliminating the controls when they are no longer needed. This is not to argue that legislators are always on morally high ground in terms of what they want the agencies to do—they may insist that a contract go to a specific company for example. Rather, the argument is that agencies should be extremely careful to avoid abusing grants of discretion, and legislatures should use the minimum amount of control necessary to regain compliance should they detect such abuse.

Notes

1. U.S. Congress, Senate, *Joint Hearings before Committees on Government Operations and on the Judiciary, Impoundment of Appropriated Funds by the President*, 93d Cong., 1st sess., 1973, 411; quoted in Louis Fisher, "The Effect of the Budget Act on Agency Operations," in *The Congressional Budget Process After Five Years*, ed. Rudolph Penner (Washington, D.C.: American Enterprise Institute, 1981), 173.

2. Frank Draper and Bernard Pitsvada, "Limitations in Federal Budget Execution," *Government Accountants Journal* 30, no. 3 (Fall 1981): 23.

3. Fisher, "Effect of the Budget Act," 156.

4. Ibid., 157.

5. U.S. Congress, House, *Hearings before a Subcommittee of the Committee on Appropriations, DoD Appropriations 1981*, 96th Cong., 2d sess., 1980, pt. 4, p. 308.

6. Ibid., 246.

7. Ibid., 309.

8. U.S. Congress, House, *Hearings before Subcommittees of the House Appropriations Committee, Supplemental Appropriation and Rescission Bill, 1981*, 97th Cong., 1st sess., 1981, pt. 4, p. 31.

9. Ibid., 119.

10. U.S. Congress, House Committee on Armed Services, *Full Committee Consideration of Reconciliation Recommendations and Hearings on Reprogramming Process and Procedures*, 99th Cong., 1st sess., 30 September 1995.

11. U.S. Congress, House Committee on Armed Services, *Full Committee Organizational Meeting and Consideration of Defense Department Reprogramming*, 100th Cong., 5 February 1987, 10–11.

12. General Accounting Office, *Budget Reprogramming: Opportunities to Improve DoD's Reprogramming Process* (Washington, D.C.: Government Printing Office, July 1989), 14–15.

13. U.S. Senate Committee on Armed Services, *National Defense Authorization Act for Fiscal Years 1990 and 1991*, Report to accompany S. 1352, 19 July 1989.

14. U.S. House, *Defense Authorization Act for Fiscal Years 1990 and 1991*, Report 101–21, 841, in *U.S. Congressional and Administrative News*, 101st Cong., 1st sess., vol. 3.

15. See P.L. 101-89.

16. U.S. Congress, House Appropriations Committee, *Hearings on Defense Appropriations for 1991*, pt. 6.

17. Of which there were many.

18. U.S. Congress, House Appropriations Committee, *Hearings on Defense Appropriations for 1991*, 124.

19. Ibid., 125.

20. P.L. 101-510.

21. *Congressional Record*, 22 June 1993, 7551 ff.

22. See The Defense Appropriation for 1996, P.L. 104-61, sec. 8070, and

the Intelligence Authorization Act, H.R. 1655, the authorization of the secret portion of the budget. Amendments 2881, 2882, 2883, and 2884 were discussed en bloc in the Senate, as reported in *Congressional Record,* 29 September 1995.

23. Fisher, "Effect of the Budget Act," 150.

24. Allen Schick, *Congress and Money* (Washington, D.C.: Urban Institute Press, 1980), 403.

25. Ibid., 406.

26. Fisher, "Effect of the Budget Act of 1974," 170.

27. Ibid.

28. Cited in ibid., from U.S. Congress, House, *Hearings before the Committee on Appropriations, Departments of Labor and Health, Education, and Welfare and Related Agencies Appropriations for Fiscal Year 1980,* 96th Cong., 1st sess., 1979, 175–76.

29. Fisher, "Effect of the Budget Act," 171.

30. Hale, "State Budget Execution," 284.

31. Ibid., 285.

32. *The State Legislative Appropriations Process* (Lexington, Ky.: Council of State Governments, 1975), 36.

33. ACIR, *The Question of State Government Capability,* 116.

34. Ibid., 117.

35. Tony Hutchison and Kathy James, *Legislative Budget Procedures in the Fifty States: A Guide to Appropriations and Budget Processes* (Denver: National Conference of State Legislatures, 1988), 108.

36. This case is taken from Royal S. Van De Woestyne, *State Control of Local Finance in Massachusetts* (Cambridge, Mass.: Harvard University Press, 1935).

37. This case is taken primarily from Raymond Atkinson, "The Effects of Tax Limitation upon Local Finance in Ohio, 1911 to 1922" (Ph.D. dissertation, Columbia University. Printed in Cleveland, Ohio, 1923, n.p.).

38. National Performance Review, *From Red Tape to Results: Creating a Government That Works Better and Costs Less* (Washington, D.C.: Government Printing Office, 1993), chap. 1.

39. Charles Dempsey, "The Inspector General Concept: Where It's Been, Where It's Going," *Public Budgeting and Finance* 5, no. 2 (Summer 1985): 39.

40. Mark H. Moore and Margaret Jane Gates, *Inspectors-General: Junkyard Dogs or Man's Best Friend?* (New York: Russell Sage Foundation, 1986), 11.

41. Ibid., 11.

42. Ibid., 12.

43. Ibid.

44. Dempsey, "The Inspector General Concept," 40.

45. Thomas Novotny, "The IG's—A Random Walk," *Bureaucrat* 12, no. 3 (Fall 1983): 35.

46. Ibid., 39.

47. Ibid.

48. For accounts of these events, see Chester Newland, "A Midterm Appraisal—The Reagan Presidency: Limited Government and Political Administration," *Public Administration Review* 43, no. 1 (January/February 1983): 1–21; and Novotny, "The IG's."

49. Novotny, "The IG's," 38.

50. *Congressional Record,* 21 December 1995, S.19138.

51. Ibid.

52. See William Barr, Assistant Attorney General, Office of Legal Council, "Testimony," *Oversight Hearings of the Operations of the Inspector General Offices,* 267–85; and Office of Legal Counsel, "Authority of the Inspector General to Conduct Regulatory Investigations," policy memo, 9 March 1989.

53. James Naughton, "Authority of Inspectors General to Conduct Criminal Investigations Relating to Regulatory Programs," *Oversight Hearings,* April 1990, 147–200.

54. *Oversight Hearings,* 10.

55. See Barbara Hinkson Craig, *Chadha: The Story of an Epic Constitutional Struggle* (Berkeley: University of California Press, 1990), 40–46.

56. *Oversight Hearings,* 103.

57. The complexity of federal programs and the inevitability of some waste, fraud, and abuse are the central points made by John Young, "Reflections on the Root Causes of Fraud, Abuse, and Waste in Federal Social Programs," *Public Administration Review* 43, no. 4 (July/August 1983): 362–69.

58. Novotny "The IG's," 37.

9. Budgetary Decision Making and Politics

Budgetary decision making includes five distinct but linked clusters: revenues, process, expenditures, balance, and implementation. Describing each decision stream separately tends to emphasize their independence. This chapter is more about how they fit together into one decision-making process. Looking at the decision strands together also permits an examination of their common themes and differences.

Real-Time Budgeting

I call the pattern of decision making that results from the integration of the five streams of decision making *real-time budgeting*. "Real time" refers to the continual adjustment of decisions in each stream to decisions and information coming from other streams and from the environment. Budgeting, like the complex computer programs aboard spaceships, continually readjusts, in real time, for changing information.

Budgeting is characterized by semi-independent, overlapping streams of decision making that depend on one another for key pieces of information. What makes this process complex and interesting is that the clusters are not timed sequentially to feed into one another. The clusters occur at different intervals and last for different lengths of time. In order to make the key decisions in any one stream, actors may have to look backward, to the last time the decision was made in another stream, or forward, to anticipated decisions, or even sideways, to decisions being made at the same time. Much of this information is tentative; it can and does change as the budget moves toward implementation.

Budgetary decision making takes the shape it does because of the characteristics of public budgeting described in chapter 1. First and foremost, budgets are open to the environment—to the economy, to the weather, to a variety of emergencies, and to changes in public preferences and political leadership. Openness to the economy means that estimates of revenues, and to some extent estimates of expenditures, may have to be revised several times during the budget process as better information becomes known. Budgeters cannot make one estimate at the beginning of the budget process and stick to it. Openness to change in political leadership and public opinion means that budgets that were generally agreed to may need to be redone.

A second characteristic of public budgets is that a variety of actors with different goals compete for limited resources. Policy decisions that feed into the budget may cause controversy and delay. Budgets have to be able to deal with policy conflict among these actors and with competition between them. Some budget actors may want to limit revenues, which has implications for the expenditure stream; some actors may want to increase particular expenditures, which has implications for the revenue stream; the goals of these actors may clash. The result may be long-delayed decisions. Budgetary decision making has to accommodate this kind of conflict and this kind of delay. Budgets have deadlines. The later they are, the less use they are, so the problem of late decisions has to be handled in some way.

The solution to the problems of changing information and late decisions is a budget process that features fragmentation, with semi-independent decision streams, and interruptibility. Parts of the decision making may proceed without the rest in order to complete the budget in a timely manner. The different strands of decision making proceed as if they were independent, referring to one another, bargaining when necessary to reach accommodation. If one decision-making strand gets stuck, such as when a tax increase is being considered but no decision is yet made, other decision streams can proceed with their work, by making assumptions about what will occur in the revenue stream and adjusting their own work when the final outcome is known in the revenue stream.

The decision clusters are mostly independent, but they need information from one another to complete their work. The revenue cluster cannot proceed without some knowledge of spending requirements and balance constraints. Decisions about how to reduce a deficit are dependent on revenue estimates and spending estimates. Spending estimates depend on revenue, balance, and implementation streams. Implementation depends on decisions throughout the process to that point, especially on the degree of underestimates of revenues or overestimates of expenditures, and the constraints of balance and handling of deficits. Revenues, expenditures, balance, and implementation all depend on the process stream to organize them and allocate power to them.

Information coming from other decision streams may appear as a constraint, but one that is flexible rather than rigid. Thus a figure for estimated revenues already fed into the expenditure stream may change if the prediction of the economy changes. Or it may change if a decision is made in the expenditure stream that requires more revenue.

Constraints from other decision streams are flexible not only because the environment changes but also because actors in one stream can sometimes force a change in another stream. Actors who want to spend more money may be able to force a change in the tax structure or even in revenue estimates; they may also be able to force a change in the definition of balance. Actors who want to reduce revenues may act to cut expenditures and define balance to suit their purposes.

Budgetary decision making is not linear and sequential, in the sense that some decisions are made first and form the frame for the other decisions. A simple model of decision making would argue that the definition of balance, the budget process, and the revenue estimates should be in place before the beginning of the decision making and that the decision making should begin with targets for spending that keep within revenue estimates. Then spending decisions should be made. Real budgeting does not look like this model for three by now familiar reasons. First, the budget is open to the environment, so new information becomes available at intervals. Second, decisions in the budget take different amounts of time to make and are remade at intervals that may be impossible to predict or schedule. Third, actors in one decision stream can jump over into other decision streams and force a change there in the middle of the decision making.

Consider, for example, recent revenue decisions at the local level. In Illinois, two recent changes in state laws have affected local revenues. In one case, the legislature passed a change in the law for tax increment districts, which is a form of project funding that uses the increased tax yield from property as a result of public development efforts to pay off the initial project costs. The state had agreed to help share the costs of redevelopment by offering increments from the state sales tax to the cities that had sales tax increment districts, but then found that some cities drew up their districts not to maximize development but to maximize the state funding offer. The size of the local demand on state funds was larger than anticipated. The state balked; it was no longer clear what proportion of the promised funds the state would provide. In the middle of a budget year, the state announced its revised guidelines and reduced funding levels. Spending decisions that had already been made had to be remade, and projects had to be reprioritized in the light of the changed law.

A second example occurred when the state changed the sales tax law to merge locally raised sales tax with the state-collected sales tax, requiring a uniform set of exemptions, but giving cities a little over two years to prepare for the change. The result for some cities would be a loss of revenues, because they would have to conform to the state exemptions. They would have two years to decide what to do and how to adapt and design alternatives and implement them. They might or might not get the decision making in the revenue stream accomplished in time. In any case, the decision began two years ahead of the event, and was thrust on the cities by the state at an unpredictable moment.

An example of a decision that may be remade in the middle of budgeting occurs when actors try to define or redefine balance during the budget process. If it appears that there is a conflict between the amount of revenues available and the amount of spending desired, and the conflict cannot be easily reconciled, one option is to attack the definition of balance and loosen it. For example, a requirement that budgets balance each year may be stretched out to balance over the life of the program. In the Highway Trust Fund, proponents of additional spending argued that if they spent more money now than was in the trust fund, they would just continue to collect user fees after the end of the building program and pay off the debt later. The intent was to redefine balance from an annual reckoning to a period of fifteen or twenty years.

Efforts to redefine balance were continuous at the national level for most of the 1980s. Gramm-Rudman-Hollings made this effort explicit by defining balance as a moving target of deficits of smaller and smaller sizes. Each year, then, the target for balance was to change. Unfortunately for the linear model of decision making, it was not clear that Gramm-Rudman-Hollings was constitutional, which made its targets somewhat dubious; and the response to its limits was to make the deficits look of appropriate size rather than be of appropriate size. The result was a shifting goal of balance that got defined each year as part of the budget process.

Budgetary decision making is not and cannot be made sequential. The solution is to make the key decisions in five parallel sequences and link them to one another for necessary information. The system of decision making by linking clusters in real time is wonderfully adaptive. Real-time decision making allows the streams to be disrupted, or interrupted, and repeated. Decisions can be adjusted or remade.

Budgeters have to have many contingency plans to deal with missing information or late decisions. To respond to missing information, they may rely instead on the last, most recent decision. If individual policy decisions are too slow, they may simplify and speed up the decision making by grouping many decisions together. They may push up the urgency of decisions that are causing roadblocks by linking them to other urgent matters. The overlapping nature of decision clusters allows solutions in one stream to resolve roadblocks in another stream. A solution in the revenue stream may unlock a problem in the expenditure stream; a change in process may solve problems of linkage between the streams.

A Comparison of the Decision-Making Streams

The focus of this book is to make clearer the nature of politics in public budgeting. After examining each of the five decision streams, one would have to say that what politics looks like depends on where you look. In some areas of budgetary decision making, narrowly conceived interest groups compete with one another for tax breaks or spending increases; in others, coalitions of interest groups that approach class interests compete for control of the scope of government services; in still others, interest groups play little if any role. Some areas of the budget are policy laden, while others appear policy neutral and technical. From one perspective, changes in the budget process itself define the political maneuvering and coalition formation; from other vantage points, the politics of process seems to have little to do with the outcomes. To get anything like a realistic view of politics in the budget requires a look at each strand of budgetary decision making.

Revenue politics is characterized by both a policy orientation and active interest-group participation. The policy issues include who will be taxed and what the level of taxation will be. Narrowly defined interest groups get involved in trying to deflect taxes from their constituents; broader coalitions of interest groups get involved in efforts to determine the distribution of taxation between income groups and the overall level of taxation.

The politics of process revolves around two policy issues and bargaining among the actors. The first cluster of policy issues includes, ironically, how much of a policy focus the budget should have, how clearly policy issues should be articulated and, concomitantly, how much conflict should be expressed and resolved during budget decision making. The second and related policy issue is how much articulation of citizen and interest-group preferences the budget process should engage in. How much access should individuals, interest groups, agency heads, and the press have to budgetary decision making, and how much secrecy should there be? The result of these policy choices influences not only the level of accountability in the budget process but also, presumably, the level and nature of public expenditures and the amount of discipline in the budget process. The politics of process also revolves around the bargaining between budget actors for more power over budgetary choices. The bargaining over the distribution of power and the choices on key policy issues are often intertwined.

The politics of expenditures reflects several different aspects of politics. There is active interest-group involvement, as well as extensive bargaining and competition. The competition between interest groups generally prevents interest-group determinism. When budget actors manage to insulate their programs from competition, however, the result looks more interest-group dominated. At times, there is a compensating emphasis on policy, in the considered choice between programs and emphasis on formulating and achieving public goals. Legislators can resist even powerful interest groups when they choose; they use the budget process to insulate themselves.

The politics of budget balance is primarily a politics of policy. Three key issues are the role of the budget in managing the economy, the scope of government programs, and which level of government will balance its budget at the expense of which other level of government. These issues are often defined in terms of the target level of unemployment, the level of social services provided by the public sector and the number of programs or services provided by the public sector that could be provided by the private sector, and the degree of progressivity of the taxes that pay for governmental services. The outcome of each of these policy decisions is far reaching. As a result, coalitions of interest groups representing wide segments of society take different stands on the politics of balance; liberals and conservatives, Democrats and Republicans, take opposing stances. The politics of balance is often a partisan issue.

The politics of implementation is a contest between the technical goals of maintaining accountability and implementing the budget almost exactly as passed and the insertion of policy changes in the budget during the budget year. Generally, the technical model is triumphant, but at the cost of considerable effort in monitoring potentially policy-laden budget adaptations.

In short, no one view of politics in the budget stands alone. There is bargaining among actors in budget decision making, but it is framed by policy concerns expressed through the budget process; there are interest groups active in budgetary decision making, but they are controlled, or can be controlled, both by competition among themselves and by the budget process that gives or denies them access to decision making. There is a contest between more technical and more policy-oriented approaches to budgeting, but in most areas of budgeting there is a balance between them. There are policy issues in the budget, but they may be played up or toned down by the budget process and format.

The description to this point has been of a lively decision process that may occur over a period of years, but it says nothing of the patterns of change over time. Some of these patterns are cyclical, while others alternate, like a pendulum, between extremes.

Dynamics of Budgeting over Time

A number of long-term patterns have been identified in this book. In the revenue stream, tax breaks gradually eroded the tax base of broad taxes such as income and sales taxes, and encouraged honest taxpayers to cheat on their taxes because the system seemed so inequitable. When the savings from eliminating tax breaks was sufficient to distribute in the form of tax reductions to a broad base of citizens and interest groups, tax reform passed, cleaning the slate, and readying it for new demands for tax breaks.

Another pattern in the revenue stream was the attempt to put beyond consideration taxes that would hurt some particular class of people. While some interest group or class was in power, it would try to find the longest-term protection for itself, often a constitutional prohibition of some tax that threatened its membership. Such restrictions have kept some forms of taxation off the agenda for many years, but many such restrictions have gradually been eroded or eliminated.

In the expenditure cluster, there was a long-term tendency toward trust funds, locking in revenue sources for particular expenditures to reduce competition with the rest of the budget. Other devices for reducing competition were also noted, including the establishment of public enterprises and the design and implementation of entitlement programs. Even right-based entitlements can be reduced over time if their legitimacy is eroded. Competition does not cease once programs or expenditures have achieved some privileged status; others find a way to latch on to the successful program's success. Thus mass transit managed to horn in on the Highway Trust Fund for a number of years.

The politics of process was also marked by long-term patterns. When debts or expenditures got out of hand, there was a tendency to blame the legislatures for lack of discipline and give increased budget power to the chief executives. If and when that power was used to thwart the policy intentions of legislators, the legislators often took back some of that delegated budget authority. Although the shifts have sometimes been extreme, the overall tendency in recent years has been toward balance, with the executive and the legislature each having staff capacity and overlapping budgetary powers.

When Congress is trying to reassert its budgetary power, it has to create both a policy capacity and a mechanism to coordinate revenues and expenditures; it has to exert some central discipline over legislators. When the president is trying to assert budgetary power, he is likely to exert more central power over the executive branch agencies. There is alternation between more top-down and more bottom-up approaches to budgeting in both branches, with a moving balance between individual or agency interest and a number of broader policy concerns.

The politics of balance has been marked by reaction after the fact to growing deficits. There has been a tendency to react through apparently rigid budgetary requirements, often written into constitutions or statutes. Such restrictions may ban or severely limit borrowing, or require budgets to be balanced when submitted. Over time, these restrictions are often by-passed.

The patterns in budget implementation have been clearly marked, beginning with a broad grant of spending discretion to the executive, followed by some scandal or attempt to bypass the policies established by the legislature. The conflict results in increasingly detailed legislative controls over spending. The agencies may gradually try to evade the controls, or the legislature may gradually relent in the enforcement of the detailed controls.

Common Themes: The Roles of Competition and Secrecy

Much of what goes on over time in budgetary decision making has to do with the channeling, control, and even elimination of competition. Competition in budgeting is strong and always present, but handled in different ways. The allocation of proportional shares of new money to existing departments or programs is one way to limit competition, but it is not the only way. Competition is limited also by the tendency to compare seriously only items in the same part of the budget. Paper supplies typically are not compared with garbage trucks; soldiers are not traded off for buildings and grounds maintenance staff. Within each capital budget, or within each department, even dissimilar items may be compared. Thus the capital budget is intensely competitive, and competition within departments is keen, with some program requests cut back and others expanded. Competition sometimes occurs between portions of the budget, but this kind of competition occurs only occasionally.

The level of competition is so high within portions of the budget that those seeking to protect programs try to reduce the level of competition by getting out of those areas of the budget. Thus program supporters try to set up trust funds, entitlement programs, or public enterprises, which buffer a program or project from competition.

The level and kind of competition vary correspondingly with the kind of interest-group involvement. The budget implementation period is not generally seen as highly competitive; the spending stream of decisions is seen as highly competitive. There is a difference in kind between many small interest groups each pleading for some benefit and groups that represent broad political and social cleavages competing for control over policy. Thus competition between classes and regions of the country over the form of taxation is of a more enduring and important sort than competition between clusters of small interest groups. Competition between business and labor over the definition of balance and the scope and role of government services is also deep and enduring.

Controlling the demands of multiple small interest groups can be achieved either through directing their competition against one another or structuring the budget process to buffer their direct demands. This restructuring has often involved some level of secrecy. The competition between social classes over the form and level of taxation and the competition between business and labor over the scope of government and the definition of balance are not curtailable in the same sense; they are part of the broader political process. Over time, the domination of one set of interests or the other brings one solution or another to the fore, creating some of the typical patterns of change over time.

Competition is one general theme of this book that cuts across several streams of decision making. A second general theme is the level of secrecy in the budget and the role of the budget as a tool of public accountability. There is inevitably some selectivity in all public budgets; it simply is not possible to tell all in a public budget. In addition to this minimum level of selectivity, however, there are three other sources of secrecy. The first is the effort to buffer the budget process from interest-group pressure; the second is the effort to spend taxpayers' money differently from the way taxpayers would choose to spend it; the third is the effort to cover up attempts to avoid hard choices between cutting spending and increasing taxes by running deficits.

The budget process can be insulated from interest-group pressure by closing the proceedings, or by concentrating decision-making power in a small group of powerful decision makers who may choose to exclude interest groups. Meetings can be held at inconvenient times and places. The budget document can describe expenditures in such a way that it is difficult for interest groups to see if they have won or lost; agencies can be organized in such a way that interest groups have to lobby for their programs in half a dozen or more places. It can be made difficult for them to know who has decision-making power, or who exercises discretion.

Budget decisions may be insulated from the public at large and its preferences by too high a level of secrecy. Expenditures that take from all taxpayers and benefit a narrow group of citizens or companies or a specific geographical area are likely to be controversial unless positive spillovers to others can be demonstrated. Under these circumstances, potential competitors for funds may be bought off or included, or the source and amount of funding may be obscured.

Most governments, most of the time, balance their budgets; when they do not achieve balance, it may be for both good and temporary reasons. Nevertheless, when governments run deficits because they lack internal discipline, or ignore or redefine the constraints of balance, they may be embarrassed by the consequences, and in the face of what would be widespread public disapproval, and in view of the politically unpleasant tasks of cutting expenditures and raising revenues, they sometimes choose to hide the deficits.

Although there are continuing sources of secrecy in budgeting, there are also continuing pressures for maintaining openness and accountability. Expenditures that seem to benefit broad groups of people and programs that citizens can easily imagine themselves using or needing tend to generate little controversy and can use resources that are highly visible. And budget implementation is generally very close to the budget that passes in full public view; there is very little behind-the-scenes redoing of the policy choices in the budget. Actors who need to come to agreement on the next budget do not wish to see the last set of agreements come undone or be remade by someone else during the budget year. To keep the whole decision-making process going, the budget actors need to believe that their previous agreements will be implemented without change. The end of the Cold War has helped to reduce the level of secrecy in the Defense Department; pressure from the deficit to find and reduce waste and shrink the scope of programs has also contributed to congressional pressure to take programs out of the black budget.

Reconceptualizing Reform

This description of real-time budgeting and the patterns of change over time is intended to contribute to a descriptive theory of public budgeting. The theory is suggestive of how the politics of budgeting works and what kinds of reforms are likely to be desirable or effective.

The description of budgeting offered here suggests that there are multiple actors, with differential power over time, and that the actors' motivations are multiple and variable. Legislators are interested not only in constituency benefits but also in maintaining their own power and the power of the legislature. Equally important, at times they are interested in providing for the public good. When their individual interests clearly clash with the public good, they are often able to opt for the public good. Sometimes they do not see a problem coming or they underestimate the severity of the public consequences of their individual actions, but they learn from disasters and are often able to restructure their processes to increase discipline or delegate decision making to a location that is more buffered from interest groups. This pattern suggests that more of reformers' attention might be profitably directed to making clear the consequences of similar actions taken in the past or documenting the likely outcomes for the future. Restructuring can be successful when there is a consensus that it is necessary to avoid a disaster.

The swings in budgetary decision making suggest there are some internal mechanisms for balance, but they are not well regulated. They depend on knowledge of outcomes that is often not there. When constraints are devised, they usually address the last huge swing, not the next potential one. For example, when cities and states ran extraordinary amounts of debt, the response was to limit the amount of borrowing and to make state and local governments incapable of an activist role. States live with outmoded restrictions in their constitutions for decades or even centuries. The initial problem is extreme, the response in turn is extreme, and the quality of government is reduced. In recent years, at the national level, huge deficits have prompted calls for a constitutional amendment; again, a problem was allowed to get out of control, and the proposed solution is extreme in its constraints and duration.

The historical pattern suggests that research and reform should concentrate on identifying the places and times, the mechanisms, that allow balances to swing wildly or too widely, and the turning points or mechanisms that have historically brought the extremes back from danger or uncontrolled spiraling outcomes. It may be that the size of the swings can be narrowed.

For example, a more careful monitoring of deficits and intense publicity about early warning signs may be helpful in averting the huge accumulation of deficits that sometimes occur when small deficits are hidden or overlooked. A belief that all budgets should balance and that most do balance has left the public sector without a series of fallback positions and triggers for corrections. Building a consensus about what kinds of deficits will be acceptable and for how long may be helpful; devising a series of measures of deficits and counting how many of them are in the "red zone" may also be helpful. This may help avert the argument that deficits are not harmful, so we can allow them or ignore them. It may be that we are willing to accept deficits from some sources but not others, for some periods of time but not longer than a certain number of years. If the conceptual murk can be cleared by a series of definitions, each acceptable to some major groups, then the level and degree of deficits may be plainer, and the efforts to eliminate them more effective.

A second theme for reform that emerges from this book has to do with the interchangeability of budget roles. Reforms that simply gave the executive more power were not long-term solutions to budget discipline or balance. Governors sometimes played restrictive roles and sometimes expansionary ones; similarly, legislatures were sometimes restrictive and sometimes expansionary. History does not support the position that increased power to the executive will solve deficits or other budgetary problems.

Reform, in the sense of changing budget processes that shift the location of budget power, changes the outcomes in the short run by shifting power to actors who have a particular point of view. If there is a reform governor and an unreformed legislature riddled with corruption and eager for pork, then shifting power to the governor may bring about short-term improvement. But endless reinforcement of the governor's powers does not bring ever more budget improvement. Illinois may have the strongest governorship in terms of budget powers, but Governor Thompson shifted from more to less fiscally conservative accounting, he routinely hid deficits, and he was oriented to patronage spending for capital projects. Under his leadership the state ran deficits despite the strong executive budget.

A balance of power between the executive and the legislature, so one actor can catch the other at bad practice, is probably more sound over the long run than the weakening of one and the continual strengthening of the other. The arrangements of the mid-1800s, when distrust of government drastically curtailed the powers of both the governor and the legislature, were not particularly successful; it is not weak government that is required, but fairly balanced powers. This conclusion has echoes of the debate over the founding of the nation. Over the past decade, supporters of increased presidential power have argued that the president needs more budgetary power to control the deficits. The argument is that Congress is profligate, and only the president can exercise discipline. The experience of the states suggests that shifting more power to the president is no long-term improvement.

Overall, this book suggests that there is a relationship between budget process and outcomes, but that there is no one ideal process that will guarantee balance and limit taxation over time. The budget process allocates power to different budget actors, each of whom has ideologies, values, and goals. When the budget process shifts power more to one actor than to another, it influences the likely outcomes. The process also tends to reinforce or weaken top-down control. That control may be narrowly political, in the sense of maintaining the power of a small elite of legislative and executive branch officials, or it may be broadly policy oriented, in the sense of trying to control spending or shift spending priorities. It may be intended to buffer budget actors from certain kinds of demands, or it may emphasize budget balance over the achievement of constituency services or the delivery of capital projects. But budgetary reform that emphasizes discipline has to have the serious support of key actors in order to work; if the recognition of the need for discipline erodes, or if the case is never well made, the process will not create the desired outcome. Process does not sit out there by itself exerting discipline on unruly and unwilling actors. The actors create the process and try to abide by it once it exists, but if it is not working, they change the process, formally or informally.

This book offers no clear guidance on reforms that would alter the degree of secrecy in the budget. Secrecy performs several functions, some of which are more legitimate than others. Secrecy may simultaneously reduce the role of interest groups and help maintain the integrity of budget processes, while it blocks out the role of the public and minimizes accountability. What is done behind the cover of secrecy is, of course, not always known. Openness in budget processes may reduce the level of hidden subsidies or politically unacceptable subsidies, or it may force more reliance on user fees to break the linkage between public disapproval and spending for narrow interests.

A third suggestion about reform concerns budget formats and the amount of information for decision making. Traditional efforts to reform budgeting by including broader consideration of the options and making sure that there is enough time and enough easily accessible information to make intelligent decisions are still reasonable in the framework of this book, but perhaps less urgent, since the book does not portray much or all of budgetary decision making as routine, mindless, and opaque. If there is a demonstrated need for clearer formats or consideration of additional options, then those formats and options should be advocated. There is nothing impossible or necessarily undesirable about this kind of reform. It may increase the burden of work, however, and hence should address only clear needs and not be done excessively. It may increase the level of competition, but competition can be handled in many ways. It may be better public policy to allow a controversy to be stated than to use the power of budgeting to prevent an issue from reaching the public, where it can be dealt with and resolved. Budgeting handles controversy all the time; it is designed to cope with the interruptions resulting from unresolved and controversial policy matters.

Avenues for Research

This book suggests many avenues for productive research, for students as well as scholars. It also suggests some lines of inquiry that probably will not be productive. Studies that compare last year's total appropriations to this year's total appropriations are unlikely to contribute much understanding of budget processes; they examine too small a portion of the budget, and over too short a period of time. Studies of budgetary tradeoffs may well produce major insights, if they adopt a realistic view of the way budgeting works.

That is, they must assume that revenue constraints are variable, not fixed; that most routine tradeoffs occur within departments and within the capital budget, rather than across sections of the budget; that major changes in spending priorities occur only over fairly long periods of time; and that budgets are structured so that some expenditures are much more flexible than others. The kind of expenditure makes a difference, since much of the politics of budgeting revolves specifically around the degree of flexibility and the attempt to lock in some expenditures.

The descriptive outline of budgeting presented here needs to be documented, elaborated on, and filled in. Much more research is needed on municipal and county budgeting, and on the linkage between the decision clusters. One issue glossed over in this book for lack of information is the relationship between microbudgeting and macrobudgeting. Given a particular set of budget processes, what strategies do budget actors use, under what circumstances? How effective are these strategies? Once it becomes clear that strategies are highly variable, not fixed, the way is opened for exploring those variations and the success of those strategies. How do budget actors anticipate or measure the environment, and how do those estimates affect their strategies? To what extent does the allocation of power implicit in the budget process determine the outcomes independent of strategies?

Another issue barely touched on is the tension between discretion and control. This book describes a discretion-and-control cycle for budget implementation, but does not deal in any detail with the ways in which administrators re-create discretion within a control budget. More needs to be described about these internal dynamics and the different political value of different resources depending on the degree of discretion they entail. New money, unencumbered money, money without strings, has a special value in a tightly controlled budget, so that there may in fact be two budgets, one with less and one with more discretion. Administrators may strive to get more money into the budget with greater discretion. When circumstances reduce the discretionary money, the impact on the politics of budgeting may be very different from a reduction in the more tightly controlled portion of the budget. The elimination of revenue sharing (unencumbered money with virtually no strings) from state and local governments' budgets thus provides a test case for observing how officials adapt to sharp reductions in the more discretionary portion of the budget.

A third theme that warrants future investigation is the process of locking and unlocking decisions. Budgeting involves a number of decisions that budget actors at the peak of their power try to make permanent. There are often attempts to unlock decisions, to reverse them, once they are made. Under what circumstances do locking or unlocking strategies work? More study needs to be made of these processes, such as the efforts to put bans in state and national constitutions on certain forms of taxation, or the establishment of trust funds or public enterprises. Efforts to create right-based entitlements need more explicit study. In each of these cases, more attention should be focused on the processes and circumstances for undoing them or reversing them.

A fourth theme of the book that needs further exploration is the relationship between the technical and political aspects of budgeting. The technical concerns of the budget include accurate estimates of expenditures and revenues, realistic evaluations of the economy, compliance with balance requirements (no matter how formulated), timely completion of decisions, prevention of overspending by agencies, and the creation of a plan that puts enough resources in the right places to get mandated work accomplished. The political concerns of budgeters include establishing and enforcing priorities, getting sufficient support for taxation to allow expenditures to occur and balance to be achieved without being thrown out of office, the creation of a workable budget process, the design and implementation of rules of balance, and the satisfaction of perceived needs for constituency benefits. These functions are not neatly divided into those performed by elected officials and those performed by career bureaucrats. Who performs which functions? How do they balance? When does political distortion of projections of the economy become so severe as to force the creation of an alternative, more neutral projection system; when do technical efforts to achieve balance cause major policy changes? Whose responsibility is it to maintain the informational integrity of the budget and its usefulness as a tool of accountability to the public? How far can that integrity be eroded before counterpressures are exerted?

These suggested topics are only a preliminary list; there are many more possibilities. Such research could meaningfully be quantitative or qualitative, as long as it had a sufficiently long time span, viewed budget constraints as flexible, and was sensitive to the different kinds of resources in a budget and the different streams of budget decision making.

Summary and Conclusions

Public budgeting is highly political, but it is not the same thing as politics in general. It represents a special corner of politics, with many of its own characteristics. The peculiar politics of extraction called taxation may illustrate broader political desires to avoid unpopular decisions, but the process of turning taxation into distributive politics through the award of tax breaks and the eventual need for reform, the tension between spending and taxing, and the occasional passage of new or increased taxes are unique to the politics of budgeting. Real-time decision making is peculiar to budget decision making with its intense sensitivity to the environment, its interruptibility, its nested options, and its time constraints. Budgeting has a bottom line and a due date, which distinguish it from many other political decisions. Budgeting carries in itself a way of measuring failure that creates pressures for action and reaction over time.

Budgeting is a particularly important arena of politics because many policy decisions are meaningless unless they can be implemented through the budget process. When political actors want to enhance their power, they often focus on power over budgeting as a way to do it. Consequently, battles over budgeting processes, which might otherwise seem dry, technical, internal matters, turn out to be lively contests. Individuals try to get into positions of budgetary power and then try to enhance the power of the positions they hold. Budgeting is the setting for major contests over the separation of powers and the balance between the legislature and the executive. Legislative committees battle with one another for jurisdiction, budget power gets highly fragmented, and coordination becomes a major issue.

The budget document itself plays a unique role in the political system. It is a management document designed to help plan expenditures and maintain financial control; it may reflect major policy decisions made during the budget process and thus represent a summary of major government actions; and it presents to taxpayers an explanation of how their money is being spent. The role of the budget in providing public accountability is a crucial one in a democracy. Yet budgets do not always play this role well. Budgets sometimes change during implementation; the figures in the budget are not always accurate; and the information may be displayed in such a way as to obscure rather than elucidate key decisions. Budgets have to remain somewhat flexible, which may reduce their usefulness as tools of public accountability; secrecy in making decisions may be necessary in order to buffer decision makers from the pleadings of special interests; and secrecy may be used to do something desired but formally prohibited.

The level of secrecy in budgeting needs to be carefully monitored, but at present, it remains relatively low. Most public budgets are fairly accurate representations of the activities and spending decisions of their governments. They thus provide an excellent vantage point from which to observe government and a way of holding government accountable. Citizens may be forced by the coercive power of government to pay taxes for programs they do not want, but this is a democracy, and citizens may and do rebel. Citizens are important budget actors.

Index of Names

Index of Subjects